DAILY LIFE IN

ARTHURIAN BRITAIN

Recent Titles in
The Greenwood Press Daily Life Through History Series

The Progressive Era
Steven L. Piott

Women during the Civil Rights Era
Danelle Moon

Colonial Latin America
Ann Jefferson and Paul Lokken

The Ottoman Empire
Mehrdad Kia

Pirates
David F. Marley

Arab Americans in the 21st Century
Anan Ameri and Holly Arida, Editors

African American Migrations
Kimberley L. Phillips

The Salem Witch Trials
K. David Goss

Behind the Iron Curtain
Jim Willis

Trade: Buying and Selling in World History
James M. Anderson

The Colonial South
John Schlotterbeck

A Medieval Monastery
Sherri Olson

DAILY LIFE IN

ARTHURIAN BRITAIN

DEBORAH J. SHEPHERD

The Greenwood Press Daily Life Through History Series

 GREENWOOD

AN IMPRINT OF ABC-CLIO, LLC
Santa Barbara, California • Denver, Colorado • Oxford, England

Library of Congress Cataloging-in-Publication Data

Shepherd, Deborah J.

   Daily life in Arthurian Britain / Deborah J. Shepherd.
      pages cm. — (The Greenwood Press daily life through
   history series)
   Includes bibliographical references and index.
   ISBN 978-0-313-33295-1 (hardcopy : acid-free paper) —
ISBN 978-0-313-03852-5 (ebook)   1. Anglo-Saxons—Social
life and customs.   2. Great Britain—History—Anglo-Saxon
period, 449–1066.   3. Great Britain—Social life and customs—To
1066.   I. Title.
   DA152.2.S528   2013
   942.01′4--dc23   2013011677

ISBN: 978-0-313-33295-1
EISBN: 978-0-313-03852-5

17   16   15   14   13   1   2   3   4   5

This book is also available on the World Wide Web as an eBook.
Visit www.abc-clio.com for details.

Greenwood
An Imprint of ABC-CLIO, LLC

ABC-CLIO, LLC
130 Cremona Drive, P.O. Box 1911
Santa Barbara, California 93116-1911

This book is printed on acid-free paper ∞

Manufactured in the United States of America

CONTENTS

Introduction   vii

1. The Setting   1

2. The People   25

3. Towns and Countryside   59

4. Social Identities   89

5. Making a Living on the Land   117

6. Making a Living in Crafts and Trade   147

7. Keeping Order   183

8. Matters of Life and Death   235

Glossary   285

Bibliography   293

Index   307

INTRODUCTION

WHAT DOES "ARTHURIAN BRITAIN" MEAN?

King Arthur is the stuff of legend. In the popular imagination, he
is a high medieval knight and ruler, living in a fantasy castle with
many spectacularly armored knights in his retinue. Arthur is the
king of all the Britons—or all England, depending on the story-
teller—but while he rules his people with justice, he is also the
authority figure behind the legendary heroes who set off on quests
to save distant maidens and seek after impossible prizes. Much
of Arthurian legend deals with these heroic quests and romantic
encounters, ignoring the mundane matters of real kingship. Some
of the romance turns dark with magical entanglements or the illicit
desires of Lancelot and Arthur's wayward queen, Guinevere. Mer-
lin, Arthur's teacher and magical advisor, is defeated by a powerful female force. Women's reputations do not always fare well in
Arthurian legend. Be that as it may, very few of these later tales
concocted by medieval storytellers, many originating in France and
other countries, resemble either English history or daily life.

The real Arthur, if such a man existed, would have been nothing
like this. Historians have agonized for generations over the question of Arthur's existence, and the mystery is unlikely to be solved.
Only an array of contemporary historians giving eyewitness
accounts of Arthur's deeds would verify his existence to our now

skeptical minds, yet we have not found one reliable contemporary source, let alone an array. This is partly because a real Arthur would have been active during the fifth century—that is, after the year 410, when Roman authority withdrew from Britain—and he would have lived in a land experiencing numerous political and economic upheavals while at the same time also under assault by external enemies. Few people, if any, holding living memories of those times had the leisure or the ability to write their stories down. Even if such writing had occurred, the many subsequent years of turmoil would have made its survival unlikely. Any surviving text would have had to be safely stored and cared for in archives in order to be read in our own century. More likely, we would only know of this text if some scribe in a later century had taken the trouble to make a new copy of it. Some early medieval texts rescued from the decay of old age were copied and recopied many times over during the intervening centuries, but only if they were thought important. These have survived down to the present day.

Many texts were not so fortunate. Consequently, the only known narrative of British life and circumstances written soon after the Romans departed comes from a work written several generations later by Gildas, a learned cleric of the Church. Gildas made clear his disgust and anger over the behavior and motivations of the earlier Britons who he felt had greedily rejected the good and lawful Roman rule they had been honored to receive in exchange for a chance to grab power for themselves. He was in no mood to glorify any British heroes, and if he mentioned earlier leaders by name, it was only to vilify them for their criminal deeds and evil choices. Some modern reviewers have suggested that Gildas, whose resentment of early British leaders was clear, knew of Arthur but hated him so much for his unlawful deeds that he deliberately left out all mention of his name. Perhaps this is modern wishful thinking: if only Gildas had written down that one name.

So the Arthur who intrigues us lived, if at all, at the beginning of this shadowy and turbulent time of the fifth and sixth centuries. He may as well be a legend like his later, more glamorous, manifestation because his post-Roman existence cannot be proven. Ironically, he is, or would be, a full 800 years older than the vision projected in the popular legends of late medieval and modern times. Why this confusion? How can the legendary Arthur be eight centuries younger than the real Arthur?

Part of the answer lies in this far earlier time when Britons were in need of real, living heroes. Contrary to Gildas's view, "bad"

British behavior bore only part of the blame for the departure of the Romans, though how large a part can be debated. Rome was beset on all sides by enemies, including rebellious armies from Britain, and needed to use its troops and administrators stationed in Britain to more urgent purposes. Although seemingly confident at first of their ability to self-govern, the Britons' efforts to survive on their own after separation from the Roman Empire failed within a generation or two. The Anglo-Saxons arrived and ultimately dominated most of British territory. Britons fled to other lands, moved to remote western and northern reaches of Britain, or merged with the Anglo-Saxon people through marriage and by adopting the Germanic culture. The Britons who settled in the western and southern territories of Wales and Cornwall remembered their losses and, using fragments of collective memory, nurtured a vision of a British hero who had almost defeated the invaders. The vision of Arthur appears to be comprised of true and embellished stories about many men and women, stories that were gathered together into an oral tradition of one great hero, valiant and victorious in battle, who in his time could beat back the enemies of the Britons and preserve their land and freedom. There was even a promise that he would return to do the same again one future day. As Viking and Norman invaders arrived in later centuries, belief in a returning hero became even more compelling. The core vision of a once great king of England remained the hopeful story of a time when the Britons were victorious over their enemies and might be again someday.

The origin of Arthur's story leads us to the purpose of this book. The need for a hero king tells us something about these times. From the historian's point of view as well as the archaeologist's, Arthurian Britain, properly speaking, is the story of post-Roman Britain and its struggle for survival against a political vacuum left by the Romans; the growing incursions of Saxons; the violent, spasmodic raids of neighboring Celtic tribes; and the internecine conflicts among British leaders seeking to dominate the remnants of their Roman world. Britain foundered for several generations, unable to maintain for itself the controls and comforts of Roman law and order, but the nation did have the potential to recreate itself politically and economically if it were not for the continuing stream of incoming Saxons, who, according to Gildas, were first invited as mercenaries to fend off external tribal attacks. In the end, most of Britain fell to Anglo-Saxon domination, with the remaining Britons emigrating to western territories—modern Wales and Cornwall— and across the channel to Brittany. This book gives the story, pieced together from fragments of history and archaeology, not of the events themselves but of life in those turbulent times.

THE SCOPE OF THIS BOOK

The intent of this book is to bring the environment and daily life of ordinary people living in the turbulent post-Roman centuries in Britain to life. The focus is on the fifth and sixth centuries, but reference is made as needed to earlier and later times in order to demonstrate continuity. Geographically, the focus is on modern England and Wales, but developments in neighboring Scotland and Ireland are covered where they connect with the people of the focal lands.

Daily life consists of the succession of mundane activities of building homes, planting crops, caring for children, and doing everything else necessary to survive and thrive. It does not immediately include the momentous events of political change—the battles, the conquests, and the defeats—but since these crises do necessarily have an impact on the lives of everyone they touch, major events are considered whenever applicable. The rebellions and struggles for power in the fourth century led up to the departure of the Romans, ca. AD 410. Loss of Roman authority and military presence had profound effects on people throughout the British provinces. Trade diminished because of the loss of ready currency and secure markets. Travel along the roads and the transportation of valuable goods became dangerous. Britain lay at the far northwestern reaches of the empire. With political disruptions occurring closer to Rome on the continent, Britain received increasingly less attention and opportunities for connections with the outside world. Urban settlements collapsed, and much of the population lived dispersed around the countryside living as self-sufficiently as possible.

Into this new set of circumstances arrived the German mercenaries. Written history declares that the Britons had invited the Germans to come to Britain essentially to provide the armed security that Roman soldiers had once provided. In particular, the cities and trading emporia required defense. It was common knowledge that the defenses of Britain were down and disordered. Many British officers and soldiers were on the continent trying to take advantage of other power vacuums as Rome began to lose control of its outer provinces. Britons at home were not prepared to fend off the expected attacks by external tribes, but they did feel wealthy enough to pay mercenaries. The early arrival of Anglo-Saxon mercenaries can be vouched at least circumstantially by archaeological discoveries of early fifth-century Germanic camps outside the walls of London and York.

From the beginning of the fifth century until the changes that mark the early seventh century, the text follows the interactions and conflicts of Britons and Anglo-Saxons as decades of immigration swelled the numbers of new settlers to some tens of thousands. Most of the immigrants were males who took British wives, settled down, and began farming. Many of the new Anglo-Saxon farms were established on lands that had been abandoned as the Romano-British population moved to the continent, principally to Brittany, while those communities remaining behind slowed dramatically in growth. The times were uncertain, people were cautious and on their guard, but there was no large-scale slaughter or enslavement of Britons as past scholars have imagined. However, later laws and documents show that the Anglo-Saxons ultimately saw themselves as the conquerors of an inferior population and used the justification of imagined superiority to take away lands and rights from the Britons in their midst. This process had begun by the sixth century in all likelihood.

Throughout the sixth century, the two sides coalesced into separate political forces composed of multiple kingdoms and leaders who lacked unity of purpose. The Britons formed kingdoms in the far north, the west including modern Wales, and the southwest where modern Cornwall and Devon are situated. The Anglo-Saxons organized kingdoms first along the eastern and southeastern coasts and then began pushing west into Wessex and Mercia. Fragments of documentary records indicate that they fought themselves seemingly as much as they fought each other. The Arthurian legend is correct on one point. The Britons needed a leader to unify them, but then, so did the Anglo-Saxons. The Anglo-Saxon push to take all the land finally stalled at the western borders of Wessex, Mercia, and Northumbria. The Britons held power and were relatively secure in Dumnonia (Cornwall and Devon), Gwynedd and Powys (Wales), and Rheged (Cumbria), and this is where we leave them both at the end of the sixth century.

THE SOURCES: HISTORY, ARCHAEOLOGY, AND SCIENCE

Very little historical record exists for this time period. Scholars make use of everything that is available. Few contemporary writings have survived, and these inevitably tell only one side of their story. Only one manuscript, *De Excidio et Conquestu Britanniae* by a cleric named Gildas, comes from Britain. He asserted that a leader of the Britons, Vortigern the tyrant, who was clearly not Arthur but someone who gathered political power to himself shortly after the departure of the Romans, called a council of other local leaders to determine how to handle Britain's defense. Under Vortigern's influence, as interpreted by Gildas, the leaders decided that for the defense of Britain, they would invite German mercenaries to Britain's *civitates* to provide security. Gildas hated Vortigern and heaped scorn on his actions, but to the consternation of many modern readers of the *De Excidio*, the cleric never mentioned the name of Arthur. With the exception of one Welsh poet (to be discussed in a moment), no surviving contemporary source mentioned Arthur by name.

Scholars have speculated if and why Gildas hated Arthur more than Vortigern or the other leaders. Such hatred would account for why he refused even to record Arthur's name for posterity although he must have been aware that many stories were being told about Arthur and his battles against the invaders. What Arthur could have done to be so hated by Gildas may have involved some offense against the Church, or it may have been the way Arthur seized power. According to Christopher Snyder, Gildas labeled Vortigern and the other leaders "tyrants" because in his view, they claimed power that was not theirs by right. Gildas did not understand power as something that came from the people and was bestowed on a worthy leader. Power, to Gildas, came from a higher authority, such as the Roman imperial government. Gildas blamed the Britons for driving out the Romans, a view that we now know to be inflated. If the Britons had repudiated their lawful government, then Gildas believed that any leadership set up in place of the Romans was unlawful and tyrannical.[1]

Several documents of the period from the continent mention Britain. These are considered in the text. There are also small details about migrations of individuals and their religious beliefs that can be gleaned from inscriptions on memorial stones or on portable objects.

Some of the works of two sixth-century Welsh poets, Taliesin and Aneirin, have survived. The surviving poems provide glimpses of history, rulers, and battles conducted in the sixth-century northwestern lands. It was Aneirin who made an enticing mention of a battle leader who "brought black crows to a fort's/Wall, though he was not Arthur" (stanza 102).[2] This warrior is given the name

Gwawrddur, and Aneirin praised him for his slaughter of the enemy in battle. Or did he? The one surviving manuscript of "Y Gododdin," the *Book of Aneirin*, was written by two scribes from possibly three sources in the late 13th century. Some scholars are concerned that the line about Arthur was a later interpolation by some scribe enamored by the legends. Then again, there is no real stylistic reason to suspect that the line is not original.

The seventh through ninth centuries provide the works of the Anglo-Saxon cleric and historian Bede, the British history by the so-called Nennius (his identity is debated), and the earliest preserved Anglo-Saxon law texts. The *Laws of Ine*, originating from Wessex, have been studied for what they reveal about contemptuous Anglo-British cultural relations.

People tend to write about the news of their time. They eulogize dead kings. They create chronicles describing critical events and major battles in annual entries to mark the passage of the years. Sometimes they expound on their religious beliefs. This was just as true in the early medieval period. No one thought it of any value to write about matters of daily life, such as what they ate for dinner and where it came from, what styles they wore and why, how their children were growing and learning, what they thought about the Christian missionaries passing through the village, how often they visited a market and what they bought, whether or not they felt safe traveling on the roads or if they had anywhere to go, how much they feared migrating warbands, and so on and on. To answer these questions, even in part, we must turn to archaeology for additional clues. Archaeologists have excavated cemeteries, old Roman villas, parts of the old Roman towns, temples, monastic sites, hill forts, and many farmsteads. The more the results are compared and analyzed, the better we are able to understand the preserved fragments of ancient life. Archaeologists try to identify the common people and their local environments, as well as the royal treasures of kings and buried hoards of chieftains. Both the ordinary objects of common lives and the luxury items of the wealthy are studied for place and time of origin. The questions of how they ended up in their place of deposition and all the related clues are fitted together to see what big picture can be made out of them. In many respects, the post-Roman past reconstructed from historical and archaeological sources is a detective story.

Archaeology relies on more than just the mere excavation of sites. Geographers, geologists, soil scientists, ecologists, zoologists, botanists, chemists, molecular biologists, and forensic anthropologists, among others, are called to look at the evidence. In the text, I frequently highlight the results of excavations that illustrate the points under discussion. I give examples of meaningful landscape, soil, faunal, floral, insect, metals, pottery, DNA, and skeletal analysis and explain how these scientific inquiries contribute to our practical understanding of post-Roman history. The scientific dating of objects, principally in this time frame by radiocarbon and dendrochronological techniques, is exceedingly important for sorting the information that archaeologists uncover.

Putting together all these sources, we endeavor to gain a picture of the real lives of the post-Roman Arthurian Britons as well as their Anglo-Saxon neighbors. In some ways, the two become inseparable. Culturally, they created the foundation of Britain today.

NOTES

1. Christopher A. Snyder, *An Age of Tyrants, Britain and the Britons, A.D. 400–600* (University Park: Pennsylvania State University Press, 1998), 78 ff.

2. Joseph P. Clancy, *The Earliest Welsh Poetry* (New York: St. Martin's Press, 1970), 64.

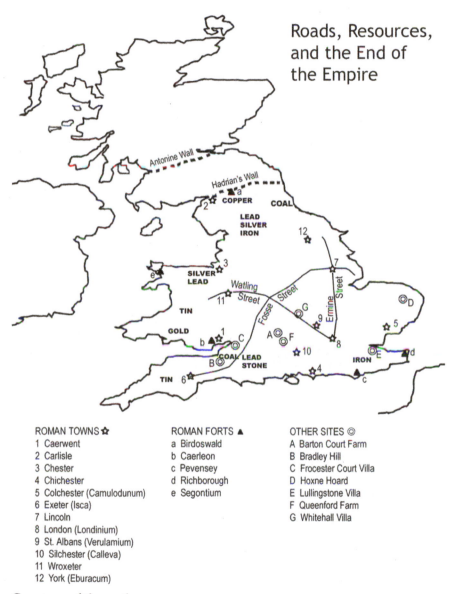

Roads, Resources, and the End of the Empire

Antonine Wall

Hadrian's Wall

COPPER
COAL

2

LEAD
SILVER
IRON

12

7

SILVER
LEAD

3

Watling Street

Fosse Street

Ermine Street

G

D

11

TIN

GOLD

b

1

C

A

F

9

5

8

COAL LEAD
STONE

B

10

IRON

E

d

TIN

6

4

c

ROMAN TOWNS ☆
1 Caerwent
2 Carlisle
3 Chester
4 Chichester
5 Colchester (Camulodunum)
6 Exeter (Isca)
7 Lincoln
8 London (Londinium)
9 St. Albans (Verulamium)
10 Silchester (Calleva)
11 Wroxeter
12 York (Eburacum)

ROMAN FORTS ▲
a Birdoswald
b Caerleon
c Pevensey
d Richborough
e Segontium

OTHER SITES ◎
A Barton Court Farm
B Bradley Hill
C Frocester Court Villa
D Hoxne Hoard
E Lullingstone Villa
F Queenford Farm
G Whitehall Villa

Courtesy of the author.

Post-Roman Britain

Picts

DALRAIDA

STRATHCLYDE

BERNICIA
(NORTHUMBRIA)

RHEGED

16

Carvetti

ISLE OF MAN

DEIRA

1

Brigantes

(ELMET)

ANGELSEY

6   3

GWYNEDD
Ordovices

7

MIDLANDS

17

POWYS
Cornovii

Dobunni

Sparse, early Anglo-Saxon Settlement

DYFED

Silures

9

8

Under British Control?

5

11

10   14

12

DUMNONIA

15

Durotriges

13

Dumnonii

4

2

1 Aldborough
2 Bantham Sands
3 Bryn Euryn
4 Castle Dore
5 Congresbury
6 Degannwy and
    Conwy Mtn.
7 Dinas Emrys
8 Dinas Powys
9 Gateholm
10 Glastonbury Tor
11 Lamyatt Beacon
12 Lankhills Cemetery
13 Poundbury
14 South Cadbury
15 Tintagel
16 Whithorn
17 The Wrekin

Traces of Dykes ———

Courtesy of the author.

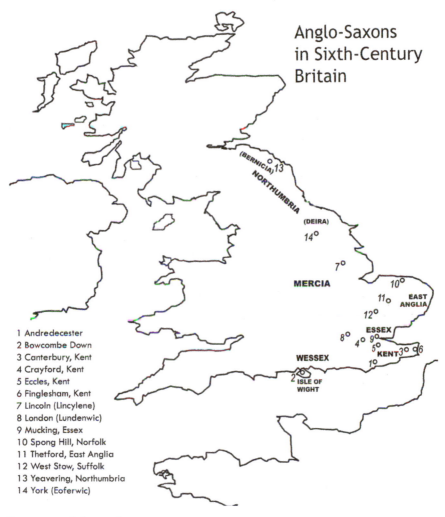

Anglo-Saxons
in Sixth-Century
Britain

(BERNICIA) ○ 13
NORTHUMBRIA

(DEIRA)
14○

7○

MERCIA

10○
11○ EAST ANGLIA

12○

ESSEX
8○ 4○ 9○

WESSEX
KENT 3○ ○ 6
5○
1○

2 ○
ISLE OF WIGHT

1 Andredecester
2 Bowcombe Down
3 Canterbury, Kent
4 Crayford, Kent
5 Eccles, Kent
6 Finglesham, Kent
7 Lincoln (Lincylene)
8 London (Lundenwic)
9 Mucking, Essex
10 Spong Hill, Norfolk
11 Thetford, East Anglia
12 West Stow, Suffolk
13 Yeavering, Northumbria
14 York (Eoferwic)

Courtesy of the author.

1

THE SETTING

LANDSCAPES AND PEOPLE

Every landscape contributes to the psychological and cultural character of its occupants. The land of Britain presents a wide range of landscapes from low-lying marshes to low, but rugged mountains. These landscapes offer a complex of wet and dry environments, assorted vegetations and soils, and a wide range of natural fauna. Although famously described as an island, Britain has never been isolated but rather has withstood continual interaction with peoples and cultures in all directions. The barrier presented by surrounding water is an illusion. It was the water and the seafaring knowledge shared by all northern and Mediterranean peoples that allowed exceptional access to and from Britain beginning far back in prehistory.

Britain was and is an attractive green land. Its adequate rainfall and moderate temperatures today create a diversity of lush landscapes, both rugged and rolling, and the land was accommodating to different ways of living—from hunting and fishing to herding and cultivating crops—depending on the local ecology. In order to better understand the conditions shaping the lives of Britons, the past environment of the land must first be explored. In this first chapter therefore, the physical environment of Britain is presented as a necessary prelude to considering the lives of the Britons during the fifth and sixth centuries.

People thrive on rich vegetation and plentiful sources of water, both of which Britain has in abundance. Its rivers support bountiful aquatic bird and fish life. These waterways are often small but can grow and flood rapidly when rains come. Overnight, a seemingly tame stream in the northern valleys might overtake its banks and flood entire fields, collapsing stone hedge walls onto roads. Then, within a week, the water returns to the riverbed as if all had always been peaceful in the valley.

The soils of southern and eastern England are in many areas a thin cover over chalk downlands. The chalk formations create rolling hills of lower elevation notable for the quantities of natural flint and chalk lying below the surface and in readily visible outcrops. The streams found on the chalk lands are often exceptionally clear and shallow waterways and excellent for trout fishing, a major pastime today but an important food source in the past. The land is covered with rich natural vegetation yet was easily cultivated even four millennia ago during Neolithic times. The downlands have also long been notable for their endless picturesque flocks of grazing sheep. Rocks comprised of compacted chalk surrounding flint cores are so plentiful that they have been widely used as building stone in these regions. Flint is also an extremely useful stone for making sharp blades, weapon points, striking fires, and other essentials of daily life. Its prevalence in southern England contributed to the early settlement there.

Bogs are found throughout Britain, in both highland and lowland areas. A bog is produced when soil forms over dense rocks and therefore cannot drain well. Bogs develop very slowly because the static waterlogged conditions allow for very little oxygen to feed the bacteria and fungi in the soils. Bacteria and fungi decompose plant material into the humus of which the bog soils are comprised. The dead plant material accumulates while the water in the soils becomes increasingly acidic. Over time, the lower layers of plant debris, compressed under the weight of the upper layers, become peat, which can be burned as fuel. Mosses of various kinds especially sphagnum, spiky grasses, and occasional trees grow on the acidic soils of bogs. Many areas are covered by widespread "blanket" bogs that are rare outside of Britain.

It is easy to forget that Britain has mountains as well as rolling lowlands with fields, streams, and forests. The mountains may seem like overgrown hills when compared to the great mountain chains of the world, but an athletic hiker determined to climb one of the taller northern or Welsh peaks can find snow in July. Although the elevations are modest, the steepness of the slope from base to summit and the rapid climatic changes that the climber will experience make the British highlands, also known as fells, spectacular in appearance. These highlands are among the windiest in the world. Some can also be extremely wet locales, experiencing frequent gales. In regions such as Cumbria, the mid-elevation fell tops are dotted with bogs. Within these bogs, over the millennia, peat layers have been deeply compacted. Peat was once used in large quantities as a heating fuel. In the 19th century and even earlier, peat cutters climbed high along narrow tracks to the high peat deposits in order to collect this fuel for sale.

Another stunning element of the British landscape is the heath lands and the varied heathers growing there. In late summer, these fields are awash with shades of purple and pink. The tough heath vegetation thrives in poor, acidic soils and in climates that are both cool and wet. In the past, there was more heath, created by widespread human-controlled grazing and controlled burning of upland vegetation. As far back as 2000 BC, humans cleared forests and burning old scrub for pasture lands. The burning process also boosted the local populations of grouse and other wild fowl desired by hunters. Careful burning removed old woody stems without damage to the roots so that new and nutritious shoots can grow for the benefit of the browsing cattle. Once trees were removed from poor acidic soils to create pastureland, tough colorful vegetation, including shrubs, prevailed. If birch and other trees tried to return to these fields and pastures, cattle ate them immediately. The warm, lowland heaths are today much diminished by the encroachment of modern housing, but the cold, damp upland heaths, often called moors, continue to thrive and are a haven for sheep.

Surrounding Britain is a wide variety of coasts from rocky cliffs to broad, unstable sandy beaches. Other beaches are entirely rocky. Salt marshes, home to wild species of fowl, exist in sheltered bays. Elsewhere, the landscape is more forbidding. Off the northwestern and northern coasts are numerous windswept islands grouped as the Inner and Outer Hebrides, the Orkneys, and the Shetlands. These have long been occupied by dispersed communities of native and immigrant fishermen adept at sailing boats in harsh seas.

FORESTS AND WILD LANDS

By medieval times, England was divided into town lands, villages, farm lands, pastures, managed woodlands, and wild, unmanaged lands. Some of the forests were utilized for the cutting of timber. Certain desirable species of tree were encouraged to grow in dense distributions, while other species of vegetation were removed. Close-spaced growth created tall, straight trunks that were cut down at the right times for the best quality lumber, while grazing animals that might do damage to the trees were kept away. Management of a lumber crop had already become a widespread business in many of England's forests by the Middle Ages. Historians have assumed that such management systems arose a long time after the Roman period, but this view is now changing to encompass a realization that much of the land-use pattern in Britain first appeared in the Roman period or earlier. By the fifth and sixth centuries, nearly all of the available land of good agricultural quality was cleared and developed, and the wild lands were mostly confined to barren or rocky soils, high elevations, and marshy lowlands.

Ancient forest clearance in Britain, whether for agriculture or other purposes, left traces upon the landscape. Close observation of surface features in some well-settled areas has revealed patterns of field boundaries dating as early as pre-Roman times. These field systems expanded in Roman times, when the climate was milder than today, and more land was farmed than in any other period. Some of these cultivated Roman fields reverted back to woodlands beginning around the fourth century AD and have remained in this condition ever since. Aside from clearing forests on a large scale for farming, the Romans also needed a steady supply of timber. Although the impressive Roman architecture that is familiar to us featured stone and brick work, such structures also required timber frameworks and scaffolding during the building process, and many lesser buildings were made completely of wood. The Romans quickly used large portions of the British forests for their building operations.

Another requirement for wood that increased substantially during the Roman period was for the production of charcoal to fuel pottery kilns, iron-smelting furnaces, and similar operations requiring high-heat fire. Smelting iron ore into metal depended on reaching and maintaining a temperature of approximately 1,300°C. A wood fire is insufficient for this task. Great amounts of charcoal, a product processed from wood chunks, were required to heat

Woodlands are still sometimes managed by foresters in parts of Britain. In the valley of the River Esk in Cumbria, northwest England, oaks are encouraged to grow close together and struggle upward for a break in the dense canopy. The results are unusually long, straight trunks with fewer knots in the lumber. The broad-leafed bracken on the forest floor is a detrimental weed that spreads rapidly and has been determined to be both toxic and carcinogenic if consumed. It has proliferated due to human activity. (Courtesy Deborah Shepherd)

cone-shaped smelting furnaces made of clay to the immensely high temperatures required for melting iron ore into a remarkably useful metal. Iron ore was plentiful in Britain, and the Romans had a huge appetite for iron from which they made both tools and weapons. Iron production must have decreased by the fifth century AD with the rapid slowing of the economy following the departure of Roman administration, but the desire for iron tools, weapons, knives, horse gear, nails, and all manner of personal and household accessories, to which people had become accustomed, would have kept local iron-smelting and blacksmithing occupations active to some degree. The habit of managing specific wooded areas for the production of either timber or charcoal, and keeping these managed woods separate from other areas where animals might forage freely, was already thoroughly ingrained.

WEATHER CONDITIONS

Although not the entire explanation for the fate of the Britons, climate change had an impact on life in Britain after the Romans left. The worsening climate may also have been one reason why the Romans departed—or to take a broader view of events, why the Roman Empire as a whole contracted in the fifth century. By the fourth century, people were already aware that conditions in Britain were deteriorating, for neither the crops nor the farm animals flourished as before.

Written records tell little about weather conditions in Britain at this time, but other kinds of evidence can reveal details about the weather. Tree rings are a useful indicator of climate change. Most people know that the age of a tree can be determined by counting the number of growth rings seen in a cross section of its main trunk. However, these rings are also useful for determining the quality of the growing seasons during which the tree achieved its growth. Good growing seasons with the right amount of sunlight and rain produce thick growth rings, while poor growing seasons produce the opposite effect. Too little rain paired with temperatures that are too low will stunt growth. Too much rain may make a tree sickly or cause it to die altogether if it cannot tolerate flooded conditions. If conditions remain changed for a long time, the array of species in an area will change to reflect the new conditions. Consistently wetter and colder weather will foster the expansion of trees and plants suited to those new conditions. Researchers can identify the plant species of a past landscape by looking at the pollens trapped in ancient soils. More will be said about this later.

Additional evidence for colder temperatures in fourth-century Britain can be found in today's glaciers. Traces of broad global climate change can be found in deep cores extracted from ice sheets. Analysis of the ice sheet core from Camp Century, Greenland, shows a distinct drop in arctic temperatures occurring from prior to AD 400 until about AD 600.[1] This drop in Greenland indicates that a corresponding drop in temperatures must have occurred in Britain during the post-Roman period. Elsewhere, studies of Alpine (Switzerland) and Norwegian glaciers corroborate that northern European weather became considerably cooler at this time. As a result, the European glaciers were growing at a rapid pace. Near Grindelwald, Switzerland, living trees were uprooted literally by advancing glaciers. Radiocarbon analysis and other scientific dating methods date the glaciers' advance to approximately AD 300, and the climate changes continued until the mid-eighth century. It was only during the most severe temperatures of this period that the Britons found themselves in serious difficulty. For the first century of colder temperatures, the British economy was able to compensate for lower agricultural production. By the fifth century, however, the strategy of working harder and making do with less was no longer a sufficient response.

Weather conditions interfered with travel and long-distance transport of goods in many places. Efficient travel and transport required good roads. The Roman Empire had founded much of its success on its extraordinary system of durable roads, but as the empire decayed and was no longer able to maintain the roads through its political and military channels, both neglect and environmental conditions contributed to many breakdowns in road connections. If roads, bridges, and the safety of travelers were maintained at all, it was up to local authorities to do the work, but in some cases, not even human intervention could be of use. In the Alps during Roman times, both soldiers and ordinary people were active travelers on the roads while mining operations brought in numerous laborers. After the fourth century, however, not only were the Roman trackways and signposts overtaken and covered by advancing glaciers, but gold mining as a commercial enterprise in Austria was also disrupted. A local alpine legend told of a kingdom overtaken by ice, and H. H. Lamb has suggested that the "king" might in fact have been the commander of a high-altitude Roman guard post forced to retreat from the advancing ice to lower elevations.[2] With roads and trackways at the higher elevations and the lands at more northerly latitudes becoming seasonally or permanently blocked by snow, ice, and cold conditions, communications and trade over long distances disintegrated.

The expansion of European glaciers is just one line of evidence for worsening climate. The bogs of northern Europe also indicate the commencement of a wetter climate accompanied by cooler temperatures, beginning around AD 400. These colder conditions were a part of more devastating storms coming off of the Atlantic Ocean. Bog sediments in northwestern England became increasingly saline due to these ocean-borne storms, commencing around the fifth and sixth centuries.

Other parts of Britain show flooding. In the east of England, where is located the low-lying marshlands of the Fens, flooding increased gradually during the third and fourth centuries. Rising waters reclaimed agricultural land that had been opened for cultivation to meet Roman needs for expanded production. The unrelenting flooding of fields forced farmers westward from the Fens to higher ground as early as the third century. Many farmers switched to cultivating oats because that grain grew better in wet soils. The late Roman period saw increased accumulated surface water across much of England. Villas built in the third and fourth centuries throughout the south were sometimes situated conveniently by water sources that are now completely dry. The wetter weather made for a higher water table in late Roman times, and wells of that date were often of minimal depth, too shallow to reach the water table today but clearly able to reach it in the fourth century.[3]

Lowland flooding can also be observed at archaeological sites from Somerset and Wales in the west to Yorkshire in the northeast. In Dorset, fourth-century pottery sherds have been found buried deep under four feet of silt left behind by floodwaters.[4] At London, the Saxon wharves of probable late fifth- or the sixth-century date were relocated on higher ground at points inland from the older Roman wharves and docks due to the higher river level. With the coastline and river courses inundated by heavy rains and high waters, there can be no doubt that communications, travel, markets, and production of all kinds were hindered. The long-term onslaught of difficult weather conditions strained much of the economic and political organization that the Romans had brought to Britain and would have done so even if Roman administrative control had remained. Fertile agricultural regions, necessary for the feeding of a larger population and its attendant armies, were made useless, not merely disrupted for a season. Unpredictable conditions forced farmers to abandoned, flooded, and windswept lands that were once dependably productive. People had to give up their homes and livelihoods and move elsewhere in a bid for survival. Large movements of population destabilized the economy, and military defense organization quickly fell into disarray.

PLANTS AND FARMING

Information about the spread or decline of cultivation, as well as what cultivated or wild plants were growing can be gleaned, with limitations, from the study of plant pollens trapped in bogs and underwater sediments. Pollen grains found in all plants are extremely durable and can survive centuries of burial in sediments even though almost all the other parts of the plant quickly decompose. Pollen specialists can then identify what plants were present in soils of different ages.

From AD 400 to 800, cereal crops and grains, particularly different types of rye, were common British crops along with hemp and buckwheat.[5] The fibers of hemp were the essential raw material for making strong rope and weaving sturdy baskets and mats. Hemp seeds are about 30 percent oil, and the oil could be used to make paints, varnishes, and soaps, as well as for cooking. Buckwheat was a useful crop in Britain because it grows comparatively well in cool climates and matures quickly, thus making efficient use of the short, northern growing season. Buckwheat has several valuable uses. The plants attract bees (important for the collection of honey) and can also be grown in order to be simply plowed under as a kind of fertilizer for the next cultivation season. Finally, it was incorporated into human foods as buckwheat flour while also being fed to poultry and other livestock. In times of shortage, buckwheat flour has often been mixed with wheat flour in order to stretch the scarcer, but more desirable wheat flour further. After the Roman period, cereal grain cultivation in Britain declined somewhat on account of the worsening climate and diminished population. The practice of cultivating of rye was retained primarily in southeastern England, although rye had previously been harvested as far north as Hadrian's Wall near the modern Scottish border.

Variations in topography throughout Britain combine with corresponding climatic effects to produce widely varied cultural landscapes. These regional landscapes are here considered in turn.

Southeast. In southeastern England where the immigrant Anglo-Saxons came early and settled in large numbers, the changes in landscape use are difficult to explain. In some areas, villas and farms appear to have stopped producing any crops, while elsewhere, the farming of grain crops continued more or less at the same levels of production as before. However, just because crops were no longer being grown at some villa estates and farms does not mean that these lands had been abandoned as was once thought by those who pointed to pollen evidence for forest rejuvenation. Expanding forests necessarily meant that cultivated fields would be fewer, but rural peasants could still pasture their animals in the renewed forests. There was always a living to be made by the pasturage of domestic cattle and sheep, but the Britons were not accustomed to living by animal products and wild plant food sources alone. Lacking the former supply of cultivated grains, there would not have been sufficient food resources containing the carbohydrates necessary for daily energy. Without these carbohydrate sources, population decline was inevitable. Even in the southeast of England where cultivation remained relatively strong, the population must have decreased in order to avoid the dangers of malnutrition and starvation.

East. In East Anglia, where Anglo-Saxons also settled early and in large numbers, the spread of woodland in formerly cultivated areas was already evident during the late Roman period. Pollen evidence from the Fens, situated at the head of the Wash and today measuring about one million acres stretching from Cambridge to Lincoln, demonstrates that cereal grain cultivation there did continue until the fourth century, after which the land was flooded by the rising seas. The increasingly wetter climate also was a factor in the noticeable decline in cultivated crops elsewhere in eastern England. On the other hand, pollens from lake bed cores show that grasses grew more abundantly throughout the east. We can guess based on this evidence that a dispersed population of farmers was depending on maintaining pastures and raising livestock for meat and dairy products with only minimal energy expended on the cultivation of crops for human consumption.

The study of pollen, or palynology, reveals more than the mere presence or absence of cultivation. It can also provide a rough guide to which species of grasses, trees, and other plants—whether domestic or wild—are increasing or diminishing over time. One grass that has traditionally been valued for pasturage is ribwort plantain, and ribwort profiles in the pollen cores expand at this time. However, ribwort is also a plant that spreads quickly over cultivated fields left fallow between crops, so it is difficult to determine from ancient pollen core evidence alone whether pasture usage was truly expanding or fields were just left unused.

Crops deplete the nutrients of the soil in different ways depending on the type of plant. Repeated cropping of the same land with the same or similar crops destroys its ability to produce an acceptable harvest, usually within a few growing seasons. Modern farmers often add chemical fertilizers to obtain the desired nutritional content in the soil. Traditional farmers of early modern Europe and America usually added manure from their domestic herds to their crop fields after each harvest, but many medieval farmers did not own sufficient numbers of herd animals to provide their fields with enough manure. Another solution was necessary. Aside from the use of manure, it is also possible to rotate a series of different crops in the same field, each crop returning to the soil a different set of nutrients as by-products of the growth cycle. Successive crops benefitted from the particular nutrients left in the soil by crops planted in the previous year. Or, the simplest method, as also used in temperate Europe and believed commonplace in post-Roman Britain, was to let the field rest, or lie fallow, and regenerate itself naturally. This fallow year would have to be scheduled once every two or three years as needed given existing soil conditions and crop needs. The fallow method was usually not enough by itself, but it did work well in combination with crop rotation and at least minimal manuring.

Southwest. In southwestern England, at the Somerset Levels, however, we see the opposite trend occurring. Cultivation of grains increases. Cereal grains in pollen cores actually exceed any previous level observed in this region from the fifth century onward. Out on nearby Exmoor, on the other hand, agricultural activity appears to decline in the centuries after AD 400. The important difference between these two areas is found in their elevation: the Somerset Levels are lowlands, while the Exmoor fields lie higher. The variation in altitude exposed the crops to two different kinds of climate. Farmers could still grow crops successfully in the lowland areas that were not overwhelmed by too much rain. The higher upland fields, however, were too exposed to colder, windier, and wetter weather that dominated Britain in these centuries. Not only were the lower fields warmer and better protected from storms, but they would also have had fewer frost days, allowing the crops more opportunity to mature.

Midlands. In a region called the Midlands at the center of England, pollen evidence points to the farming of hemp, buckwheat, and other cereal grains in the post-Roman centuries. Forest regrowth is uncommon, but new forests are indicated by pollen samples in one region of Derbyshire. Hemp was a crop whose fibers had a variety of important uses, while it could also be processed for cooking oil. Buckwheat cultivation might have been necessary to produce livestock fodder. Overall, the pattern of land use in the Midlands is variable with some farmers still persevering in the cultivation of grains for human food.

North. In northern England, we find substantially different climate and soil conditions from those encountered in southern England. Roman period farmers had expanded northward in their need to produce greater harvests for a fast-growing population, but the more challenging environmental conditions had always required adaptation of traditional farming practices taken from the south, even in the best of times. In the Roman period and earlier, settlers in this region had cleared the forests, but after AD 400 or so, pollen cores show that the clearance process began to reverse. To the north by Hadrian's Wall, land formerly used for agriculture no longer seemed to be producing grains except very sporadically, but forest regrowth does not occur either. The old northern fields remained clear of trees, and we can only assume that the land was now used mainly for grazing. Further to the south, however, some open lands were allowed to revert to forest. When cereal grains are grown in the northern counties, analysis of the pollen species shows that the crops were mostly types of rye. Hemp, as elsewhere, was also grown. The raising of livestock supplemented by a few field crops, what is traditionally called a "mixed farming" economy, seems to have continued throughout the post-Roman period, though not with the density of settlement and nor with the rapid expansion that had occurred during the Roman period.

The Romans had given the impetus for all the agricultural expansion in the northern region of England and in southern Scotland, wherever the land was suitable for farming. At the height of Roman political and economic domination in Britain, farmers also attempted to push into the rugged northern lands still

One of the granaries at Housesteads, a Roman fort situated along Hadrian's Wall in Northumberland, northeastern England. Granary floors were generally elevated to discourage the entry of burrowing rodents. The stone pilings revealed by archaeologists supported the wooden floor. The circulation of air under the floors also kept the grain dry and free from mold. (John Miller/iStockphoto.com)

occupied by warlike native tribes. Hadrian's Wall was built around AD 136 in order to protect Roman settlement to the south from these unruly tribes in the north that Rome did not seek to subdue, and the land north of the Wall is roughly equivalent to modern Scotland. In AD 142, the Antonine Wall was built a bit further to the north in order to move the border of the Roman claim about 100 miles north of Hadrian's Wall. This additional territory was abandoned shortly thereafter (by AD 196) when the beleaguered Roman garrisons finally retreated once again to the defenses of Hadrian's Wall, not having been able to push back the northern tribes any further. Meanwhile, farmers had already moved into the area north of Hadrian's Wall. Not only did the general Romano-British population under Roman rule desire more land for farming, having already learned of the comforts of the Roman agricultural villa lifestyle, but the Roman government also required increased food production. Creating an adequate local food supply was necessary for the support of the garrisons of soldiers housed in the many new forts established along both of these walls and the other provincial borders. The Antonine Wall had 19 forts along its length, while Hadrian's Wall had numerous forts, fortlets, and towers along a length estimated at 73 miles. The dedicated agricultural activity, associated with Roman military facilities, quickly lost its market when the empire withdrew its soldiers. As would be expected, pollen evidence suggests that at least some of the field clearances in southern Scotland made during the Roman period reverted to woodland immediately after the Roman retreat back to Hadrian's Wall in the second century, while later withdrawals are similarly reflected in the core data.

West. Wales, west of the Midlands, resembles Scotland, in that it has some impressively rugged terrain and rocky uplands. What Wales lacks in many areas is the kind of level landscape and fertile soils most appealing to cultivators. In northwestern Wales, the post-Roman woodlands may have been converted into pasture. In the rarer lowland areas of Wales where suitable soils for cultivation did exist, farmers still grew cereal grains in scattered fields. The effort to increase the grazing opportunities for livestock has been interpreted to mean that Britons from elsewhere were moving into Wales. These immigrants could have been refugees from lands suffering adverse climate changes, and the possibility of growing unrest due to difficult weather conditions and the absence of Roman control should not be discounted.

HUNTING AND HERDING

Although Britons had some domestic animals, their herds were usually small and devoted mainly to dairy and wool production. In order to put some animal protein into their diets, people normally hunted and fished. Archaeologists often find the remnants of bones and even fish scales in trash heaps left near houses and in villages. Other evidence may come from natural deposits of dead animal and marine life remains in lake and river beds or from peat bogs where animals may have become trapped. Identifying these wild animal and fish species reveals the potential human food sources. Archaeological deposits such as trash heaps containing bones provide more straightforward evidence of what was for dinner and which domesticated species—cow, sheep, pig, goat, dog, or other— were kept or purchased at the market. Not all animal species present at human habitations were intentional visitors. Insects and vermin inevitably infested rural habitations, town structures, and stored food supplies everywhere. Preventing the damage they caused was a constant problem for the Britons, but for archaeologists, even identifying the species infesting storage areas can provide some information about living conditions, environment, and diet.

RODENTS AND INSECTS

Archaeologists generally think in terms of two categories of animal remains: microfauna and macrofauna. The microfauna include small species such as insects, worms, snails, various rodents, bats, and other small animals that might colloquially be called vermin. Macrofauna commonly included the local wild species of mammals, birds, and fish; domesticated animals including pets; and predator carnivores such as wolves. Micro- and macrofauna are usually considered separately in archaeological reports.

The small animals, or microfauna, are an important source of information because they are more sensitive to climatic and environmental change. Insects, rodents, and bats are naturally attracted to human settlement sites. We would not expect these types of creatures to have been deliberately brought to farms and villages by humans. Some rodents and insects can grow to a much larger size if adequate food and water are available. Therefore, the size and numbers of these creatures can show whether conditions are wet. They can also show that humans have been around, since humans may always be relied upon to leave trash and garbage lying about, thus providing all the comforts of home for insect pests and vermin.

At the city of York, the identification of a third-century Roman bathhouse built of wood was based on the presence of a certain species of insect that thrived in warm, rotting wooden beams, such as would be expected to be found in a structure of which the primary purpose involved water. Historic structures that were typically wet or damp retain evidence of their ancient wetness in the form of insect, mollusk, and fungal traces. Certain essential settlement features, such as latrines, can include waterlogged layers of deposits packed with abundant traces of ancient microfauna, especially if the water table has remained high. Constant, uninterrupted wetness due to waterlogged conditions provides an excellent medium for the preservation of most organic substances.

WEST STOW: THE ANIMALS

When the first Anglo-Saxons came as invited mercenaries to help the Romanized Britons fight off the barbaric invaders coming out of the north, these same mercenaries stayed and eventually settled down in small communities amid the existing British settlements. What had been intended by the Britons as a temporary measure became a permanent condition of life and society in Britain. Over the ensuing decades, many small waves of Germanic warriors of various tribal origins—summed up by Bede as Angles, Saxons, and Jutes and most easily referred to as Anglo-Saxons upon their settlement in Britain—arrived, looking for a chance to gain some wealth and property on which to settle down. The migration once started could not be stopped. At the early Anglo-Saxon farmstead and village site of West Stow, in Suffolk, a large assemblage of domestic animal bones has been recovered and analyzed. Here, we see the usual collection of cattle, goat, sheep, pig, poultry, and goose bones, as well as bones of horses, a valuable domestic animal used primarily for transportation and labor. Nevertheless, the early Anglo-Saxons ate all of their animals that died. There were not so many animals of any kind that these people would be choosy about the origins of the meat they ate. Cut marks made by iron knives on horse bones found in refuse heaps show that these animals as well were butchered for human consumption. Such cut marks made by knives leave distinctive grooves on fresh bone from a recently butchered carcass. The grooves are different than the marks (also identifiable) that might be made by a carnivore, such as a dog that gnawed at bones thrown from the dinner table. Each kind of marking, and its source, can be identified by specialists with the aid of a high-powered microscope.

The West Stow people naturally did not limit themselves to eating only domestic animals. Wild species found at West Stow—all of which are likely to have been hunted for food, pelts, or both—are bear, red deer, roe deer, hare, fox, beaver, and badger. Deer were the most numerous. Humans always tend to destroy or drive off the natural predators of deer—wolves, lynxes, and bears (all were once found living throughout Britain)—because these hunters are potentially dangerous to both humans and their domestic animals. This action incidentally allows the deer to multiply. In their turn, deer feeding habits became destructive of the cultivated fields, pastures, and managed woods, so that humans have an additional reason to hunt deer. Celtic heritage harbored a strong hunting tradition. The ancestors of the Britons had hunted for sport, food, and even ritual. The sacrifice of animals for religious reasons was also important. Signs of these rituals appear today as archaeologists find the bodies of sacrificed animals buried in pits dug into the thick chalk layer that lies below the topsoil in many parts of southern Britain.

Red deer are red in summer but a dull brown in winter. They are Britain's largest land mammal. Today, they are most numerous in Scotland, but isolated populations remain in the west, especially in the southwest. These animals are herbivores and graze on a wide variety of plants from grasses and heather to shrubs and trees. Their natural predators were bears, lynxes, and wolves, all now extinct in Britain. Eagles and foxes occasionally prey on very young calves. (Rupert Kirby/iStockphoto.com)

Although West Stow is identified as an Anglo-Saxon settlement, the village and farm is likely a good model of contemporary British practices as well because the animal-keeping practices observed at West Stow, particularly with regard to the selection of animal species and the method of management, show more similarity to what had gone on in Roman and earlier Iron Age Britain than to contemporary practices in the Saxon homeland. The Anglo-Saxon immigrants in Britain did not try to reproduce their lifestyle from their homeland but rather learned from the British natives how best to farm and keep or hunt animals within the specific environmental conditions of Britain. In other words, they adapted their accustomed daily routines to the British landscape and available resources.

CLIMATE CHANGE

This chapter has emphasized climate change. Not all historians are yet in agreement that climate change was a major factor in post-Roman Britain, but much counterargument centers on the concern that "climate change" is just too easy an explanation. As evidence mounts from archaeological investigations, this concern is losing ground. For those who believe that a colder and wetter climate was indeed a major concern in late and post-Roman Britain, the patterns of changing rural land use provide substantiation. The Romans when they first arrived had found the British countryside already to be largely deforested and cleared for farming. What land was not suitable for cultivation was already opened up for grazing, particularly in the lowlands of the south and the east. In the northwest, major forest clearances continued to occur from AD 250 to 400, as demonstrated by pollen core sequences showing a rise in the pollens of cultivated grains and field weeds. These lands, cleared at later dates, included more elevated marginal lands in the valleys of the Lake District and the Yorkshire Dales and amid the hills of the Pennines and southern Scotland. Such land development in the face of presumed worsening climate requires some explanation.

The new lands where late-Roman agriculture expanded were marginal for agriculture, even by present standards and with modern farming technology. Few landowners today bother to cultivate crops in the Lake District, and the many picturesque sheep grazing on the hillsides are mostly for impressing and pleasing the many tourists who come each summer to enjoy the idyllic landscape; little of their coarse wool is profitably marketable. In modern Britain, the northern populations can easily depend on food and other

necessities shipped in from southern markets connected to international commerce networks. Although the Romans had made an
impressive start in creating international trade networks that bol-
stered settlement in many outlying, marginal areas, as political
and environmental conditions caused these network connections
to break down as early as the second century, many regions found
themselves becoming increasingly self-sufficient. The northern
Britons might have preferred to get their grain by trade, but if trade
became impossible, then grow their own grain they must. It was
labor-intensive work, often carrying great uncertainty of success,
to pull a reliable crop out of northern soils every summer without
fail. The extra land clearances were an effort to plant enough so that
famine could be avoided. The farmers knew that some of their crop
would fail each season. Which fields would be most damaged by
the elements depended on the vagaries of annual weather patterns,
so planting in a wide variety of locations, and perhaps even arranging the crops in different ways, helped to ensure that there would
be a harvest. The one certainty was that a greater amount of effort
had to be expended for less harvest every year.

The problems encountered while farming under wet conditions
were many. The escalating rainfall leached the nutrients out of the
soils and left the bottomlands too poorly drained and bearing rot-
ted crops. Attempts to escape damp, mildewed soils and move
fields upslope to looser, healthier soils faced the dilemma that crops
were then exposed to colder temperatures. The fall in ambient temperatures resulted in fewer warm days and a yet shorter growing
season. At higher elevations, weather conditions became too variable. All this made successful farming in Britain more problematic
than ever.

MARGINAL LAND

In earlier Roman times, the use of marginal lands for cultivation was necessary to support the growing population, but such
production was unpredictable. Crops grown on marginal land not
only did not grow easily or abundantly, but also might completely
fail due to any sufficient change for the worse in either temperature
or rainfall. The occasional crop failure in the north meant urgent
demands, especially by the large military garrisons, for shipments
of staples from the south. Such occasional but urgent demands,
in turn, required southern food producers to make available a

substantial surplus of foodstuffs on a regular basis. This was not always possible since adverse weather conditions in the north of Britain were also likely to affect the south. Therefore, supplying surplus grains to the north in bad years was always an arduous undertaking. The Romans had pushed Britain's agricultural productivity to its limits with the farming technology known at the time, and there was very little margin left for coping with disaster. A slight drop in temperature might be enough to cause great damage. One estimate suggests that average temperatures in late and post-Roman Britain dropped by more than 2°F (1.5°C). Although seemingly minimal, such a drop would shorten the effective growing season by as much as 30 days. With 30 fewer days to bring a crop to maturity and harvest, many marginal farms could no longer operate.[6]

In parts of the Lake District in Cumbria, northwestern England, a temperate rainforest climate prevails today. Although sunny days in the summer are not unusual, typical weather is overcast and misty. Light rains are frequent. The high humidity and precipitation produce lush and mossy vegetation on the forest floor. Here, moss covers the remains of uninvestigated medieval stone ruins. Climate conditions and local species of vegetation leave the soils too acidic for productive cultivation. Historically, the land has been used primarily for sheep-raising. (Courtesy Deborah Shepherd)

Some historians suggest that the Britons under Roman rule had been encouraged to expand their agricultural base too rapidly, without thought to the carrying capacity of the ecosystem. Given the farming technology of the era, Britons were dangerously over-extended and too populous even when production levels looked fine. The legions and the growing population demanded increasingly more food and other materials for trade. Forests were cleared too quickly without adequate reforestation plans; attempts were made to cultivate and depend on completely unsuitable soils; and in many areas, the severe erosion of topsoil from too extensive land utilization was a problem. Places that are now wetlands and wholly unsuitable for agriculture (e.g., the Fens and the Somerset Levels) were drier in Roman times and put to the plow. For a while, populations grew on these lands, but when the wetter climate arrived, these lowlands quickly became waterlogged and had to be abandoned. These lands would not become accessible again. People who had lived and farmed on the lowlands were forced to move to other parts of Britain, but there was nowhere to resettle that was not already occupied by other struggling farmers. Some sort of broad demographic crisis involving migration accompanied, to varying degrees, by wide-scale famine, epidemic, civil war, invasion, and emigration must have occurred. Historical records only hint at such events; the details are missing.

EXAMINING ANCIENT SITES

In this book, key elements of the narrative will be illustrated with detailed examples from archaeological sites in order to show how we know what we know. Barton Court Farm excavations revealed the effects of climate and shifting ownership on a rural farm in midlands Britain.

Barton Court Farm

This farm site near Oxford, originally established in the Roman period but occupied as late as the fifth century, shows evidence of progressive human adaptation to a wetter climate. As successive house structures deteriorated and required replacement, the occupants of this farm moved the location of the new house to a higher elevation. Their reasoning could have been that the ground under the house was getting soggier, or they were moving the new house closer to their new fields tilled on higher slopes. The first phase of farming at Barton Court continued into the mid-second century, at which point the property was abandoned apparently for several generations. Closely datable finds from this archaeological site, which would tell when major changes occurred, are rare, but the excavators believe that new occupants arrived at and built a new farmhouse during the third century. The new house, occupied in the third and fourth centuries, was later robbed of stone to be used in building other houses in the vicinity. By the fifth century, the second structure was left a ruin and its belowground cellar filled in with dirt and rubble, presumably so that no person or farm animal would fall in. Other smaller structures to the southeast of the abandoned house indicate, however, that farming at Barton Court continued in post-Roman times. The final residence to be built at Barton Court contained, among other things, a hoard of coins buried on the premises for safekeeping during the fifth century.

We don't know if that post-Roman Barton Court farmer buried his coins because he feared being robbed or merely wanted a safe place to store his wealth, but he died or went away without taking his treasure or telling anyone else where to find it. Although not commonplace, hoards are reported frequently enough among excavation finds to suggest that people had a reason to secure their wealth. By the middle of the fifth century, new people using artifacts of German type—certainly a group of Saxons—moved in and began farming at Barton Court. This was precisely the time when the Saxon settlement in England began.

Barton Court Farm was occupied intermittently from Roman until well into Saxon times. During the late Roman period, the farm family built and used a construction that archaeologists have interpreted as a "corn-drying" oven. Such ovens were used to dry out wet, harvested grain so that it could be stored without quickly developing mold. (The term "corn-drying" stems from the British definition of "corn" as any kind of grain, particularly wheat or oats, and is not to be confused with the American corn plant.) The fields of Barton Court were low lying, and plant seeds recovered from early Roman soil layers at the site show weeds typical of extremely wet soils, while later crops included flax that is itself suited to damp ground. Soil wetness was clearly a problem at Barton Court, even in the second century when the farm was first abandoned. That first abandonment may have been due to the owners obtaining better drained land elsewhere. They may have simply moved to the higher ground at another nearby farm. The late Roman return to lower ground reflects later attempts to increase the likelihood of a harvest in adverse conditions by planting more fields at different elevations and on varied soils despite their probability of partial failure. Nevertheless, it was a losing battle. The mid-fifth-century Saxons seem to have decided that planting crops would not be a profitable use of their energy, and so they concentrated their efforts at Barton Court on pasturing animals.[7]

Barton Court Farm demonstrates well the difficulties that Romano-British farmers and their post-Roman successors experienced due to changing climatic conditions. It is unclear whether the Britons left the farm because they felt pushed out by a growing Anglo-Saxon community or they were disgusted with the poor growing conditions and moved in search of better lands. The abandoned hoard raises questions we cannot answer, but there are no signs of violent takeover of the farm.

Historical Accounts of Climate

The written evidence for the post-Roman centuries of Britain is sparse in the extreme. Texts were written on parchment, a very expensive and rare commodity made of animal skins. Few people outside the Church were literate at all, and of those, fewer still had the liberty to compose original scholarship. Once written by hand, a manuscript existed as a single copy unless it was deemed important and interesting enough to be laboriously copied by a scribe onto additional sheets of valuable parchment. Although highly durable, parchment could wear out from use or be damaged by fire, water, or insects. A damaged copy might simply be thrown away. We have no way of knowing what texts were available in medieval times, but that were lost due to a lack of surviving copies. Occasionally, scholars today read within manuscripts references to other written sources that the author consulted and referenced, but that are entirely unknown today. Frustrating as this reality is, the tracking down and piecing together of the surviving fragments of ancient manuscripts, some actually found reused as bindings of unrelated manuscripts, is a fascinating field of study in its own right.

The best-known text covering post-Roman Britain is the manuscript by Gildas, thought by most historians to have been a monk or clerical member of the Church. He wrote a short commentary describing the harmful effect of changing climate in Britain among other calamities, and it is known as the *De Excidio Britanniae*.[8] According to most scholars today, Gildas lived from ca. AD 510 to 570 (estimates of his birth year vary). Historian Nick Higham and others have challenged these dates, placing Gildas as much as 60 years earlier,[9] but the arguments are complex. In this book, we will use the commonly accepted dating for Gildas.

As for the calamities suffered by the Britons, the reader has to suspect that Gildas was not entirely objective in his account. In chapter 20 of *De Excidio,* he wrote in Latin, "The Romans, however, could not assist [the Britons], and in the meantime the discomfited people, wandering in the woods, began to feel the effects of a severe famine, which compelled many of them without delay to yield themselves up to their cruel persecutors, to obtain subsistence." The "cruel persecutors" were the barbarians, identified in Gildas's chapter 19 as the Picts and the Scots. Again, in chapter 25, Gildas wrote of the Britons falling under attack by barbarians on all sides. There was murder, famine, enslavement, perpetual fear, and self-imposed exile to remote and wild places.[10]

Among the images of war, Gildas painted a picture of famine as a harsh reality in the recent memory of his people. Many Britons had hidden in the hills and wildernesses of their island while some escaped overseas, and others fled to "the rocks of the seas." Wales, the southwest, northern England near Hadrian's Wall, and the island chains surrounding Britain did see new settlement beginning around the fifth century, according to archaeological finds. Despite the poor quality soils, unfavorable weather, and remote isolation of these places, Gildas's story revealed Britons searching for a safe and fruitful place to call home amid the inevitable population shifts of turbulent times.

NOTES

1. Michael E. Jones, *The End of Roman Britain* (Ithaca, NY: Cornell University Press, 1996), 190.

2. Jones, *End of Roman Britain,* 193.

3. Jones, *End of Roman Britain,* 198.

4. Jones, *End of Roman Britain,* 201.

5. Petra Dark, *The Environment of Britain in the First Millennium A.D.* (London: Gerald Duckworth and Co., Ltd, 2000), 134–154.

6. Jones, *End of Roman Britain,* 222, 223.

7. David Miles, ed., *Archaeology at Barton Court Farm* (Abingdon, UK: Oxford Archaeological Unit [Report No. 3] and Council for British Archaeology [Research Report No. 50], 1984), 25.

8. Jones, *End of Roman Britain,* 230.

9. N. J. Higham, *The English Conquest: Gildas and Britain in the Fifth Century* (Manchester, UK: University of Manchester Press, 1994), 229;

Christopher A. Snyder, *An Age of Tyrants: Britain and the Britons, A.D. 400–600* (University Park: Pennsylvania State University Press, 1998), 45.

10. Gildas, *De Excidio Britanniae, Six Old English Chronicles, of which Two Are Now First Translated from the Monkish Latin Originals,* edited by John Allen Giles (London: G. Bell & Sons, 1891), accessed from Paul Halsall, *The Internet Medieval Source Book,* http://www.fordham.edu/halsall/basis/gildas-full.asp.

2

THE PEOPLE

The Romans were accustomed to the barbarians of the outer provinces living in well-defined tribes governed by regional chiefs. When the legions came to Britain, they collected information about tribal organization and sent reports back to Rome listing numerous tribes and their rulers. Today, some researchers wonder whether the Britons were organized with as much political order and stability as the Romans represented or modern readers assume. The tribes were not enduring entities like nations today are presumed to be. A British tribe described in one document might no longer be found in a similar document dated 50 years later. A tribal leader, even those referenced in documents as "kings," might have no known predecessor or successor. The likely conclusion is that tribal power was fluid and depended on a strong, charismatic leader for consolidation. "Kings," in this context, resembled powerful chieftains who held considerable influence over several groups of people, each with their own subking or leader. After the loss of such a leader, the tribe might elect a new king from its ranks, or fission into separate parts, or fuse with another group under a different king.

WRITTEN EVIDENCE

A particularly useful source of information for tribal identities and the names of important persons is found in the texts carved on memorial stones. The many fragments of information from surviving memorial stones, often of unknown date, tell bits and pieces about the kings, warriors, and kingdoms of Britain, but they are like pieces of a puzzle that refuse to fit together.

Medieval record-keepers of history—monks or clerics who commonly added a dose of religious instruction to all of their writings—valued the wisdom and supported the authority of kings. The historical accounts emphasize the role that kings and other supreme leaders played. The times and the people of any nation were often judged by the quality of their leaders. Gildas, the earliest recognized British historian, wrote in the mid-sixth century and dwelled on the issue of the legitimacy of power. He questioned the legal authority of some of the rulers in his nation's recent past and concluded that they could only have been usurpers of authority. The early post-Roman leaders in Britain had stepped in to fill the power vacuum left by the departed Romans, but did they have the rightful authority to do so? Gildas did not think so, for he declared that they lacked proper connection with the earlier Roman regime from which all legitimate right to rule emanated.

In the eighth century, the Venerable Bede wrote *The Ecclesiastical History of the English People,* or *Historia Ecclesiastica Gentis Anglorum,* from the Anglo-Saxon point of view. A churchman who represented the new Christianity among Anglo-Saxons, Bede was most interested in demonstrating how God had selected his people, the English, to be God's people in Britain. Historian N. J. Higham suggests that Bede "invented" the English nation in a very deliberate and creative way. In the eighth century, contemporary Britons still held onto the belief that the land of Britain belonged to them alone and not to the immigrant Saxons who by Bede's time already controlled large portions of the country.[1] Bede's text was an effort to propagandize his preferred view that the German immigrants were the English people of Britain and the dominant nation of the island. Bede's insistence on Anglo-Saxon domination and rightful ascent to national power can equally suggest, if read between the lines, that British opposition to the Anglo-Saxons was still dogged and determined. To a contemporary observer, there was still argument over who held claim to Britain.

Another influential early work of British history was *The History of the Britons,* or *Historia Brittonum,* written in Wales ca. 829–830 and attributed to Nennius, an identity that many now believe to be a pseudonym. Nennius is well known to modern readers due to his assertion that Arthur was a *dux bellorum* who fought with the British kings against the Saxons. The title *dux bellorum* in Latin translates literally as "duke of war," a type of chief military commander. The mention of Arthur by name has been intriguing to many professional and amateur historians. The more general implication of the statement is that the Nennius envisioned an alliance of British kings under the command of one chosen leader. This alliance of Britons confronted the Saxons in organized and effective fashion. However, Nennius is writing of events occurring about 14 generations or 350 years before his own time. That is a very long time in an age when most traditions were still preserved orally rather than as written records. Oral traditions are easily embellished or confused with other stories. Was his *dux bellorum* a real person named Arthur whom he had seen described in manuscripts now lost, or was Nennius simply recording popular tradition?

When reading historians such as Nennius, Gildas, and Bede, modern audiences should take care to understand the intent and motivation of the writers. One portrays Britain as ruled by powerful leaders able to raise and support a standing army. Another paints the Britons after the departure of the Romans as a dismal people who had sunk low and quickly withered into nothing of consequence. The third declares that Britain belongs to the Anglo-Saxons. All are convincing. The truth lies somewhere between the lines.

The Roman departure from Britain caused much of its existing administrative and economic organization to malfunction but not necessarily to collapse altogether. While some increase in social unrest may be expected, the possibility of a severe disruption of society should not be overplayed. The greatest threat may have come from other Britons who had always been outside the Roman sphere of influence. Natives, who had formerly been pushed to the west and the north, now saw an opportunity to regain territory from the disorganized Britons. Some began raiding along the edges of the former Roman territory and could no longer be kept at bay in the absence of the trained and equipped Roman military. Taxes were no longer likely to be collected without Roman enforcement, leaving government services to disappear and infrastructure to decay. Roads were not repaired or patrolled so that their use became increasingly difficult and dangerous. Manufacturing centers providing essential products often could not get the raw materials they needed, nor were there markets for selling mass-produced wares. Large, central markets could no longer expect to operate in safety or serve as outlets for reliable suppliers. Customers no longer had

High-quality Roman-made Samian ware and repaired pieces found at Richborough Roman Fort in Kent. Samian ware was highly valued for its fine grained and evenly red color. Being no longer able to replace broken pieces, the fifth-century owners resorted to attempting repairs. Note the label "Germanii" on the lower left fragment. This piece probably depicts a past victory over the German tribes on the continent. (Charles Roach Smith. *The Antiquities of Richborough, Reculver, and Lymne, in Kent*. London: John Russell Smith, 1850)

a steady influx of Roman coins with which to pay for necessary or luxury purchases. Many political, social, and economic changes began happening at once, and the Britons had to adapt quickly.

ARCHAEOLOGICAL EVIDENCE

Historical sources may give us misleading details, but archaeology, on the other hand, gives us a picture painted with very broad strokes. The ambiguity of the archaeological evidence derives from problems of preservation, excavation, and interpretation. Many items of daily use are unrecoverable. Some materials such as stone and fired ceramics survive quite well in the ground. Bone and iron may survive well, but in acidic soils, both will fragment and disintegrate. Softer organic materials, such as wood, plant fibers, textiles, and food debris, rarely survive. The material remains that have been found and identified after nearly 15 centuries of burial are only a small sample of what people used in the post-Roman era. The sample may not be representative. Excavation is a time-consuming and expensive activity. Only the smallest sites are entirely excavated. Instead, archaeologists usually sample sites by investigating carefully selected areas. Investigations over a large area often are planned using a randomized sampling strategy so that all hidden areas of a site have an equal chance of being excavated even though perhaps 10 percent or less of the site is exposed. Interpretation always requires careful reasoning and is based on preestablished research design and strategy. Despite the difficulties, archaeology reveals matters of daily life that no chronicler would have bothered to record. Commonplace knowledge from farming techniques to home furnishings were known to everyone and did not need to be described in writing. Archaeology brings some of these details back to light.

Another problem faced by archaeologists is the destruction of sites by later human activity. In Britain, villages and villa estates were abandoned when conditions became too wet and cold. Where land continued to be put to agricultural use or was later cultivated once more, fields were plowed in later centuries by larger, heavier equipment pulled by oxen. The deeper furrows cut into the shallow remains of rural dwellings from earlier centuries. Later, farming activity sometimes obscures the clues revealing why these farms and villages were abandoned in post-Roman times. Until recently, archaeologists were not able to find much good evidence for fifth- and sixth-century British life.

TRIBES AND ROMANS

The Roman tactic of dominating conquered populations through negotiations with and coercion of their own leaders into cooperation often also served to increase or solidify the power of native leaders over their own people. The conquered ruling class had little motivation to struggle against the Romans when they found that they might continue to occupy positions of status under the new regime, though not every ruling family benefited equally. The Roman arrival and conquest transition set into motion many local power struggles.

Tribes in Britain controlled home territories as exclusive property and claimed additional territories where they asserted their hunting, fishing, and other resource collecting rights. Tribes occasionally battled locally over territorial boundaries or resources, but they were not skilled at forming effective or long-term alliances against external threats. No single leader had enough authority to command people beyond his own territories. All British political interests and organization were maintained on a relatively local level without a centralized authority. This is why the Britons were unable to band together to resist the Romans when the legions arrived in Britain in the first century AD. Each tribe instead attempted to fight the Romans individually and lost.

Before encountering the Romans, the Britons had no idea what central authority or kingship looked like or how it worked. They had never been willing to let any one person or family dynasty have so much power. After living the next four centuries under Roman rule, the Britons learned to understand and value a stronger, centralized form of government and to appreciate the services and security it could provide. The conquering Romans pushed north and west until they had secured a larger single portion of Britain than any of the conquered peoples had imagined as a single territory. This new political reality had a profound effect on the Britons' view of themselves.

By the end of the Roman occupation, the Romano-Britons were thoroughly adjusted to Roman ways of social and political organization. The loss of Roman rule forced Britons accustomed to the imperial lifestyle to find ways to continue the services of communications (roads), security (military), and trade in manufactured goods (factories and markets) that had been organized under the Romans. Later, they faced the threat posed by the unconquered tribes who had once been pushed into marginal areas and now sought access to the fertile lowlands.

Britons

The Britons spoke a Celtic language. This language later evolved into the Brythonic group of languages represented today by Cornish, Welsh, and Breton. The emergence of Welsh, Cornish, and Breton as separate languages probably took place during the fifth and sixth centuries AD and was a result of the German invasions of Britain. When the Romans took charge, the language of government and official documents became Latin because public officials were Romans or descendents of Romans. The Romans also imported many other languages as spoken by army recruits from all over the empire and by foreign merchants and other visitors who came to the new British ports and towns. The native people continued to speak their Celtic language. Even after the Romans left Britain, Latin remained the language of administration and learning. Those Britons who received schooling learned to read and write in Latin. Churchmen used Latin. Only in the eighth century were texts first written in Brythonic dialects that were adapted to the familiar Latin alphabet.

The bilingual and bicultural situation in Britain contrasted with the relationship between the Romans and the Gallic people of what is now France but was the province of Gaul. Conquered by the Romans somewhat earlier than the Britons, the people and culture of Gaul, for reasons that are not easily understood, were far more profoundly changed. In the process, the common people of Gaul let go of their native language and began speaking Latin just like the Romans. Was it because Gaul was part of mainland Europe and in much closer economic and cultural contact with the cosmopolitan Empire? In a world where people from all parts of the known world on the three continents of Europe, Asia, and Africa could travel the roads and seaways, Latin was the international language of communication. The Britons situated on the outer edge of the known world of culture and commerce may have retained their native language because they were more isolated from foreign contact and less pressured to communicate beyond their boundaries.

Latin never became as much a part of native British society as it did elsewhere in the empire. Latin's insignificance to the daily routines of the British Celts is underscored by the fact that virtually no words were borrowed into Latin from the language of the Britons. The dominant speakers of Latin were not comfortable with British words and did not rely on British expressions or terminology. All that needed to be said or written for administrative purposes could be found in the vocabulary of Latin. Many Latin speakers were probably not Britons at all. Britons, however, used Latin and borrowed words for describing the new innovations introduced by the Romans and for which Celtic language had no words. Such words as *fenestre*, for the window as designed by Roman architects, and *mercatus*, for market, found their way into native British speech.

Britain's Celtic identity has shifted to the background over the centuries, but one area of Britain that is still demonstrably Celtic is modern Cornwall. In Roman times, Cornwall was the provincial region of Dumnonia and held the honor of being the westernmost region, or *civitas*, of the Roman Empire. Dumnonia was not as Romanized culturally as the rest of occupied Britain, but ironically, it became more culturally Roman during the fifth century after the

Romans had left.[2] The city of modern Exeter, then called Isca, was the central town of Dumnonia and of the people called the Dumnonii. Dumnonian territory, marked by distinctive house types and pottery styles during the Roman period, extended to all of Cornwall and to the lands around and just east of Exeter. Farmsteads in Roman Dumnonia resembled the pre-Roman Celtic settlements of the region characterized by round buildings surrounded by earthen embankments. Roads ran through Dumnonia, but only a small area had Roman-style villas with long rows or enclosures of rectangular buildings. Roman or Romano-British temples were completely absent, implying that the natives did not adopt the Roman gods. Romano-British pottery types were also uncommon.

Dumnonia had one feature that made it particularly valuable to the Romans. The land held tin deposits, and profitable tin mines were already in operation during Roman times. Tin was valuable for creating the alloys of bronze and pewter. Bronze was formed by the addition of tin to copper, while lead mixed with tin made pewter. In each case, the addition of tin enhanced strength and durability in the alloy. British tin was shipped far and wide in the empire at great profit.

In the fifth century, tin production under the control of the Dumnonians continued. The famous fortified site called Tintagel dominated the region. At Tintagel, archaeologists found over a hundred rectangular buildings. Trade activity left behind remnants of valuable and exotic items, some from as far away as Mediterranean and Byzantine cultures. The pottery received in trade, including storage jars and jugs, held valuable foreign wines, oils, preserved food stuffs, and other desired rarities. The people who lived at Tintagel enjoyed a rich and prestigious lifestyle. Large burial mounds thought to be post-Roman in date have been excavated near the site of the later Tintagel parish church situated on a cliff overlooking the sea above Tintagel Head. Tintagel is believed by many to be the chief royal Dumnonian estate in the fifth and sixth centuries.

Romanized Culture

In Roman times, Britain was dependent on military garrisons housed in Roman forts to provide civic order and security. Many of the soldiers who filled the garrisons were brought in from outlying provinces of the Roman Empire, some from as far east as Asia Minor. After many years, when their obligations to the army were finally over, foreign conscripts often chose to settle down in Britain.

Many had already started families with British wives. During the Roman centuries, a wide range of immigrants were added to the native population.

The native population changed of its own accord. Britons living under Roman rule had growing opportunities to participate in trade and the production and sale of goods. They also enjoyed Roman public entertainments in urban amphitheaters and other leisure activities such as the public baths. Some Britons accumulated wealth and enough servants to maintain their spacious new Roman villas. The British upper class learned to emulate their conquerors.

The key to economic wealth and success is large-scale production and trade. The Romans discovered that Britain abounded in valuable metal ore deposits such as tin, copper, lead, iron, and silver. Using Roman techniques and organization, these ores were mined in quantity, processed into metal ingots, and traded to other parts of the empire or used in Britain at other large manufactories where iron-, tin-, or bronzewares of quality were mass produced. Other objects of Roman lifestyle made of glass or high-quality ceramics were produced by specialists at other manufacturing centers. Britons learned these skills and understood how much better the quality and quantity of wares achieved would be if craftsmen were specially trained and worked full time. The Roman system demanded a monetary economy so that workers could be paid wages and in turn purchase their own personal necessities with coin. Wealthy Britons must have held responsible economic positions and had ownership of lands and manufacturing resources. Masses of goods were shipped to faraway markets for profit. Archaeological finds of British goods from Ireland demonstrate that Britons engaged in trade with the Irish.

Religion also marked the status of individual Britons. The urban and estate–dwelling Britons adopted public deference to many of the religious beliefs and customs of the Romans. Roman culture not only had its own beliefs and deities but readily assimilated foreign religions. Several major cults, including the cult of Mithras, were imported into Britain by the Romans. Soldiers conscripted from eastern provinces brought religious ideas and celebrations of their own. Archaeological remains of shrines to various deities have been discovered throughout Britain. One religion in particular began gaining in popularity after its arrival on the island around the third century. Despite early Roman opposition, Christianity gained a foothold. The Romans viewed Christians as dangerous political malcontents bent on undermining the authority of the emperor, but

Near Carrawburgh Fort on Hadrian's Wall stands a fascinating temple to
Mithras constructed in the third century. The worshippers of the Persian
god Mithras were members of male-only cults arranged in military-like
orders. Mithras appealed to high-ranking officers and members of the military perhaps because his myth told of the release of life-giving forces after
Mithras killed a divine bull. Temples and altars to Mithras were common
along Hadrian's Wall. (Robert Estall/Corbis)

Emperor Constantine reversed Roman suppression of Christianity
in AD 313 when he issued the Edict of Milan legalizing Christian
worship. By the time of the Roman departure from Britain, many
Britons were openly Christian, and the numbers of their ranks were
increasing. To what degree they were properly Christian and formal followers of the teachings of Christ is open to debate. Scholars
strongly suspect that the personal beliefs of common people were
a complex mixture of Christian teachings and ancient pagan ideas
full of seasonal rituals to promote healthy crops and magic charms
to protect children and ward off evil spirits.

Imported Soldiers

Roman policy held that it was safer to bring foreign soldiers to
keep the peace rather than to recruit natives. Foreign soldiers had
no loyalties to local families that might conflict with their duties to

Rome. Britons who joined the Roman army were assigned to other provinces. Although logical, this policy failed when in the course of their military service, foreign soldiers met and established marital relations with British women. Many eventually lived out the rest of their lives in Britain. In this cosmopolitan society, Latin naturally became the common language of international trade, government, learning, writing, and elite status. Brythonic language was not suppressed, but it became associated with the lower classes and dwindled in importance. Many Britons were likely to be bilingual, knowing at least enough Latin to get by, especially if they traded their goods with the army or at the larger markets.

Later Religious Influences

Romans and those working and trading for Rome brought Christianity to Britain. After the end of Roman rule, many Britons retained the Christian religion they had adopted. Beginning as early as the third century, Christianity had spread into Britain. Many Britons and other Celts were exposed to informal teachings of Christianity. With the breakdown of continental connections in the fifth century, British Christians became isolated from continental communities, and they developed interpretations, practices, and rituals that differed from the standards approved by Roman Church leadership. When the two Churches reconnected after the mission of St. Augustine reached Canterbury in the late sixth century and began debating their differences, the method for determining the date of Easter became a particular sticking point. However, there were other important conflicts.

A useful source for the fifth century is the *Life of Saint Germanus*, bishop of Auxerre. Historian E. A. Thompson believes that Germanus died in AD 437. He first visited Britain in AD 429 and arrived a second time just before his death. His *Life* was composed by Constantius of Lyon sometime between AD 480 and 494, so memories about Germanus were still fresh at the time of writing.[3] The purpose of a saint's "life," or *vita*, is to inspire readers to greater faith, not necessarily to teach them history. However, with caution, modern readers can glean some history from stories of saints' lives. Constantius makes it very clear that Germanus preached in Britain in order to strengthen the faith of British Christians. Germanus also intended to correct the heretical beliefs of Christians who had been misled by British heretic, Pelagius. Germanus was not so intent on converting pagans. His goal was to prevent heresy, for the Church was afraid

that heresies—improper and unsanctioned beliefs—were prolif-
erating throughout the Roman frontiers. The fifth-century British
monk Pelagius taught that human nature is essentially good. Insist-
ing that humans had free will, he argued against commonly held
beliefs that humans were weak and prone to sinning. The doctrine
of human frailty tempted too many people to claim inherent weak-
ness as an excuse to behave immorally only to ask for forgiveness
later. Building further upon these arguments, Pelagius and his followers also denied the Church's doctrine of original sin, which was
the basis for the necessity of infant baptism. The rebuttal of major
doctrine and sacrament was too much for the Church, and Pelagius's teachings on human free will were declared heresy. However, since Pelagius had originated in Britain and developed his
doctrines there, his ideas remained popular there, both in the rural
countryside and the towns. Among his supporters were some rich
and influential men.[4] As a result, Germanus was sent to correct the
growing problem of Pelagianism.

Germanus's visit underscores how fluid Christian ideas were
during the fourth and fifth centuries. Christian communities whose
members often lacked formal education were held in thrall by
traveling preachers whose words might or might not meet with
approval from Rome. Other people were not members of communities but simply adopted Christian beliefs as they had heard them
described. There was also the obvious problem of language. Teachers like Pelagius spoke the native language of the people. Germanus did not. Nor was there any indication in his *Life* that Germanus
attempted to communicate directly to the common people. Instead,
he contented himself with talking to the local rulers, the tribal
kings, and heads of leading families, who usually heard his words
through an interpreter.[5] Naturally, these limited efforts did little to
impact the religious beliefs of the laboring rural population.

Roughly contemporary to Pelagius was Patrick, the first bishop
of Ireland. The future patron saint of the Irish was raised from boy-
hood as part of an organized Christian community in Britain. He
wrote of himself in his *Letter to Coroticus*—the title possibly refers
to a king whose land lay just north of Hadrian's Wall—that he
was born the son of a *decurion,* a man whose office was to collect
taxes and arrange for the provision of town services. Even as the
Romans were leaving, Patrick's father may have been among those
administrators who continued to look after the welfare of town
residents using such taxes as could still be collected to finance
repairs and customary services. Patrick further described himself
as "freeborn" and of noble rank. He presented himself as a citizen

of Rome, and he similarly addressed the soldiers of Coroticus as "citizens" in the Roman manner. The fifth-century Bishop Patrick was a product of the old Romano-British world, but unlike Pelagius, Patrick had no public falling out with the Church on matters of doctrine. Instead, many miracles are associated with Patrick's missionary work in Ireland, and the legend of how he banished the snakes from Ireland remains a popular story.[6]

POST-ROMAN CHANGE

The traditional date for Rome's abandonment of Britain is AD 410, but Roman withdrawal had started earlier. The empire had been failing. Imperial troubles from barbarian attacks, provincial revolts, and internal power struggles combined with a declining economy forced Rome to downsize. Britain itself had been the source of more than one revolt, so one way to be rid of the problem was to cut Britain off. The army was withdrawn and forts abandoned. In a few instances, Britons moved into the empty forts, sometimes to continue the work of defense against external attack. Perhaps, not all of the Roman legionaries were willing to leave their British families behind. However, Britain's defenses became localized and piecemeal. Likewise, the administrative machinery of the towns fell apart. Some services continued for a time, but little new growth or repair of old structures took place. Gradually, the Britons reverted to their old ways and shook off the trappings of Roman life.

Causes

A popular but mistaken interpretation of the Roman departure from Britain holds that the Romans willfully abandoned the country that they had held under their control. On the contrary, Romano-British generals were struggling in the fourth century to seize power for themselves, and several attempts were made to expand that power beyond Britain's borders. Destructive rebellions made Britain too difficult for Rome to govern. In part, the Romans chose to leave, but they were also pushed out. British leaders were anxious to rule their own country, but self-rule was plagued with problems, chief among which was the inability to agree on who should be in charge.

Another view holds that it was not the leadership but the ordinary Britons who rebelled against the Roman authority. Why would the ruling Britons who had benefited the most as members of the Roman ruling class be anxious to expel Roman power? Perhaps, they imagined that they could retain their power but not have to share their wealth with the Romans in the form of taxes. The elite Britons would have been shortsighted if they thought that compensating for the loss of the Roman army was simple. The large landowners and manufacturers—the leaders in economic power—should have known the dangers posed to markets by the loss of the Roman infrastructure. Whether it was the lower or upper classes who rebelled, support for the theory of British rebellion is often taken from Zosimus who recorded in his *History Nova* that the "Britons therefore took up arms, and braving the danger on their own behalf, freed their cities from the barbarians threatening them. And all Armorica [Brittany] and the other Gallic provinces followed their example, freed themselves in the same way, expelled their Roman rulers and set up their own governments as far as lay within their power."[7]

There is a problem with the word "cities" in the preceding quote. The Roman-built towns were already walled and could be defended against attacks, including those mounted either by peasants or neighboring tribespeople. The town dwellers themselves were well off and had no real motive for rebellion. Instead, the places being rid of barbarians may have been the districts surrounding the towns.[8] On these lands, farmers labored to feed not only themselves but also the townspeople to whom much of the farm produce went. These farmers were the most heavily taxed portion of the British population and the least likely to have appreciated Roman overlordship, particularly if demands on them were increasing just as bad weather and other factors reduced crop yields. Furthermore, farmers were more exposed to losses when actual raiders—whether Pictish, Irish, or German—overran the countryside. When Roman military units departed to protect the empire's core from foreign invaders and civil unrest, troublesome tribes surrounding Britain took advantage of the power vacuum. The immediate consequence of Roman withdrawal was an escalation of danger experienced by the farming peasantry. When domestic military leadership passed in quick succession through three "usurpers," culminating in a general who took the name of Constantine III, the soldiers behind these upstart rulers came at least in part from the countryside. The farmers were not neutral in these struggles. Zosimus's remarks about Armorica and the other Gallic provinces seem to corroborate the notion of widespread popular uprisings in the western empire.

However the events of the early fifth century transpired, the Britons could not maintain their accustomed lifestyle for long. The complex Roman provincial economy collapsed in the fifth century. Large-scale manufacturing and long-distance distribution of products declined rapidly. Nearly, all production and distribution was reduced to small-scale, local activity.

Economic Change

The economic collapse included the end of any practical monetary economy in Britain. Coins still remained in people's possession, but they were no longer in mass supply nor used for making everyday transactions. Prior to AD 402, Roman coinage was regularly imported in large quantities as wages for the Roman garrisons. Coins also arrived through trade with many parts of the empire, throughout the Britain via public markets and as payments for wages and services. When new coins stopped arriving, people responded by hoarding their coins rather than spending them. The circulation of coins steadily diminished. Whenever possible, individuals preferred to pay for goods by bartering other goods rather than relinquishing scarce coins. Some of the remaining Roman coins in Britain were undoubtedly melted down for their metal content, but many were buried as hoards in the ground for safekeeping. Hoards buried shortly after AD 402 contained mostly contemporary Roman coins. Similar hoards were buried for over half a century. The latest hoard yet discovered to contain a predominantly Roman coins is called the Patching hoard. Judging from its most recent coins, it was buried after AD 461, but some of the coins in the hoard were minted as early as AD 337, well over 100 years prior to its burial. Clearly, Britons were holding onto old as well as new coins if for nothing else than their metal value. Such hoards were the best insurance against hard or dangerous times.

The transition away from a monetary economy was not immediate, but an absence of new coinage supplies impacted the way people lived at both the elite and peasant levels of society. Ordinary transactions were less frequent. Markets dealt mainly in necessities. Merchants brought few, if any, costly imports from overseas. Foreign traders came less frequently to British shores. All areas of Britain were affected, but the southeast and east felt the brunt of the impact. There are signs that some eastern Britons moved westward going as far as crossing to the continent and settling in Brittany.

Western Britain experienced the Roman absence differently. Although western Britain had from the Roman point of view been a cultural and economic backwater because Roman cultural influence had been strongest in the east, the western regions including Wales now had a somewhat stronger monetary economy. Archaeologist Ken Dark has suggested that the use of coinage persisted longer in western Britain than in eastern Britain where increasing numbers of German warriors and settlers were disrupting Romano-British society.[9] The German immigrants were not accustomed to using coins and did not have any interest in them except for their raw metal value. Saxons in eastern Britain were more likely to take coins out of circulation and melt them for jewelry and other ornamental objects. In the west, the Britons, both the original occupants and the transplanted refugees, continued to thinks of coins as money for a while longer.

Fifth-century markets in western Britain still functioned locally with fewer goods made by specialists or imported from overseas.

Roman mosaic floors like this one from Bignor Roman Villa in Sussex, England, often depicted subjects that were offensive to or too ostentatious for Christians. Pagan images such as Medusa, the snake-haired Gorgon, were probably removed from buildings that continued to be occupied by British Christians. The latest archaeologically confirmed occupation of Bignor Villa was in the fourth century. A number of its mosaic floors have survived. (Laurence Gough/Shutterstock.com)

Markets did not disappear, but styles became strangely frozen in time. Even at the end of the fifth century, makers of pottery and personal ornament continued to copy the styles and fashions of late Roman Britain. Archaeologists have found evidence suggesting that some large, industrial-sized kiln sites continued to mass-produce the old pottery until after AD 450. Local artists and craftspeople continued to produce and copy the well-known Roman fashions. Professionally produced pottery, as opposed to the crude, rough, homemade variety, was available in western Britain for decades longer than in the east and southeast. Just as coinage retained its intended purpose longer in the west, so did Roman styles. The west suffered fewer cultural disturbances brought about by Anglo-Saxon immigrants.

An additional reason for downsizing the British economy is that the Britons no longer had a large Roman military system to support. The Roman army had been a huge consumer of food, metal goods, leather goods, raw materials of all sorts, human labor, and animal labor. The Roman army paid for goods purchased and paid its soldiers' wages in coin. When the army departed, a major consumer of British production was gone. Because the British did not create their own defensive military force on the same scale, no new consumers of products and services came forward. Instead, British leaders hired German mercenaries to fill the void left by the departed Roman army.

Not every aspect of Roman fashion was retained. The growing public acceptance of Christianity changed the way people chose to live. The pagan Romano-Britons of earlier centuries had enjoyed elaborate mosaic floors and ornately painted plaster walls inside their houses. These forms of artistic expression often depicted scenes from pagan mythology. As Christianity gained a following in Britain during the fourth century, the well-to-do citizens began eliminating overtly pagan designs from their villa decor. Christian ideals demanded aesthetic simplicity. Aside from frowning on mythological scenes, Christian practice encouraged plain floors and white, undecorated plaster walls. Statuary, once a common feature of both domestic and public spaces, virtually disappeared. The colder annual temperatures and rainier weather of the fifth century encouraged the use of woven floor and wall coverings, decorative in a less likely offensive or ideological way and cozier for the building occupants. Woven coverings were a logical and historically common solution for overcoming chilly indoor temperatures, but their complete deterioration over time has made the surviving plain

and undecorated interiors of post-Roman residences look impoverished to modern eyes. The missing wall textiles provide the illusion
of a much diminished lifestyle in distressed circumstances. All the
plain walls really demonstrate is a change in religious belief and
behavior.

In the early and mid-fifth century, western British society appeared still hopeful of being able to maintain its accustomed social
order and to recover its former days of Roman glory—if only the
annoying tribes to the north and west could be fended off and the
German mercenaries be contained.

Western Refuges

By no means all Britons were happy to be free of Roman government and taxation. The breakdown of provincial government left
a power vacuum that, according to the cleric Gildas, precipitated
bloody civil conflict among the old British families struggling for
control. Soon, tribes in Scotland and Ireland realized that British
lands were disorganized and ripe for attack. Britons who wished to
avoid impending troubles immigrated to western lands including
Wales and Cornwall in the southwest. Others left altogether, traveling across the channel and settling in northwest Gaul in a region
that is now appropriately known as Brittany but was then called
Armorica.

Scoti and Picts

Never conquered by the Romans, the Celtic tribes of Ireland and
Scotland were quick to take advantage of British disorder. The
ancient names—Scoti and Pict—are confusing to modern readers.
The Scoti originated in Ireland but crossed the Irish Sea in a northeast direction to settle in Scotland. Eventually, the Scoti dominated,
and the land took on their name. The Picts lived in Scotland prior
to the Scoti arrival and diminished as an organized people after the
sixth century. When the Romans penetrated Wales, they built fortifications along the coasts. Further west, the Romans never made
headway against the tribes of modern Ireland. The Irish Sea became
the Roman boundary. As for the north, Roman dominance never
extended more than a short distance into Scotland. There was no
convenient natural barrier to defend. Instead, two large fortified
walls were constructed to mark the limits of the Roman domain and
to keep the northern tribes at bay: the Hadrian and Antonine Walls.

Gildas, the sixth-century British cleric, recorded that the Picts of Scotland and the Scoti of Ireland were the chief enemies of the Britons after the departure of the Romans. In fact, the Picts and the Scoti had been raiding Roman Britain since the Romans laid claim to the land and militarized their borders. Roman documents indicate that border troubles escalated in the fourth century. However, the raids from the north and west did not necessarily originate out of a desire for new land. The Picts actively raided but rarely settled. The reasons for this behavior are not clear.[10] The Scoti from Ireland raided also, yet made only limited settlement in Britain. The main destination of Scoti settlers was Scotland north of Cumbria. A few early church dedications suggest that some Scoti also immigrated to western Cornwall. Contemporary inscriptions and place-names from the Isle of Man, an island found between the British mainland and Ireland, are also closely related to the language of the Scoti and may indicate Scoti settlement there as well.

Both Irish and Pictish raiders were capable of long-distance voyages, and their most effective routes of attack were over water. It may have been the wealth of Roman Britain that enticed them, but there is no evidence that the raiders took any valuables back home other than slaves. British or Roman items made of silver, bronze, and other precious metals and stones have failed to appear in Pictish hoards of the period. The acquisition of slaves may have been the real impetus for the raids. With slaves providing more labor, the Picts, Irish, and Scoti could increase production on their farms. More production led to wealth, increased landholdings, and greater social status.

Tyrants

Who were the leaders of the Britons? Gildas was certain that the troubles experienced in Britain were divine punishment for wrongdoing and wrong ideas. These troubles included a period of civil war during which members of the British elite vied for ruling control of Britain or for autonomy in their own region. In addition to general sinfulness and inadequate faith, Gildas attributed the ensuing power struggles between leading Romano-British families to rampant greed. He argued that most of the contenders lacked any right to the power they sought. In his mind, only a few individuals or their families had the legal authority invested in them by the Romans to fill the void left by the Romans. Authority must be handed down as if no break with Rome had occurred. Any other effort to rule was unlawful.

To emphasize his bias toward Rome, Gildas used the term *tyrannus,* where "tyrant" should be understood as a "usurper," one who takes authority he does not have. In *De Excidio Britanniae,*[11] Gildas depicted a disorganized British upper class struggling for the power to govern while the Irish and Picts took advantage of disorder.

The problems were not just political. Agricultural production was hampered by deteriorating weather conditions, another of God's punishments. Markets and roads were no longer safe, worsening climatic conditions led to famine, and people were migrating to other parts of Britain seeking both safety and better farming options.

The Irish may not have come always as raiders. Some of the Irish in western Britain were probably hired mercenaries, just like the Germans in eastern Britain. Hired Irish warriors were perhaps put in place to fend off their countrymen on missions to seize land. Evidence for Irish movement into Britain appears at all the natural crossing points where sailing distances are shortest. Irish personal names and place-names are found in Galloway in Scotland, at Angelsey and Holyhead in northern Wales, and at Dyfed in southern Wales. Concerning Dyfed, there are also somewhat later written sources of both Welsh and Irish origin that appear to describe the settlement of several tribal groups in former provincial areas. For whatever reason the Irish came, their place-names and personal names carved into memorial stones and written in the ancient Irish script called Ogham are numerous in southern Wales.[12] This distinctive Irish influence in southern Wales persisted into the seventh century.

In southwestern Scotland, the Irish retained their cultural identity the longest. They established perhaps in the late sixth century a small kingdom or group of polities called Dalriada. From this political center, the Irish language spread northward through the highlands of Scotland, gradually becoming Scots Gaelic. The Gaelic language overwhelmed and supplanted the native Pictish language. Elsewhere, English eventually overtook the remaining traces of indigenous Pictish speech. Historical tradition provides some stories about the people of Dalriada. According to one source, the Dalriadan king came to County Derry in AD 575 to negotiate a political settlement with the king of Ulster. Perhaps, the Dalriadan kingdom had until then spanned the Irish Sea to include Irish and

Scottish territories on both sides of the water. Archaeologically, the Irish connection is not so apparent, leading an occasional researcher to conclude that the Dalriadans originated from the same population as the Picts.[13]

Roman writers were responsible for labeling the indigenous people of the north the *Picti*, and the linguistic origin of the name is uncertain. The common belief that it came from the natives' habit of tattooing or coloring their bodies, with blue woad or other pigments, cannot be supported.[14] Nevertheless, the name was widely known and was used by prominent writers including St. Patrick in the fifth century, Gildas in the sixth, and Bede in the seventh. As a population, the Picts were linked to eastern Scotland. Pictish place-names are found from Inverness in the north to the Firth of Forth in the south. The Picts may even have occupied the Orkney Islands for a time. They were mainly farmers, much like other contemporary people, and built their houses of stone with rounded walls. Additional rooms were built tangentially to the main room in an agglomerative pattern often referred to as cellular.[15]

The southern Picts were partially converted to Christianity in the fifth century. However, the strength of their Christian convictions was challenged by St. Patrick who complained that they were engaged in the trafficking of other Christian converts as slaves. He called the Picts apostates for having converted to Christianity but then choosing to disregard their oaths. Such behavior is not surprising. Conversion of an entire people was, as always, a gradual process spanning a number of generations. People do not change their beliefs quickly or easily. The northern Picts did not seriously adopt Christianity until late in the sixth century when they were visited by the Irish monk St. Columba. Despite coming late into Christian society, very little is known about pagan Pictish religion. Once Christianity became the dominant religion among the Picts, all traces of the ancient religion were systematically wiped away.

Unlike Irish sources that provide a contemporary glimpse into the sixth century, texts about the Picts are all of later date. Many of these texts are king lists or other records with little informational value.[16] The purpose of king lists was to record the lineage of ruling families, but where information was missing, as inevitably was the case, the identities of ancestral rulers were blithely embellished. Names were added or replaced to satisfy current political rivalries. King lists can be revealing documents, but they must be interpreted with care and not taken for straightforward history without confirmation from other sources.

Pictish Symbol Stones

Among the better-known attributes of Pictish society are the Pictish symbol stones. These stones are difficult both to interpret and to date. One group of stones exhibits an assortment of symbols or images that are often abstract or else appear to render half-human and half-animal forms representing figures from mythology. Some scholars believe these stones date from the fifth and sixth centuries. Certain symbols may be pictographs for personal names. The repetitious patterns of symbols imply that they combine to convey a message. Some stones appear to have been burial markers, while others are likely to have been memorials to absent persons, deeds, or events. In Pictish cemeteries, stone cairns contain objects evident of prestige, wealth, and status. The men and women buried in the cairns were local elite members of Pictish society. Some Pictish symbol stones could have been meant to reinforce the status of ruling elite families or to glorify the memory of their ancestors. Later Pictish stones added Christian symbols and descriptive images of aristocratic life such as scenes of riding or hunting activity. Forms of highly skilled labor, such as metalsmithing, were also depicted.

The Christian elements in Pictish life were due to missionary influence. Many unknown preachers of the Christian faith traveled north from Britain as well as east from Ireland in the post-Roman era. The conversion of the Picts was described in some hagiographies, the biographies of individual saints written for the purpose of teaching the reader about the exceptional Christian qualities of the saint. Such stories should not always be taken literally, but an example from the life of St. Kentigern serves to underline the probable extent and limited success of missionary activity among the Picts.

Composed by Jocelyn, 12th-century bishop of Glasgow, the life of St. Kentigern recounted how Kentigern traveled to Glasgow after being named the first bishop to the Strathclyde Britons. Many of the neighboring Picts had already been converted to Christianity by St. Ninian. However, they had let their faith slide, and St. Kentigern converted them again around the beginning of the seventh century.

In the fifth century and perhaps later, the Picts were mostly pagan and ruled by local kings. Certain contemporary Pictish structures are often interpreted as royal forts or strongholds. Since British kings had royal forts, Pictish forts could have been influenced by the British pattern. However, no Pictish fort is securely dated to either the fifth or sixth century. Also, some post-Roman Pictish forts may not have been forts at all but rather operated as pagan religious centers. The most convincing examples of the religious interpretation are found on promontories overlooking the sea.[17]

The religious center argument is based on liminality. Although early medieval defensive forts often occupied promontories, the combination of high elevation and location near a body of water was also characteristic of pagan sacred sites. Scholars have long recognized that ritual places have "liminality"—that is, they stand at the edge of some imposing physical boundary at a point of transition from one type of environment to another. Standing on a boundary is symbolic of transitioning from one world to the next. This applies to birth, death, religious conversion, and other great transitions. Other possible liminal boundaries are found at the edge of dense forest (especially around a clearing within the forest), any river or lake shore, or a promontory edge. Whether these structures were liminally placed for spiritual reasons or built for military defense against attack remains to be determined.

The Votadini

Another people residing in southern Scotland were the Votadini. By all appearances they had maintained friendly relations with Roman Britain. The Votadinian stronghold, one of the largest hillforts in Scotland, is known today as Traprain Law, where "Law" derives from Old Norse *hlaw*, meaning "hill." Traprain Law was used for defense until the mid-fifth century. In 1919, a large silver hoard containing many valuable pieces of Romano-British origin was discovered there. How the Votadini could have acquired so much silver is curious, and it has been suggested that they were paid to protect those Britons settled south of Votadinian lands against incursions by northern tribes. Alternatively, others suggest that the last people to occupy Traprain Law were not the Votadini but the Picts, and the silver hoard of Traprain Law was the loot *stolen* from neighboring Britons. Yet, another view asserts that the Votadini migrated to northern Wales in the fifth century where they played a role in expelling the invading Irish, after which effort the Votadini brought home treasure.[18]

German Mercenaries

Even before the Romans departed from Britain, Germans and Frisians had already arrived and settled, having initially been conscripted into the Roman army and sent to serve at British posts. Once their long terms of service were over, the veterans stayed. The retirees frequently settled together in their own ethnic communities, probably still speaking their native languages, and were recognizable archaeologically by their culturally distinct burial rites, ornaments, pottery, tools, and weapons. In surviving Roman and British sources, these people were usually lumped together under the label *Saxones*. Modern writers use the terms German, Saxon, or Anglo-Saxon.[19]

The single contemporary document describing the coming of the Germans to Britain was written by an anonymous Gallic chronicler on the continent. The document is known in English as *The Gallic Chronicles*. The two relevant entries were dated to AD 410 (the first arrival event) and 452. The latter entry purports to describe past events during AD 441–442 when the British provinces were *incursione devastatae* or "devastated by an incursion of Saxons" and *in dicionem Saxonum rediguntur* or "yield[ed] to the power of the Saxons."[20] In reality, German incursions began in the south and east progressing slowly and haphazardly until the seventh century when the British and Celtic communities were at last able to draw firm boundaries marking off Cornwall, Wales, and Scotland as the homelands of native kingdoms that the Anglo-Saxons did not or could not challenge.

De Excidio Britonum described the main influx of German arrivals more than a century after the fact. Gildas alleged that some British elites sought to control the external threat of Irish and Pictish incursion by hiring foreign mercenaries. German warriors who were invited for this task soon rebelled against their hosts, and there were rumors that some British settlements were taken by force from their owners. Much later, historians envisioned exaggerated incidents of violence.

Visions of violence in modern histories notwithstanding, Gildas was neither a witness nor a reliable interpreter of these events. There is no record of why the German mercenaries chose to come to Britain, how they thought they would be compensated, or whether they felt the Britons had cheated them. Remember that this was not a contract between nations in the modern or even the medieval sense. At most, letters or emissaries requesting aid and promising reward might have been sent to various German leaders. Word spread. Men seeking fortune and prestige answered the call. One possible piece of evidence comes from Gildas's description of a special council of British leaders. These leaders were said to have issued such an invitation to the Germans. Vortigern was the alleged leader of that council, but other regional leaders could have independently taken similar action. Bands of unrelated German warriors, seeking fortune and following ambitious chieftains who had the means to organize the transport ships, began to arrive. New groups continued to arrive throughout the fifth century. The immigration was a slow trickle of small, mostly unconnected warrior bands, not the arrival of a single massive army.

Apparently, the Germans were by and large satisfied with their end of the deal for nearly all of the fifth century. Archaeology and history both suggest that the relations between Britons and Germans were cooperative for a while, but by the 490s, the Germans in Britain, some of whom would have been born in Britain and possibly of British mothers, rebelled against their employers and demanded a more permanent status accompanied by the right to landownership. Although there was a clear British plan to import German mercenaries, too little, if any, thought had been given to the problem of sending them home again after a job well done. German settlements initially resembling soldiers' camps evolved over time to include buffer communities of families and offspring whose presence and determination to hold onto their lands continued to protect and shield the Britons living behind them from unexpected attacks. After the passage of more generations and a lifelong commitment to the new land, those Germans, now more appropriately called Anglo-Saxons, felt they had a natural right to stay in place.

The earliest archaeological evidence for Germans in Britain derives from burials. Because the German mercenaries were not Christian, they buried their dead with the possessions that had been important to them in life and that were necessary for their continuing activities in the afterlife. Warriors needed their weapons: swords, spears, shields, and battle-axes. Farmers needed their tools. Everyone was buried with their personal knife, and the buckles, brooches, rings, armbands, beads, and pins that were integral parts of clothing and accessories. In all likelihood, most people were buried in their best clothing and jewelry that was not bequeathed to survivors. Many graves contained pottery that probably held food for the dead. In cremation burials, the ashes of the dead along with their burnt possessions were gathered from the pyre and placed in a pottery jar or other container.

Several distinctive styles of brooch used to fasten cloaks and other articles of clothing mark the presence of the earliest mercenaries. The oldest finds of German fasteners come from burials in East Anglia dated to the early fifth century. Like the burial practices back home, the dead were cremated and their ashes placed in pottery urns. The urn was then buried in the cemetery ground. Very quickly, however, changes began to occur. Contact with the Britons led to the adoption and adaptation of new burial ritual. Some Germans, especially those who moved into the southern Midlands, were buried in the late Roman or Christian manner, called inhumation where bodies were buried whole into the ground either in coffins or wrapped in shrouds.

A specific German burial preference is called weapon burial. Many German males were buried with their weapons, a custom that was not at all known in fourth-century Britain. Interestingly, the weapon graves appear to increase in proportion to other types of graves after ca. AD 450. Some interpret this development to mean that after 450, either a proportionately greater number of warriors were coming as mercenaries into Britain or it became even more fashionable in German society to be buried with a set of weapons, especially if one was considered an important person. This suggests that the symbolism of weapon burial was increasingly used as a sign of general high status, even among those who might not have been illustrious warriors but were more renowned for wealth or political leadership. In other words, weapons became a badge of office, thus increasing the number of presumed "warriors" in cemeteries.[21]

Mercenaries and Towns

Despite changing burial symbolism, after AD 450, the number of German mercenaries positioned to protect British domestic security seems to have increased. Cemeteries reveal their presence near former Roman towns and cities. Although these urban settlements of earlier centuries were no longer home to large populations, they remained occupied, and some scholars speculate that limited administrative and economic functions continued within their walls and amid their crumbling buildings.

At London, remains of mid- or late fifth-century German cemeteries show in maps as a ring around the southern perimeter. Pottery sherds identified as German-made have been found within the city walls near St. Bride's Church. Finds at the site of Mucking, Essex, suggest that there were other Germans positioned there to guard the mouth of the Thames River. Early German cemeteries were also placed close to Roman roads and near towns and harbors that were strategic locations in the late fourth century. It stands to reason that many of these locales remained strategic a century later, justifying the need for mercenaries. Although archaeologists have found some German artifacts in London, possibly obtained through trade, there has been no evidence of actual German settlement *within* London's walls. To all appearances, the Germans around London were invited warriors working under contract, and they behaved appropriately by staying outside of town.[22]

This pattern of early German occupation is also noted elsewhere. Similar evidence showing German encampment around major towns has been documented at the urban centers of Lincoln and York. Like London, these centers retained their importance to the fifth-century Britons and were therefore assigned a German guard force. By the end of the fifth century, the Germans were strategically positioned around the administrative centers of the Britons, and they may well have outnumbered the remaining British occupants of these towns.

Population Change

Part of understanding social change involves understanding population change. The study of demography in times when very little documentation is available can begin with questions such as *how many people were there, and how did the separate populations compare in size?* The first difficulty encountered is the problem of identifying ordinary Britons. The rural peasant Britons who farmed the land throughout the Roman period left behind few durable artifacts for archaeologists to study. What they did leave—house foundations, plain pottery, and a few metal fragments—lacks stylistic character and is therefore very difficult to date even to the correct century. Not only is there uncertainty whether or not certain artifacts date to the fifth or sixth century, but it is also sometimes impossible to distinguish among pre-Roman, Roman, post-Roman, and medieval objects. British artifacts, compared to Roman or German artifacts, lack the distinctive style and ornamental traits and, in some cases, durability when buried in the ground. As a consequence, it is difficult to recognize the ordinary British people who left behind plain and indeterminate possessions in the archaeological record. Yet, the Britons were there. The latest excavations conducted with a much closer eye to detail and alternative forms of evidence do not support old claims that the Germans had killed off the Britons or driven them all away. Although movement occurred, Britons were still living in all parts of Britain.

Many scholars accept that the troubles of the fifth and sixth centuries led to population decline, but making population estimates for Britain based on the known datable finds and sites is problematic.

One early estimate settled on about half a million people but is viewed today as too low. Current estimates range from two to six million people for all of Britain. This number includes Britons, Germans, Picts, Scoti, and other ethnicities.

Estimating prehistoric population is accomplished by analyzing the demographic potential of small individual landscapes. Archaeologists mark known sites on maps, count the number of known burials, suggest which parts of the landscape were likely to be settled and farmed, study the distribution of stray artifacts found scattered and not associated with any site, and estimate how much evidence has been undiscovered or destroyed by human activity. Some landscapes of Britain are better researched than others, so estimates from well-known landscapes are sometimes applied to other areas showing similar characteristics.

The greatest challenge to making accurate population estimates is the accurate dating of artifacts, sites, and other cultural remains. Working within a short time frame requires close dating, but many post-Roman objects and structures, as well as human remains in burials, are hard to assign to a short range of years since styles changed so irregularly. Dating by style, when it can be accomplished, is called typology. Without close dating, the population estimates lack historical usefulness. Contemporary styles of pottery and ornament do not mark out the decades or even the half centuries. Of many object types, the best that might be said is that they could be post-Roman, or not.

Radiocarbon dating helps to assign a closer time frame to some objects and features, but it can only be used on artifacts that are organic in origin, such as bone, wood, or plant material. Radiocarbon dating works best on materials burnt at the time of use. Charcoal, made from charred wood, works well for radiocarbon dating, likewise, bones burnt in a cooking fire. Even so, such dates are not exact and can be distorted if the dated material was long exposed to weather or other chemical-altering conditions.

Dendrochronology, the study of tree-ring patterns, is used to assign dates to wood when enough tree rings can be seen in cross-section to connect the tree growth pattern to the present or a known event. However, if the soil of the archaeological site is too acidic, as soils often are in Britain, wooden and bone remains are usually too decomposed or damaged to study.

Many post-Roman sites were occupied for only a short period, no more than a generation or two. Neighboring sites may overlap in time or have been occupied in quick succession. In such cases, the archaeologist tries to determine whether nearby farms were occupied by two different families at the same time, by the same family at different times, or even by different families at different times. To illustrate some of these problems, three examples of excavated sites from the post-Roman period in Britain— Glastonbury Tor, Spong Hill, and Frocester Court Villa—are presented below.

ARCHAEOLOGICAL STUDIES

Glastonbury Tor

The town of Glastonbury in Somersetshire and its famous abbey have claimed Arthurian connections for centuries. Glastonbury Tor, a hill rising over 500feet and much altered by human activity, may have been occupied in the fifth century as a defensive stronghold. Such was the interpretation offered by archaeologists in the 1960s. From those limited excavations, it was decided that several wooden buildings had once stood on the Tor, and one contained a metalsmith's furnace complete with a bellows inlet for increasing the heat of the fire by blowing in air. People came and went upon the Tor, but no cemetery has been discovered save for two isolated graves containing adolescents. There is no apparent explanation for the lack of adult burials or the presence of the two youths. Trash heaps containing many animal bones indicates considerable eating, even feasting, taking place on the Tor, and sherds identified as pieces of sixth-century Mediterranean amphorae, or jugs meant for the long-distance transport and storage of wine, attest to the importation of a luxury commodity that had surely become rare in Britain. Where did the wine-drinkers come from, and why were they on the Tor?

Some people think that the Tor may have been the site of a fifth-century monastery occupied by hermits, but the fact that the only two burials found are oriented in the pagan manner, from north to south rather than east to west as preferred by Christians, argues against a monastic interpretation. On the whole, the opinion that this is a secular defensive stronghold maintained by a local chieftain seems more likely if not entirely suitable. If Glastonbury Tor does turn out to be a monastery, then it is the oldest known Celtic monastic site in Britain.[23]

Spong Hill Cemetery

The cemetery at Spong Hill is situated in East Anglia where many of the earliest Anglo-Saxon arrivals were received. The site has been thoroughly excavated and includes remains from several periods: a prehistoric burial mound, Roman, Anglo-Saxon, and late medieval. The early Anglo-Saxon immigrants buried their dead in the pagan manner by cremation. There are at least 2,400 cremation burials at the Spong Hill cemetery spanning from the mid-fifth century through the sixth century, and the excavators believed that people from a number of German settlements in the region brought their dead to Spong Hill cemetery. There are also some later burials, including inhumations, placed away from the earlier remains.

Cremated remains were buried inside specially made pottery urns. Such urns, or large jars, were made solely for the purpose of holding human remains. Personal possessions were also burnt and buried with the body. Many women had their jewelry and personal household tools such as spindle whorls for making yarn. Men were not buried with weapons but with the ordinary objects of daily life such as razors, knives, and dice for games. Only the males in the late inhumations were given spears, swords, and shields in burial. Archaeologist Catherine Hill suggests that in the final period of Spong Hill, the local elite used the cemetery and marked out a separate area for the high-status interments of the dead. Inhumation of the body might have been one way to show that the deceased person was powerful in life. It may also show that these later Anglo-Saxons had been influenced by Christian practice although they continued to give grave gifts to the dead. Early Christians were very clear about labeling cremation burial a pagan and abhorrent custom. Similarly, they opposed the burial of objects with the dead.

Many of the Spong Hill burial urns were observed to be similar in style to urns used further north in Lincolnshire and Yorkshire. This and other evidence suggests that the immigrants maintained communication with their counterparts throughout Britain. Communication enabled the sharing of cultural traits so that consistent styles and rituals were maintained over long distances.[24] Despite coming from dispersed parts of the continent and in small, unrelated groups, Anglo-Saxons formed a unified and coherent society in their new homeland.

The nonmilitaristic character of the early cremation burials at Spong Hill is striking. It could mean that some early immigrants came to fifth-century Britain with the intention of farming and raising families. Settling down was not an afterthought once mercenary employment had ended. Perhaps, some Spong Hill occupants never intended to be mercenaries. Alternatively, these Germans did not at first think of weapons as suitable grave gifts. Their economic value or status symbolism may have made it necessary to bequeath weapons to heirs. Not being a part of British society, the Germans were unconcerned by the legalities of prior property ownership. Anglo-Saxon sites like Spong Hill, sometimes occupying former British farms, became numerous in eastern Britain.

Frocester Roman Villa

In the Roman period, large farming estates, or villas, were owned and operated by wealthy landowners. Excavations conducted at some villas have shown continued habitation and building use during the fifth century. In western Britain, at Frocester in Gloucestershire, the fifth-century occupation of Frocester Court villa is seen in the presence of datable burials and timber structures put in place after the Roman period ended. Some fourth-century residents had lived in stone-built dwellings. The stone structures were abandoned perhaps because they had fallen into disrepair and were too hard to keep up. Britons preferred to build with wood after the Romans left. At Frocester, one long and narrow timber building was constructed without upright supporting posts. This lack is revealed archaeologically by the absence of postholes in the ground. Without support posts, it was a flimsy structure. Many sherds of coarse pottery were found strewn about on the floor. Was it a temporary warehouse for storing goods, some of which were kept in the now-fragmented pottery containers? A second timber building was more solidly built and could have been used as a residence. Four bodies were buried nearby.

The excavator, Carolyn Heighway, has suggested that the villa was for a time put to use as a marketplace serving the surrounding countryside.[25] The long narrow building is especially suggestive of a structure erected for the safe temporary storage and exchange of goods in all weather. A former Roman official who remained behind could have moved a local market held elsewhere to this secure but abandoned villa and kept it organized and functioning during his lifetime for the benefit of the surrounding settlements as well as his personal income.

NOTES

1. N. J. Higham, *King Arthur, Myth-Making and History* (New York: Routledge, 2002), 99.

2. Ken Dark, *Britain and the End of the Roman Empire* (Charleston, SC: Tempus Publishing, Inc., 2002), 150.

3. E. A. Thompson, *St. Germanus of Auxerre and the End of the Roman Empire* (Woodbridge, UK: Boydell Press, 1984), 1, 2.

4. Thompson, *St. Germanus*, 26.

5. Thompson, *St. Germanus*, 16.

6. P. F. Moran, "St. Patrick," in *The Catholic Encyclopedia* (New York: Robert Appleton Company, 1911), http://www.newadvent.org/cathen/11554a.htm.

7. S. Ireland, *Roman Britain: A Sourcebook* (New York: St. Martin's Press, 1986), 168, 169.

8. Thompson, *St. Germanus*, 34, 35.

9. Dark, *Britain and the End of the Roman Empire*, 54.

10. Edward James, *Britain in the First Millennium* (New York: Oxford University Press, 2000), 103.

11. Gildas wrote, *De Excidio Britanniae, translated to modern English as "Concerning the Ruin of Britain."*

12. James, *Britain in the First Millennium*, 104 and Lawrence K. Lo, "Ogham," *AncientScripts.com: A Compendium of World-Wide Writing Systems from Prehistory to Today*, 1996–2012, http://www.ancientscripts.com/ogham.html.

13. W. A. Cummins, *The Age of the Picts* (Stroud, UK: Sutton Publishing Ltd., 1999), 54–56 and Dark, *Britain and the End of the Roman Empire*, 222–225, 228.

14. Dark, *Britain and the End of the Roman Empire*, 212.

15. Dark, *Britain and the End of the Roman Empire*, 212–214.

16. Dark, *Britain and the End of the Roman Empire*, 211.

17. Dark, *Britain and the End of the Roman Empire*, 220–222.

18. Cummins, *Age of the Picts*, 72.

19. I prefer to use "German" in reference only to the earliest generations of mercenaries and settlers. After that they can be best lumped together as "Anglo-Saxons."

20. Christopher A. Snyder, *An Age of Tyrants, Britain and the Britons, A.D.400–600* (University Park: Pennsylvania State University Press, 1998), 35–36; the source of the translations is Theodor Mommsen et al., *Monumenta Germaniae Historica, Chronica Minora*, Vol. 9, bk. 1 (Berlin, Germany: Weidmann, 1826–), 617–666.

21. Deborah J. Shepherd, "Archaeology and the Social Meaning of Bearing Weapons in Anglo-Saxon Society before the Christian Conversion," in *Ancient Warfare*, edited by Anthony Harding and R. John Carman (Stroud, UK: Sutton Publishing, Ltd., 1999), 219–248.

22. Dark, *Britain and the End of the Roman Empire*, 51, 52.

23. Snyder, *Age of Tyrants*, 178, 179.

24. Catherine Hills, "Spong Hill," in *Ancient Europe, 8000 B.C.-A.D. 1000, Encyclopedia of the Barbarian World*, editors-in-chief Peter Bogucki and Pam J. Crabtree, Vol. 2 (New York: Charles Scribners' Sons, 2004), 496, 497.

25. Snyder, *Age of Tyrants*, 196, 197.

3

TOWNS AND COUNTRYSIDE

The loss of reliable transportation networks changed urban life in post-Roman Britain for the worse. Towns and rural areas in Roman Britain were tied together by an intricate network of roads. In many ways, the foundation of Roman culture everywhere was its road system. No towns could be supplied, no fortresses built and garrisoned, and no territory "Romanized" without the efficient and durable Roman roads and the directional signposts that pointed the way and measured the distance for travelers. The road network connected British destinations so well that many modern highways follow the same conduits. In some less-traveled areas, the ancient highway construction survives in use.

POST-ROMAN DECAY

The Roman standard of living required excellent roads, safe and well-defended towns, functional harbors, clear and navigable waterways, aqueducts for reliable freshwater, sewers for urban sanitation, and a variety of public structures such as markets, temples, courts, and barracks to house the defending garrisons. Such basics form a society's infrastructure. Maintenance of the infrastructure requires supervision by a recognized authority and the funds or labor, usually collected in the form of taxes or conscription, to perform the work.

Even before the fifth century, administrative authority had begun to break down. Caretaker officials were not always appointed or sufficiently salaried. The infrastructural elements of communication and urbanization started to show neglect bit by bit. Once the Roman core of Britain's government was absent, towns depended on a few dedicated local officials using their own wits and resources to look after public services. For a while, towns continued to operate with the resources already in place, but eventually their services began to diminish. Commonplace attributes of Roman life—aqueducts providing plentiful water, markets supplied with goods and craft specialists from near and far, forums for gathering, temples, amphitheaters, warehouses, granaries, and ultimately the roads themselves—began to fall into ruin or were roughly transformed into other structures to meet more urgent needs.

THE ORIGINAL ROAD SYSTEM

The Roman road system by the end of the fourth century was massive. Road building began soon after the conquest. By the mid-second century, after only 100 years of Roman occupation, an estimated 8,000–10,000 miles of road had already been laid in order to facilitate the movement of troops and supplies. Naturally, these roads were also put to use for local traffic to and from villages, villas, mining camps, manufacturing centers, and towns.

The provincial Roman government recognized four categories of roads ranging in order from the most important to the least: public roads funded by the state, military roads built at the army's expense but also used by the public, local roads on which less engineering effort was expended, and private roads that were built and maintained by their owners. The latter two categories encompassed roads and tracks of varying quality.

Before the Romans built roads, the ancient trackways of Britain had followed the natural terrain seeking the easiest ground to traverse wherever it was found. Such tracks often detoured around marshy areas, hills, or ravines. Romans did not like to waste effort laying out long, meandering roads, so they ignored the older routes, preferring instead to move in the straightest line possible except where major obstacles in the landscape left no choice. Since Roman roads usually connected such new places of military importance as forts, towns, and administrative centers, the old trackways often did not take the desired direction. There were a few exceptions. Silchester was one of the pre-Roman centers of British activity reused by the Romans. There, the old native roads connected to the new road system.

Laying roads the shortest distance by going through obstacles required a great investment of labor. If a hill stood in the way, earth was hauled away until the land was leveled. If a wetland needed to be crossed, earth was moved in to build a causeway. Construction was systematic. A dependable road required a solid foundation. Roman roads were constructed with thick layers of tightly packed stones and gravel sorted for size. The larger stones formed the bottom layer, while layers of progressively smaller gravel filled in and leveled the roadbed. The final result was well over a foot thick and resistant to the wear and tear of heavy traffic and severe weather. More important roads were elevated above the surrounding land surface and provided with ditches on both sides so that the road surface would never flood. Elevated roads were so well fabricated they did not collapse or become rutted even in the worst rainy seasons. Upright curb stones buried in a line along the sides reinforced the road surface keeping it stable. These elevated roadbeds formed the original "highways" of Britain and were much used until modern times.

A surviving paved Roman road in the Greater Manchester region, England. The road bed is slightly elevated due to the thickness of the paving. The central drainage ditch helped to control water runoff during heavy rainfall. Surface cobblestones are meticulously fitted. (Robert Estall/Corbis)

Construction methods varied according to the official status of the planned road, but certain techniques were distinctly Roman. The careful layering and tight packing of selected gravels and other materials to form the roadbed is called "metalling." Many different materials were used, depending on their availability and suitability to local subsoil conditions. Sand was added to keep the road from becoming too rigid and prone to cracking. In areas where iron ore was smelted into iron, the rock-hard chunks of slag, produced as a waste by-product during the smelting process, were added to the layering material. The iron content of the slag pieces had the added value of rusting over time. The rust would physically combine and harden with adjacent stones and sand to create an extremely solid, concrete-like mass. Heavily used roads were resurfaced from time to time. The final road metalling performed at the end of the fourth century sometimes resulted in a total road thickness of about three feet.

POST-ROMAN ROADS

The making of roads was more than the laying of pavement. Services for travelers encouraged long-distance travel. Along the major roads, wayside staging posts sprang up to assist the movement of Roman troops and supplies. Civilian settlements frequently arose in conjunction with Roman military sites or along major roads because of the lucrative business opportunities available for provisioning both the military ranks as well as the civilian travelers. Additional food, personal necessities, luxuries, and leisure items were always needed and desired. Roman soldiers were paid their wages in coins and only needed a convenient opportunity to spend them.

Roman roads in the fifth and sixth centuries continued to carry traffic, but roads do not choose their travelers. Historians speculate that the existing road system enabled a quick penetration of southern and eastern England by Germanic newcomers. The road system also allowed the entire population of Britain to move about in response to foreign threats and changing weather conditions. Townspeople left for the urban amenities of the continent. Merchants sought markets and customers in safer jurisdictions, while farmers migrated to drier and warmer fields. The old Roman roads retained their importance in successive medieval centuries, too. Even where they did not remain in use as roads, the lines they imposed on the landscape often became boundaries for parishes and other significant administrative or private land units. The well-known Roman highway Watling Street in Northamptonshire now serves as the line for a number of modern administrative boundaries.[1]

Most of the roads, however, were used because they went to places that remained important. Medieval Watling Street along with Ermine Street, Fosse Way, and Icknield Way were all former Roman roads that continued in use for local trade and travel along their routes. Roads were no longer used as highways of long-distance travel. By late 11th-century Norman times, the importance of land routes for commerce had much diminished. Long-distance transport in the Middle Ages relied mostly on shipping over internal rivers and along the coasts.[2] Water transport was cheaper, easier, and especially when the hauling of heavy goods was concerned, more efficient.

WATERWAYS

Use of waterways required boats and barges, but otherwise, water transport systems necessitated less effort for construction and maintenance than roads. In the fifth and sixth centuries, however, all forms of transit were diminishing. Land travel slowed. Markets localized and then disappeared, and no one made much use of the waterways. Later, around the eighth century, no central government existed to provide organized road maintenance, so a shift to the transport of cargo by water made sense. Wharf piers and storehouses would appear in towns fortunate enough to lie along suitable rivers. Some of the new shipping skills were brought by Viking invaders. Vikings were much more accustomed to water travel than Anglo-Saxons, but all that change lay four centuries in the future.

REMAINS OF ANCIENT ROADS TODAY

Archaeologists and historians have made much progress over the last century mapping the Roman roads of Britain. Mentions of roads and routes in written sources, coupled with the discovery of both known as well as undocumented road surfaces during archaeological fieldwork, have provided a comprehensive picture of Roman transportation networks.

By contrast, the ancient trackways of Britain are much harder to map, since these routes were constructed only by the wear and tear of persistent use rather than through any deliberate and durable construction methods. The continual wear by foot, hoof, and cartwheel often provided the only signs marking most lengths of ancient track. Only occasionally would stones be positioned in a recognizable way to shore up the track base or create a more stable footing in wet conditions. If left untraveled, these tracks soon disappeared through natural erosion. Even when ancient tracks can be spotted in the landscape today, it is hardly possible to determine their age. There is nothing about their appearance that reveals their antiquity. Many now serve as private roads on rural farmlands or as hiking paths on public lands. Such folk trackways have looked much the same for millennia.

URBAN CENTERS

Much of the Roman character of Britain, at the time of the departure of the legions, ca. AD 410, lay in its administrative organization and public services—the creation and maintenance of the road system, protected and planned towns and markets, established public authorities making and enforcing laws, aqueducts and public baths providing an adequate urban water supply for concentrated populations, sewers and latrines supplying large-scale sanitation services, temples, and public entertainments—all these services and conveniences were the accoutrements of city life introduced by the empire.

Nevertheless, urban life was always somewhat precarious in this outer imperial province. The urban system, thoroughly dependent on the maintenance of a strong regional authority manifested both in military forts and appointed governors, sat perched atop a traditional and self-sufficient rural culture. Garrisoned forts guarded strategic points of the landscape, and agents of government oversaw production and commerce in and around the towns. Urbanization relied on the interdependent relationships of towns, forts, and countryside. Towns and forts depended on the smooth movement of people and supplies, but the countryside was able to care for itself.

DECLINE IN IMPORTANCE

As the fourth century wore to a close, stresses within the Roman Empire made its grip on Britain increasingly tenuous. With major Roman capitals and governments under assault on the continent, the central imperial power in Rome could not afford to expend energy and limited military resources on the preservation of distant Roman outposts such as Britain. During Britain's last decades as an imperial province, the tendency toward self-reliance in the countryside had already begun to reassert itself.

In defiance of these trends, some towns and their rural neighbors in late fourth-century Britain seemed to have thrived together. Local political ties and economic networks remained strong for some decades more. Several reasons account for town survival. First, the original system of administration motivated itself to keep going. The Romans were adept at recreating their society from the ground up wherever they went. They established major urban centers to administer to the economic, legal, and other public needs for entire regions. Second, smaller towns were positioned to provide markets for essential goods, production of everyday items such as tools or shoes, shipping and warehousing of common food stuffs, religious shrines, and public meeting places. These amenities were desired by Britons, whether rural or urban. Finally, agricultural production in the countryside was well organized so that there should be enough food surplus transported to cities and towns, as well as to military camps and garrisons, to support all those consumers who were not themselves farmers. Everyone relied on this system in order to be well fed and satisfied despite occasional local shortages.

TYPES OF TOWNS

In order to understand British society at the end of the Roman era, we need a clear picture of how the Romans organized urban Britain.

Coloniae

The dominant urban centers in the fifth century were the result of nearly four centuries of town development. Before the Romans came, the Britons maintained groups of hillfort settlements with defenses. Some of these forts were larger, more complex, and functioned as tribal centers. Neither the form nor, in many cases, the location of the major hillforts suited the Romans for their urban centers, so the new Roman towns were usually built elsewhere. The redundant and abandoned old settlements lay dormant during the Roman period.

The Roman towns were divided into four types depending on their originally assigned purpose. Some of the most important centers in Britain were initially founded as *coloniae*. These settlements were created and given over to the legionaries discharged from military service after the successful completion of their service. *Colonia* formation often occurred when the entire garrison of a fortress was decommissioned. The settlement layout in a *colonia* was designed according to Roman urban planning concepts. It began when the Roman army deeded over a block of land grants to a defined group of discharged legionary veterans. Each veteran received a land plot for a house in town (which was still in the planning stage) and another plot outside of town for his fields and pastures. The veteran's army rank determined the amount and location of the land deeded to him. Higher-ranking veterans received better deals. Altogether, the surrounding agricultural territory assigned to the *colonia* and its inhabitants was substantial.

A *colonia's* land usually matched, more or less, the lands controlled by the decommissioned legionary fortress where the discharged veterans had served. The modern cities of Colchester, Gloucester, Lincoln, and York all evolved from *coloniae*. Colchester, as was typical of Roman town settlements, was laid out on a rectangular grid with a surrounding defensive wall.[3] Roads entered the town through four main gates—facing four different directions. Other prominent amenities included a basilica for public gatherings and a temple for public worship. *Coloniae* were granted a charter of independence allowing their appointed magistrates, who were Roman citizens, to make and enforce suitable laws for governing the town inhabitants, both army veterans and British natives. This policy allowed the local judicial system in Britain to deviate from the legal systems in use in Italian towns according to their differing cultural traditions and needs.

Municipia

A *municipium* had different origins than a *colonia* but might gain similar importance in time. *Municipia* were not pre-planned, nor were their original inhabitants drawn from a specific part of society. Instead, *municipia* grew out of local economic needs. The large and important *municipia* might be promoted to the political status and rights of *coloniae*. London was possibly chartered as a *municipium* late in the first century but was promoted to a *colonia* by the early fourth century. Another *municipium* of note was Verulamium. However, it was also one of few major urban centers of Roman Britain that did not survive as a modern city.

Civitates

Below the rank of the *municipia* and *coloniae* were as many as two dozen sizable British towns of lesser rank.[4] The administrative organization of these towns provided mainly for local government and markets. Their locations, size, and function often coincided more closely to original tribal settlements and boundaries than did the *coloniae* or the *municipia*. Because of this local connection, such smaller towns, known as *civitates*, became an avenue for continuing the political influence of local leading British families. Each *civitas* was incorporated with local rights and authority but lacked independence and self-governance.

The leading families of the Britons controlled at least some of the *civitates* and benefitted from their revenue production, but the provincial governors ruled over all. Like the higher-ranking urban centers, the *civitas* capitals were still visibly Roman: they were laid out on a grid, surrounded by defensive walls, and provided the usual public structures of forum, temples, and baths. Their purpose being largely economic, substantial areas of the *civitates* were given over to commercial activity, including manufacturing, a wide range of services, and shops.

The later towns, especially the *civitates*, were largely occupied by Britons who had taken to town life. The Roman method of conquest involved using a permanent military presence to subdue the native population until such time that the natives gave up rebelling against the inevitable and showed willingness to cooperate with Roman authority.[5] Once an adequate level of coexistence was achieved, the imposing and expensive military fortresses were gradually replaced by towns. The function of the remaining military installations changed to providing protection for the towns and the surrounding countryside. With viable towns in place, the native leaders discovered that towns were the perfect base for increasing their own local power and economic advantage. By the fourth century, leading Britons lived in the towns in order to promote agricultural production, manufacturing, and trade in their domains. Economic success brought wealth to these families. The Britons had become fully invested in the Roman economic system.

Vici

Some small settlements began simply as offshoots of military forts. The needs, wants, and spending power of officers and soldiers encouraged the growth of civilian settlements on the outskirts of forts. This kind of settlement, or *vicus*, thrived on providing simple craft wares, repairs, and other services for the fort. Textile, clay, metal, and leather goods were produced or mended, and civilian labor was available for hire, augmenting the workforce for the reg-

ular maintenance duties required of soldiers. Some *vici* grew large.
At Cirencester, Dorchester, Exeter, and Wroxeter, the *vicus* outside
the fort evolved into a much larger *civitas* ultimately overwhelming
the fort.

TOWN LIFE

The Britons voluntarily and enthusiastically took to town life.
The advantages of urban services provided impetus to encourage
the creation, maintenance, and proper governance of town communities. All that new settlements needed to do was conform to
Roman models of urban organization. The Romanized towns of
Britain thrived, even during the fourth century when imperial fortunes were waning.

Running a Romano-British town was no simple matter. Administrative activities took place in a basilica complex often connected
to a forum where an open-air market appeared regularly. In this
basilica complex, offices and numerous storerooms housed the
legal and accounting services, goods, and foodstuffs necessary to
supply the townspeople on a daily basis. Taxes, fees, and duties on
goods sold were collected and distributed to support the costs of
town administration.

Some of the income paid for the necessary maintenance of streets
and the aqueducts that brought freshwater into town. Plumbing
was provided by lead or ceramic pipes or simply by directing running water into open channels lined with stone. Sewers and drainage ditches were regularly cleared of excess waste. Although most
residences lacked personal plumbing, public facilities were conveniently available. Public latrines, some flushed with running water
by virtue of being situated above a sewer ditch, and heated bathhouses, open to all social classes and separated by sex, made up for
the lack of these amenities in all but the most elite private homes.
Basins providing drinking water for the public were set up at
numerous accessible locations. Recreational and educational facilities might also be provided. Remains of amphitheaters still survive
at Chester and other Roman towns.

COSMOPOLITAN TOWNS

Signs of continuing cosmopolitan ties to the continent are clear.
A recent study of the architectural designs found in late Romano-
British buildings reveals that distinctive and ornate architectural

styles can be traced to *increased* contact with widespread parts of the larger empire. This is particularly true in southwestern Britain. The southwest maintained a successful ongoing commercial relationship with Mediterranean lands during the fourth century[6] and, it is now argued based on recent archaeological work, also in the fifth and sixth centuries. The unusual architectural influences found in the late and post-Roman southwest are described as so authentically "exotic" that apparently Mediterranean or North African architects and skilled construction workers were imported in order to produce certain structures.

It might be argued that either the southwest was more independent of Roman control or that Dumnonian leaders were more powerful. The Roman departure had less impact on this region. Native rulers appeared to maintain order without difficulty. The Britons of the southwest, particularly in the counties of Cornwall and Devonshire, managed their own defenses and had no dealings with mercenaries. They benefited from a wealth of natural resources, predominantly in metal ores. As they had been less dependent on outside Roman support all along, their economic, political, and social networks, both internal and international, suffered little apparent disruption at the turn of the fifth century.

TOWN WALLS

City walls were an integral part of the urban landscape in early Britain. Since the first and second centuries, defensive walls built of stone blocks by skilled masons surrounded the larger *coloniae, municipia, civitas* capitals, and also some lesser settlements.[7] Town wall masonry might be as thick as 100 feet and include towers and a walkway along the top.

Around AD 370, a major military reorganization was undertaken in response to devastating barbarian attacks by sea from Scotland and Ireland. At the same time, many existing walls were repaired and fortified. Britain was already suffering from inadequate military manpower, so how effective the defense of these new walls was in the event of attack remained questionable. Nevertheless, army detachments were placed in towns and even at some large villas. At Catterick, around AD 370, researchers found that space was made for new troop barracks by forcing civilian residents and shop owners to move.[8] The danger of attacks from the north put Catterick, in northern Yorkshire, in a strategically important defensive position.

Detail of the flint and tile construction of the Roman city wall surrounding Verulamium, the remains of which are now situated on the southwest side of modern St. Albans, in Hertfordshire, England. In many parts of southern England, flint rocks are so plentiful in the soil that they are a nuisance for farmers. Luckily, they also could be used as building material. Although not easily shaped for a close fit, plenty of cement held the stones together. Builders in flint cracked stones in half and positioned their reflective inner surfaces as the outer face of walls for visual appeal. The row of red brick tiles was probably another decorative feature. Such stripes are seen in Roman walls. (Natalie Tepper/Arcaid/Corbis)

POST-ROMAN TOWNS

Britons immediately faced two serious problems: (1) destructive power struggles involving different factions of leading families and (2) raids by opportunistic tribes from across the northern and western borders. The Roman departure left a power vacuum, yet town life continued in the first decades of post-Roman Britain indicating the Britons could indeed survive without the Romans. According to Gildas, the majority of power eventually fell to a man named Vortigern. In order to protect the towns from raiders, British leaders under Vortigern allegedly hired German mercenaries as guards.[9] At first, the plan worked well, but soon these same Germans became another foreign enemy wishing to conquer a piece of Britain.

The two most important early written records of this period are Gildas's *De Excidio et Conquestu Britanniae* and *The Anglo-Saxon*

Chronicle. Neither is contemporary. Sixth-century historian Gildas wrote with contempt about the power struggles among Britons, yet he did not give much information concerning the actual events of several generations earlier.[10] The *Chronicle,* told from the Anglo-Saxon point of view, imparted a long-remembered oral history of Anglo-Saxon beginnings. The tale of Hengist and Horsa told of two brothers leading an invading army and achieving decisive victories in battle. Their conquest led to the founding of Kent, the first Anglo-Saxon kingdom. The story promotes a legendary and patriotic version of the arrival of German mercenaries in Britain. Linguistic arguments have supported the idea that Hengist, at least, may have been an historical leader of the first decades, but little of his legend is factual.

In the east, British leaders were apparently unable to raise adequate troops to defend the towns. For too long, they had depended on Roman soldiers to perform that task. Although some soldiers stayed behind when Rome relinquished its hold on the island, many had gone to fight on both sides of the continental rebellions. There were not enough trained men or material support from the towns to continue the task.

The first mercenaries are better known archaeologically than historically. By the early fifth century, German mercenaries camped around the outer defenses of major urban areas, in particular around London, Lincoln, and York. At the town of Mucking downstream on the Thames River from London, German camps guarded against attacks coming upriver from the sea. From such strategic locations, the mercenaries protected the important towns. Their camps and cemeteries are easy to identify. Because they were pagans, their burials contained personal possessions for use in the afterlife, making the remains easy to recognize as German. British Christians, by contrast, left nothing in burials but the body.

Soon many more Germans, including women, arrived, and new generations were born on British soil. Although many Britons were accustomed to town life, the immigrants were not. Wherever early Germanic settlement prevailed, farm and village life, typical of the settlers' homeland, dominated. Only gradually did this pattern change.

Once the immigrants put down permanent roots in Britain, it is common to refer to them as Anglo-Saxons although the term is not ethnically accurate. Nevertheless, it is a convenient name. While Britons lived in towns, Anglo-Saxons lived in rural farms and villages. As the facilities of British towns fell into decay and the towns were abandoned, Anglo-Saxons sometimes moved into town areas but only to occupy the space in their own way. This happened at Winchester and other urban locations. What little evidence has been found of early Anglo-Saxon activities in towns indicates that the primary attraction of the old towns were their defensive walls. Unrest and raids were plaguing the Anglo-Saxons as well. They too were struggling to carve out and defend territorial boundaries. The town walls had many uses.

Although the towns were reoccupied, services were not reinstated. Markets did not revive. Specialized craft and manufacturing activities were not pursued. The Saxons did little to rebuild or repair but merely took over the remaining standing structures and ruins as their strongholds.

The *Anglo-Saxon Chronicle* tells of three great battles comprising the Anglo-Saxon conquest of Britain. In reality, many small skirmishes accompanied small-scale settlement activity. As town life crumbled, many Britons emigrated from the south and east as the Anglo-Saxon population expanded. Others moved to rural settlements and were absorbed into local Anglo-Saxon culture. Tradition holds that ca. AD 449, the Anglo-Saxons rebelled against their British employers and began to take what they could in both lands and goods. In the same year, an invading Anglo-Saxon army led by Hengist and Horsa won a major victory in Kent, after which their people settled those lands. Around AD 471, a group of Anglo-Saxons annihilated a British force defending a former Roman fort at Pevensey, Sussex. The fort, once known by the name of Anderida, was called Andredescester by the Saxons. Anglo-Saxon dominance slowly expanded inland. The last of the three traditional conquests occurred in AD 495 when Cerdic and Cynric arrived near the Isle of Wight or Portsmouth on the south coast, marking the foundation of the Anglo-Saxon kingdom of Wessex centered on Winchester.[11]

REFORTIFICATION

Few forts saw their stonework repaired in the fifth century although old forts were reoccupied and mercenaries guarded the still-standing town walls. Although town walls throughout Britain had been reinforced during the fourth century, the fifth-century rapid decline in active garrisons left many walls undefended or manned only by informal troops lacking training. Unmanned town walls were not much use against attack. By the mid-fifth century, settlement within town walls was no longer urban in character since nothing worth defending could be protected inside the towns.

That is not to say that no new defenses were built. Britons reverted to a reliance on the earthen hillforts of past tradition. Scholars are not certain when Britons began to build new defenses in the ancient Celtic earthwork fashion, but earth and timber defenses may have been constructed by the early fifth century. Efforts to build defensive earthworks cannot be well dated unless some suitable construction or organic material is found within the earthwork layers that can be radiocarbon dated. Unfortunately, radiocarbon dating is not as precise as would be convenient. Without clear tree-rings for counting and calibrating to specific years, scientific dates of earthworks usually point to a wide range of decades or several centuries. Distinguishing early from middle or late fifth-century remains under such circumstances is difficult.

ARCHAEOLOGY OF URBAN CENTERS

Scholars have debated whether urban centers continued to function in post-Roman times under the control of Britons. Logically, if remnants of the urban or provincial administration of Britain survived into the fifth century, then its presence should be detectable in the late provincial capitals. London, York, Lincoln, and Cirencester are the most likely candidates among the *civitates* to have remained operational. Archaeologists have sought evidence that administrative tasks were still undertaken at these locations. The persistent use of higher-status residences and working quarters occupied by chief administrative officers are also telltale signs. Some of the evidence so far discovered is tantalizing.[12]

LONDON

At the end of the Roman occupation, London's defensive wall was in good repair with some recent additions including the Tower of London. Extramural cemeteries continued to receive new interments, and neighborhoods of native wattle and daub dwellings for the working class arose. The city was still operational, but some Roman buildings from previous centuries fell into disrepair. A new basilica-like Christian church, built possibly after AD 400, was made of stones plundered from abandoned structures. The quarrying of new stone was not attempted, yet the construction effort indicated that manpower could still be mobilized on an impressive scale for a large public works project.[13]

Urban occupation in the later fifth century is hard to ascertain. Stylistic differences in British pottery and other recoverable cultural artifacts disappear, so it is hard to know whether Britons remained present and how late in the century this was true. Most of the found objects are strictly functional in appearance. However, the dead continued to be buried in the cemeteries demonstrating that life of some kind continued in London.

Recognizable fifth-century Anglo-Saxon pottery and other objects of German origin have also been found within London. Perhaps, Anglo-Saxons living or working in the town left them behind, or British residents traded their own possessions for some artfully pleasing pieces. When two ethnic groups live in such close proximity, they commonly share the use of each other's possessions, and this natural behavior makes assigning ethnic identity to archaeological remains hazardous. Who made and who used the objects can be very different people.

One reason for the popularity of Anglo-Saxon pottery inside London may be that British town dwellers suffered from a growing shortage of usable pottery. The average Briton had been accustomed to buying wares made by professional potters working in Roman factories. When the markets were no longer supported by vibrant urban populations, those factories, already struggling to find enough customers during the general fourth-century decline, closed down. Pottery will nevertheless break with regularity, and as household supplies ended up in pieces on trash heaps, Britons sometimes turned to their Anglo-Saxon neighbors for serviceable pots and plates. The new immigrants were accustomed to making their own pottery and were therefore able to produce wares adequate and pleasing for daily use.

As generations passed, the Anglo-Saxon presence in London became more obvious. In the decades of the middle and late fifth century, a series of Anglo-Saxon cemeteries formed a partial ring around the south side of London. The cemeteries were close to Roman roads and other strategic features and were the result of mercenary camps positioned there for the benefit of the inhabitants still within London's walls.[14] Their presence signaled that a major authority remained in charge who was probably British and concerned with the protection of London.

Evidence from London several generations later shows a different picture. Late fifth-century activity shifted to different parts of the town, and a distinct Anglo-Saxon settlement appeared to the west of the old City of London. This immigrant village was more civilian in character than mercenary and showed that Germans had settled in to stay. Along London's waterfront on the River Thames, archaeologists have found signs of increased settlement outside the old walls but not inside. This extramural land development might be the work of Anglo-Saxons who did not wish or were not allowed to live within the walls. However, the evidence of both artifacts and old place-names found in and around London does suggest a thriving mix of Anglo-Saxon and British population.

YORK

In York, the elite and freeborn residents of towns, particularly the skilled artisans and shopkeepers among the latter, were living side by side in the fourth century. The accumulation and spread of dark earth layers representing abundant human activity around the wealthier Roman town houses show that the houses remained occupied. Among archaeologists, "dark earth" refers to soil layers, especially living floors, exposed to significant human activity. As humans drop trash and other organic matter, the soil becomes darker in color. Although people still occupied houses in York, the public buildings were no longer in use. Already, the administrative functions of York were noticeably diminished. Some reuse of public space did occur. One building, the imperial military headquarters, was converted to a craft production area. In the courtyard of the old headquarters, a small church might have been built.

Like London, York had been selected for mercenary protection after the Roman army left. German cremation cemeteries outside the city walls were the last resting place for many mercenaries stationed outside York. This group came from a different region of the German homelands than the London contingent, and their possessions showed stylistic and cultural distinctions. The British call for warriors went out widely and attracted men from different northern territories of the continent.[15]

York's role as an urban center may have been overtaken by the Brigantians (also called the Brigantes), the British tribe dominant in the York region prior to the Roman invasion. Although the Romans began subduing Britain in earnest in AD 43, it was not until the decade of the 70s, after the defeat of a Brigantian rebellion led by Venutius, when this tribe finally came under Roman control.[16] Some scholars believe that northern troubles at the end of the second century were instigated by another Brigantian revolt.[17] The Brigantians did not consent easily to Roman conquest. Even after several centuries, the Brigantian identity remained strong in the north. In Rome's absence, it would be no surprise to see Brigantians commandeer the defenses and remaining economic power contained within York's walls. The similar reemergence of other native tribal groups in the fifth century fostered the civil wars, which have been thought to have done so much harm to British political stability.

York was also connected to the continuing defensive activity along the border at Hadrian's Wall. Although some of the wall forts were briefly abandoned around AD 400, Britons returned to most of the strategic places and guarded them for several decades against invading northern tribes. Along the highway leading south to York from the wall, a string of smaller forts were likewise in use from time to time. If the Brigantians took over the city of York in the fifth century, they must have defended that northern road and would necessarily have taken over the defense of the entire region north of York. This power arrangement could have existed even into the sixth century. Although history does not record the continuing status of post-Roman York, records show that the city was the northern regional administrative center in both the fourth and seventh centuries. Like as not, York's administrative role continued in the intervening centuries.

These case studies of London and York demonstrate how the former Roman capitals adapted to changing political and economic conditions. For some decades, at least, their defenses were strengthened, local market and production activity supported, and urban populations sustained. As time went on, urbanization waned, and urban areas lost importance. Although small populations continued to live within town walls, they behaved increasingly like rural village populations depending on self-sufficiency and lacking all but the most local connections. The town functions most likely to continue even as urban populations and networks dissipated were group religious meetings and occasional small markets. Christian churches and a few cemeteries were used by their membership communities. As the fifth century drew to a close, archaeological evidence of town life becomes so scarce that it is no longer possible to prove or disprove continuing activity. Not until the seventh century did some of the old cities once again come to life, this time as centers of the growing Anglo-Saxon kingdoms.

WROXETER

Wroxeter, once known to the Romans as Viroconium, is a Shropshire village in western England. Although counted among the largest towns in Roman Britain, no later town or city disturbed its ruins. For that reason, Wroxeter is among the best preserved and most archaeologically accessible of the Roman towns. Excavations have revealed that people continued to live in Wroxeter for a short time in the fifth century. When these people left, the settlement was abandoned. It is unclear why Wroxeter was so successful under the Romans and fifth-century Britons but did not attract later

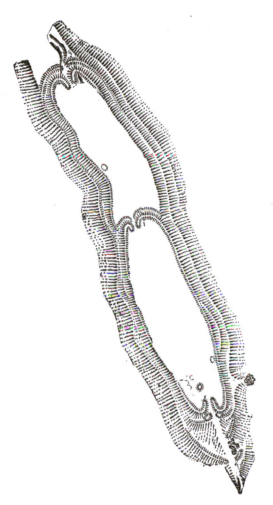

The Wrekin in Shropshire, diagrammed in aerial view and situated east of Wroxeter, demonstrates how an advantageous natural feature, in this case a long rocky ridge, could be improved and further fortified by humans. The Cornovians, who became the post-Roman central power forming the Kingdom of Powys, originally occupied the town of Wroxeter when the Romans left. In the fifth century, they abandoned the town and its walls designed for Roman-style defense in preference for the Wrekin. Britons all over the west moved to hillfort defenses at this time. (J. Charles Wall. *Ancient Earthworks*. London: Talbot, 1908)

occupants. Normally, good locations for urban settlement remain good locations from one period to the next. The only unusual aspect of Wroxeter's location is that its surrounding farmlands were not useful for harvesting crops although animals could be pastured.

The Wroxeter region was settled in Roman times by the native Cornovian people who farmed extensively and built small earthen hillforts of the type that provided residential space for no more than a single extended family. The tribe also mined nearby deposits of copper, lead, and silver. These valuable ore sources provide the key to understanding Wroxeter's economic success in Roman times.

The advancing Roman army eventually forced the Cornovians into submission and established Wroxeter as their *civitas* capital. From there, Cornovian leaders assisted in regional administration. As was typical under Roman rule, the Cornovians retained considerable control of their land after consenting to acknowledge Roman overlordship.[18] Roman domination came with the advantage of greater trading opportunities, and the Cornovian elite recognized how access to greater wealth could strengthen their own political power. Like other western tribes, the Cornovians did not struggle overmuch against Roman rule nor were they greatly inconvenienced by it. This was in contrast to the more violent and devastating tribal resistance that took place in eastern and northern Britain. The Roman presence in the west was a thin veneer by comparison to the east and north. Western rule was less intrusive. Roman lifestyles were not visible outside of urban centers or beyond the edges of the major roads. Villas were rare. Roman styles of dress, pottery, and customs were not typically adopted by the western rural populations.

Roman demand for the wealth of mineral deposits controlled by the Cornovians brought more power to the tribal elites. The rural population found a new economic opportunity in producing and selling animal and other products to both the army and the growing number of town dwellers. Numerous new farms and villages working to meet growing demand soon surrounded Roman Wroxeter.

Evidence of the Cornovian upper class is visible in town but only occasionally seen out in the countryside. One rural exception is Whitley Grange villa, home to a wealthy family. The Roman-style residence, built of stone, included a large bathhouse (75 feet long) with an interior swimming pool. Despite the obvious high-status lifestyle, not many of the usual indications of wealth were found. Only four coins and a very small number of pottery sherds were uncovered during excavations. Such objects are usually abundant at excavations of villas but are missing at Whitley Grange. The villa was not in fact occupied by a wealthy Roman family but instead by upper-class Cornovians who adopted Roman ways only selectively. Both the architectural form of the villa and the luxury of the bathhouse appealed to the wealthy native owner, but Roman pottery and a coin-based economy were unnecessary. Household management of Whitley Grange must have differed substantially from villa operation in eastern England, but exactly how is uncertain.

Inside Wroxeter, preservation of post-Roman remains is remarkable due to the lack of modern construction on the site. Here, archaeologists have found clearer traces than seen anywhere else of the timber-built structures typical of the fifth-century Britons. In addition to dark earth layers, rare timber remnants and foundations have also come to light. Enough is preserved to see that the design of the timber buildings actually resembled that of older Roman buildings constructed in stone. The fifth-century builders were in fact copying in wood the look of the no longer inhabited and decaying Roman stone buildings.[19] One particularly

Reconstruction of an upper-class Roman town house at Wroxeter (known to the Romans as Viroconium), in Shropshire, England. Built using only Roman technology and methods, the authentic construction took six laborers six months to complete. The design employs such structures and materials as wattle and daub walls, oaken beams, mud and straw bricks, plaster, hypocausts, and wooden panels. (Denis Kelly/Dreamstime.com)

substantial and intricately designed timber building is thought to be the fifth-century Cornovian ruler's residence.[20]

The switch from stonework to timber construction reflects a number of social and economic changes. Stone production at the quarries mined in Roman times was an industry that could no longer be maintained on a regular basis. Even if stone were quarried, organizing the manpower, draft animals, and wagons, sledges, or rafts needed to move the desired quantity of stone to Wroxeter and other still-occupied towns was not logistically possible. The economy could no longer support large-scale quarrying projects. Assembling the skilled laborers able to build in stone and the food and supplies and shelter needed to support them presented great difficulties. For all these reasons and more, construction in wood was both prudent and realistic.

Unmanned town walls were not much use against attack, but it soon did not matter. In post-Roman Wroxeter, the distinction between the town and countryside quickly diminished. The Cornovians were more interested in defending the outer boundary of their wide territorial claims than in fortifying the walls of their city. The larger defense plan required hillforts and earthen dykes placed at strategic locations. Hillforts often began as small natural hills or promontories reinforced with a surrounding ditch, like a castle moat of later times. The ditch lay outside an elevated ring, or rampart, of earth. Together, the ditch and rampart slowed down attacker so that they could be picked off or pushed back. For added defense, sharpened timbers were placed in the ditch to impale enemies falling from the rampart, and a palisade of timbers on top of the rampart provided yet another obstacle. Dykes were an extended ditch and rampart work marking the boundary of a territory.

Historically known dykes were built near Wroxeter somewhat later, and one dyke in particular served to bar the entry of aggressive tribes from the west. This dyke, or series of dykes, is called Offa's Dyke, named after the Anglo-Saxon king who refurbished an existing dyke to protect his kingdom of Mercia from the Welsh of Powys in the eighth century. By then, the Wroxeter region belonged to Mercia. Another dyke, named Wat's Dyke, is better connected to post-Roman Britain. It ran for 40 miles along a boundary line parallel to Offa's Dyke. Although once assumed to be the same age as Offa's, radiocarbon dates taken from charcoal and burnt pottery sherds found within the earth of the dyke have shown Wat's Dyke to be much older. In fact, it dates to the fifth and early sixth centuries, coinciding with the post-Roman occupation of Wroxeter by the Cornovians.[21] The Cornovians used Wroxeter as a dramatic central place for councils, ceremonies, and markets, but their obligation as rulers was to keep other tribes further to the west from crossing the boundary of Wat's Dyke and also to protect the rural farmers settled on the east side and who owed allegiance to the Cornovian leaders.

CAERWENT

A *civitas* capital like Wroxeter, Caerwent is situated in southern Wales near the headwaters of the Bristol Channel. As at Wroxeter, British elites occupied the old Roman town in the fifth century. The Silurians, much like the Cornovians, had at first opposed the Roman invaders but soon submitted to Roman rule in the second century. At their *civitas* capital, then called Venta Silurum, a forum basilica was built around AD 120, probably marking the beginning of a major urban building program. Substantial town walls of stone were added in the third and fourth centuries, and Venta Silurum thrived. Rows of shops and large town houses with courtyards displayed prosperity. One particularly massive fourth-century town house had 2 courtyards and more than 16 rooms. With so much wealth and power present in the last Roman century, it is not surprising that Caerwent continued as a Silurian seat of power in the fifth century.

Urban renewal at Caerwent continued in the late and post-Roman era. One large central structure was partially demolished and then renovated. A part of the structure was given central heating and converted into what may have been administrative offices. Another part was made into blacksmithing and metalworking shops that could have produced tools and even weapons for the population of both town and countryside.[22] Like the Cornovians, the Silurians adapted their town to support the needs of their territory, rebuilding Roman civic structures to fulfill other needs.

All of the changes that began in the early decades of the fifth century made it a time of upheaval. Everywhere people were moving to seek better conditions or hunkering down to protect themselves and their property. Worsening climate and lawlessness convinced some Britons to emigrate. Others feared and fought the Anglo-Saxon newcomers, while their neighbors chose to settle among them. Many Britons ultimately blended in with their new neighbors. Romano-British society in the east began to disintegrate in a generation or two, succumbing to the dominant Anglo-Saxon presence, but in the west, the old British tribes and many aspects of their ancient culture were in resurgence. Life was not easy, for other Celtic tribes further west and north—from modern Ireland and Scotland—tried to take advantage of the departure of the Roman garrisons by raiding British territories. Defensive mobilization may have unified western Britons more quickly as they provided for their own protection without seeking the aid of mercenaries. Descendants of British tribal leaders seized their regional *civitas* capitals and reclaimed or even expanded their ancestral territories. British-style earthwork defenses rapidly replaced Roman walls and forts, and the western Britons for a time looked as though they might prosper as independent kingdoms, fully capable of withstanding any onslaught that invaders could bring against them.

RURAL LANDSCAPES

Although many rural places in eastern England were eventually settled by the families of mercenaries, the transition from a "British" to "Anglo-Saxon" settlement landscape is not easy to map. Culturally identifiable artifacts from settlement sites are usually too few to determine who was living there even without the problem of answering *when* they lived there.

Another difficulty has been a particularly faulty but common bias held by past researchers. Early excavators of villa sites assumed that many villas were abandoned in late Roman times and then reoccupied decades later by Anglo-Saxons, so that is how they interpreted the evidence. In the 1970s, archaeologists began to argue what is now obvious, that British society between the Romans and the Anglo-Saxon kingdoms really did exist.[23] Archaeologists began to look harder to find the remains of post-Roman Britons. The faulty assumption and conclusion guided for many years how the evidence was interpreted leading to interpretations of massacre and panicked flight in the face of vast invading armies.

When the ruins of villa buildings appeared to be the result of deliberate demolition, a common interpretation saw signs of battle. A less violent scenario asserts that villa economy depended on the opportunity to buy and sell products in markets. Villas operated like large businesses, not as single-family farms. What can look like violent demolition was only relocation and gradual ruin. In some cases, actual demolition occurred in the act of taking dressed stones from abandoned buildings for use in new construction. Careful tracking of stones around the British countryside has revealed that high-quality Roman stonework was not left to lie about but was eagerly reused for new purposes. This renewal process began in the fourth century if not earlier. Careful examination of villas proves that they were not abandoned all at once. Villa populations declined leaving some buildings unnecessary. Traces of violent destruction or demolition by fire at villa sites are rare. Conquest by force rarely came into play at the old villas.

Another interpretation visualizes deliberate British migration westward and the formation of British political units. Some wealthy villa owners in the east, faced with a decline in market opportunities and accustomed to managing a large-scale business operation, might have rejected the option of reducing operations. For those with ambition and nerve, a move westward to lands where independent British power was in the process of consolidating held promise of more opportunity. Other villa owners stayed put and downsized so that what had once been a large-scale agribusiness now resembled a number of rural family farms that might nevertheless remain networked together for certain economic advantages such as sharing the use of oxen. In current opinion, some of those "Anglo-Saxons" who allegedly took over "abandoned" British villas were really the same British landowners and their dependents adapting to changing conditions and trading with the newcomers so that Anglo-Saxon-made objects became part of their possessions. Meanwhile, in the western counties, the British population grew and reorganized.

Three changes occurred on villas. Structures were abandoned or converted to other uses, and large estates were split up into smaller properties. Smaller farms continued to connect with each other. With the disintegration of long-distance and regional trade networks, the movement of foodstuffs and basic goods became undependable. Villas built to produce large quantities of food and goods for trade had no reliable markets. Self-sufficiency was more important to survival than quality mass production. Villa owners downsized by splitting estate properties among the resident households. This created the appearance of individual-family farms. Many stones were taken from old villa buildings to lay foundations at new farms nearby. Fewer people were living at the original villa center, but the villa population simply dispersed over the estate landscape.

At the new farms, timber or wattle-and-daub houses were sometimes constructed according to traditional native patterns.

Wattle-and-daub could be cozier than the large and drafty stone houses favored by Romans used to a much milder Mediterranean climate. For example, Barton Court Farm consisted of farmhouses and buildings (described in Chapter 1) that were built, abandoned, and replaced in the normal course of events. No disaster or violent attack played a part in this process. The rapid natural decay of wattle and timber buildings explains the need for frequent new construction. If a wide swath of countryside around Barton Court could be thoroughly investigated, similar farms should be found. Archaeologists try to amass landscape data in this way. As the results of landscape-oriented investigations accumulate, the post-Roman process of splitting villa estates will become clearer.

As for the new immigrants, Anglo-Saxon settlements were characterized by small, frequently moved farmsteads where the occupants replaced buildings or changed locations every generation or two. The pattern has been seen clearly at Mucking and West Stow.[24] This kind of shifting settlement behavior is not unusual and in fact constitutes the norm in societies where land is not densely utilized and simple agricultural techniques deplete soil nutrients from the fields. Manuring the fields was not an option because scarcely any farmer had sufficient livestock to collect enough manure for the job. As soils became overused, new land had to be cultivated while the old fields rested. The process of opening new fields usually increased the distance between field and homestead. Since Anglo-Saxon houses, like British houses, were neither costly nor difficult to build, it made more sense to build a new house nearby rather than walk long distances to work.

After a generation or two, the old fields recovered their fertility naturally by having lain fallow, and it was then no surprise to see someone reoccupy the original homestead. The European system of shifting agriculture—or crop rotation as it is sometimes termed—is necessitated by the planting of a single food crop in a field. This practice strips the soil of certain nutrients. Each plant takes and gives back different sets of nutrients. Allowing a field to revert to natural vegetation made up of many natural plant species permitted nutrient content in the soil to normalize.

LANDOWNERSHIP

An unknown number of the old villa estates, once run as large independent business entities, became corporate family holdings consisting of a collection of related family farms working cooperatively. British society still remembered its tribal heritage, even after four centuries of Roman influence. Tribal values emphasized the fulfillment of familial duties and responsibilities. In the matter of managing villa lands, large extended families included cousins, in-laws, all their siblings, and offspring linked backward and forward through several generations. Extended families could number between 50 and more than 100 persons. When the Roman garrisons left, people had to provide for their own security. Well-organized extended families were the answer, for they had the numbers to repel marauders, and one's relatives could be relied upon to look out for the welfare of related family units. Lands within the estates were parceled out to individual households by the leading members within the group. So long as the group organized itself with minimal argument and disorder, the system worked well. This model fits the archaeological evidence for shifting households and matches later landownership patterns in Britain. The alternative explanation of independent small landowners owning and managing their own lands self-sufficiently without governmental protection lacks the element of physical security provided by the corporate family model.

CLIMATE CHANGE

Climate change played a large role in rural life (see also Chapter 1). In some areas of Britain, formerly productive farmland started to suffer from weather conditions that were too wet and too cold in most years for reliable harvests. Farmers located on low-lying and now waterlogged soils were forced to move to drier land at higher elevations or to land where underlying bedrock created drier topsoils. Marshy regions such as the Fens and the Somerset Levels became too wet to support any farming at all. Although farming had once been common on these lands, traces of agricultural activity disappeared completely in the fifth and sixth centuries. Northern farms, or farms at higher elevations, which were already prone to greater rainfall, became too cold and wet. Frosts were more frequent and growing season too short for crops to ripen. Such farms had to be abandoned. In general, northern farmers moved to the south or to lower elevations and valley bottoms. There they found a localized climate that was warmer and less stormy. Farmers living in the south moved to higher elevations where soils had better drainage in order to escape too much wetness. Overall, British lands suited for the growing of crops diminished in acreage, but farmers adapted by relying more heavily on raising animals for meat, dairy products, eggs, wool, and hides. Domesticated animals were more tolerant of the colder and wetter climate than were crops. Obviously, the daily diet of Britons (and Saxons too) had to adapt to these changes in production, and that, of course, is what happened.

NOTES

1. Martin Jones, *England before Domesday* (Totowa, NJ: Barnes & Noble Books, 1986), 153.

2. R. A. Dodgshon and R. A. Butlin, eds., *An Historical Geography of England and Wales,* 2nd ed. (San Diego, CA: Academic Press, 1990), 144.

3. John Wacher, *Roman Britain* (Toronto, ON: J. M. Dent & Sons, Ltd., 1978), 65.

4. Wacher, *Roman Britain,* 67.

5. Gil Gambash, "To Rule a Ferocious Province: Roman Policy and the Aftermath of the Boudican Revolt," *Britannia* 43 (2012): 1–15.

6. Bryn Walters, "Exotic Structures in 4th-Century Britain," in *Architecture in Roman Britain,* edited by Peter Johnson with Ian Haynes (Walmgate, UK: Council for British Archaeology, 1996), 152–162 (CBA Research Report, 94), 159.

7. Wacher, *Roman Britain,* 99.

8. Wacher, *Roman Britain,* 100.

9. Christopher A. Snyder, *An Age of Tyrants, Britain and the Britons, A.D. 400–600* (University Park: Pennsylvania State University Press, 1998), 102–106.

10. S. Ireland, *Roman Britain: A Sourcebook* (New York: St. Martin's Press, 1986), 168–172.

11. Stephen Johnson, *Later Roman Britain* (New York: Charles Scribner's Sons, 1980), 122.

12. Ken Dark, *Britain and the End of the Roman Empire* (Charleston, SC: Tempus Publishing, Inc., 2002), 50.

13. Dark, *Britain and the End of the Roman Empire,* 50, 51 and for an example of archaeological evidence of demolition and reuse, see T. Brigham, "A Reassessment of the Second Basilica in London, A.D. 100–400: Excavations at Leadenhall Court, 1984–1986," *Britannia* 21 (1990): 77–81.

14. Dark, *Britain and the End of the Roman Empire,* 51, 52, 99.

15. Dark, *Britain and the End of the Roman Empire,* 52, 53.

16. Johnson, *Later Roman Britain,* 3 and Barry Cunliffe, *Iron Age Communities in Britain, an Account of England, Scotland and Wales from the Seventh Century BC until the Roman Conquest,* 2nd ed. (London: Routledge & Kegan Paul, 1978), 343.

17. Nick Higham, "Literary Evidence for Villas, Towns and Hillforts in Fifth-Century Britain," *Britannia* 25 (1994): 171.

18. Roger White, "Wroxeter, Rich in a Wealthy Land," *British Archaeology*, no. 17 (September 1996), http://www.britarch.ac.uk/ba/ba17/ba17feat.html.

19. Martin Henig, "Roman Britons after 410," *British Archaeology*, no. 68 (December 2002), http://www.britarch.ac.uk/ba/ba68/feat1.shtml.

20. Charles Thomas, *Celtic Britain* (London: Thames and Hudson, Ltd., 1986), 48.

21. Anonymous, "In Brief: Dyke Redated," *British Archaeology*, no. 49 (November 1999), http://www.britarch.ac.uk/ba/ba49/ba49toc.html.

22. Neil Faulkner, *The Decline and Fall of Roman Britain* (Charleston, SC: Arcadia, 2001).

23. Philip Rahtz, "How Likely Is Likely?" *Antiquity* 49 (1975): 59–61.

24. Dark, *Britain and the End of the Roman Empire*, 64.

4

SOCIAL IDENTITIES

SOCIAL CLASSES AND THEIR OCCUPATIONS

British society at the end of the Roman era consisted of the wealthy elite class, artisans and craftspeople of all kinds, soldiers, peasants, common laborers, and slaves. Bishops and priests were included among the elite, while itinerant preachers and monks held lesser status. Those who continued to live as professional soldiers were, like artisans, revered for their skills. Slaves continued to exist where hard manual labor was need, especially if they were foreign born and not Christian.

Slaves

Slavery was essential to the Roman world. The Roman economy was preindustrial. It depended on labor input rather than on labor-saving technology. Many people were required to supply the unskilled labor necessary for all the services and goods required by urban dwellers. The Roman military needed the service of many men to support wars of conquest or defend established borders. Men from conquered territories were often conscripted by force into the Roman armies and then shipped off to distant legions where they had no choice but to serve. The wars also produced war captives who might be made into slaves outright.

The continuing importance of slaves in the empire is reflected in changes made to the laws. In AD 533, Emperor Justinian updated laws governing fugitive slaves. The new passage of the Justinian Code made landowners legally at fault for employing a fugitive slave. By the sixth century, the main function of slaves was to work the land, harvest after harvest. These slaves were used as serfs, that is, peasants who were required to remain all their lives on their owner's land where they raised crops for the landowner. Runaway serfs committed the crime of depriving their owners of essential labor, but if a landowner knowingly employed runaways, this act was also a crime of stealing labor from others of their class. Landowners were now made responsible for turning in any suspected fugitives to the authorities.[1]

In Britain, the situation was somewhat different. Neither archaeological finds nor the written records have shown evidence of a significant serf population working the fields. More likely, the countryside was populated by small farmers who were free. However, the workers on the large villa estates may have lived more like serfs, in that they were tenants with little freedom of movement. After Roman authority broke down, the status of villa workers becomes unclear. As already considered, post-Roman villa operation may have transferred into the hands of large, extended families, but other villas may have brought together unrelated serf families cooperating as a collective.

Written sources scarcely acknowledge slavery in Britain. Slavery had less economic importance because the supply of captives was not so plentiful. Nevertheless, raids among tribes and Britons were an ongoing problem. St. Patrick famously recorded that as an adolescent he was enslaved and taken off to Ireland—twice. The saint did not find the circumstance of slavery at all unusual, but he did show indignation for having been forced into slavery. The man, yet to be a saint, left hints in his surviving writings that he came from a wealthy background—his father owned a villa, and Patrick only reconciled to the humiliation of slavery by viewing it as God's judgment on him. This formative personal experience fired his hatred of slavery, at least where the enslavement of fellow Christians was concerned. Describing Christians who persevered in their faith during dark times, Patrick observed, "Those who are kept in slavery suffer the most." Patrick said of himself as a missionary, "even if I wanted wealth I have no resources, nor is it my own estimation of myself, for daily I expect to be murdered or betrayed or reduced to slavery if the occasion arises."[2] His words portray slavery as commonplace. It is likely that small numbers of slaves assisted alongside free laborers on many farms and former villa lands. There would also have been foreign-born slaves with special talents or education who were imported to serve in skilled positions such as secretary or tutor.

Finding evidence of slavery is difficult. Even in later centuries, slavery was an ever-present condition that often left no physical trace. Five centuries after the post-Roman era, William the Conqueror took the throne of England and ordered that information about lands and resources in his new kingdom be compiled and recorded in the *Domesday Book*. This undertaking revealed that 10 percent of the English population was then living as slaves or serfs. Post-Roman Britain may have had as many or more slaves.

Free People

To the medieval mind, the category of free men and women did not include all free persons but rather only those free people who were not at the same time noble, wealthy, or powerful landowners. The upper classes did not need to be also distinguished as "free." The *other* free people in Britain, the small farmers, craftsmen, and skilled or semiskilled laborers in the towns were the "free" people. Men working as professional, paid soldiers were also considered free.

The best way to learn about this middle social status in Arthurian Britain, since written sources drop only the vaguest of hints, is to look closely at burials in cemeteries. Although Christian rules forbade the old practice of leaving gifts and personal possessions with the deceased because to do so was deemed pagan, there are still hints about identity and status to be found in the manner of burial. The investigation of Queenford Farm Cemetery (discussed below) illustrates the life of the free through death.

The Upper Class

The lives and residences of the upper classes reflected the rapid and widespread changes happening throughout British society. The Roman villa of Lullingstone is part of a dense concentration of villa sites in Kent. The original Lullingstone buildings were constructed around AD 75. The land was good for farming and had in an earlier generation been home to a British family. The villa buildings were rebuilt several times during a long and successful occupation. The final expansion of the villa compound occurred around AD 280. Several decades later, a Romano-Celtic temple was constructed by the villa owner on a nearby plot of land. During the fourth century, the villa continued to prosper and was renovated with the addition of expensive mosaic floors. About AD 360, several generations after the pagan temple was built, a separate Christian chapel appeared. Progress came to an abrupt halt in the early fifth century when the villa burned down. The reason for the fire is unknown. No sign of an enemy attack has been found, and the catastrophic fire could have been accidental.[3] Until the fire, Lullingstone had been a successful villa operation. Contrary to earlier scholarly opinion, fourth-century Romano-British villas were not in general decline. The occupants of many villas were thriving until shortly after AD 400 when many villas were either abandoned or transformed into different kinds of landholdings.

A view of the excavations conducted at Lullingstone Villa in Kent during 1950. First discovered in 1939, the villa has been the subject of many investigations. Lullingstone may have been the home of governors of Britain during the second century. Publius Helvius Pertinax, who was governor of Britain before becoming Roman emperor in AD 193, may have lived there as evidenced by his portrait bust found during excavations. In post-Roman times, a Christian chapel replaced a pagan shrine. (Bettmann/Corbis)

What became of these wealthy fifth-century landowners? Without active long-distance commerce, they were unable to market their products. Villas were more than just large farms; they were corporate production centers employing many free workers and slaves for a variety of manufacturing activities in addition to agricultural labor. Even if villa owners could find enough laborers to generate their products, profits depended on continental trade connections. Villas were abandoned, not overnight but over a period of years or decades, simply because they did not make the profits to support the large community of people needed to maintain production levels. Villas were not self-sufficient. Most relied on trade to sell wares and obtain essential supplies. If these supplies could not be acquired through trade, it was difficult or even impossible to continue the villa economy.

Not least, political disturbances were a factor. Some villas in regions of conflict found the unrest around them too dangerous. Villas represented large accumulations of wealth and had depended on the Roman military to provide a stable and safe environment in the countryside. Villas never had and were not prepared to maintain their own personal armed guard. All these factors taken together contributed to the breakup of large villas into smaller, more economically efficient and self-sufficient landholdings.

In western Britain, signs of native wealth actually increased in the fifth century. In the absence of Rome, British communities absorbed some immigrants from the east and solidified their political territories. Some towns, such as Wroxeter and Caerwent, were occupied by urban dwellers for a while longer (Chapter 3). Later, the towns were abandoned while hillfort and rural settlements grew. Town life was unprotected and unsustainable under the new conditions, but hillfort centers were capable of sounding alarms, mobilizing warriors, and protecting peasant families and farms from raids. The militaristic needs of a watchful defense were the reality of British existence.

IMPORTANCE OF CEMETERIES

Post-Roman British cemeteries are difficult to identify and to interpret because the burials lack objects. Christian teaching forbade the inclusion of grave gifts for use by the dead in the afterlife. In practice, nothing could be buried with the dead for any reason. In the early centuries, the dead were not even dressed in clothing but buried in a winding sheet or shroud. Christian burials were empty of shoes, buckles, straps, pins, or any kind of jewelry. Although a lack of grave goods raises the probability that a cemetery or burial contained a Christian who was therefore likely a Briton, negative evidence is not sufficient. Slaves, whether belonging to British or Anglo-Saxon owners, and regardless of their religion or place of origin, were usually buried with no possessions. The poor might also be given nothing to take with them, or at least nothing to leave any observable trace after burial for 16 centuries. If the deceased were buried with a loaf of bread and fruit or with baskets, such gifts can no longer be detected.

The lack of grave goods, although an important sign of post-Roman British communities, also makes dating a burial or cemetery much more difficult. Pottery and jewelry show stylistic changes that are helpful for close dating by decades rather than rough centuries. When bones or wood (if a coffin were used) are found (some soils are too acidic for these remains to survive), the material can be dated in a radiocarbon laboratory. Radiocarbon testing, also known as carbon-14 dating, is expensive, and the results produced give only a range of years, not as an exact date. There is always some variance due to a variety of environmental factors. Radiocarbon dates are truly helpful when it is hoped to narrow down a time frame from the late Roman through medieval centuries. Then, for example, gaining the information that the object is early rather than late medieval is important.

Sometimes, archaeologists suggest the age of medieval cemeteries based on what is known about the local landscape: when farms and villages were settled, what pagan or Christian sites were in use, the location of ancient roads, mining or other industrial activity, and similar clues. Developing the big picture of the history of settlement over a cohesive area provides probable dates for some sites lacking in concrete evidence.

Queenford Farm Excavations

The cemetery at Queenford Farm by Dorchester-on-Thames in Oxfordshire is reliably dated to the late- and post-Roman centuries. The site of the modern village of Dorchester was once a small, walled Roman town. The cemetery at Queenford Farm was one of two cemeteries associated with the Roman town. Additionally, burials of fifth-century German immigrants were found near the town. As typically happens to archaeological sites in densely settled areas, the Queenford cemetery was largely destroyed by modern activity before archaeologists could examine it. Despite such losses, as many as 164 burials were excavated and analyzed. The known graves are estimated to represent a mere 7 percent of the original number. Large sections of the original cemetery were damaged beyond recovery.[4] This means that vital information about the demographics of the community that could have been determined from the cemetery layout has been lost. Groups of burials in cemeteries may represent families, social classes, or occupations. With only one small area excavated, the picture from Queenford cannot be considered informative of the entire population.

The Queenford Farm dead, like those at other contemporary cemeteries, were mostly buried in wooden coffins in accordance with Christian practice. This involved the laying out of the body on its back with head oriented to the west. The dead were interred at a shallow depth of only two to three feet. Originally, all the Queenford graves were enclosed by a cemetery boundary ditch, but later, graves were placed outside the boundary as well.[5] The human remains recovered from the surviving bit of cemetery revealed a normal demographic sample with regard to gender and age. There are approximately equal numbers of adult males and females with about half the men living past the age of 40 and somewhat less than a third of the women reaching the same age. Young adult female deaths were often due to childbirth complications, seen when female burials were accompanied by an infant or fetus not yet born. Such a pattern is typical of premodern societies. Of the children, most died under the age of five. If they lived to be 5 years old, they were likely to reach age 15 or so. Few young infants were buried in the cemetery, but certainly many died. Infants must have been disposed of differently.[6] This pattern of missing or otherwise placed infant burials is typical in Roman and post-Roman cemeteries. At Queenford, infants were not given regular burial unless they were in their mother's grave or perhaps deposited in the destroyed portion.

The bones from the excavated part of Queenford have been studied in detail. Multiple cases of inherited anomalies, or odd deformations of the spine and other skeletal and dental abnormalities, show that certain groups of individuals were likely to have been related since they shared unusual hereditary traits. A number of men and women over the age of 30 had osteoarthritis. The damaged bones were often not symmetrically affected on each side of the body; for example, the right wrist might be more arthritic than the left. Such uneven skeletal damage was likely to have been caused by specific repetitive labor. Most arthritis occurred on the spine indicating that these persons habitually carried heavy loads. The men of the Queenford sample were more likely than women to suffer bone fractures and other traumatic injuries to bone. This is a sign that the men were engaged in more dangerous activities, although warfare is not indicated as one of them. Weapon injuries were not found, at least not on the excavated skeletons.

The Queenford Farm cemetery was in use for 100–200 years. Depending on the exact length of the usage period, the population served numbered approximately between 250 and 500 persons; a shorter time frame would point to a larger living population.[7] However, it is difficult to be certain about the average life span and fertility rates of the Queenford people since so much of the cemetery and all the infants are missing. The surviving burials are interesting, in that they appear to be part of a sizable community of Christian peasants who lived simply and worked hard. None of these people seemed to have had special social or occupational status. As a group, their life spans and health problems were similar. The pattern of female and child mortality matches that of a hard-working farming population lacking luxuries. There are no signs of a stigmatized servant or slave class, although it is also possible that a few servants or slaves were treated with relative equality to the rest of the population in burial or that they were buried elsewhere. The skeletal remains show no sign of death by intentional violence, no injuries from weapons of war, and no unusual spikes in the death rate, either from battle or epidemic. From all appearances, the Queenford Farm people lived hard but undisrupted lives for as many as 10 generations.

These graves do not necessarily hold the dead from one farm complex or one village. More likely, families from the local area all gathered to use the burial ground at Queenford Farm. Such practices of sharing grew into the formation of parish cemeteries during the Middle Ages.

COMPARING BRITONS AND SAXONS

As the German presence grew in Britain, Britons and Anglo-Saxons began to form two ethnic groups, each with its own culture. They sometimes interacted, intermarried, and shared cultural objects and activities, and at other times preferred separation.

Living with foreigners was nothing new for the Britons after four centuries of Roman rule. As with the Romans, who came from all parts of the empire, the Anglo-Saxons came from many parts of Germany and were mostly male. Although legionnaires in the Roman army were given land upon retirement and many settled down in Britain rather than return home, those who married British wives and raised families were not so numerous as was once thought.

Recent DNA studies of the modern British population[8] have shown that four centuries of Roman rule did relatively little to change the genetic makeup of the native population. Distinctly, Roman genetic stock is barely detectable. The Germanic genetic component in today's Britain is much more significant with roughly a 15-percent share of modern genes due to Anglo-Saxon forebears. Some expected this number to be higher since the Anglo-Saxons became the ruling class in England by the seventh century. The small 15-percent share suggests that the major of the nonruling classes throughout England remained identifiably British for generations. Although some Anglo-Saxon males may have brought their own women with them, the men successfully raised families and increased their numbers rapidly. However, if they took British wives, then their children, although raised to live like Anglo-Saxons, became increasingly British, in terms of genetics but not culture, with each generation.

The Anglo-Saxons were not the only newcomers. With the unrest accompanying the departure of Rome, some groups of Irish and other Celtic tribes came into British territory and settled in outlying regions of the north and west. Their small numbers were soon absorbed into the general population.

Lifestyle Differences

Many clues help to identify Britons and Anglo-Saxons in the population of the early post-Roman centuries. The most obvious difference between Briton and Anglo-Saxon was in their houses. Many Britons reverted to building the traditional house form common in the pre-Roman centuries: the wattle-and-daub round house with a conical roof of thatch. Anglo-Saxons also used a timber frame but preferred rectangular longhouses.

Christians grew rapidly in numbers throughout the empire once Christianity was decreed a lawful religion under Galerius in AD 311 by the Edict of Toleration and more widely in AD 313 under Constantine by the Edict of Milan. Britons had already begun secretly adopting the faith. Abandonment of Romano-Celtic temples from the late third century onward was followed by construction of Christian churches and chapels. One consequence to conversion was that Christian belief changed the way people wished to live in their homes. The once popular Roman floor mosaics and wall paintings, often bearing pagan themes, were removed or covered over. The naturalism and physical exuberance of Roman art did not sit comfortably with Christian Britons. Even those who had the means to live luxuriously in the late Roman period often opted for simpler surroundings than their predecessors.

Contrasted with the wildly ornate interiors of earlier centuries, the utilitarian appearance of late Roman interiors gave the homes of Christian Britons an impoverished appearance to modern eyes. However, the simple white walls and undecorated floors were not left barren by the owners. Decorative carpets and wall hangings, embroidered or intricately woven and appealing to Christian aesthetics, kept homes cozy. The textiles would also have contributed to a warmer, less drafty interior as British weather deteriorated in the fifth century. Given the economic conditions, wall hangings and carpets were also preferable options because the artisans with the skills to create quality textiles were more likely to be locally available. None of these textile coverings survive, but their use is so logical that it is unreasonable to discount it. Like the colorful paint that once adorned classical marble statues, perishable substances might make all the difference in how a work of sculpture—or a home interior—would appear.

Housewares

Other lifestyle changes revolved around manufactured goods. The provincial administration probably survived on its own for a while since many local officials were British ruling elites and inclined to do what they could to preserve the status quo. However, one important part of the economic system did collapse quickly: large-scale manufacturing. Regional markets were likely to have folded at about the same time because markets depended on a regular and consistent supply of wares, the existence of customers, and above all, on reliable and safe transportation for both wares and customers. Increased danger on the roads, no military policing, and the rapid loss of a monetary economy when Roman coins ceased to be imported via military channels—all these changes made regional markets untenable. Production reverted to small-scale or home-based operations intended to meet local needs. The markets were likewise local and limited.

Until the end of the fourth century, Britons were accustomed to obtaining mass-produced pottery from a small number of large workshops. With the breakdown of the transportation and commercial systems, pottery businesses could no longer see their wares safely distributed to markets. The lack of Roman currency flowing into Britain made commercial sales all but impossible to transact. The factories were forced to disband or greatly reduce their output and workers, but it is hard to say how quickly this happened. At one pottery workshop at Harrold, north of London, a number of kilns have been excavated. The kilns continued in use until some-time in the fifth century although the date of their abandonment cannot be clearly determined from the physical evidence.[9]

Serviceable pottery could be made at home. Since many home-made pots were not well made or durable, their remains decayed and crumbled in the ground. Such pieces are not seen in muse-ums. Furthermore, poor-quality sherds found in excavations, being mostly undecorated and uninteresting from an aesthetic point of view, were unlikely in past generations to have been collected, cata-logued, and published.[10]

With no opportunity to buy more, Britons took care of their remaining high-quality Roman ceramics. Some pots and jars were even repaired, showing how irreplaceable good wares of Roman origin had become. This is why a late fourth-century pot or plate fragment found at an archaeological site does not indicate that the object was last in use in the fourth century. The vessel or plate could have been broken and finally discarded decades and generations later. The site cannot be dated on the basis of the pottery. Ceramic styles in Britain become static. There is no discernible develop-ment of post-Roman pottery styles. Archaeologists often depend on artifact styles to help date sites. Without active ceramic factories and markets, there was no style development in pottery. From the beginning of the fifth through the sixth and even into the seventh centuries, the use of pottery evidence for dating sites is problematic.

Britons did not rely on just clay for their containers and cooking pots. Other likely materials for serviceable vessels were wood and leather. Stone, glass, basketry, and metals—such as iron, tin, and bronze—were also used to hold food, liquids, and other content.

Styles and Identity

Many object categories from the fourth century disappear from archaeological view in the fifth century because those items were no longer received in trade or manufactured. This is another reason why it was erroneously concluded that many Britons died. The fifth-century disappearance of items categorized as British property is connected to the problem of identifying the people who created and used existing objects. Archaeologists try to follow the destiny of different populations by identifying certain types of commonly found objects with distinctive styles, such as jewelry, pottery, or weapons, and associating the styles with specific groups of people. Today, it is argued that mistakes were made in the past in the way ethnic identities were assigned to users of certain fifth and sixth century artifact types. In other words, the objects assumed to have belonged to Anglo-Saxons or to Britons may not be matched correctly. One wrong assumption can lead to many others.

Pottery again provides a good example. Most fifth- and sixth-century pottery found in Britain has been labeled Anglo-Saxon, but is this identification accurate? Some "Anglo-Saxon" pottery is probably British-made pottery, but the potter copied popular Anglo-Saxon styles. Other Anglo-Saxon pottery was undoubtedly used by Britons because they acquired it in trade. Pottery would easily pass between the two groups since it often held the foods or other substances that were exchanged in trade. Since Anglo-Saxon men frequently took British wives, these women naturally made some of the jars and bowls used within their homes. Methods for making pottery and styles of decoration became mixed. When two populations live for generations side by side as well as intermarry, it naturally becomes impossible to separate them according to artifact styles. Much of what has been classified as Anglo-Saxon pottery is more appropriately labeled Anglo-British pottery.

An alternative explanation suggests that Britons were not very skilled at making pottery because they had grown to rely on Roman pottery factories to fulfill all their needs. When these factories closed down and existing Roman-made wares became scarce, individual British households were not able to supply their own needs as well as they would have liked. Saxons, on the other hand, were accustomed to making their own pottery. Although not as nice as Roman wares, Anglo-Saxon pottery was solid and serviceable. Britons used what Anglo-Saxon pieces they could get for that reason.

These same problems of correctly identifying pottery producers apply also to the users and owners of jewelry, weapons, and any

Anglo-Saxon saucer brooches, fifth to seventh centuries AD (gilt bronze). Found in a female grave during excavations at Bidford-on-Avon, Warwickshire. Archaeologists have uncovered an early Anglo-Saxon cemetery having so far revealed over 200 inhumation burials and 32 cremations. The shape and scroll-like design of these brooches illustrate typical Anglo-Saxon style preferences. (Warwickshire Museum Service/The Bridgeman Art Library)

other objects with distinctive styles. In the past, it was assumed that dress ornaments, hair pins, buckles, and other personal items made of bronze, bone, or iron were useful ethnic markers. One only had to distinguish between Anglo-Saxon and British styles. Present opinion holds that beginning quite early in the fifth century, new composite styles, reflecting both Anglo-Saxon and British preferences, became increasingly common. Because these objects were deliberately made to appeal to both Britons and Anglo-Saxons, they were more easily shared or exchanged. Furthermore, people are often intrigued by foreign styles. Although most post-Roman period jewelry, personal toiletry items, and weaponry were in the past identified as Anglo-Saxon, they were probably made, owned, and used by both groups.

Illusion of Poverty

Surviving material culture from the early fifth century is rare, but is that poverty? Romans kept a great many personal possessions compared to other people in the ancient world. Romans simply had more *stuff* than anyone else. What looks like the impoverishment of post-Roman British society can instead be argued as a return to normalcy. The Anglo-Saxons had a similar lack of possessions. The primary difference between the Britons and the Anglo-Saxons was in their graves. The British dead, since they were Christian, were buried with nothing, while the pagan Anglo-Saxon dead were often given a wide array of personal, household, and occupational objects to take to the afterlife. Little wonder that the museum exhibits of Anglo-Saxon artifacts, which come mostly from Anglo-Saxon graves, are so much more plentiful and interesting to view.

A final thought on fashions and styles: Britons no longer closely followed the fashions of the Roman continent. Their connections to the continent, if not severed, became far more distant. Older, familiar Roman styles remained popular, and traditional Celtic styles were revived. Old, worn-out objects were sometimes replaced by carefully crafted reproductions, and these new copies remained in use for generations. As is to be expected, a number of finds have been dated to the late fourth century based on their styles, but such dates could be too early by decades or generations. Careful consideration of context has revealed instances of anachronistic styles persevering through the copying and reuse of objects.

In short, the poverty of fifth-century Britons, particularly in the latter half of the century, may be something of an illusion. The Roman lifestyle diminished, but Britons had an older culture to fall back on and new Christian ideals to express. Many Britons took to living in less durable houses built in the round, native style and utilizing wattle and daub walls. Wall hangings and carpets, which left behind no archaeological trace, replaced the more durable paintings on wall plaster and mosaic floors. Lack of evidence by no means proves poverty of cultural environment. Rather, Britons are to be admired for adapting and thriving during such rapid and far-reaching social, cultural, political, and economic upheaval.

Changing Use of Space

It should be no surprise that buildings and civic places used by fourth-century Britons, including amphitheaters, were rejected by fifth-century Britons. The forums, basilicas, warehouses, and office spaces were abandoned or used for other purposes. Some structures, such as public bathhouses, had fallen into disuse long before the end of the Roman period.[11] Nor is it true that Britons had lacked access to these structures all along and therefore did not care for them. According to historian Nick Higham, St. Patrick's own words from the fourth century are deliberately self-deprecating in a well-educated, classical tradition unfamiliar to modern under-standing. Patrick consistently described himself as poor, a rustic, "least of all the faithful and contemptible to very many." Modern readers should not be fooled by this language and way of express-ing one's self. Patrick used a diminutive Latin word, *villula*, to describe his father's villa lands. Yet, by using this word, Patrick was

This large fragment of a Romano-British sepulchral monument was found at some time before 1842 during railway construction near York. The fig-ures appear to be a father and son. Urban Britons in the early fifth century probably continued to wear Roman-style clothing, as illustrated here, for a few decades. After that time, there is no available information about Brit-ish clothing. Simple Anglo-Saxon styles may have been adopted by some Britons living in Anglo-Saxon areas. (Charles Wellbeloved. *Eburacum, or York under the Romans*. York: R. Sunter and H. Sotheran, 1842)

deliberately informing his readers that his father did indeed own a villa—not just the building but the entire estate that went with it— and that Patrick's own social status by birth was by no means humble. He was born of the upper class.[12] There were wealthy Britons, and British choices were not due to poverty but to cultural preference, following a pattern of native behaviors that had reappeared long before AD 410 and was influenced by Christianity.

Ethnic Identity and Political Power

Modern scholars recognize the difficulty of tracking ethnic groups in prehistory. This text has been careful to explain all the ways that interpreters of objects can misidentify their owners and users. Objects do not necessarily reveal who their producers are. Rather than kept and used by the people who made them, objects are more likely to reflect political and economic relations and alliances. In the fifth century, the fate of the Britons and how, when, and where Anglo-Saxons spread through England are inevitable questions. By the sixth century, however, ethnic identity due to intermarriage and other factors was already too complicated to determine with accuracy. Instead, the new questions posed ask: who has seized power and how is society realigning itself. On the eastern and western extremes of Britain, some power centers were already consolidated, and Anglo-Saxons had their sights on taking control of the central regions.

Keith Matthews argued that native British identity was a result of the Roman invasion in the first century.[13] The Britons saw themselves as a united entity because the Romans treated them as such. The two populations became polarized. By the seventh century, two polarized populations had reappeared: the Britons and the Anglo-Saxons. Matthews suggests looking at the eighth-century writings of Bede on the history of his own people, the English, to get a sense of what the Anglo-Saxons thought of their own identity.

Bede famously wrote about the arrival in Britain of the Angles, Saxons, and Jutes. In Bede's view, three groups of German immigrants with distinct homelands came to Britain and settled in separate territories. The Anglo-Saxons somehow maintained their tribal identities for more than two centuries. From past experience with histories of immigrant groups worldwide, this degree of continuity is highly suspect. Archaeologists have tried too many times to separate Anglo-Saxon material finds into Jutish, Saxon, and Anglian categories. The effort always fails. Bede's worldview of tidy discrete groups continuing through time mirrors the thinking of Roman historians writing about the barbarian tribes of Europe but does not match reality.

The linguistic evidence does not support Bede. The country ultimately took the name of the Angles. The Saxons' name was not used in Old English documents but only appears occasionally in Latin, British, and Gaelic language sources. When Old English texts refer to the Jutes, they are called *Geatas*, but the sources are talking only of the Geatas living on the continent. If Bede were correct, a more equitable use of nomenclature in the sources would be expected.

People do not behave by society's rules. Societies may forbid or frown upon intermarriage across ethnic lines and the mixing of social classes, but individual ideas and desires create many exceptions. Only the strictest of social consequences can prevent the number of infractions from being widespread. People will mix. Anglo-Saxons may have mistrusted Britons and the feeling was returned, but there was little to stop the early mixing of Anglian, Saxon, and Jutish populations. Since the immigrants were mostly men, little could stop the pairing of Anglo-Saxon men with British women, whether actual marriage was involved or not.

Mixing bloodlines is not the whole story. People also select their social identities. Children with parents from different groups usually select one of the groups to which to belong, and it is not always the father's line that is followed. So long as the child is allowed membership with the chosen group, the social identity becomes 100 percent even though the biological identity is split fifty-fifty. The history of race relations in America and throughout world history has been filled with such calculations.

Matthews defines a third type of social identity that is fluid according to context. Within a small group, both Anglo-Saxons and Britons identified according to their allegiances to local leaders and tribal concepts. On the larger landscape of Britain, the local units of population lined up, more or less, as natives and immigrants. From the perspective of those living on the European continent, the primary distinction was between the continent and the population living across the channel in the British Isles. A merchant trader sailing to Britain to exchange valuable wares was not concerned if his customers were Anglo-Saxon or British so long as the trade was fair.

In many ways, the difference between the fifth century and the sixth century is that both sides began to see the larger context. Their allegiances on both sides were less localized. Although they were far from uniting into two well-managed political entities under strong central authorities, movement in that direction began.

Polarized Conflict

Why the British and Anglo-Saxons refused to merge peaceably and instead separated into two hostile camps has been a subject of discussion for decades. Although many Britons appeared willing to absorb Anglo-Saxon culture, the opposite is not true. As Bryan Ward-Perkins noted, "by an act of extreme arrogance, [the Anglo-Saxons] even termed the Britons *wealas*, or 'foreigners,' on their own island." This word eventually became the English word for Welsh and held the secondary meaning of "slave." No better indication of Anglo-Saxon opinion of Britons can be given. Aside from the names of some water features, the Anglo-Saxons did not even adopt British words or learn to speak their language. Only about 30 words in Old English are believed to derive from Brittonic.[14]

Where it is apparent that native and immigrant were intertwined, both sides chose to ignore the implications. Three names in the early genealogy of the Wessex kings were British: Cerdic, Ceawlin, and Caedwalla, but the British did not claim connections while the Anglo-Saxons pretended there were none. In Northumbria, it was recorded that King Oswiu made a marriage alliance with British Rheged royalty by marrying a king's daughter named Rhiainfellt. Other marriage alliances must have occurred, but such actions did not change the ethnic animosities expressed in written documents. As late as the 10th century, nationalistic poetry on both sides scorned the other side and boasted of victories—both past and prophesied for the future—in which the hated opposition would be defeated and driven out.[15]

A number of authors, including Ward-Perkins, believe that given the overlord position assumed by Anglo-Saxons, many Britons chose to blend in rather than retain their British identity and suffer the social and economic consequences. The oldest written Anglo-Saxon laws stipulated compensation payments as punishments for theft or bodily harm. If the victim were a *wealas*, the payment would be only a fraction of what an Anglo-Saxon would receive for the same damages. It is little wonder that someone with mixed ancestry would choose to pass themselves off as Anglo-Saxon. Ine's Laws from sixth-century Wessex reveal ethnic polarization. Ine's people were Saxon, but the laws referred to them as *Englisc*. Britons were called the *Wylisc* (Welsh). The laws were taking an "us" (all German people) versus "them" (all foreigners) stance. As further evidence, late sixth-century Catholic missionaries to Kent found a majority of people to be pagan, far more pagans, as it appears, than there were biological Anglo-Saxons. Part of the blending process found Britons shedding their Christianity, at least in the southeast.[16]

How Many Anglo-Saxons?

The Anglo-Saxons arrived with plenty of new material goods and flamboyant styles of their own. Not only did these objects make the Anglo-Saxons very visible to the archaeological record, but also the goods that they brought to Britain in successive waves of arrivals sometimes came into the possession of Britons through trade. Superficially, this process made the Anglo-Saxons much more "obvious" in the archaeological record than their real numbers merited. Actual Britons owning Anglo-Saxon objects could be mistaken for their neighbors. Older studies on this subject suggested that hordes of Anglo-Saxons overran and obliterated the Britons. Since the 1980s, a much more minimalist picture has been adopted with estimates of Anglo-Saxon immigrants ranging from 25,000 down to less than 10,000, but this is not the final word on the subject.[17] Regardless of the exact number, the Anglo-Saxons were a minority group who became politically and linguistically dominant.

Population Flux

Times of uncertainty inevitably bring hesitancy and population decline. Late and post-Roman Britain was no exception. Historians postulate several generations of population reduction, at least among the Britons. Although there were signs of German mercenary arrivals prior to AD 410, the influx accelerated by the midfifth century. The first Anglo-Saxons came primarily in all-male warbands. Only later did families and entire communities travel to settle new lands. At first, they did not carve out separate territories. Immigrant settlements were scattered among the native farms and villages. Heinrich Härke postulates that since there is little sign of new forest clearance to accommodate the new settlers, the landscape must have had a sufficient number of abandoned farms to provide ready real estate for Anglo-Saxons looking to settle down. There was often no need to push Britons off their own land.[18] However, the Anglo-Saxons did not compliantly fit in with

British society and adopt British ways. Quite the opposite occurred. The immigrants had no interest in changing their own ways. They were the warriors invited to do what the Britons could not do for themselves: fight off invaders and keep order. Changing their ways had not been part of the bargain.

Skeletal data can be used to make a rough comparison of immigrant and native numbers. Analyses have shown a ratio of one Anglo-Saxon to three Britons where immigrant populations were their densest. This number reduces to 1 in 5 elsewhere in eastern and southern England and to as low as 1 in 10 or less in the north, west, and southwest. Studies of mitochondrial DNA also show that no more than one-fifth of the population in any region was Anglo-Saxon.[19] Yet, the Anglo-Saxons dominated.

Anglo-Saxon Status

Treasure hunters, antiquarians, historians, and archaeologists have all been intrigued by the early weapon burials found in Anglo-Saxon cemeteries. Buried weapons included swords, seaxes (single-edged battle knife), shields, axes, and spears. Ordinary knives, although useful as weapons, were common tools of daily use also carried by women and older children, so knives did not count as part of the weapon assemblage. Swords were the most valuable weapon conveying the highest status; spears apparently the least. Some men were buried with only a spear, while others had a full complement of weaponry.

A statistical analysis conducted of the male Anglo-Saxon graves in England showed that 48 percent of males from the fifth and sixth centuries had been buried with weapons, but only 23 percent of the seventh-century males took weapons to the grave. Looking only at the males who were given a sword for the afterlife, the percentage did not change over time. Six percent of the graves in both periods were sword burials. One interpretation of these numbers concerns the changing definition of legal freedom. The possession and the privilege of bearing arms was a symbol of legal freedom. With fewer men taking weapons to the grave, the numbers of free men in Anglo-Saxon society might be falling. An alternative explanation suggests that the meaning of weapons in graves changed. At the same time that fewer men were given weapon burials, beginning approximately with the advent of the seventh century, settlements took on a more hierarchical character. Categories of settlements increased, ranging from hamlets to royal estates such as Yeavering in Northumberland. Small kingdoms were forming. Family status within kingdoms was defined by more than warrior identity. Male status was judged within the context of family, community, and relationship to local and regional leaders. The new royalty claimed the majority of status recognition for themselves and their associates, while mere heads of lesser households no longer qualified for weapon burial status.[20] The evidence from cemeteries supports the perception of growing Anglo-Saxon kingdoms found also in the written sources.

Anglo-Saxon Gender Representation

Much has been made in recent decades of bodies from Anglo-Saxon weapon burials containing female DNA and alleged female burials with feminine object producing male DNA results. There are rare but clear-cut cases of these phenomena. The application of DNA tests to the bones and the resultant surprises were all the more disturbing to historians and archaeologists because the burial symbolism seemed so assertive in its declaration of sexual identity.

This is not the only time gender roles have been transposed in premodern societies. Native American studies have ethnographically documented the acceptance of contrary gender roles for certain individuals by a number of tribes. Absence of clear information does not mean that some gender switching did not occur among Anglo-Saxons and their contemporaries. Christian rules of behavior tended to erase gender complexity in a number of societies.

In higher-status Anglo-Saxon graves with grave goods, standard kits of items are clearly associated with each gender. Gender distinctions are in the accompanying objects, not in the grave construction or location. The male weapon graves have already been described. Elite women were buried with jewelry items including several brooches, sleeve clasps provided in pairs, beads that were originally strung, bangle bracelets, rings, and pins. Brooches and pins were not only ornamental but served to hold clothing together; there were no buttons, hooks and eyes, or snaps for that purpose. Additionally, clothing was sewn together, tied, and belted.[21] Women who ran households were buried with tools befitting their status: a personal knife, keys to the household storage chests containing valuables, spindle whorls for making thread, loom weights for weaving, and weaving battens for keeping the loomed threads straight and tight. Wives of landowners were generally the key guardians. Men only rarely carried a single key. Men also used fewer personal ornaments and pins or brooches. The details of male clothing are much harder to discern.

Besides weapons, some men also took to their graves more mundane tools for metal- or woodworking, if such were their skills. Some men were given special items such as horse harnesses, ceremonial drinking horns, gaming pieces for board games, and musical instruments. Both genders carried their personal knives, tweezers, fire steels used like matches for striking sparks, boxes, and vessels for food and drink.

Heinrich Härke suggested that the strict gender divisions of early Anglo-Saxon burial rites were a reaffirmation of boundaries that had become blurred in real life. Migration and mobility, adjustments to new environments, and resettlement are all forces that upset the daily routines of life. Men and women must share duties and behave differently toward each other. The different social classes must mix more closely. Social rules are frequently broken. Therefore, according to Härke, the strict differentiation of the burial rite in Britain was a reaffirmation of who each individual truly was.[22]

Overlapping gender roles do not imply switched sexual roles. The same blurring of gender boundaries is easily seen in the American West of the frontier period. Widowed women took over the operation and defense of the farmstead. Women traveled and did business alone and carried weapons because they had no available male relatives to escort them. Widowed men raised children without the help of nannies or servants. It is not hard to understand that similar gender-bending adaptations could have occurred in early Anglo-Saxon society. The burial rite was designed to put all cultural norms back to rights again.

As the seventh century approached, elite males and females as young as entering puberty at time of death were given the trappings of adult status.[23] These teenagers had inherited their status from their parents. In the past, respect, wealth, and power had more often to be earned as one grew older. Inheriting adult status before reaching adulthood introduces complex changes in the way society operates.

Not all burials got the full complement of gender-related grave goods. Some had no more than one recognizable item. In the sixth century, roughly half of Anglo-Saxon burials had gender-identifying objects in them. A somewhat larger proportion of these graves contained women. In the seventh century, the weapon rite declined quickly while goods in female graves gradually lowered in frequency. Going to such effort to represent the deceased's gender in burial may have had more purpose than to give the dead their possessions to take with them. The burial rite served as a public reminder of the deceased's social status and family associations. If inheritance were involved, these arrangements had to be finalized in public, and what better time and place for the process than at the funeral. In short, funerals then, as now, are for the survivors to say good-bye, settle accounts, and restabilize community roles. Why the practice remained more conservative with women than with men is a matter for conjecture.

DNA Studies

In recent years, the ability to extract and analyze DNA from centuries-old skeletal samples has improved. Two techniques allow researchers to follow the movements of populations.

One of these techniques is the mapping of Y-chromosome types. All humans have 23 pairs of chromosomes in their DNA. One of these pairs contains the sex chromosomes: XX in females and XY in males. The Y-chromosome is small and contains only 27 active genes. Since no female carries any part of a Y-chromosome, the simple conclusion is that the Y-chromosome passes down the male line from father to son usually without any mutation.[24] Armed with this knowledge, researchers assumed they had found the Y-chromosome of Genghis Khan when they discovered a single chromosome type emanating out of Mongolia and currently possessed by an estimated 16 million males throughout Asia and elsewhere. Since records suggest that Genghis may have born children by hundreds of women as part of his plan of conquest, all of his sons had the potential to pass on his Y-chromosome, thus accounting for the most common Asian Y-type.[25] Approximately, 153 Y-chromosome groups are currently defined worldwide.[26]

The second technique looks at females. Both men and women carry mitochondrial DNA (mtDNA) in each of their cells. Unless a mutation has occurred, everyone inherits the same mtDNA carried by their mother. Thus, maternal lines can be traced through mtDNA. To study female lineages in Britain, Bryan Sykes took over 800 DNA samples from volunteers from all over Europe. Since Britain's population has descended from prehistoric invaders and immigrants originating all the way from Asia, Sykes hoped to capture all the major British lines by this method. The results fell into seven distinct mtDNA sequence groups. In order for a line to exist today, there must have been daughters surviving in every generation who in turn became mothers of the next generation of daughters. Although the sons of the mothers also carried the same mtDNA, sons cannot pass the trait on to the next generation.

Sykes's seven maternal lineages were theoretically founded by an actual woman. Sykes gave names to the imagined ancestresses and called the lineages Helena, Tara, Jasmine, Xenia, Velda, Katrine, and Ursula, each defined by a distinct mtDNA type. Mitochondrial DNA, like the Y-chromosome, comes in different types because it can mutate but does so very rarely. Nevertheless, the rate of mutation is consistent. Using careful calculations, molecular biologists can estimate the passage of time by measuring the numbers of known mutations. The estimates determined that Ursula's line was the oldest at 45,000 years, while Jasmine was the youngest, being only 10,000 years old. Where they had lived required looking for the location where their individual types were most common and where the number of mutations within the lineage were greatest. This place would be the presumed homeland for that ancestress. As a result, Velda was placed in northern Spain, Ursula in Greece, Xenia in the Caucasus Mountains, Helena in southern France, Katrine and Tara both in northern Italy, and Jasmine in Syria.[27]

Using this kind of data, Sykes found a number of interesting patterns, and a few of his results are summarized here. The chromosomes show that the Anglo-Saxon immigrants were decidedly male. There was no great influx of Germanic mtDNA. Instead, the Anglo-Saxon Y-chromosomes were joined with Celtic mtDNA deriving in part from the ancient lineages just mentioned. Although the Anglo-Saxon Y-chromosomes had more success monopolizing Celtic females for some centuries because they were the conquerors, the Celtic Y-chromosomes did not disappear and are still present throughout the British Isles. Sykes was surprised that he found very few identifiably Roman Y-chromosomes. However, the majority of legionaries holding the military posts in Britannia were not actual Romans but came from other parts of the empire.[28]

In another study, Mark G. Thomas et al. looked closely at the Anglo-Saxon Y-chromosomes in England. Whereas the immigrants represented less than 10 percent of the population by archaeological estimates, their genetic contribution affected about 50 percent or more of the modern English gene pool. The authors' computer simulation models required that an extreme situation was required in order for the Anglo-Saxons to gain such a high reproductive advantage. They determined that an "apartheid-like" situation occurred whereby Anglo-Saxon males had the ability to produce many children and to demand extramarital sexual liaisons with British women, while more impoverished British males had fewer opportunities to produce and raise children who survived to adulthood. The Laws of Ine recorded in the seventh century made the punishment for raping a British woman minimal. In this way, Thomas et al. estimated that the spread of Anglo-Saxon genes to 50 percent of the population happened within 15 generations or less.[29]

One opponent of the apartheid argument is John E. Pattison. He points out that Germanic Y-chromosomes in the modern English population did not come just from the Anglo-Saxon immigrants. Germanic lineages have been immigrating to Britain since prehistoric millennia. The Belgae and German legionaries among the Romans arrived before the Anglo-Saxons. Pattison believes that the apartheid argument is not necessary to achieve the levels of Germanic Y-chromosome groups present today in England.[30]

The science of the DNA research and these two opposing arguments have been outlined here to make the point that archaeology and history do not stand alone in the study of the population changes during the post-Roman centuries. Insight can come from a great many directions, including molecular biology. Although there is disagreement on how to interpret the present DNA data, more studies and more analytical advances will soon be made.

NOTES

1. From P. Krueger, ed., *Codex Justinianus* (Berlin, Germany: Berolini, 1877), 983; reprinted in Roy C. Cave and Herbert H. Coulson, eds., *A Source Book for Medieval Economic History* (Milwaukee, WI: The Bruce Publishing Co., 1936; reprint ed., New York: Biblo & Tannen, 1965), 264, 265; and found at Paul Halsall, *Medieval Sourcebook: Codex Justinianus: Return of Fugitive Slaves & Coloni, c. 530 [XI.48.xii.]* (1998), http://www.fordham.edu/halsall/source/codexXl-48-xii.html.

2. *The "Confessio" of Saint Patrick,* chapters 42 and 55, http://www.ccel.org/ccel/patrick/confession.html.

3. John Aylett, "Roman Britain: The Villas," *British Heritage* 24, no. 5 (September 2003): 49, 50.

4. T. Brigham, "A Reassessment of the Second Basilica in London, A.D. 100–400: Excavations at Leadenhall Court, 1984–1986," *Britannia* 21 (1990): 36–40.

5. Brigham, "Reassessment of the Second Basilica," 40, 41, 45.

6. Brigham, "Reassessment of the Second Basilica," 60.

7. Brigham, "Reassessment of the Second Basilica," 62, 63.

8. Bryan Sykes, *Saxons, Vikings, and Celts, the Genetic Roots of Britain and Ireland* (New York: W. W. Norton, 2006); Mark G. Thomas, Michael P. H. Stumpf, et al., "Evidence for an Apartheid-like Social Structure in Early Anglo-Saxon England," *Proceeding of the Royal Society, B: Biological Sciences* 273 (2006): 2651–2657; Mark G. Thomas, Heinrich Härke, et al., *Limited Interethnic Marriage, Differential Reproductive Success and the Spread of "Continental" Y Chromosomes in Early Anglo-Saxon England* (Cambridge: McDonald Institute for Archaeological Research, 2008), 61–70; and John E. Pattison, "Integration Versus Apartheid in Post-Roman Britain: A Response to Thomas et al. (2008)," *Human Biology* 83, no. 6, article 4 (2011), 1–14, http://digitalcommons.wayne.edu/humbiol/vol83/iss6/4.

9. Ken Dark, *Britain and the End of the Roman Empire* (Stroud, UK: Tempus Publishing, Ltd., 2000), 54, 55.

10. Today, archaeologists are careful to record every pot sherd, but there is often no way to date these very plain, crumbly, and often indistinguishable fragments.

11. Dark, *Britain and the End of the Roman Empire*, 57.

12. Nick Higham, "Literary Evidence for Villas, Towns and Hillforts in Fifth-Century Britain," *Britannia* 25 (1994): 229.

13. Keith J. Matthews, "What's in a Name? Britons, Angles, Ethnicity and Material Culture in the Fourth to Seventh Centuries." *The Heroic Age* 4 (Winter 2001).

14. Bryan Ward-Perkins, "Why Did the Anglo-Saxons Not Become More British?" *English Historical Review* 115, no. 462 (June 2000): 514.

15. Ward-Perkins, "Why Did the Anglo-Saxons Not Become More British?" 516.

16. Ward-Perkins, "Why Did the Anglo-Saxons Not Become More British?" 524.

17. Summarized in Heinrich Härke, "Kings and Warriors: Population and Landscape from Post-Roman to Norman Britain," in *The Peopling of Britain: The Shaping of a Human Landscape (The Linacre Lectures 1999)*, edited by P. Slack and R. Ward (New York: Oxford University Press, 2002), 145–175.

18. Härke, "Kings and Warriors," 146.

19. Härke, "Kings and Warriors," 147.

20. Heinrich Härke, "Early Anglo-Saxon Social Structure," in *The Anglo-Saxons from the Migration Period to the Eighth Century: An Ethnographic Perspective*, edited by John Hines (Woodbridge, UK: Boydell Press, 1997), 125–170.

21. For those who are interested in period clothing design, consult Gale R. Owen-Crocker, *Dress in Anglo-Saxon England*, rev. ed. (Woodbridge, UK: Boydell Press, 2004) and Penelope Walton Rogers, *Cloth and Clothing in Early Anglo-Saxon England, AD 450–700*, CBA Research Report 145 (York: Council for British Archaeology, 2007).

22. Heinrich Härke, "Gender Representation in Early Medieval Burials: Ritual Re-affirmation of a Blurred Boundary?" in *Studies in Early Anglo-Saxon Art and Archaeology: Papers in Honour of Martin G. Welch,* edited by Stuart Brookes, Sue Harrington, Andrew Reynolds, and Martin G. Welch, British Archaeological Report No. 527 (Oxford: Archaeopress, 2011), 104.

23. Härke, "Gender Representation in Early Medieval Burials," 101.

24. Sykes, *Saxons, Vikings, and Celts,* 99–101.

25. Sykes, *Saxons, Vikings, and Celts,* 125, 126.

26. Y Chromosome Consortium. "A Nomenclature System for the Tree of Human Y-Chromosomal Binary Haplogroups." *Genome Research* 12, no. 2 (February 2002): 339–348, http://genome.cshlp.org/content/12/2/339/F1.expansion.

27. Sykes, *Saxons, Vikings, and Celts,* 106, 107.

28. Sykes, *Saxons, Vikings, and Celts,* 286, 287.

29. Thomas et al., *Limited Interethnic Marriage,* 61–70.

30. Pattison, "Integration versus Apartheid in Post-Roman Britain," 1–14.

5

MAKING A LIVING
ON THE LAND

FARMING

British soil productivity produced results for early farmers. Depending on the soils, they produced good harvests or where planting was not profitable, pasturing animals made for an alternative living. The climate was relatively mild: wet and warm enough in the summers and not too cold in the winters. Before the Romans came, the Britons thrived while using the simplest of farming tools and methods.

The Romans quickly understood the potential for food production in Britain, particularly when enhanced by their methods. Bountiful harvests were a key element in the success of Romano-British administration. Not only must the people be sufficiently fed, but the army and the bureaucracy, the cities and towns, the craftworkers, and all the other specialists who did not spend their days producing food must be fed as well. Hungry people were a dissatisfied and rebellious people. British farms ultimately fed the Romano-British population and more. During the Roman period, food surpluses were shipped to the continent to feed other parts of the empire.

British and Roman Farms

The pre–Roman British farmhouse was typically a multipurpose round structure made of strong wooden support posts forming the outer wall, wattle and daub to fill in the spaces between posts, and thatch on the roof, enclosing a single living space about 40 feet in diameter. The round houses were usually surrounded by storage pits. Occasionally, small four-post buildings that are thought to have served as aboveground granaries were also nearby. The Romans, however, used a very different kind of farm layout. They introduced to Britain the idea of additional special-purpose buildings and a large rectangular layout of rooms for the farm residence and main work area. Collectively, these structures and spaces were called a *villa*. The idea of having separate barns, byres, granaries (for the storage of grains), and various other storage and work sheds built in a rectilinear plan with a central courtyard safely bounded by the walls of the outer buildings presents at the same time both an orderly spatial arrangement of tasks and an effective defense against all persons and unknown dangers lurking beyond the villa. Visually, the two types of rural settlement were immediately differentiated by the round shapes of the Britons and the rectangular shapes preferred by the Romans.

Forest Regrowth

At some villa sites, farmland was completely abandoned and left to revert to forest. The villa buildings tell the same story. The villa at Withington in Gloucestershire was occupied and altered perhaps as late as the early fifth century, at least within the bathhouse structure, but after that event, no evidence of occupation in the area survives. Nevertheless, the villas did not completely disappear. Even though forests reestablished themselves over old villa sites, those secondary woods did not contain the same species of trees as virgin forestland. To early medieval farmers, the difference in tree species would be clear. Former villa lands could easily be identified by their trees.[1] When the need for more farmland presented itself, the old villa fields were once again cultivated. Farmers knew that those plots would still be clear of rocks and major root systems. Since the fields had been used repeatedly in the past, they likely had and would still have good drainage. Some villa fields were brought back under the plow in a few generations. Other villa lands lay dormant for some centuries. Anglo-Saxons also took advantage of old fields. Studies of known Celtic and Anglo-Saxon place-names for farms and villages in the counties of Cheshire and Shropshire demonstrate that the Anglo-Saxons typically moved into areas previously occupied by the Britons.

Land Charters

Examining the earliest surviving land charters also reveals continuity of land use. Roman villa boundaries can be mapped by landscape archaeologists who plot out the positions of visible structures and historic field ridges formed by the repeated plowing of the same land over many generations. Surviving middle and late Anglo-Saxon land charters describe the positions of the boundaries of their estates. In the southern Avon valley, at a place called the Vale of Wrington, the later estates were found to correspond to the lands belonging to earlier Roman villas. The modern field boundaries, marked by hedges, match in many respects the original Roman fields.[2] This close level of boundary continuity since Roman times occurs in many parts of Britain.

Villages

Towns need villages for support. Villages contribute basic foodstuffs. Additional labor is another service villages can supply at need. Deserted medieval village sites dot the British landscape today. These settlements once thrived but were later abandoned when they became unneeded or insupportable. Deserted villages are particularly interesting to archaeologists because the absence of later buildings on top of the early medieval levels makes it easier to excavate the remains of life in earlier times. In villages and towns where people continued to thrive, build, and change the patterns of streets, the older layers were all but destroyed or else too covered over by later structures that disturbed the older layers.

Once thought to be a fruitful source of information about the early post-Roman period, deserted villages have presented an unexpected history lesson. Most were founded in the 11th century or later as a result of a Norman period population expansion. Their abandonment occurred with the great 14th-century plagues—the Black Death—that reduced the British population by at least a third. Archaeological examination of the deserted villages revealed no information about post-Roman centuries except as a reminder that the arrangement of settlement upon the landscape is not a random thing. Villages and farms were not quickly or easily carved out of the wilderness, but tended to stay in the same locations with only minor adjustments. As population numbers grew or ebbed, the lesser quality lands were retaken or abandoned as needed. These late medieval deserted villages were founded on marginal lands of poor quality and were never again resettled.

Farming Life

The majority of Britons worked on the land. Occasionally, they had the advantage of a local market for obtaining everyday staples but not often. Many Britons had to be self-sufficient in most things. Primary dependence was placed on crops and animal husbandry. Fishing, though water resources were plentiful, was not a common pursuit, although finds of shells of edible shellfish at some sites such as Dinas Powys in Wales reveal that people did not ignore this option. Hunting was a supplemental source of food, but the numbers of wild animals were limited compared to the size of the population. Wild plant foods, such as berries, were likely to be gathered regularly. Farmers grew grains, legumes, and root crops throughout Britain, and animals were raised for dairy, meat, wool, fats or oils, and other useful products.

The farmer's life was built around an annual cycle of tasks relating to sowing and harvesting. Major crops were wheat, barley, rye, peas, beans, and flax. Cattle, sheep, and pigs were the primary domestic animals. Goats and poultry were also raised for food. Horses, dogs, and cats were kept mostly for the assistance that they gave with farm work, but horses were sometimes also eaten.

Fields

English Heritage, the national organization that protects historic and prehistoric monuments, uses the term "Celtic" field to refer to small rectangular fields, the edges of which have become raised due to repeated plowing. In these fields, repeated plowing has pushed some soil to the edges of the field as the plow breaks up and turns the clods of earth. This raised bank is called a "lynchet." Obviously, not all square fields with lynchets are actually Celtic in origin. Fields labeled "Celtic" because of their appearance have been found to date as early as the Bronze Age (2500–750 BCE). Some were in use as recently as Roman times but not later. The name has caused much confusion, leading to the expectation that all Celtic farmers produced square fields with lynchets. The truth is that the lynchet effect is a result of the design of the plow in use. By post-Roman times, plow technology had changed.

For the Roman period, field shapes have been studied at both villas and small farms. The small farms were probably home to the less-wealthy farming families, while villa operations produced many goods for sale and were profitable enough to employ a number of workers. Villas were widely spaced, but when small farms dominated a landscape, they were positioned in close proximity, often only 400 to 800 meters distant. They also typically followed the less-traveled folk trackways rather than occupy the more valuable lands along the major roads.[3] In the Roman period, fields of various shapes are reported, ranging from small rectangles to long,

Strip lynchets, caused by ancient plowing, in the Renscombe Valley near Worth Matravers, Dorset. (Michael Allen/Collections Picture Library)

narrow strips up to five times longer than they were wide. The strip fields were grouped together into blocks of parallel fields.[4] Contrary to expectation, the shape of the field does not predict whether it is managed by a small farm or a villa. Most likely, selection of field shape depended on soils, topography, crop under cultivation, and plowing technology in use.

The preferred location for all fields during Roman times was on valley bottoms and downlands. The downlands, situated at a higher elevation than the valley bottoms, are characterized by light soils lying on top of geologic layers of chalk and limestone. Downland soils were well drained and easy to cultivate, and the landscape also supported sheep and cattle. Strip fields were common on the downlands, but small, square "Celtic" fields, on the other hand, were more likely to appear in rougher landscapes such as the uplands of the north, the Pennines, the gravels of the Midlands, and among the wetlands of the Fens.

As rural properties transitioned from Roman to post-Roman economies, field use sometimes changed. In some cases, the fields continued to be used although the main villa or small farmhouse was abandoned. Increased rainfall forced some farmers to build new homes on higher ground. Others moved to a safer or more convenient location. Farm owners sought fields with better soil conditions and abandoned the old fields. Settlements commonly shifted location to follow the fields under cultivation.

Once Saxon immigrants began settling down in eastern Britain, they left their own stamp on the rural countryside. Most Saxon fields were long and narrow. The expansion of Saxon farms and hamlets dotting the landscape coincided with a general disappearance of small square fields. There is no record of how the early Saxons organized their fields. Some scholars have tried to project backward in time from the 11th century and suggest that the early Saxons kept open fields with rights common to all families in a village. This means that different people could begin working different parts of the common land after it was no longer producing a crop. Open fields normally had no internal hedges, walls, or fences. If the early Saxon fields were truly held in common, labor was more likely to be pooled for major tasks such as sowing and harvesting.

Grains

Grain used for making bread, cooked cereals, and as a thickener in other preparations provided the carbohydrate energy staple of the British diet. In the southeast, where Anglo-Saxon and British settlements were taking up positions on the formerly villa-dominated landscape, the selection of wheat, rye, barley, and oats for cultivation depended on local conditions. Of these grain crops, rye and barley were the hardier species, best fit for sowing in the cool, short summers of northern Europe. Whatever farmers chose to plant, they had to take into consideration that the fifth-century British growing season may be sufficiently wet, but it usually did not allow crops much time to mature and ripen. An unusually cold or rainy season produced only crop failure and famine. On the plus side, the long midsummer days at this relatively high northern latitude provided extra sunlight and made up in part for the shortness of the season. To be safe, farmers preferred grain types that would be most likely to reach full maturity and ripeness under British weather conditions. Peas and beans were also cultivated and provided essential vitamins and minerals in the diet.

Barley was the most common grain. When converted to malt, barley was also an essential ingredient for brewing beer. The crop was sown in the spring, and both naked and hulled types were used. The cultivation of barley had its origins seven or more millennia earlier in the Near East. Although no longer preferred by Europeans and Americans, barley is nutritious. It was particularly valued in Britain because of its superior adaptability to climate variation. Barley can be grown, with luck, in environments ranging from sub-tropical to sub-Arctic because it can ripen in the shortest amount of time of any cereal while maintaining its resistance to excessive dry heat or cool moisture.

The primary form of barley in Britain was the hulled six-row variety called *Hordeum vulgare*. To use this grain, the hulls must be removed and first parched with heat before threshing so that they become brittle and break away more easily. The naked, and much easier to use, variety of barley was available, so it is curious that Britons in increasing numbers chose to grow the hulled type. The most probable explanation is that the hulled barley was grown for animal feed since animals can eat the grain without threshing.

Wheat was a desirable food grain but not so easy to grow or process. The plant comes in several varieties, and the types that were probably grown in Britain during Roman and later times were not like the wheat we know today. One type, called einkorn, was more resistant to temperature extremes, drought, fungoid diseases, and bird predation, but its yield was lower than yields from other types of wheat, such as emmer and naked (modern) wheat. Wheat of all types is more particular of temperature and rainfall than barley. Nevertheless, there was some flexibility in planting wheat.

Depending on the climate or the type of wheat, it might be sown in the fall or the spring. Spelt was native to Britain and used since the Bronze Age, but it has the poorest yield of all wheat types because the grain is mostly husk and of no nutritional value to humans. Threshing processes were never thorough, so bits of husk remaining in breads and other foods caused some long-term dental wear and damage. Observations of teeth from burials reveal severe wear of the enamel. Some of the wear might also be due to other practices such as chewing on certain plant and animal materials to process and soften them for use, but grit and husks in food were not helpful to dental health.

A new type of wheat gained popularity during the first millennium AD. This was a bread wheat variety known as *Triticum aestivo-compactum*. It was suited to heavier soils, especially the clays.[5] The lighter soils were easier to work, but with oxen and a suitable plow, it was possible to till the clay soils. Having a wheat that grew in such fields was important. Few other crops cultivated in the Roman period could be successfully grown on the heavy soils. This *Triticum* type, like naked barley, was free threshing, meaning it did not need parching beforehand in order to force the hulls to break off. The free threshing trait makes finding recognizable traces of *Triticum aestivo-compactum* more difficult. The process of parching the hulls left them charred, which in turn increased their chances for long-term preservation in the soil. Archaeologists can recover charred hulls when they use flotation processes to sort organic matter out of soil samples, and since the charred hulls were better preserved, they were more easily recognized under a microscope. Uncharred hulls from bread wheat do not provide either of those advantages to researchers. The best evidence of bread wheat comes from the excavations at Barton Court Farm in Oxfordshire.[6] In most places, bread wheat did not gain in significance until Anglo-Saxon times.

Rye had its uses as well. Many populations of the world have relied on rye for their principle bread-making grain. Rye cultivation is over 8,000 years old and has been a mainstay in western Asia and central and northern Europe. As a crop, it adapts well to relatively poor soils and climate conditions and works as a winter crop when even winter wheat would fail. Of all the grains, rye has the greatest stamina during northern winters. Besides providing a flour for bread, rye can be used for livestock feed. It is high in carbohydrates, supplies quick energy for humans, and also provides limited quantities of protein and the B vitamins.

Oat crops are common to cool, temperate climates worldwide, and the plant is the only one believed to have been first domesticated in Europe. Oats are said to have originated as an invasive weed of barley fields in western Europe, but it turned out to be an advantageous weed. Oats follow rye in the capacity to produce in poor sandy and acidic soils. For humans, oats have always been popular in porridges and as a thickener for stews. The plant, from grain to stalk, has been used as livestock feed and animal bedding. Oat grains contain many nutrients including calcium and a high proportion of protein.

Direct evidence for the use of oats and rye as crops intended for human consumption does not occur in Britain until the Roman period. Earlier, the plants were present, but they could not be distinguished from weeds growing in fields of other cultigens. In the Roman period, when farmers were trying to expand the quantity of land under cultivation, the hardy oats and rye plants, which were not too particular about the quality of soil on which they grew, were sometimes sown in old nutritionally drained fields, while bread wheat grew in the new fields on heavy soils.

Other Food Crops

Peas come in hundreds of varieties of which the common garden pea is today the dominant form in the western world. Classed as legumes, peas have been known as a food in Europe for at least four millennia and grew wild in Britain as recently as medieval times. Some varieties, called sugar peas or snap peas, grow inside edible pods and are eaten whole. Peas thrive in cool weather and can be eaten raw, cooked, or dried and ground into a flour. Dried peas can be stored for later reconstitution in water and help provide a varied diet during other seasons of the year. Lentils are a similar plant that has traditionally been treated much the same way as peas. Both are high protein foods and an excellent source of potassium and B vitamins. They also contain complex carbohydrates for consistent energy reserves and more dietary fiber than grains.

Beans are another family of legumes among which the variety called the broad bean, or fava bean, was much valued by early Britons. Like peas, fava and other beans, if dried, can be stored for long periods of time. The bean likewise provides an excellent source of protein plus iron and some B vitamins. The fava bean prefers cooler weather and even survives slight freezing. In early Britain, it could be a spring or fall crop in the south, but due to its cold tolerance, the plant could also be grown further north and at higher elevations than other legume crops. Traditional farming economies around the world instinctively combine beans with grains in the diet. These two food groups actually form a valuable symbiotic nutritional relationship because their respective amino acids are complementary and assist in protein production within the human body. Britons took advantage of this healthful relationship of foods.

Other foods were grown in family gardens, just as farm wives have traditionally kept their own home gardens. Herbs, including dill and coriander, show up in the pollen records from rural archaeological and geological investigations. Pollen analysis has also revealed that effort was made to grow grapes in Britain. At Wollaston in Northamptonshire, grape pollen was found associated with a series of planting rows.[7] Most likely, these Wollaston residents were attempting to produce their own wine, but grape production generally requires a warmer, sunnier climate.

Nonfood Crops

Two nonfood crops of importance were flax and hemp. Pollen assemblages, dating to the fifth through eighth centuries and obtained from the study of soil cores taken from British lake sediments, occasionally show high levels of hemp pollen. The presence of high pollen levels in lake beds probably means that hemp stalks were left to soak in the water until the strong fibers were loosened and could be more easily separated. The fibers were then woven into ropes, mats, and other essential objects including sturdy sandals. Flax fibers were similarly soaked and separated in order to make threads for weaving linen cloth. Flax seeds provided linseed oil for a myriad of preservative and medicinal uses. Hengistbury Head is one of many archaeological sites where evidence proving human use not only of flax but also of peas (*Pisum sativum*) and fava beans (*Vicia faba*) has been documented.

Drying was a form of food preservation essential for maintaining life during the winter months in temperate climates. Without refrigeration, few options besides drying or dehydrating were available for preserving foods. Some foods could be pickled, fermented, or packed in oil in relatively airtight containers, but drying was still the most cost-effective and widely applicable method. The winters could become distressfully hungry times if insufficient food was not stored. Structures found at villas and other large residential sites from the Roman period have been interpreted as corn driers. "Corn" in this case refers to any grain, not just the specific cob-producing plants known to Americans as corn. Furthermore, the drying method could be applied to foods other than grain. Because of the large quantity of dried and parched grains, beans, and other food remnants found inside these oven-like fixtures, archaeologists have concluded that they were meant for drying out the fresh harvest in order to prepare it for long-term storage. Of course, this kind of drying could be accomplished without an "industrial"-sized corn drier, which is probably why large driers are not found at post-Roman sites. Nevertheless, the need for food drying remained unchanged. The large corn driers were meant for processing large quantities of produce such as would be brought in from the fields of a villa.

Plows and Field Tools

No discussion of crops is complete without considering the technology of cultivation. Chief among essential agricultural implements was the plow. The first light wooden plow in Britain, a simple device sometimes called an ard, may have appeared during the late Bronze Age. The remains of an ard have been found at a site in Ireland. Otherwise, wooden tools such as ards have not survived in archaeological conditions. Most likely, broken ards were burnt as firewood. There would be no reason to bury one, and in most soils, natural decay would destroy the wood. The types of plowing implements in use prior to the 11th century are not well known. However, analysis of the shapes of field systems reveals that some sort of plowing device was used in order to make long, even rows.

Ards, common in Roman times and for a short while later, merely cut shallow rows into the earth and could be operated by one man. Early plows were used to break up light soils and might be pulled by draft animals. They did not have an attached moldboard for turning the earth over as later medieval plows had. The moldboard was a labor-saving accessory for use in heavier, clay-like soils. Romano-British farmers did sometimes tackle heavier soils while attempting to expand wheat cultivation, but it appears that they did not yet have a suitable plow for the task.

Most of the evidence for early ards and their construction comes from ards lost in Danish bogs where organic objects are uniquely

Medieval manuscript illumination of a farmer teaching his son to plow, from Alphonse Le Sage's *Las Cantigas*, late 13th century. (Gianni Dagli Orti/Corbis)

well preserved. Other well-preserved finds in the bogs are human bodies deliberately deposited either as ritual sacrifices or as punishment. Ards basically did no more than scratch the surface of the soil and required the extra process of cross-plowing to fully break up the soil and make it more productive. Nevertheless, this simple action was usually enough because cross-plowing broke apart and loosened the roots of the weeds so that they did not interfere with the growth of new plants. The weeds did not even need to be removed from the soil since their root systems functioned to hold the lighter soils stable and prevent harmful erosion. Most uses of the ard were on light soils that would otherwise erode rapidly.

Maintaining good draft oxen was essential for the operation of plows. As in medieval times, many a farmer could not afford to own and maintain two such expensive animals for his own personal use. Draft teams were kept and shared, just as open fields and pastures may have been shared, by entire villages. The need to share expensive yet indispensable resources is an important factor behind village communal organization.

Other common agricultural tools in use during the fifth and sixth centuries were scythes and sickles, two variations of the cutting instrument made of iron and necessary for harvesting grains. Both tools have curved blades attached to handles, but the scythe has a longer blade that is attached at an angle so that it is able to cut the stalk at a point closer to the ground. Remains of scythes and sickles have been found at Romano-British sites and at Roman forts, so there is every reason to assume that later Britons and early Saxons had these tools as well.[8] Examples have also been found from contemporary archaeological sites in northern Europe where the preservation of iron objects in less acidic soils is better. At the village of Vallhagar on the island of Gotland in the Baltic, one sickle and four scythes have been found as well as pieces of a single plow. Vallhagar dates to the fifth and sixth centuries.[9]

Animals

Because animal bones usually preserve well and are relatively easy to identify in the garbage pits and burials of excavated sites, we tend to know a quite a bit about the animals used by Britons. Experts in zoology can identify animal species from bones and sometimes determine the sex and age of individuals. Like the continental Europeans, Britons relied mainly on domesticated cattle, sheep, pigs, goats, and fowl. Sheep and particularly pigs became more numerous in the fifth century. These latter species are low-maintenance, sturdy animals and survive well in the cool northerly climate. Sheep could wander about out of doors most of the year feeding on the natural grasses, while pigs were allowed to root at will in the forests. Cattle and goats were more sensitive to cool damp weather and required more attention including provision of shelter and extra feed. Such effort was worthwhile only because of the value of their milk to human nutrition. Milk was infrequently drunk directly. More likely, milk was processed into a range of storable dairy products, principally cheeses and butter, which provided proteins, fats, and other nutrients. The relatively quick proliferation of sheep and pigs at human settlements also indicates a desire in the fifth century to increase the locally available meat supply, not to mention the supply of wool to convert to clothing, blankets, and other warm comforts. Pigskin may have been used to cover window openings since glass windows would not be available for centuries to come. Stretched taut pigskin protects from the more severe elements of nature but still allows light to come through.

Domesticated Species

Cattle. In Europe, a wild species of cattle called the aurochs roamed for millennia. From this animal, cattle were domesticated. The native cattle breed most common to Britain was the Celtic Shorthorn (*Bos longifrons*). When the Saxons settled in Britain, they introduced other breeds of cattle from the northern continent, but they also used the native cattle. Occasionally, cattle got away from their owners and wandered feral and wild in the forests. The wild British aurochs had disappeared long before the Romans came to Britain, but even today, a few herds of feral white cattle, whose origins are uncertain, can be discovered. Early cattle roamed relatively freely all the time. Before the enclosure of private pasture lands with fences, stone walls, and hedges beginning in the sixteenth century, cattle mated haphazardly with available bulls, and selective breeding was rarely achieved. Early domestic cattle did not produce as much milk or meat as modern, selectively bred cattle. Most native breeds were smaller in the past and remain rather small today.

Some of the native breeds, especially the shaggy Highland cattle, are well adapted to harsh cold weather and can graze on the available scrubby vegetation much like the local sheep. The Highland cattle live contentedly out in the open even on the cold windy islands off northern Scotland's coast. Similar cold-adapted animals may have already been kept on British farms by the fifth century.

Pig. Pigs are difficult to control and were often allowed to roam freely. German immigrants brought many pigs to Britain. Genetic stocks were enhanced when Anglo-Saxon pigs had opportunities to mate with wild boars living in nearby forests. Feeding pigs generally consisted of leaving them in fields to graze on grass and clover or turning them loose in forests in the autumn when they could eat the acorns and beech mast (nuts) lying on the ground. This autumn diet helped the pigs to grow fat. In the process, the pigs cleaned up the forest floor and improved the ecosystem. At other times, pigs happily ate the garbage for which there was no other use, such as the dregs of barley left over from beer-making. Pigs reduced outdoor insect infestations by eating certain grubs. They also ate the brambles that choked out other, more desirable vegetation. These handy animals were kept for meat and especially valued for the amount of fat they could produce. The fat was important because in premodern times, fat was often seriously lacking in human diets—a situation that is far removed from our present-day dietary situation.

Pigs were customarily killed when they reached maximum body weight. Because they were able to eat their fill in nuts off the forest floor in the fall and winter months, pigs made an excellent winter source of protein and fat. An easy way to store pig meat for large concentrations of people, such as a garrisoned fort, was in the form of salt pork with the bones removed. Bacon preparation was well known in later Saxon times and would likely have been around in earlier centuries. Smoking or salting meat might be either an individual or a communal operation, and such meats could then be taken to a local market or shared out to family members. Since the bones were removed in the preparation, salt or smoked pork rations, prepared at one location and then transferred to another for consumption, would leave no bones in the consumers' trash heap for archaeologists to find. For this reason, the archaeological evidence for meat consumption is often incomplete; an absence of pig bones does not mean a lack of pork in the diet.

Sheep. Sheep come in all shapes and sizes in Britain, and they sport an amazing variety of horn arrangements and shapes. Today, there are separate breeds for meat, milk, and wool production, but early sheep were not nearly so specialized. The Romans brought long-haired sheep to Britain. Their different-textured wool fibers have been found in some Roman period textiles. The small, hardy, and agile Soay breed is considered to be similar to the ancestor of most if not all modern sheep, and isolated flocks still live today on the west coast of the Scottish Highlands where they have existed for four millennia.

Sheep were slaughtered for meat at a relatively early age, sometimes as young as four years old. That timing, however, does not take into account the slaughter of lambs whose use for meat would allow the sheep owner to regain access to the mother ewe's milk for human consumption. Choices had to be made whether an increased herd or greater milk supply were desired. Dairy sheep also were not kept for many years, but because their milk was an important food source, they were kept as long as they were good producers. Those animals that were kept for the use of their wool and manure were allowed to live the longest since their ability to produce valuable product did not diminish so quickly with age. Slaughtering patterns and age at death are determined from the close examination of sheep bones found in trash heaps. Such characteristics as tooth eruption pattern, tooth wear, and bone development are reliable indicators of age.

Sheep's milk is very nutritious and contains twice as much calcium, phosphate, and zinc than the same amount of cows' or goats' milk. Sheep's milk also has 50 percent more solids that are useful for the making of cheese and butter. Ewes will get nervous when milked, but most can be trained to cooperate. The most valuable sheep for heavy fleece are the castrated males, called wethers. Sheep were valued by southern English grain farmers for their manure. The denser fat of the animals was used for candle-making or as lamp oil.

Goat. Goat's milk was much more important to the post-Roman diet than it is today in western society. Since cow's milk was somewhat rare due to the scarcity of dairy cows, people depended on goats and sheep for what milk they drank. Goat fleeces, like sheep wool, were used for textile production and made into clothing, blankets, and rugs. Goats are destructive browsers of greenery but otherwise are able to fend for themselves in finding food during most of the year, making them a relatively easy animal to keep.

Archaeological assessments of goat and sheep bones are complicated by the fact that even an experienced zooarchaeologist has difficulty distinguishing between the two species. Often, the excavation faunal reports list goat and sheep as a single category because the opportunity for error in discerning which is which is too great. Despite their value, however, goats existed in smaller numbers than sheep in Britain.

Poultry and Other Birds. Chickens were the most important form of domestic poultry, both for meat and for the renewable resource of eggs, although the familiar birds of today, the ubiquitous big white hens, are modern creations of selective breeding. One Roman writer mentioned cockerels (the male bird) as good for eating. Chickens were an efficient meat source. Some poultry grow quickly and can reach market weight in about four months so that their meat is relatively plentiful even though the animal is comparatively small when compared to the meat on individual pigs or sheep. In short, chickens were a reliable complement to the host of farm animals. Of course, due to their smaller size and fragile bones, recognizing chicken dinner garbage in the village trash heap is a difficult task for the zooarchaeologist.

Other birds commonly kept for their eggs or reared for meat were ducks and geese. Geese have the advantage of looking after themselves very efficiently by grazing on grass. However, they must be penned at night for their own safety.

One last type of bird that may have been kept by some individuals for its hunting abilities was the hawk: either the peregrine falcon or the sparrow hawk. Occasional hawk bones are identified on archaeological sites.

Horse and Donkey. Domesticated horses reached Britain during the last centuries BCE before the Romans arrived. The Celts used horses for riding and pulling chariots, especially in battle. Since the Celts, unlike the Romans, did not use saddles but preferred to ride bareback, they could not fight directly from horseback, being too easily thrown off. Instead, they typically jumped down from their horses when confronting the enemy and fought on foot. The Romans with their saddles and horse bridle equipment had a better purchase on horseback, but even they did not know about the use of stirrups that give the rider far greater stability. Late period Anglo-Saxons did use stirrups, but they still didn't achieve good stability, according to descriptions of battles. Only the Normans fully benefited from the advantages of fighting on horseback.[10]

Many British horses were small and not suited for heavy farm work or the moving of large loads. In any event, there is no evidence that they were harnessed as draft animals. Eriskay, Exmoor, Fell, and Welsh ponies are among the original native horses known to fifth- and sixth-century Britons. Their principle value was as a mode of human transportation. In medieval times, larger breeds were imported for heavier work and for carrying fully armored knights. Horses imported by the Romans were also larger, and limited interbreeding had enlarged the size of the native stock somewhat. Occasionally, horses were eaten, as seen from butchery marks on horse bones found at the Anglo-Saxon site of Sedgeford, but they were generally too valuable to be used as food.[11] Sometimes, horses escaped from their owners and wandered feral and half wild in the forests.

Donkeys were introduced to Britain by the Romans. Donkeys have been domesticated for millennia because they are smaller and slower than horses and therefore easier to control. They are also declared to be patient, are certainly sure-footed, eat less than a horse, and live longer (approximately 40 years). They can be put to work carrying burdens according to their size or pulling carts. Mules are the hybrid, infertile offspring of donkeys and horses.

Dog. Among the earliest remains of a dog known in Britain were bones from the site of Star Carr in Yorkshire dated to 7600 BCE. The pre–Roman Celts kept huge mastiffs that they trained to assist in battles. The mastiffs would fight and protect their masters, especially if wounded. The Irish and British nobility continued the practice of using war dogs for centuries. Other breeds trickled into Britain over the centuries. The Romans brought a variety of hounds with them, including the greyhound, and some toy breeds that were meant only as pets. Dogs were useful for hunting a variety of other animals as well as for herding sheep and other unruly farm animals. It is difficult to prove the antiquity of other uses of dogs. Only occasionally were they eaten and probably only in dire circumstances of hunger.

Dogs were common residents at Anglo-Saxon settlements, perhaps more so than at British homesteads. Dead dogs were consigned to the trash pits with the rest of the refuse, but they were not eaten. When a whole skeleton is found intact and articulated without knife marks, the bones cannot have come from an animal butchered for food. Anglo-Saxons depended on dogs for hunting and farm work. At least 14 dog skulls, belonging to large retriever-like animals, were recovered from the village of Thetford in Norfolk.

Ferret. Another hunter, although not nearly so domesticated as dogs, was the ferret. Ferrets were used to force rabbits and rats out of their underground burrows.

Cat. Pet cats were popular with the Romans who brought this animal to Britain in the first century AD. The animal's best working skill has always been to rid houses and storage buildings of mice, rats, and other vermin. Larger rats were often best dispatched by dogs, some of whom are talented as ratters. Cat remains are also common on some Anglo-Saxon sites. At least 18 cats and kittens were found at Thetford.

Bees. Kept for their honey-producing abilities, bees provided a much-loved sweet condiment for the table. Sugar was unknown and not introduced to Britain until the Middle Ages after which it remained a scarce commodity for centuries. Honey also formed the basis for fermenting a sweet alcoholic beverage called mead. In short, there was never enough honey.

Wild Species

Fish. Fish, shellfish, and other edible marine life were extracted from the seas, lakes, and rivers. At the Welsh hillfort site of Dinas Powys, limpets, oysters, and whelks were among the shellfish on the table. The acidic Dinas Powys soils were not kind to fragile fish bones. Whatever quantity and variety were once dropped into the trash heaps, most of the bones have long since disintegrated beyond recognition. Nevertheless, several larger fish species were still identified from the hillfort site. Residents of Dinas Powys dined on salmon and sea trout. In eastern England at Thetford, cod, plaice, and freshwater perch occasionally were served. Eels were another marine food source mentioned by early medieval writers as part of the British menu.

Deer. Fallow deer had become extinct in Britain but were reintroduced by the Romans. Only the red and roe deer species have remained native to the island. Deer are reliably prolific, as anyone who lives in deer-hunting territory knows. If humans remove the deer's natural predators—wolves, lynxes, and bears—then the deer must be hunted lest they proliferate to the point of starvation. Since farmers tend to remove the predators for the safety of their domestic herds, deer hunting becomes both a necessary and pleasing solution since the animals are desired for their meat, hides, and antlers. A harder material than bone, antler can be turned into small intricate tools, such as sewing needles or awls, and it can be carved with designs for ornamental work. Red deer is one of the two species of animal depicted in objects from the seventh-century Saxon royal burial of Sutton Hoo in Suffolk. A small bronze red deer stag was attached to one of the royal accessories, possibly the ceremonial whetstone or scepter. The particular arrangement of the antlers' tines on the Sutton Hoo figurine were traditionally known as "royal," so it is significant that the royal design is used in this famous early Anglo-Saxon burial.[12]

Animals Used Mainly for Their Pelt. Beavers became extinct in Britain in the 15th century but had flourished there earlier. Valued mostly for their water-resistant pelts, beavers were commonly seen in eastern England, particularly in East Anglia, the Fens, and Lincolnshire. Other valuable pelts were taken from otters and pine martens. Hares and rabbits could be eaten and their soft pelts used for small items. Brown hares originated from Asia and were possibly imported by the Romans.

Birds. Peacocks, cranes, wild duck, and other wild birds were hunted for meat and also feathers.

Carnivores. Some animals were hunted because of the damage they did. Wolves were targeted since Roman times for sport and to restrict the harm they inflicted on herds. Probably more hated by farmers than any other animal, the wolf acquired a sinister reputation. An Anglo-Saxon outlaw was called a "wolf's head" because, like his namesake, he was not protected from harm by law or human morality and so therefore was fair game to be killed by any of his enemies. The red fox, a great predator of domestic sheep and poultry, was hunted for similar reasons. The population of wild bear in Britain was probably already greatly reduced in Roman times when many of the cubs were captured and reared in captivity for export. It was fashionable among the extremely wealthy and powerful ruling elite of Europe and beyond to keep a trained bear for entertainment and as a status symbol. Other bears, especially the adults, were hunted simply so that they would not harm humans or livestock. All of these carnivores bore thick pelts, which made an excellent addition to winter clothing or coverings.

Elk. Wild elk still dwelled in the forests and were hunted from time to time although they were not numerous.

Boar. Wild boar once flourished in British forests. Boars were hunted with spears, dogs, and nets not only for meat but also for being a pest. They destroyed crops and property. The wild boar is the second of the two species depicted on objects found in the East Anglian Sutton Hoo burial. The boar was associated with the Anglo-Saxon god of war, and a representation of a boar appears on the war helmet of the buried warrior or king. Other Saxon war helmets have been found also bearing boar symbolism, and similar helmets with boar crests on the heads of dead chieftains are described in the poem *Beowulf,* known from a single manuscript in Old English dating no older than the eighth century.

Diet

In general, food was bland. A small number of native herbs were cultivated in gardens for seasoning. Salt was available though not plentiful, and it was prized both as a preservative and as a flavor enhancer. When stronger, more exotic spices became available through international trade in later centuries. These were prized, even by the upper classes, for their power to disguise the bad taste of somewhat old or moldy food that was nevertheless eaten. Despite all efforts to keep the food supply from rotting, humans fought a constant battle with microbes over the contents of the storage sheds and pits, and few could afford to throw out food that had not gone overly bad when the only alternative was hunger.

So long as food was in adequate supply, most people's diets in the fifth and sixth centuries maintained a reasonably healthy balance. A variety of grains was used in cooking, and bread—flatbread if

Kitchen gear from a presumed house site near Shefford in Bedfordshire. These reconstructed objects resemble the traditional cooking tools of Roman and post-Roman times. The large pottery jar with pointed bottom on the left is a Mediterranean amphora and held wine, olive oil, or a similar commodity when it was purchased from foreign merchants. The iron stand with long links supported a kettle at varying heights over an open hearth. The two-posted stand supported a spit, or possibly two, for roasting meats over the same hearth. The bar, or spit, illustrated at the top has a loop on each end for hooking onto the stand. (Sir Henry E. L. Dryden. "Roman and Roman-British Remains, at and near Shefford, Co. Beds." *Publications of the Cambridge Antiquarian Society*, Vol. X. Cambridge: University Press, 1845)

not loaves—was baked from wheat. Beans and peas provided the majority of vegetables, available fresh or dried throughout the year, while fruits, especially berries of assorted kinds, could be found wild in season. Meat came from wild and domestic animals with pork, ham, and bacon being perhaps the most often consumed though few people would eat meat on a daily basis. Wild game provided lean meat, but even domestic animals other than pigs lacked fat. Fresh- and saltwater fish and shellfish were harvested where accessible. Cow, sheep, and goat milk was mostly converted into different kinds of cheeses and butter. Honey, salt, and native herbs improved taste. Beverages included beer, mead, milk, and water. Other drinks may well have been made from local fruits and plants. Wine was imported by the wealthy, although some industrious landowners seem to have attempted to grow their own grapes and probably fermented other berries for drink. Climatic deterioration after the Roman period probably made grape cultivation impossible. Other exotic food items, such as olives, were imported from the Mediterranean region along with wine. Salt packing, dehydrating, and smoking techniques were used to preserve food for later consumption. A few products such as oils and wine could be sealed in airtight containers.

Woodland Management

Tree conservation was recognized as a necessary task. Britain is not a large geographic area, and its native forests have been cleared and cut back for millennia in order to make room for fields and pastures to support a growing population, yet there was always a daily demand for wood that must be met. Timber was the primary building material and source of fuel. Coal and peat came into large-scale use much later. The prehistoric Britons understood the need to cultivate the woodlands so that a good supply of wood of different species and forms never ran out. They learned how to encourage preferred patterns of wood growth, tailor-made for specific uses. Woodland management was a rural task engaged in on a part-time and seasonal basis by many individuals.

Britain has a long history of "farming" trees. Woods were typically managed by deliberate close planting and by coppicing. To encourage the straight growth of oak and other trees suitable for the strong main posts and beams of timber buildings, farmers protected existing oak stands and encouraged the close spacing of new trees so that their trunks quickly grew straight upward in search of sunlight. Seedlings that were too close to a larger tree to reach the light were removed. Seeds were planted where the best growth was expected. Mature trees were selectively removed at the proper time. These are all ancient practices of tree cultivation that came naturally to farmers. In modern centuries, management continued as landowners benefited from the controlled culling and sale of timber off their lands. Trees grow well on upland areas where farming is unrealistic. Sheep and, in the past, pigs grazed and fed off the undergrowth and dropped mast, which only helped give the trees more room to grow while efficiently imposing multiple uses to the land.

One method of woodland management is coppicing. Widely utilized in Britain, coppicing is the practice of cutting a younger tree down to ground level in order to encourage new shoots from its base and, of course, to use the timber of the original tree. If these shoots are allowed to grow, one stump rapidly produces several or many long, straight narrow trunks. Today, such narrow shoots are of no practical use except perhaps as campfire wood. In landscaped yards, they are a nuisance to homeowners. But in ancient and medieval Britain, there were many uses for straight rods of wood, and coppicing encouraged their rapid and continuous growth.

Narrow wooden rods were needed for the weaving of wattle panels to form parts of walls, which were then lashed to the timber framework of a building and plastered over with specially prepared mud, or "daub," to create completed houses and other structures. Rods were also lashed together to make sturdy walking platforms and pathways over wetlands or seasonally muddied areas, especially within settlements or along frequently traveled trackways. In a western wetland called Somerset Levels, a number of panels of prehistoric walkways made of wattle have been found through excavation. These were well preserved in the permanently wet environment. Some panels have been dated by radiocarbon methods to 4,000 or 5,000 years of age, and deliberate coppicing practices date that far back as well in order to supply all the wattle then in use.

Charcoal

When the coppiced rods weren't put to use as wattle, they served readily as wood fuel. Wood may be burned directly, but much of it was turned first into charcoal in order to achieve a more lasting and hotter fire. The traditional method of making charcoal involved an earth-covered kiln constructed conveniently near the wood source. Kiln sites can be detected archaeologically because they were often reused, and the charcoal stains in the soil remain for many centuries. Successive firings of wood pieces into charcoal actually improved the ground foundation so that the kiln worked better. Care was taken to prevent the interference of strong winds, and sometimes wind breaks were constructed. Wood was prepared by cutting it into similar lengths—three or four feet lengths were common. After cutting, it must be left for six months to dry thoroughly before the kiln was built. The wood pieces were then packed tightly into a mound or cone shape about 10 feet in diameter, and a thick post was inserted in the center. The entire mound was then covered with earth, forming the kiln, but small vents were left at the bottom to let in a little air. The center post was then removed to leave an open chimney. From a wood fire lit outside of the kiln, the burners took glowing embers and placed them into the open chimney, after which the kiln was closed up. The vented structure then allowed the fire to burn steadily.

The goal of charcoal burning is to maintain a slow, even burn but also to allow as little oxygen into the kiln as possible while not losing the fire altogether until all that remained of the wood inside is as thoroughly charred as possible without being burnt up. Charcoal is wood with all its internal moisture, saps, and resins removed. Sometimes, the saps and resins were also collected as they flowed out of the kiln and then used for making such products as tar. The whole process took several weeks and had to be tended constantly to ensure that the kiln did not break apart and that the fire continued to burn at the proper level and did not waste the wood. An experienced charcoal burner could tell by the smell of the smoke how the burn was progressing.[13] In early modern times, professional charcoal burners were paid wages to produce burns for large landowners and fuel merchants who wished to convert a large quantity of wood to charcoal on a regular basis. Centuries earlier, smaller scale burns were typically carried out by individual homesteads to create personal supplies of charcoal for fueling hot fires in the home or workshop. As charcoal demand grew greater, professional burners took over much of the work, and homeowners purchased their charcoal.

FARM SITES

Bradley Hill

Many of the rural activities discussed in this chapter occurred at the late fourth-century Romano-British farmstead of Bradley Hill in Somerset. The owners had reoccupied an early Roman farm abandoned since several centuries earlier. For whatever reason, the land had not been utilized. The new occupants were of ordinary social standing. They took over three buildings, two of which were multiroom houses while the third was an animal barn. A cemetery was maintained on the property, which eventually held 55 burials.

Building 1 was built with stone walls and a rectangular foundation in Roman fashion. Although it had multiple rooms, these were completely walled off from each other, by an absence of any internal doorways, and each room could only be entered from an outside door. Because some pottery fragments found within the building were late Roman in style and design, the excavator concluded that the building was abandoned in the first half of the fifth century. Building 1 was deliberately demolished, probably so that its stone could be reused elsewhere. The largest room contained a hearth. In the smallest room, the burial of an infant was discovered under the floor.[14] This find is not unusual because it was a common Roman custom to bury infants indoors.

Building 2 appears somewhat similar to Building 1. After a short period of use, it was refloored, or perhaps the first occupation had occurred before the building construction was completed. Three infant burials were discovered under the floor of the smallest room in this structure. Some of the structure was destroyed by much later plowing. The estimated date for its abandonment is late fourth to early fifth centuries.

Building 3 was constructed as an extension onto Building 2 and therefore must have been built later. Part of Building 3 collided with earlier burials, and some of these old burials were moved out of the way where later burials were also placed. Inside were found animal stalls, and a drain for removing wash water had been inserted in the floor. After this byre was no longer used for animals, 21 infants were buried under the floor; each was buried separately within a stone-slab cist. Based on coins also found embedded in the floor, this building was abandoned sometime in the fifth century.[15]

This farm was isolated in its location, but it did not have its own corn drier nor did it have adequate storage space, so it is likely that the people living here were dependent on supplies and services available at another location. There may have been a larger farm or operational villa nearby.

Following early Christian practice, most of the burials in the Bradley Hill cemetery were aligned roughly east to west with the head to the west. At the resurrection, the dead would then rise up and face the east. Burials following Christian practice were supposed to be completely empty of any object, article of clothing, or gear. The normal practice of preparing the body for Christian burial was to clean it and wrap it in a shroud. However, one burial in the cemetery was aligned in a north to south orientation and buried with hobnail boots. This individual was not buried according to Christian rules. Perhaps, he died while visiting the settlement but was known to be a pagan. Of the burials, a total of 49 followed Christian custom, and all of these were buried later than the non-Christian burials. The inhabitants of Bradley Hill converted to Christianity and started following Christian burial practices within decades after establishing their farmstead soon before AD 350.

The 55 burials taken together represent 10 adult males, 10 adult females, 1 young female child, and 34 infants. Once the Bradley Hill people became Christian, they buried their infants in the cemetery, not under the house floors. Assuming this is the complete burial population of the farmstead community, 67 percent of the population died before the age of 4. Newborns had a less than one in three chance of surviving infancy. The average life expectancy of males who did reach adulthood was about 42 years, while for females it was only 31 years. The high female and infant mortality statistics tell us that pregnancy and childbirth were dangerous endeavors.[16]

Given the number of burials over a 100-year time frame, the farm's population must have averaged about six people at any given time with two adults assumed to be at the head of a single family. Aside from the complications of childbirth, malnutrition may have afflicted several of the infants. One adult male may have died of a back injury. Many adults suffered arthritic damage to their joints due to constant hard manual labor, and a large number showed considerable dental decay, which itself can weaken the body's immune system and bring on illness and death.

Bradley Hill is a good example of the expansion of farming and the apparent economic growth of Romano-British society in the fourth century. Where a farm had been abandoned for several centuries, it was now reoccupied. Care was taken to build strong, Roman-style residential and byre buildings out of stone. Such buildings could not have been constructed by the occupants without outside assistance. For that reason and its lack of self-sufficient farm facilities, Bradley Hill appears to be a subfarming unit connected to a larger farm collective where certain resources and the storage of foodstuffs and other necessities was held in common. There may have been a large villa involved, but none has yet been located in the area.[17]

At Bradley Hill, a story of intermittent land usage is paired with behavioral changes relating to Christian conversion. Although there is no way to tell why a late Roman family came to live here for a few generations and then left, worsening weather patterns, a breakdown of the farm collective system, or too much local political instability may have all contributed. Whatever these events meant to the people who lived them, Bradley Hill creates a brief snapshot of life on small rural farms.

West Stow

Whereas Bradley Hill in Somerset was a British farm, early Anglo-Saxon immigrants settled the rural village at West Stow in Suffolk. West Stow was situated less than three miles from a late Roman villa, which may have also operated as a regional market center. The village consisted of 7 small rectangular timber houses in the typical Germanic "hall" design and about 70 smaller buildings of the "sunken-featured building" (SFB) type for storage and specialized work. For example, on the floor of one SFB were found heavy doughnut-shaped loom weights, making it a likely weaving shed. Early West Stow resembles closely the type of settlement the Anglo-Saxons favored in their homeland with the same kinds of structures. The styles of pottery and metal objects show that the village was occupied from about AD 420 until about 650. Perhaps, only three or four families lived there at any one time.

Throughout the site were found remains of grain crops such as wheat (including spelt wheat), rye, barley, and oats. The animal bones pointed to the presence of many cattle, sheep, and pigs, with pigs increasing over time. Saxons in their native country were not enthusiastic keepers of pigs, so their increased reliance on pigs in Britain suggests an adaptation to British conditions where pigs were found to provide ample food returns for less investment of resources and labor. Hunters contributed red and roe deer, ducks, and geese. Pike and perch were fished out of the local river, and poultry added to the diet. Some pony-sized horses (occasionally eaten) and large dogs were also kept.[18]

Aside from the pigs, another clear change in Anglo-Saxon behavior was a reduced interest in eating horseflesh. In the Anglo-Saxon homelands, butchered horse remains were plentiful. In England, not so many horses were eaten. Initially, the need for meat was replaced by pigs, but over the decades, increasingly, more cattle and sheep were consumed. The change was gradual, due to the naturally slow growth of sheep flocks and cattle herds. Part of the reason for the slow growth is biological. Cows and ewes give birth to only one or two young at a time, while pigs deliver much larger litters. At two litters per year, a sow can give birth to approximately 20 piglets annually. It was sensible for the Anglo-Saxon settlers to rely on pigs until they could increase their herds and flocks. Another reason for the gradual transition was livestock durability. Cattle needed more tending and shelter, especially in the winter, and if the pasture was covered with snow, feed must be provided since cattle cannot graze through snow.

Despite continuing to build and dress like Anglo-Saxons, the immigrants appeared to have learned many helpful survival tips from Britons. The large-scale use and maintenance of pigs, for example, was something unfamiliar to the newcomers. The author of the West Stow zooarchaeological study, Dr. Pam Crabtree, suggests two possible interpretations. On the one hand, the British population may actually have survived in this area, rather than dying in conflict or fleeing, as many scholars in the past assumed, so that the remaining Britons were responsible for the regional continuity of livestock and cultivation practices. This could also mean that Britons existed as slaves or laborers subject to the authority of the Saxons or, on the other hand, that they dwelled nearby as helpful neighbors. The answer is not easy to determine. After several generations of coexistence, ethnic differences become blurred. Archaeologists have not found evidence of Britons in the vicinity, but lack of evidence does not prove actual absence. If the Anglo-Saxons were more numerous and the Britons had chosen to blend in by living in Anglo-Saxon-like halls and using sunken-featured outbuildings, then there would be little else preserved in the ground to tell Briton from Anglo-Saxon. Only burial rite might differentiate them due to their Christian practice provided the Britons continued to practice Christianity.[19]

By the time that the West Stow settlement flourished, Anglo-Saxons had been living in Britain for generations, the first ones having arrived as mercenaries. They had ample time to observe British customs. It is not likely that the Anglo-Saxons who set up farmsteads at West Stow were unfamiliar with the territory, nor did they take their village lands by force. All the archaeological evidence indicates that West Stow was not occupied by Britons prior to Saxon settlement. Like Britons elsewhere, the Anglo-Saxons took unoccupied lands for their own use, and Britons who remained in the neighborhood were not inclined to do anything about it. This scenario was repeated a number of times in different locales over a period of several decades in the early fifth century.

NOTES

1. Leslie Alcock, *Economy, Society and Warfare among the Britons and Saxons* (Cardiff, UK: University of Wales Press,1987), 276.

2. Martin Jones, *England before Domesday* (Totowa, NJ: Barnes & Noble Books, 1986), 153.

3. P. J. Fowler, "Agriculture and Rural Settlement," in *The Archaeology of Anglo-Saxon England,* edited by David M. Wilson (London: Methuen and Co., Ltd., 1976), 25.

4. Fowler, "Agriculture and Rural Settlement," 26.

5. Ken R. Dark and Petra Dark, *The Landscape of Roman Britain* (Stroud, UK: Sutton Publishing, Ltd., 1997), 110.

6. Dark and Dark, *The Landscape of Roman Britain,* 111.

7. Dark and Dark, *The Landscape of Roman Britain,* 111.

8. Dark and Dark, *The Landscape of Roman Britain,* 106.

9. Alcock, *Economy, Society and Warfare among the Britons and Saxons,* 38.

10. Juliet Clutton-Brock, "The Animal Resources," in *The Archaeology of Anglo-Saxon England,* edited by David M. Wilson (London: Methuen and Co., Ltd., 1976), 384.

11. Clutton-Brock, "The Animal Resources," 383.

12. Clutton-Brock, "The Animal Resources," 390.

13. D. W. Kelley, *Charcoal and Charcoal Burning* (Princes Risborough, UK: Shire Publications Ltd., 1996), 5–9.

14. R. Leech, "The Excavation of a Romano-British Farmstead and Cemetery on Bradley Hill, Somerton, Somerset," *Britannia* 12 (1981): 183.

15. Leech, "The Excavation," 192.

16. Leech, "The Excavation," 196.

17. Leech, "The Excavation," 207.

18. Pam J. Crabtree, "West Stow," in *Ancient Europe, 8000 B.C.–A.D. 1000, Encyclopedia of the Barbarian World,* edited by Peter Bogucki and Pam J. Crabtree, Vol. 2 (New York: Charles Scribner's Sons, 2004), 500, 501.

19. Pam J. Crabtree, "Sheep, Horses, Swine, and Kine: A Zooarchaeological Perspective on the Anglo-Saxon Settlement of England," *Journal of Field Archaeology* 16, no. 2 (1989): 212.

6

MAKING A LIVING IN CRAFTS AND TRADE

CRAFTS AND CRAFTSMEN

Specialization

Work specialization provided better quality wares and an improved standard of living for some people. Growing food out of the soil and on the hoof was a basic task essential for survival, but other types of production also helped to solve life's problems. Fashioning iron or wooden tools, good cloth, shoes, cooking utensils, storage containers, sturdy buildings, and a variety of personal objects out of a wide range of raw materials benefitted from specialized knowledge and practiced skill. Even though many simple crafts such as textile weaving, pottery making, and basic blacksmithing could be performed to an adequate standard at home, the best-quality workmanship for producing durable items was accomplished when a skilled specialist made surplus product for sale or trade to customers.

Many of these items were exchanged through barter. The value of the things being bartered depends on personal agreements. In most instances, post-Roman trade was accomplished through barter rather than by currency exchange because the departure of the Roman army had stopped the regular influx of coins in the form of soldiers' wages. As the remaining coins were hoarded or melted down for their metal content, Britain gradually became a moneyless society.

Full-time specialists needed a more complicated support system and usually the support of a periodic and reliable market. Some specialists were fully dependent on the income of their craft and needed the assurance of a steady stream of customers and sufficient compensation for their efforts. They often lived in larger population centers where customers and supplies were plentiful. Most full-time specialists were men, for early European society did not give a woman such independence of action or movement. Full-time craftspeople sometimes traveled to where the work was found. Itinerant workers of all kinds moved from one villa estate or village to the next taking work commissions where offered. A woman was more likely to be a part-time specialist working inside the home. However, a wife might assist her husband in his full-time craftwork.

What objects need to be crafted in fifth and sixth century Britain? Below, the major craft activities of those centuries are divided into groups according to the raw materials used.

Iron

Steel is a modern invention and is made by a complexly engineered process. Until the modern invention of steel, the workhorse metal of civilization was iron. The first step to making iron was to smelt iron ore in a smelting furnace. The result of the hot and dangerous process was a small amount of iron bloom and a much larger amount of slag—a rock-like substance consisting of the many impurities in iron ore that smelting removed. The bloom was a rather poor grade of iron that was then further purified, strengthened, and shaped in a blacksmith's forge with a hammer, tongs, and anvil. The heating and hammering process, repeated numerous times in the forge, released more impurities from the bloom. Removing impurities made the iron stronger and less brittle. When the blacksmith was satisfied with the condition of the iron, he proceeded to forge the shape of whatever tool was needed.

A myriad of necessary and useful objects were made of iron by blacksmiths. Horses were harnessed with ropes and leather straps connected to iron rings and buckles. More buckles and pins of different shapes and sizes held people's clothing together. Even the pin mechanism of fancy, bronze brooches was often constructed of iron. Knives and shears were essential implements for daily life. Longer blades were fashioned for use as sickles and scythes to cut grain in the fields. Iron nails were needed for constructing

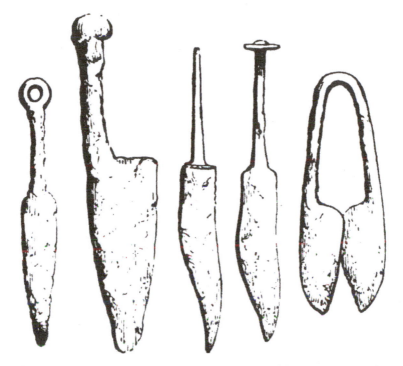

Four iron knives and one scissors, operated by squeezing the two opposing blades together, found at Richborough Roman Fort in Kent. The knife handles were once bound with cord or leather to form a comfortable grip. (Charles Roach Smith. *The Antiquities of Richborough, Reculver, and Lymne, in Kent*. London: John Russell Smith, 1850)

boats and other carpentry work. Nails found in graves once held wooden coffins together. Door hinges, locks, and other construction details were dependent on iron. Wooden buckets were held together with iron bands. And, of course, weapons for the hunt and the battlefield—fishhooks, arrow points, spearheads, swords of all sizes and shapes, helmets, armor plating, chain mail, and the framework of shields—were all made of iron.

The process of smelting, though arduous, was best accomplished by experienced smelters, but could also be done on the household scale. Simple smithy work was an essential survival task that many men could accomplish in a pinch. When the first Vikings came from Greenland to North America and set up camp at the site of L'Anse aux Meadows on Newfoundland around AD 1000, they built a forge. They probably needed to repair their tools and nails for ship maintenance. As for Roman Britain, iron smelting and smithy work occurred at many villa sites. Smelting furnaces were smoky, hot, and gave off fumes, so the work of smelting was placed away from habitation. Forges were more commonplace than smelting furnaces, but like the furnaces, they were set apart from homes and nice public areas.

Iron ore, or the raw material from which iron is made, is found in many places worldwide in deposits close to the surface. Mining is not difficult. Iron is reasonably plentiful in many parts of Britain and can be observed as red stains on mountain and hill sides in the west and north of England. The rock-like ore, once collected, must be washed and broken into small pieces. The next necessary ingredient is charcoal. This too is broken into pieces of appropriate and consistent size. Then, a furnace is constructed of clay. Both a floor and a mound shape, like an inverted bowl with thick walls, are formed. The top is left open as a chimney, and several air vents are added at the bottom. A slag trap, or pit, is built into the floor, and a larger opening, like a little door, is added so that the bloom can be removed after the smelting process is over. Most furnaces were reused at least several times before heat stress damaged them beyond repair.

The smelting furnace was designed to achieve a high internal temperature: 1,800°F was often necessary although higher temperatures were more effective. In order to reach an adequate temperature, the charcoal needed additional oxygen, so laborers used a bellows to fan the charcoal. Without the additional oxygen blown in through the vents, the furnace would not be able to melt the iron ore. Manning the bellows required nonstop effort by a team of bellows operators. Another team managed the charcoal and added more fuel as needed to maintain the internal temperature. Workers also had to look out for cracks forming in the clay walls due to the intense heat of the furnace. A bucket of slurry, or watery clay, was kept handy for patching up small cracks before they became large destructive cracks. Outside air coming in through cracks in the walls would lower the temperature inside the furnace making it too cool to melt and separate the iron ore into bloom and slag.

Roman furnaces were about three to four feet tall. By the high Middle Ages, furnaces were much taller, perhaps six to eight feet, and might have to be filled and managed by men standing on surrounding scaffolding. When the post-Roman Britons or the Anglo-Saxons made a furnace, they constructed something quite small, even less than three feet in height. Such furnaces would produce less iron but were also easier to handle and required smaller teams of laborers using less charcoal. People produced iron bloom in the fifth and sixth centuries mostly on a household scale. Not every household would have its own smelting furnace, but those involved in making iron can be expected to have placed their furnaces at a distance from other buildings and activities, since the smoke and fumes of smelting were not pleasant to human or beast. The absence of iron artifacts at archaeological excavations of household sites may be partly explained by the frugal repair and reworking of broken iron at the forge. Smithing skills were frequently put to use, and iron was recycled as much as possible.

Once the furnace was readied and the iron ore and charcoal prepared, the smelting process would take one or several days, depending on the size of the furnace. Archaeologists of the Whitehall Roman Villa Landscape Project site in Northamptonshire conducted one of many recorded experimental smelts to test their understanding of the process. They made a small furnace based on a common Roman design. This experiment took only seven hours to complete despite unanticipated technical problems.[1] The result was a usable piece of iron bloom ready to be transferred to the blacksmith's forge for further processing.

Iron was also smelted by villa workers at Chesters Villa, Woolaston, in Gloucestershire. During Roman times, villa smelters produced iron bloom on an industrial scale for general trade and foreign export. Some of the larger villas of the region emphasized industrial iron production along with agricultural production. Trade at Chesters depended on ships able to navigate the Bristol Channel to reach foreign ports. During the fourth century, sea traffic out of Bristol diminished, and that is the presumed explanation for the decline of iron production at Chesters. Villa excavators found that the later smelting activity was minimal compared to what had taken place a century earlier. During the fifth century, iron production in the industrial area ended, but occupation or use of villa structures continued. At the main villa building, some demolition had occurred, and excavators suggest that scavengers may have been looking for usable bits of iron within the structure or for discarded slag, which may yet contain some recoverable iron.[2]

Smelting activity at Chesters was largely dependent on the ability to export to foreign markets because production profits from sales in local and regional markets were not adequate. Had regional trade been sufficient, there would not have been the obvious decline of iron production in the fourth century. In the fifth century, it was no longer reasonable to run the large furnaces at all, negative evidence neither proving nor disproving the continuation of small-scale smelting somewhere in order to serve the needs of the local population. Later, or perhaps at the same time, people were taking advantage of the small amounts of iron that could be forged out of some of the more impure pieces earlier rejected and discarded into slag piles. Scavenging rejected iron bloom fragments was simpler and cheaper than smelting when need was not so great.

Post-Roman iron smelting may also have occurred at Hayes Farm in Devonshire. Located in the heart of the territory where British kingdoms were consolidated in the sixth century, this farm—with signs of occupation dating from pre-Roman times to potentially as late as the seventh century—has yielded sufficient iron slag to support claims of smelting activity.

Other Metalworking

Other metals that had high economic value in Roman Britain were copper, tin, lead, and silver. Gold was too rare in Britain to make much economic impact. The alloys, bronze, made of copper and tin, and pewter, made of lead and tin, were also produced for trade. Britain was rich in these metals, and the Romans took full advantage of that fact. The Romans organized mining and refining of these metals for their own use as well as for trade. Mining and production of these metals was a profitable activity that once again greatly diminished by the fifth century. In the southeast, metalworking industry fell off precipitately, but in the southwest where British kings and tribal territories dominated the settled lands from their royal seats atop fortified hillforts, some profitable production and trade in metals continued.

In recent decades, experts have begun to recognize certain types of ornamental metalwork as uniquely British. Circular brooches with a straight pin attachment of a type called penannular, which functioned rather like large safety pins, were common in the post-Roman centuries. These were made of bronze and decorated with a distinctive ring and dot ornamentation or enamel inlays. Use of these pins was typical of Britons and less likely by Anglo-Saxons.[3]

Other items for personal hygiene were made of metal and perhaps organic materials that have not survived among the excavated finds. Romans used metal toothpicks, ear scoops for cleaning out ear wax, body scrapers for removing sweat and grime with or without a bath, tweezers, and so on. Ear scoops were common personal implements owned by many people. Body scrapers were frequently used in the steam baths. Romans were not accustomed to using any kind of soap while bathing, so scraping the surface of the skin to remove grime loosened by steam was both cleansing and exfoliating. Combined with the sweating induced by the hot, steamy environment in heated baths, this was actually an effective way to get clean. A cold bath sealing the skin pores and rinsing the body completed the process. This sort of bathing occurred frequently in Roman Britain, but after the late-Roman decay of the public bath and villa bathing facilities, the pastime was abandoned. It is hard to know what tools of personal hygiene remained in use afterward, but one likely item, not mentioned yet, was the hair comb carved out of bone. Britons probably had these, and Anglo-Saxons had combs too. Toothpicks, ear scoops, and tweezers could easily be made from scrap metal or bone, but the manner and habits of post-Roman hygiene are unknown.

Dinas Powys

Britons in the west organized into small kingdoms based at large defensive hillfort sites some of which were royal seats. One royal seat was Dinas Powys near Cardiff in southern Wales. Excavation has revealed an abundance of first- and second-century Roman luxury items such as fine-quality red Samian ware (the equivalent today of owning a fine set of china), an ornamental La Tène-style brooch from the continent, broken glass objects including bottles and lamps, and bits of window glass. Since no direct signs of Roman habitation were found at Dinas Powys, the Roman treasures could have been heirlooms gathered to the spot in the fifth century when luxury goods were becoming scarce. Another explanation asserts that archaeologists simply have not yet found the first- and second-century residences of Dinas Powys. The second idea seems less likely since the valuable nature of the glass and foreign imports suggests that a large and well-established settlement would have been their source.[4] That settlement would not be so hard to find.

In addition to early Roman objects, excavation at Dinas Powys revealed a post-Roman settlement complete with buildings, industrial production activity, and graves. Results of radiocarbon dating tests ranged from the beginning of the fifth century through the seventh century. From the fifth century were found three industrial hearths designed for use in metalworking. An incomplete timber structure was started and left unfinished. One child's grave dated to this early phase, and imported Mediterranean pottery from the end of the fifth century or later indicated continuing foreign contacts. At the turn of the sixth century, there were signs of ongoing industrial activity, the possible construction of two buildings made of reused stone (although if that is the case, the stone was later removed and perhaps used yet again), and the presence of imported pottery from western Gaul. The last phase, during the seventh century and possibly early eighth, is mainly marked by the construction of a new ditch-and-rampart wall for defense, perhaps signifying growing political turbulence.

Metalworking held a position of importance at Dinas Powys. Bronze was worked into small ornaments and pins for personal adornment and for fittings such as box hinges and decorative plates. Tools for working bronze and iron were found within the hillfort. The occupants also left behind considerable quantities of iron ore, slag, and cinder from their iron smelting and smithing activities. The raw materials for iron smelting were locally available. At least some of the ore came from a deposit located only two miles away.[5] With all the iron smelting, smiths must have been busy at Dinas Powys. It would make little sense to transport heavy iron blooms elsewhere for smithing, and there was no logical place to take the raw iron than Dinas Powys itself. Dinas Powys was a regional center for the making and repair of weapons and tools. The leadership at the hillfort appears to have taken care to see its defenders well armed and its people well supplied for their daily needs.

Dinas Powys ranks behind only Tintagel and Cadbury-Congresbury for the amount of archaeologically recovered imported pottery from the post-Roman centuries.[6] Other recovered household objects—including stone rotary querns for grinding grain for bread, whetstones for sharpening blades of all kinds, glass and semiprecious stone beads (mostly also imported), German-made glass containers, objects bearing early Christian symbols, carved bone pins, and hair combs made out of antler—demonstrate that the residents of Dinas Powys had the time, skill, and means to acquire and make the finer things in life. They also ate well. Animals were regularly butchered. The cattle, sheep, and pig bones collected from the site number over 12,000. Excavator Leslie Alcock suggested that many animals were most likely brought as tribute payments to the military and princely court occupying Dinas Powys. In return for the tributes, the people living in the vicinity expected protection from enemy attack. When not engaged in defensive and governing activities, the court enjoyed a rich lifestyle that contributed to the employment of skilled artisans.[7] The women worked in textiles and possibly basketry. The royal seat at Dinas Powys must have been an impressive sight to all who visited.

The assumption of high status is not so easy to prove when looking at post-Roman hillforts and other sites, Dinas Powys included. The buildings were not grand breathtaking structures like Roman public buildings constructed of carefully dressed stones and carved columns, and they did not appear much different than the buildings found elsewhere in Britain at the time. Symbols of status were expressed in ways that did not always preserve well. Status was expressed by the possession of exotic objects or items made of valuable materials, certain patterns of dress, and the bearing of high-quality weapons ornamented with precious materials, along with a reputation for using them in deadly fashion. These are among the possibilities for showing one's high place in society. The fine products made by the artisans of Dinas Powys were not left about to get buried in the ground. All that was left behind were fragments of foreign pottery, glass, and bits of precious metals. The textiles, worked leather, and carved wood decayed. Metal objects were taken away for use elsewhere or possibly recycled into other objects. Despite Dinas Powys's royal status, little remains to help us picture how it looked.

Wood

Carpentry was a trade frequently in demand, but little of what was made and knowledge of how it was made has been preserved underground. Broken wooden materials likely ended up as firewood. At other times, wooden objects and construction were left to disintegrate from exposure to the elements. In the 9th and 10th centuries, Anglo-Saxons and Scandinavians were able to construct and use a simple lathe mechanism enabling even cutting and shaping for the efficient turning of wood for bowls and other round objects. The same societies could build large seaworthy boats out of well-prepared wooden planks and beams. Their timber buildings were constructed with intricate and specialized joins, and larger buildings such as wooden churches and mills displayed great competency of carpentry technique. Anglo-Saxons also split wood to make wooden roof shingles to replace the usual thatched roof.[8]

Such well-developed skills did not appear out of nowhere. Earlier centuries had their carpentry products as well. Wooden chests for storage and simple tables with stools or benches provided for basic interior furnishings. Bedding was placed on wooden platforms or otherwise raised off the ground for warmth and protection from vermin.

British and early Anglo-Saxon carpenters would be expected to have the following woodworking toolkit available to them: axes, hammers, adzes (a curved tool for shaping and dressing the surfaces of lumber), boring bits for drilling holes, chisels, gouges, planes (for smoothing wood), saws, and wedges (for splitting).[9] These tools were well known in the ancient world. They have been found preserved in hoards and burials in Scandinavia and at a few Anglo-Saxon sites of the seventh century. Comparable pieces are known from Romano-British sites. They must have been among those iron artifacts that were usually kept (not discarded), repaired, or recycled for their metal.

Clay

Articles worked in clay were the pots, cups, bowls, and jars needed for food storage, preparation, and consumption. Wood was also a likely material for making tableware objects such as bowls and cups. Clay was also for making the typical donut-shaped loom weights, which pulled and weighted down bunches of vertical warp threads on a standing loom. Since many households now wove their own fabrics for daily use, looms were numerous. However, the worn-out wooden frames of old looms most likely ended up in hearth fires. Only the clay loom weights have survived occasionally as archaeological finds. At West Stow, some loom weights left behind in a shed have been presented as evidence that a loom once stood inside, ready for weaving whenever time and threads were available. When the loom decayed, all that was left behind was a row of loom weights on the ground.

Clay was also the best material for making stable heatproof foundations of hearths, kilns, and iron smelting furnaces. Kilns and furnaces also had clay walls. The mass production of clay bricks and tiles in factories, so essential in Roman times, had ceased due to the collapse of the markets and demand. Instead, most people used local clay as a packing material when building and repairing their wattle-and-daub structures. The daub applied to the walls of wattle structures was most durable if it had a clay-like consistency.

Some Britons must have found the loss of the finer things in life frustrating. After several centuries of being accustomed to the fine ceramic wares imported by the Romans, Britons were left with a dearth of luxury goods. Gradually, the last of the Roman wares were used up or broken. It became necessary to manufacture as much of what was needed as possible within the home or village. Native Britons least impacted by the Romans, such as those living in Wales and Cornwall, were best prepared to make their own pottery, but their materials and methods were coarse and merely serviceable compared to Roman wares. Coarsely made and less skillfully fired pottery also presents a problem to archaeologists. Coarse ware tends to break down more readily in the soil so that sherds crumble to nearly nothing when exposed to the air. If not carefully excavated, coarse pot fragments might not even be noticed. Decades ago, excavators did not always bother to record or save any artifacts lacking aesthetic interest, so even if noticed, coarse ware sherds were discarded.

At some sites, stone bowls have been found, perhaps for use as mortar and pestle combinations for small grinding jobs.

Central seats of power such as large hillforts and coastal harbor sites in the west with ruling-class connections had more access to international goods than most parts of Britain. Exotic foods, wine, and oils continued to be traded in small quantities, and the pottery containers for these goods remained behind with the purchasers. This sort of trade was not ordinary market trade but a kind that might be described as a gift exchange between high-ranking social equals who wished to maintain their foreign alliances and communications. In this way, a random assortment of exotic shipping containers from the Mediterranean, western Gaul, and even northern Africa found its way to Dinas Powys. Most of these containers were large two-handled amphorae that lacked a flat bottom because they were meant to be stacked on their sides in ship cargo holds. The typically pointed bottoms were also useful for propping the amphorae upright by pushing the point into sand or loose dirt. The containers that ended up at Dinas Powys did not add up to any sensible collection of cooking and serving wares but nonetheless were put to further use. Despite all the craftwork going on at Dinas Powys, no evidence of local pottery-making has been unearthed.

The first Anglo-Saxon mercenaries to come to Britain also used the mass-produced pottery from Romano-British kiln factories. Later they returned to making their own wares. The Anglo-Saxons became prolific makers of pottery since they had brought such skills from home. In the early years, the pagan Anglo-Saxons practiced cremation of the dead. Cremated human remains were placed in decorated ceramic urns made especially for the purpose. Given that Britons and Anglo-Saxons at times peaceably interacted, coexisted, traded, and even intermarried, the best pottery was likely to have been most popular with both groups. Most homemade pottery surviving from these centuries is thought to be Anglo-Saxon made. In fact, some Britons, especially women living with Anglo-Saxon men, may have learned to make good imitations of Anglo-Saxon daily wares. In other words, the post-Roman pottery used by all occupants of Britain is dominated by Anglo-Saxon styles and methods of manufacture, but others besides Anglo-Saxons were using or making it.

Leather

Leather production, particularly for the military, had been an industry in Roman times. Containers for transporting and consuming liquids of all kinds were often made of leather. Sturdy footwear, belts, and straps of all kinds such as those used to saddle and harness horses and other transport animals were often made preferably from leather. Processed leather does not normally survive on archaeological sites unless it has become buried in perpetually waterlogged underground layers. This circumstance happened at several urban centers with low-lying wharf areas situated near the water table. York and Dublin provide particularly good examples, but their underwater remains date mainly to the eighth century or later when the trade activity at these towns accelerated under the newly arrived Viking invaders. For the Britons and early Anglo-Saxons three centuries earlier, there are no comparable waterlogged sites, but given the presence of domestic animals, the earlier leather consumption of the Romans, and knowledge of leatherworking, they were capable of making a sufficient supply.

Aside from providing material for footwear and horse gear, leather was often the product of choice whenever a strong, flexible material was needed. The application of oils and resins made leather water resistant. Skins were stretched thin enough to let light through and were then used to cover windows. Glass window panes were a luxury far in the future, but skins let in some light and protected from the elements. For those who knew how to write, animal skins could be made into parchment, the material bound in book covers, and used for manuscript texts and record-keeping before paper became known. Leather attached to a wooden frame created a bellows capable of blowing large quantities of air to maintain fires in forge and furnace.

Protective gear for battle and gloves and aprons necessary for working with hot metals were made from leather. Before the advent of chain mail and metal armors, warriors relied mostly on thick leather to create body protection from helmet to tunic and leggings. Although metal helmets were occasionally used, many warriors did not have them. The few known examples come primarily from wealthy warrior graves and appear by their decoration to have been made more for show than for protection in battle. In truth, no iron helmet would protect the head from a well-aimed sword, axe, or mace blow. Helmets were only good for light protection, so a thick leather helmet was just as useful and easier to wear. Leather head covers could be reinforced with riveted metal plates if desired.

Tanning is a both chemical and physical process by which raw skins removed from a butchered animal are turned into flexible but dry leather or suede. Ancient and early medieval tanners began the process by physically cleaning the skins in water and then scrubbing them to remove fats, blood, dirt, and other matter. Removal of hair fibers was accomplished different ways, but the use of tannins was a popular method. Sources of vegetable tannins commonly used at the time were oak bark and stale urine. A soaking in tannins loosened the hairs so that they could be scraped off. Another effect of tannins was to leach out the water from the protein molecules in the skins making the molecular structure tighter. Next, animal dung was frequently used to soften the leather product. It was either pounded into the skins directly, or the skins were kneaded in dung and water so that they absorbed the solution. Some porous skins, such as deerskin, could be soaked in fish or animal oils instead. This method produces chamois cloth, which is useful for soaking up liquids but may also be washed and then dried.

The use of stale urine as the soaking agent was well known in Roman and medieval times, so it was likely to be the common ingredient for British and Anglo-Saxon tanning as well. In Rome, urine was systematically collected for use by tanners as well as by cloth fullers (see "Textiles") from the public urinals. Both trades had a constant demand for urine. Public urinals were so handy a source for these businesses that Emperor Vespasian, in an AD 71 government fund-raising effort, declared a tax to be collected from businesses taking the contents of public urinals.

Other Animal Products

Bone, horn, and antler were excellent materials for carving small objects that were not put to too much stress. Bone had a problem with brittleness and breakage but was an abundant material and easily obtained for making replacements. Horn and antler were harder but less abundant for obvious reasons. Many of these same objects could also be carved from wood, but bone, horn, and antler were more durable and had a smooth finish.

One of the most common artifacts from ancient and early medieval societies was the bone comb. Keeping one's hair clean and combed was not merely a matter of vanity but of good health. Giving a home to lice was not pleasant. Nevertheless, vanity played an important role without a doubt. Writings from the late-Anglo-Saxon period show that appealing hair was considered an important personal asset, especially when it came to relations between the sexes. Non-Christian burials of both men and women throughout Europe frequently included a bone comb with tightly spaced teeth carved on one side. Some people had double combs with two sets of teeth positioned back to back along a center spine. Combs have been found from Russia to the western provinces. The arrangement and styling of hair is one aspect of life and culture that can rarely be recovered from vanished societies, but whenever the hair of the dead has been preserved by exceptional burial conditions, the hair styling attracts interest.

The mention of horn often brings to mind the idea of a drinking horn—a hollowed-out horn of appropriate size and shape that was used for holding drink. Since a horn could not be set down without it tipping over, it is often said that the drinker had to finish the drink all at once. Such behavior might be appropriate for ritual drinking at feasts or the jovial consumption of alcoholic beverages, but most people drank from small bowls or mugs that could indeed remain upright when set down.

Antler is a dense, hard material and can be made into sharp, pointed tools such as sewing needles and awls used for punching holes in leather preparatory to sewing it. Bone might also be used for making sewing needles, but bone needles had to be made thicker in order to prevent breakage. Both materials were used for making pin-beaters (a weaver's tool for pushing individual threads on the loom tightly together), spoons, and other household items. Bone and antler were good materials for constructing fishhooks. The wealthy might have decorative boxes and other personal objects made entirely or in part of these materials.

Another likely but thus far archaeologically unproven use of animal products is the insertion of feathers into bedding. It would be a simple matter to stuff cloth sacks with duck or goose down for pillows or warm bed coverings. Mattresses, on the other hand, were likely stuffed with straw if piles of straw were not simply slept on directly. Romans had used duck and goose down for pillows and covers, so knowledge of the practice was available to the Britons. The idea is simple, but sufficient quantities of the down were not easily come by. Regular folk may have taken advantage of its value of trading their available goose and duck down for more important essentials. Many people would have been satisfied with sleeping under covers and on pillows stuffed with the more abundant alternative of wool. Of greater concern for simple comfort was the need to keep whatever bedding was used free of insects and other vermin.

Textiles

Making cloth began with processing fibers and producing thread. Fibers were gathered from plants or wooly animals. Plant were soaked and beaten to break down the tough cell structures leaving a softer, more flexible fiber. Animal wool had to be cleaned and carded (combed through) before being spun into threads. The resulting yarns, threads, or cords were dyed with a wide range of vegetable and mineral compounds. Once threads were woven into cloth, the cloth was fulled (felted or shrunk) so that it held its final size and shape. Excavated sites from later Anglo-Saxon and Scandinavian settlements have revealed that people kept and used carding combs and spindle whorls—small, handheld weighted devices for spinning and twisting the fibers into yarn. People who made yarn also dyed and wove it.

The most common fiber available to the general populace was wool from sheep. Wool from goats was also used though it made for a coarser material. A useful plant fiber, flax, was sometimes cultivated. From its fibers was made linen, a much lighter, finer, and cooler cloth than wool to wear in summer weather. Linen required more work to produce, so wearing it was sign of wealth or status. Hemp, another plant fiber, was too coarse to be woven into cloth, but it was a durable material for making mats, ropes, and footwear. Neither cotton nor silk were known in western Europe for centuries to come.

Common people did not own many articles of clothing, and they had to make and repair virtually all that they had. No samples of cloth from the post-Roman period have survived. However, small fragments of cloth have been found in early Anglo-Saxon graves.[10] With careful excavation of present and future sites, it is likely that

Anglo-Saxon clay loom weights and cooking pot. The doughnut-shaped weights held the vertical warp threads at the proper tension in the loom frame so that the weaver could insert the horizontal weft threads accurately. (Museum of London/The Bridgeman Art Library)

more evidence will be recovered, including samples of decorative weaving patterns and clothing styles.

Thread was woven on a standing loom with a vertical wooden frame. Some household looms were such permanent, heavily used appliances that their main supports were anchored into the ground and braced against a strong wall or other anchor. With the loom standing almost upright, the weaver attached vertical warp threads to the top cross-post and weighted groups of these at the bottom by tying them to a heavy weight of some sort to keep the threads steady and taut. Weights were usually donut-shaped and made of fired clay or carved from stone. Then the horizontal weft threads were woven in from side to side, usually working from top to bottom. The wefts were pressed tightly upward with a weaving baton made of wood or bone. The baton was also metaphorically known as a weaving sword. The metaphor of a woman's sword was carried further when some non-Christian, early Anglo-Saxon women of high status and economic standing were buried with weaving batons made of iron just like their husbands were buried with iron swords. Did these women really use iron weaving batons? Wood or bone was a better material for working with threads, and an iron baton would have been a tiresome weight to manipulate. Perhaps, the iron baton was made especially as an item of status and symbolic meaning meant only to be placed in the grave.

Another tool used frequently when weaving was the pin-beater, a small polished piece of bone, about five inches long with pointed ends. This tool was handy for pushing into position individual threads in the weft so that the finished cloth was smoother.

With the weaving completed, the cloth was removed from the loom. Most pieces were probably fulled. In the Middle Ages, fullers were full-time craftsmen. Developed in antiquity, fulling improved cloth's durability. Fulling accomplished two main goals. First, the fibers of the fabric were compacted and thickened, making the cloth thicker and warmer. Repeated fulling of wool produced a thick felt, if desired. Second, the fulling process preshrunk the fibers so that the garment would not change shape or shrink further after it was sewn, worn, and became wet.

Fulling required the cloth to be soaked and pounded. The fulling of wool can also be partly accomplished directly on the wool yarns before spinning occurred. The goal, when washing and fulling the raw wool first, was to remove the oils and natural lanolin from the wool so that it no longer felt greasy. Using plain water alone accomplished this purpose in part. However, stale urine or plant ashes mixed with water enhanced the removal of oils. Fuller's earth, also known as natural potash, can be found naturally and consists of silica, magnesium, iron, and aluminum. It was used to clean and remove the oils from wool. If the mineral sources were not available, stale urine made a good substitute. Either chemical process also causes the individual fibers to open up and interlock. The resulting weave then becomes much tighter, and the final product, the woven cloth, can be cut without any unraveling.

Linen was fulled by a soaking process for improved fit and durability. One desirable quality of linen is its quick response to heat. A hot iron gives ordinary linen a sleek starched look or can create a series of decorative pleats. Rounded pieces of glass may have been used for ironing in post-Roman times and earlier. Flattened balls of glass have appeared at eighth- or ninth-century Anglo-Saxon sites. The glass, when heated, could press the linen smooth without damaging it. Even without heat, linen was sometimes folded into pleats when wet and laid flat until dry. The result was rougher than a pressed pleat but still pleasing

ARTISANS AND WORKSHOPS

In Roman times, factories, or large workshops, brought craft specialists together for the coordinated production of a steady stream of popular items. When the economy was expanding and the wealthy as well as the trades classes had coin to spare, specialty goods—high-quality ceramics, jewelry, fine knives, glass bottles, and many other small but valuable luxuries—were produced for sale even before a buyer for the item was arranged. Buyers could always be found in the urban markets. Of course, larger, expensive items such as ornate furniture would more likely be made under contract and to the buyer's personal specifications, but the makers, more than likely, still operated from organized workshops that took the orders and shipped out the goods. In a failing post-Roman economy, where the transportation routes for shipments and the markets themselves both became uncertain, craftsmen reverted to working independently and producing only items made to order. Jewelry makers owned their own tools but worked with valuable materials (bronze, silver, gold for gilt, and stones for mounting) provided by the buyer. The old workshop system, tied to profitable markets with international connections, was a good way of doing business in Roman times, but after the post-Roman economic collapse, was no longer viable.

Private workshop collectives supported by ruling families were the exception. At the larger hillforts in the west and southwest of Britain where rulers controlled surrounding territories, signs of activity by an array of craftsmen—carpenters, bone workers, and metalsmiths of all kinds—continued full time not only to meet first and foremost the needs of the ruling class but also to provide for others living in the vicinity of the fort. Sites like Dinas Powys (see above) or Tintagel were likely to have supported such organized production.

Alternatively, some craftsmen were itinerant. They traveled from location to location to stay briefly or for several months at a time while completing the projects desired locally. Other craftworkers might have traveled to seasonally contracted projects where they were employed during a part of each year. A seasonal or itinerant craftworker might bring his family with him or leave them on his land if he had a farm to be tended.

The reuse of urban spaces by craftworkers occurred in some towns but not others. At Caerwent in southeastern Wales, an abandoned Roman civic structure was partially reopened for blacksmithing

The Anglo-Saxon brooch (gold leaf on carved wood) was discovered at Mitcham, South London, and is dated to the early sixth century. The curvilinear abstract designs favored by the Anglo-Saxons sometimes represented animals and plants. The Lundenwic settlement had become a flourishing trading, production, and craftworking center located in the heart of modern London. (Museum of London/The Bridgeman Art Library)

and metalworking. It was mostly in the west that towns remained economically viable enough to maintain manufacturing or services.

The fate of towns in the east was usually different. At Colchester in Essex, near the east coast, strikingly little early fifth-century activity has been found aside from the construction of an

Anglo-Saxon hut or two within the walls. It seems probable that the town was mostly abandoned or occupied by a small number of squatters.

Colchester

Roman Colchester in Essex near the east coast was established in the first century as an early *colonia*. It had temples, a monumental arch, a basilica, shops, numerous houses, and fortifications. Over 600 burials have been mapped in its environs. A local pottery industry ran at least 40 kilns, a number that indicates Colchester must have supplied pottery for the surrounding region.

After all this success, by the fifth century, all trace of British habitation in Colchester was gone. Saxons arrived but in very small numbers. These were certainly not the sort of numbers that would have driven out an existing town population by force. No sign of destruction or burning in the town marked the coming of Anglo-Saxons. On the south side, two early Anglo-Saxon huts were located. One had pottery from the early part of the fifth century. The other hut was much later, dating to the sixth or seventh century. Inside the hut, stake holes, a spindle whorl, and a loom weight fragment suggest that it was a simple weaving shed. Aside from these two simple huts, the only other Anglo-Saxon finds were random objects from other parts of the town and burials with Anglo-Saxon grave goods located in nearby pagan cemeteries.[11]

These newcomers at Colchester were not German mercenaries. A few families had come to occupy the abandoned streets and buildings of a former Roman town. There is no sign that the town was crowded or even particularly lively at any time during the early Anglo-Saxon period. All that can be said about the people living there is that they appeared to be of German origin. The dead were buried in the pagan manner, and only Anglo-Saxon style objects were used. Some of the artifacts were imported from the homelands.

There appears to be no overlap of British and Anglo-Saxon occupancy at Colchester. Several reasons could account for this. The Britons in this part of Essex might have migrated to Gaul or moved westward shortly after the Romans left, hoping for better circumstances. Initial fear of the Anglo-Saxons may not have been a deciding factor, but perhaps a lack of men-at-arms available to manage the town defenses caused difficulty. Only the largest towns purchased mercenary help. After seeing how York and London fared with surrounding encampments of German warriors, Colchester residents may have opted to abandon their location instead.

EXCHANGE, TRADE, AND MARKETS

Trade is the exchange of goods and services on a one-to-one basis between acquaintances. In many societies, these exchanges take on the appearance of friendly gift-giving, but there is an important underlying economic basis. When two friends or neighbors exchange food or other products, they are helping each other obtain the variety of things they need and want.

In small societies where the exchange of goods is on a personal level and appears most like a gift-giving activity, there is no need to put a price on things. In fact, the people making the exchange do not acknowledge the relative value of the items exchanged. The goal instead is for each person to get what she or he most wants. This approach to trade works best within a society where no one accumulates wealth and the values of items do not vary greatly. Nothing that is traded or given as a gift is rare or valuable. The appearance of gift-giving is created because people will give when they have something to give. For example, a hunter will share out the meat from a large kill he has just made. The group understanding is that the receivers of the gift will then give in their turn when they have something that all the others can use.

When trade activity extends further afield and exchanges are more frequent, then an estimation of the value of many items becomes shared knowledge. How many bushels of wheat should be exchanged for a lamb? Everyone has a general idea of the answer. People may meet often for the purpose of making exchanges, but markets are not necessary. People can meet and trade whenever they choose. They usually know each other so that a personal relationship exists between buyer and seller. These relationships create an important basis for trust while negotiating a high-value exchange. Trading actions are much easier to negotiate if trust already exists between buyer and seller.

Larger concentrations of population benefit from an organized market that meets at regular times. Markets enable people to shop around and discover unknown purchasing opportunities. It is no longer necessary for sellers to be known to buyers, for with many sellers present, competition keeps the prices equitable. Scheduling is also a useful characteristic of markets. Knowledge of market days and locations allows people to make the most of their surpluses while also being able to plan their purchases efficiently. In sum, opportunities are expanded by markets, but they are also limited. The limitation lies in the fact that the element of trust is lost. People must deal with strangers. Rules of behavior need to be enforced so that transactions are honest. Prices need to be stated with clarity. Markets depend on a recognized administrative and legal authority for handling disputes and preventing crime.

Roman Trade

Traders specializing in exotic, foreign, and luxury goods could make fortunes, but the work was often as dangerous as it was profitable since pirates and thieves have existed as long as professional traders have been around. In the first instance—trade for necessary and commonly desired, ordinary goods—individuals in ancient times convened at a designated place and time to conduct a market where anyone may present items for exchange. As markets grew bigger, they became regular events anticipated by a great many people. Money was necessary. Coins or some other form of currency—anything from shells to iron bars have been used by different societies—facilitated the exchange of goods. Coins, metal disks imprinted by a governing authority, were especially useful because their value was determined and decreed by official declaration. So long as people trusted the government, they would not argue over the value of its coins. Coins had to be taken at face value within the realm of the government. Once a coin went outside its political home, however, its value became whatever the seller and buyer agreed, which was usually the perceived value of its metal content. Trade throughout the Roman Empire was efficient because, in theory at least, everyone from east to west used the same Roman coins according to their face value, eliminating the problem of haggling over the currency.

Although exotic luxury items, jewelry, weapons, or other decorative pieces attract the most attention, long-distance trade to and from late Roman Britain usually emphasized the transport of raw materials over finished products. Because Roman culture had spread throughout much of southern Britain, manufactured items were found in essentially the same style everywhere. Foreign buyers did not need to buy British versions of the same pottery or shoes manufactured domestically in their province, so they logically were more interested in raw materials not occurring naturally in their native country. Lead, tin, copper, silver, shells, amber, and other valuable substances with regional availability were traded at high prices. Perishables that could not be produced in every climate were also traded, but tracking cargos of consumables is more difficult since organic goods rarely leave an obvious trace. Wine, olives, oils, and fish paste are among the foodstuffs proven to have been traded in quantity via Roman harbors throughout the empire.[12] A labeled clay jar once containing fish paste was recently found in Roman layers at Carlisle in northern England.[13]

Post-Roman Trade

It has been shown that during the post-Roman era, the British currency system collapsed without the support provided by a constant influx of Roman coins. As in all times of uncertainty, people hoarded what coins and valuables they had. The lack of new Roman coins hindered payments for goods and services, thus rapidly slowing the economy. Without the authority of the Roman government, and the army to enforce peace and order, moving goods of value between towns became problematic. Long-distance trade diminished, while local economies did what they could to provide for necessities. One of Britain's most important exports under the Romans had been metals. Tin, lead, and silver mines fed the needs of the empire. Whether or not and where miners continued to work during the fifth and sixth centuries is not well known, but new information is coming to light all the time.

London

The *Anglo-Saxon Chronicle* for AD 457 records the British retreat to London after a military defeat at Creaganford (Crayford in Kent). This battle allegedly was lost to Hengist, the famous early Anglo-Saxon military leader, and his son Esk (or Esc). At this place and time, the two sides apparently did come to blows over who had rightful access to lands in Britain. The chronicle entry implies that the city confines were still a safe haven for Britons. The text states simply, "A.D. 457. This year Hengest and Esc fought with the Britons on the spot that is called Crayford, and there slew four thousand men. The Britons then forsook the land of Kent, and in great consternation fled to London."[14]

The Venerable Bede, a cleric and scholar of the Anglo-Saxon Church, writing in the eighth century, described a place called *Lundenwic* where there was a market "of many peoples coming by land and sea." No definitive evidence of an international market dating to the fifth or sixth century has yet been found within or near the Roman walls of London.[15] The settlement name itself, beginning with a Germanic version of the Roman name *Londinium* and ending in the Anglo-Saxon suffix *-wic*, probably means "dwelling place at London." Archaeologists in recent years have found that Lundenwic was indeed a thriving trading place in the seventh and eighth centuries. Documents record that the Church of St. Paul was founded in AD 604. Perhaps, Bede is right that earlier markets operated in London.

Advances in analyzing the manufacturing methods of Anglo-Saxon pottery are making it possible to distinguish early period pottery from that of the middle and late periods. Using distinctions based on the type of temper used and other characteristics, London researchers have found pieces of early pottery scattered throughout the Lundenwic area. The pottery finds show that Anglo-Saxons had settled Lundenwic as early as the fifth century. They probably conducted some sort of trade, but there is no way of knowing yet how international it was. The construction of the great church is a strong indication that foreigners were arriving in significant numbers by the early seventh century. Missionary Augustine, later the first Archbishop of Canterbury, arrived in Britain in AD 597. He had been sent by Pope Gregory to bring the Roman version of Christianity to the isles and to the Anglo-Saxons in particular. Although many Britons already practiced a Celtic form of Christianity, which was not approved by Rome, the Anglo-Saxons were pagan. The founding of St. Paul's Church in Lundenwic less than a decade later meant not only a reconnection with the Christian continent ruled by the Roman Church tradition but also hailed the arrival of foreign Christians and the acceptance of Christianity by Anglo-Saxons.

Anglo-Saxons probably did not move in significant numbers into old London until the seventh century, give or take a few decades. Village populations consisting of immigrants had grown far to the west of the walled town, in the vicinities of modern Hammersmith and Brentford. Much closer to the walls, by modern Aldwych, finds of early objects have prompted excavation along the nearby river bank where Somerset House stands today. What archaeologists found were a defensive dyke, over 60 Anglo-Saxon building foundations, lanes for both wheeled carts and walking, storage pits, small ditches for water drainage, imported pottery, and large amounts of butchered animal bone in trash heaps. This was Lundenwic, and it was thriving in the seventh century. The settlement covered a large area from the Roman wall to Westminster and north to Oxford Street on today's London map. It became the connection between the Thames and the North Sea water routes and the new Anglo-Saxon kingdom of Mercia, which did not otherwise have a harbor facing the continent. A site this large and strategic to a kingdom does not appear overnight. It would be unusual if earlier traces of trade could not be found after closer examination of Lundenwic.

The Anglo-Saxons were not naturally attracted to Roman cities. Judging from their choices, the stone building construction was seen as an obstacle to progress, not a foundation. The structures and street layout got in their way so that they seemed to prefer to locate economic activities outside of the walls rather than inside. In fact, Britons also appeared to have the same difficulty once the Roman infrastructure of urban services disappeared. The surviving city spaces were not adaptable to basic subsistence activities. When markets reappear in the old cities, we find them in new locations.

Trade Elsewhere

Trade also occurred at the village level, and not all villages were small. One early Anglo-Saxon village was established in Leicestershire, the Midlands, where the later Anglo-Saxon kingdom of Mercia formed. The location demonstrates an early advance of Anglo-Saxons inland from the southeast coast. Although not fully excavated, the village has produced remains of at least 14 houses in the classic Anglo-Saxon hall shape. Excavators also found 18 pit-houses, or "sunken featured buildings." Wooden and thatched houses will not stand for very many years. Rebuilding of houses over a number of generations occurred and is illustrated by the overlap and repositioning of foundations between old and new halls. Dating between the fifth and seventh centuries, the village was positioned along a road probably built in Roman times over which goods and people continued to travel. One destination via this road was Melton Mowbray, a village that later became an Anglo-Saxon religious center. Prosperity is seen in the volume of goods and variety of craftwork activities. Much trade also occurred in perishables, such as crops, animals, leather, or textiles.[16] Domestic animals of all sorts were driven into villages for trade purposes—a practice in medieval times called "droving." Poultry and small animals were brought in cages. Once an animal was butchered, the common ways of preserving the meat for a short period of time were salting or smoking. It was simplest to keep the animal alive until it was needed.

Finds of imported wares and other objects are usually clear indicators of trade contact. In recent years, the increasing number of imported objects found along the South Devon shore has escalated the search for more evidence of post-Roman economic activity. Archaeologists suspect that the South Devon shore was an active location for foreign traders to arrive by boat and meet with Britons who had the means to purchase expensive foreign luxury goods and also desirable items to trade for them. Possibly, the usual payment was in the form of processed metals from British mines. Two proposed "beach markets," one at Bantham Sands and another at Mothecombe, have yielded significant signs of recurring long-distance trade. The South Devon shore could, in fact, have been the primary access point for trade with and travel from British territories.[17]

Archaeologists digging in the sands at the coastal site of Bantham Sands have found the largest concentration of fifth- and sixth-century Mediterranean pottery anywhere in Britain except for Tintagel (see below). The lands of origin of the Bantham Sands pottery fragments are mainly eastern Mediterranean, North African, and the Iberian peninsula of Spain. A few sherds have also pointed to Phocaea in Asia Minor, now part of Turkey. Mixed with these pieces is some locally made pottery from Cornwall. Due to the varying proportions of pottery types and their particular places of origin, the excavators suggest that the activity at Bantham Sands was earlier than at Tintagel and Mothecombe and that the Bantham Sands trade had already ended by the sixth century.[18] The conclusion is that Britons in the west never lost contact with the Roman world.

Mothecombe was another beach market site lying a short distance west of Bantham Sands. Like Bantham Sands, Mothecombe was situated in a natural bay, a good place for anchoring and unloading cargo or passengers. Both fifth- and sixth-century pottery sherds were numerous on the site. Finds of several hearths and a posthole show that temporary shelters were erected on the beach to house those who came to trade. A 2005 *South-West Archaeological Research Framework* report describes five South Devon locales, in addition to Bantham Sands and Mothecombe, where similar foreign pottery sherds have been observed.[19] The bays of the South Devon coast, which were quieter and more accessible to the small ships of the time than the rugged Cornwall coastline, made welcoming harbors for ships from across the channel and as far as the Mediterranean.

Tintagel

Trade in luxury goods for profit as practiced in Roman times was partially supplanted in the post-Roman centuries by long-distance exchanges resembling gift-giving among regional rulers. One succession of rulers who received exotic wares lived at Tintagel. The coastal settlement of Tintagel, although once thought to be the probable site of an early Christian monastery, has been known since the 1970s as a fully secular site. Well over 100 residential huts built of stone were originally but inaccurately interpreted as monastic cells. Aside from Roman artifacts—for Tintagel has a long occupation history—a massive quantity of fifth- and sixth-century pottery sherds coming from approximately 300 complete vessels have been found. The sherds were mostly from the type of Mediterranean amphorae used to transport wine and olive oil. A lower terrace of huts likely served as workshops for craftsmen.[20] The huts were partially open-air shelters with large hearths and windbreaks suitable for blacksmithing and other activities requiring good ventilation. It also makes sense to place the smell and noise of industrial work at a lower elevation where it would be less likely to disturb the important residents.

Current opinion sees Tintagel as either a combination of a defensive hillfort and royal seat or an international port of trade. In fact, it could well have been both. The name probably came from the Cornish word for "fort"—*tin* or *din*—and *tagell*, which means "neck" or "constriction." *Tagell* describes very well the narrow-necked promontory on which the settlement was founded. Later tradition held Tintagel to have been the seat of the rulers of the post-Roman kingdom of the Dumnonii.[21] Tintagel's geographic position was certainly attractive from a defensive point of view, for it was also refortified in the 12th and 13th centuries.

As a port of trade, Tintagel may have operated only during the warm months when the weather was more favorable for sailing the seas. Winter gales on the Tintagel headland are severe, and the hillfort site lacked a sufficient freshwater supply to accommodate many people. A number of the imported pottery sherds have been discovered not in the hillfort but out on the headland where the ships arrived and their cargoes were unloaded. Trading activity occurred outside the hillfort and only when ships were in port. Cornish tin was the most likely product traded by the Dumnonii leaders in exchange for the wine and other foreign products they desired. Most goods received were taken inland to other households.

Excavations made in the 1980s out on the headland revealed traces of what is believed to have been a fifth-century wharf built out into the water to assist with boat landings and loadings. Other post-Roman period evidence from the main hillfort site includes a possible fifth-century court and yard found underneath a Norman period hall built on the same spot six centuries later. The earlier court included an area with two large hearths, a large oven, and numerous discarded animal bones along with broken pieces of valuable imported pottery, glass, and metalwork. The overall collection gives the impression of an elite residence.

As a fortress for the kings of Dumnonia, Tintagel was probably occupied in the summers by the royal court. At other times of the year, it may have lain empty. Early medieval kings followed a regular pattern of traveling with their retinue of warriors and court attendees. They would support the daily needs of this large group by paying a sequence of long visits to different parts of their kingdom. While settled at the fortress in any given area, the royal party would receive the food and supplies they needed from local hosts who in turn would have already gathered these supplies from the farmers on their lands.[22] In this way, a rudimentary tax collection system was organized with taxes in kind going first to the local elites and then shared out to the royal elites. By remaining frequently on the move, the royal court and its demands did not overtax any one location while leaving another area less obligated.

Written Communication

All growing kingdoms engaging in international contact benefit from the ability to keep records or to write messages to foreign leaders. Surviving written records from the post-Roman centuries are rare. Even the materials necessary for writing were rare. Paper did not exist, and papyrus was no longer accessible in Britain as the plant from which it was made grew in Egypt and nearby parts of the Mediterranean. The best and most durable writing material available was parchment. Made from stretched and treated animal hides, parchment was very expensive since there was a great need for leather for more urgent daily necessities. Meat consumption was very low compared to modern standards, so hides were in short supply. Writing inks were made according to recipes utilizing local plants, minerals, or shellfish for their color source.

The few manuscripts that were written were often treasures in their own right, such as a complete, bound gospel text or a historical chronicle. Those that were thought valuable were copied over when the originals became faded or damaged. The most ancient texts surviving today come down to us as later copies of lost originals. If no cleric or monk thought the text worth the trouble, it would eventually be discarded without any copy being made. Many texts were one of a kind, and if they were suddenly destroyed by fire or other disaster, the contents were gone forever. It would be astounding that no Britons had kept written records, but sadly, it is also no surprise that none of these originals were copied or have survived.

A long tradition exists of certifying written contractual agreements with a wax seal showing the impression of a signet ring or other official seal in the possession of the person ordering the creation of the text. This seal had more legal weight than a mere signature and usually sealed the document closed until it reached its intended recipient. Rarely are such seals found. In 2000, the news was announced that a garnet stone had been found at an isolated farmstead called Cefn Cwmwd on the island of Anglesey off the coast of northern Wales. The stone was engraved with a scorpion in the Byzantine style of the sixth or seventh century. The engraving identified the stone as part of a signet ring for sealing important documents. How it got to Angelsey is impossible to say. It may have been lost by a traveling merchant, or the stone was no long used as a signet and was instead being traded as an item of beauty.

The Angelsey garnet could have belonged to a merchant. A trader would use a ring to place wax seals on his cargo so that his ownership of his goods en route to market would be clear. Others had important contracts or documents to write. Since many rulers were not literate or skilled at producing properly phrased legal documents, specialist scribes were employed for this purpose. Many were clerics and could be found at monasteries when needed.

Manuscripts on parchment are not the only kind of written communication. An impressive array of contemporary memorial stones inscribed in Latin bears further witness to the continuing importance of maintaining a written record. There would be little purpose in carving such texts if only a handful of persons in the country could read them. Actual literacy levels in the population are impossible to gauge.

Few contemporary texts survive from post-Roman Britain. One possible example is a manuscript known as the *Vergilius Romanus*, containing copies of texts of Virgil and illustrated with beautiful color illuminations. The book is now owned by the Vatican Library in Rome (under catalog number Cod. Vat. Lat. 3867). Paleographers—those who study the style of manuscript-writing scripts— date the work close to AD 500. The Vatican has believed the book to have been copied in Italy, but several British scholars, including

A page illustrating Vergil's Bucolics, from the *Vergilius Romanus*, a late fifth or early sixth century manuscript believed by some scholars to have been created in Britain. (Art Media/Heritage Images)

Martin Henig, a Roman art specialist at Oxford, and Ken Dark, a historian at the University of Reading, argue that it was made in Britain. If true, it is the oldest known British book. If the *Vergilius Romanus* is British, the production of such a book long after the Romans had left shows that Britons retained their Latin literacy and interest in Roman culture.[23]

Coin Hoards

The Romano-British were accustomed to using coins for payment and wages, but after AD 402, the incoming supply of imperial coins rapidly dwindled. Most coins had come to Britain in order to pay Roman military and administrative salaries. Although existing coins continued to circulate for a long time, economic uncertainty led many people to bury their coins in the ground for safekeeping.

Such burials are called hoards. Others chose to melt down their coins for the metal that could be put to use in other ways.

The Roman Empire had for centuries depended on coins. Coinage is the most complex form of payment and requires a recognized political authority to produce and uphold its value. In the fourth century, the Romans produced the *as* (copper), *sestertius* (bronze), *denarius* (silver), and *aureus* (gold), among other coin types. In the fourth century, Emperor Constantine added the *solidus*, made of a combination of silver and gold. One *aureus* equaled 25 *denarii*, 100 *sestertii*, or 400 *asses*. These values were accepted throughout the empire. Britons mainly used foreign coins. Except for some coins of Constantine III (see Chapter 7), no native coinage was minted until the eighth century.

The Hoxne Hoard

The Hoxne Hoard (pronounced "hoxen") was found in 1992 in Suffolk. This hoard is worth discussing in detail because it is so large and well documented. When buried, the treasure was packed into a large, high-quality wooden box with silver fittings, padlocks, metal hinges, and reinforced corners. Inside were placed smaller boxes inlaid with decorative bone and ivory. All the objects had been carefully wrapped with pieces of wool and padded, probably with hay. The coin contents included 14,865 coins of which 569 were gold, 14,272 silver, and 24 bronze. Other valuable metal objects in the box included 10 gold necklaces and rings, 19 gold bracelets, 11 silver vessels, 19 silver ladles, 78 silver spoons, 3 silver strainers perhaps used to remove the usual impurities in wine, and 8 personal toilet and hygiene utensils such as ear scoops, tweezers, and one item that may have been a bristle brush for the hair.[24]

One of the Hoxne necklaces is more accurately described as a woman's gold body chain. It was meant to be worn around the back of the neck, crossed in front, passed under the arms, and connected in the back. The front and back joinings of this particular necklace were connected to decorative plaques inset with an amethyst, four garnets, and four other stones (or perhaps pearls) now lost. This chain would have fit a small woman. There are also two unusual gold bracelets decorated in repoussé with hunting scenes. Repoussé is a technique of pressing out designs on thin sheets of metal from the back side. The number of silver ladles and spoons is exceptional as is their decoration. Fifty-two of the objects are inscribed with text and Christian symbols, mostly crosses. Twenty-two inscriptions are personal names, and ten of these names are found on the spoons. The names are Roman and include Aurelius Ursicinus, Juliana, Silvicola, Peregrinus, Euherius, Patanta, and Faustinus. Samples of the silver and gold objects were tested by X-ray fluorescence for metal quality, and the results showed that the metal had extremely high purity: an average of 94.7 percent for the gold and 96 percent for the silver.[25] The Hoxne Hoard is a valuable treasure indeed.

The oldest date that can be assigned to this hoard, or what numismatists call the *terminus post quem,* is likely to be AD 408 because five silver *siliquae* among its contents were minted under the authority of the imperial usurper Constantine III during his reign from AD 407 to 411, and the coins were probably not available in Britain until AD 408. Therefore, the hoard could not have been buried earlier than AD 408. Depending on how long the Hoxne coins were kept by their owner aboveground, this hoard could have been buried in the ground anywhere between AD 408 and ca. 450. Since many of the Hoxne coins are in near mint, or uncirculated, condition, burial must have occurred closer to AD 408.

Tens of thousands of Constantine III *siliquae* have been found in Britain, and they are the last coin type to have circulated widely. However, not everyone was satisfied to use the coin as simple currency. About 80 percent of the Hoxne *siliquae* (including *siliquae* minted prior to Constantine III) have been clipped, that is, pieces ranging from slivers to nearly half the coin were cut off from the original coin at some point during its use. (See below for more about the meaning of clipping.)

A number of coin hoards found in Britain have been categorized in museum collections as "late Roman." In the case of coin hoards, it is difficult for numismatists to distinguish between "late" and "post-" Roman because it is always possible that the hoard was buried either in the same year or many decades after the minting of the youngest, or newest, coin in the hoard. Many scholars tend to be very intellectually conservative and will date hoards closely to the youngest identified coin found therein, unless there is no other obvious reason for dating the hoard differently. Since the Hoxne coins were necessarily minted no later than AD 411 (the Constantine III coinage was the last new minting in Britain until centuries later), such hoards are not truly "late Roman" but stand on the boundary between Roman and post-Roman times. When it is taken into consideration that these coins may have circulated for decades prior to burial, the dating of the Hoxne and similar hoards really should be adjusted to post-Roman times.

Another problem for numismatists is that so many hoards were found in the past when they were not protected by the recent treasure trove law, which gives the government prior claim to the hoard contents although rewards are usually given to the finders. As a consequence, the hoards were broken up and sold in small batches for personal profit. In earlier centuries, hoards were even melted down before anyone made an adequate record of what was in the hoard. Giving accurate deposition dates to the hoards found decades and centuries ago and sometimes known only through incomplete notes is often not possible.

It has been estimated that around 60 of the known "late-Roman" hoards in Britain represent deposits made in the turbulent times from AD 400 to 425. The next group of hoards that can be dated with some confidence are the sixth-century hoards, but there are far fewer of these. The current "Checklist of Coin Hoards from the British Isles, c.450–1180" published by the Fitzwilliam Museum of Cambridge University lists just five later hoards ranging in date from ca. AD 470 to ca. 600. Two are from Surrey, and three are from Kent; all come from southeastern counties where Anglo-Saxon settlement was densest.[26] In these areas, one can expect that fear of disorder and lawlessness would lead people to entrust their riches to the ground. Or perhaps, it was the Anglo-Saxons who were entrusting their stolen loot to burial.

The clipped coins in the Hoxne Hoard (and in many other hoards) raise further questions. Clipping might have occurred because people were stealing small bits of silver or other metal and still hoping to spend the coin for its full face value. On the other hand, some owners of a clipped coin may have clipped it because they worried that the coin was counterfeit or not minted with good-quality metal. To prove that it had the value claimed, they clipped a piece off the edge to judge its color and texture. Clipping showed a clean, fresh metal surface, without corrosion or dirt, by which the purity of the metal could be visually ascertained. Clippings that are mere slivers were likely to have been made for this purpose. Finally, once the monetary system had broken down more thoroughly in Britain, clipping may just have been a way to make "small change" or to spend the coins not as coins but so much as bulk metal, valued by weight. Someone wishing to spend half of a silver coin could simply cut it in half. Balance scales were used to judge the true weight of the silver.

In Roman times, the small change of the currency in use consisted of coins minted in bronze (an alloy of copper and tin), but after Britain was no longer receiving fresh supplies of Roman coins, many people would have found it more useful to melt down the bronze coins they had so that they could use the metal for decorative objects. Low-value transactions were easily accomplished instead by barter without need for coins. The rich hoarded their gold and silver in its original form for a longer period, or perhaps permanently, if they did not live or have the opportunity to retrieve their hoard, as may be assumed to have happened to the owner of the Hoxne treasure. Perhaps, many of the rich hoarders even had hopes of escaping abroad where their coins could be spent for the original face value. All these possibilities would explain why so few bronze coins appear in the Hoxne and other post-Roman hoards.

Governments then, as now, have viewed the clipping of coins as illegal.[27] Roman law passed in AD 317, and reinforced with new laws several times after that, stipulated the death penalty for anyone caught clipping coins. Clipping was considered a form of stealing from the government. However, clipping in Britain apparently accelerated rapidly after AD 408. Once Rome had left the province, the laws governing the authority over coinage were no longer enforceable.

As already stated, the Hoxne Hoard came from Suffolk on the southeast coast of England. Was it the buried booty collected by Anglo-Saxon raiders, or the hurriedly protected treasure of a Romano-British villa owner in the area? Given the careful packing of the boxes within a box, it appears to have been carefully buried by its original owners, but they never came back to retrieve it. Were they killed, taken prisoner, or did they flee in haste without having a chance to grab their treasure? Did the person who buried the box in the ground disappear or die and no other family member know where to find it? There is no way of knowing these answers. Although it is a mistake to hold on to melodramatic visions of slaughter and enslavement marking the arrival of the Anglo-Saxons, it is also not wise to take the direct opposite view of prevailing friendship and peace as Anglo-Saxons settled the countryside. In the fifth and sixth centuries, Britons and Anglo-Saxons maintained a complex and volatile relationship that could sometimes be negotiated but other times not.

Coins or Barter

Some parts of Britain on the frontier did not use much coinage even during Roman times. Barter was the rule. This was also the case where transactions of large quantities of raw materials were common. From the land of the Dumnonii of the southwest, at least 10 different stone weights, of varying sizes, have been found. These apparently were used with an industrial-size balance scale for weighing quantities of goods in barter exchanges. These weights come from late-Roman contexts and could have been used for weighing tin or copper as well as grain or wool. The southwest was already involved in Mediterranean trade with foreign vessels arriving directly in its harbors, so there was always a need for the accurate weighing and valuation of goods traded for high-priced imports.[28] Archaeologists believe that the use of stone weights for this purpose had occurred even prior to Roman arrival and simply continued in the same fashion thereafter. When foreign trade was not hindered by the departure of the Romans, barter by weight remained the most sensible solution.

NOTES

1. "Northamptonshire," *The Whitehall Farm Roman Villa and Landscape Project*, http://www.whitehallvilla.co.uk/index.html.

2. M. G. Fulford et al., "Iron-Making at the Chesters Villa, Woolaston, Gloucerstershire: Survey and Excavation 1987–1991," *Britannia* 23 (1992): 183, 205.

3. Simon Denison, "Gemstone Evidence for Late Roman Survival: Jewel Points to Trade between North Wales and the Byzantine Empire," *British Archaeology* 52 (April 2000), http://www.britarch.ac.uk/ba/ba52/ba52news.html.

4. Christopher Snyder, *The Britons* (Malden, MA: Blackwell Publishing 2003), 190, 191.

5. Leslie Alcock, *Economy, Society and Warfare among the Britons and Saxons* (Cardiff, UK: University of Wales Press,1987), 41, 42.

6. Snyder, *The Britons*, 191.

7. Snyder, *The Britons*, 192.

8. David M. Wilson, "Craft and Industry," in *The Archaeology of Anglo-Saxon England*, edited by David M. Wilson (London: Methuen and Co., Ltd., 1976), 254.

9. Wilson, "Craft and Industry," 255.

10. Wilson, "Craft and Industry," 270.

11. Philip Crummy, "Colchester between the Roman and the Norman Conquests," in *Archaeology in Essex to AD 1500*, edited by D. G. Buckley, CBA Research Report No. 34 (London: Council for British Archaeology, 1980), 78, 79.

12. Michael Fulford, "The Interpretation of Britain's Late Roman Trade: The Scope of Medieval Historical and Archaeological Analogy," in

Roman Shipping and Trade: Britain and the Rhine Provinces, edited by Joan du Plat Taylor and Henry Cleere, CBA Research Report No. 24 (London: Council for British Archaeology, 1978), 62.

13. Maev Kennedy, "Discovery of Ancient Tunny Fish Paste Gives Inkling of Roman Taste," *The Guardian,* July 9, 2002, http://www.guardian.co.uk/uk/2002/jul/09/arts.humanities.

14. John Schofield, "Saxon London in a Tale of Two Cities," *British Archaeology* 44 (1999), http://www.britarch.ac.uk/ba/ba44/ba44regs.html.

15. Schofield, "Saxon London in a Tale of Two Cities."

16. Anonymous, "Rare Early Saxon village in Midlands," *British Archaeology* 26 (July 1997), http://www.archaeologyuk.org/ba/ba26/BA26NEWS.HTML#village.

17. James Gerrard, "Recent Work on the Dark Age Site of Mothecombe," *Study Group for Roman Pottery Newsletter* 35 (November 2003), <http://www.sgrp.org/Newsletter/2003–11.htm>.

18. Paul Bidwell, "Mediterranean Pottery from Bantham Sands, South Devon," *Study Group for Roman Pottery Newsletter* 35 (November 2003), http://www.sgrp.org/Newsletter/2003–11.htm.

19. C. J. Webster, *South West Archaeological Research Framework: Recent Work on the Early Medieval Period.* Version 1.1 (January 2005), http://www.somerset.gov.uk/media/OE945/FrameworkProjectDesign1.pdf.

20. Christopher Snyder, *An Age of Tyrants. Britain and the Britons, A.D. 400–600* (University Park: Pennsylvania State University Press, 1998), 184 and Chris Morris, "Not King Arthur, but King Someone," *British Archaeology* 4 (May 1995), http://www.britarch.ac.uk/ba/ba4/ba4feat.html.

21. Snyder, *An Age of Tyrants,* 185.

22. Snyder, *An Age of Tyrants,* 185–187.

23. Ken Dark and Petra Dark, *The Landscape of Roman Britain* (Stroud, UK: Sutton Publishing, Ltd., 1997).

24. Catherine Johns and Roger Bland, "The Hoxne Late Roman Treasure," *Britannia* 25 (1994): 165, 166, 169.

25. Johns and Bland, "The Hoxne Late Roman Treasure," 170–172.

26. "Checklist of Coin Hoards from the British Isles, c. 450–1180," *The Fitzwilliam Museum,* http://www-cm.fitzmuseum.cam.ac.uk/dept/coins/projects/hoards/.

27. Andrew Burnett, "Clipped Siliquae and the End of Roman Britain," *Britannia* 15 (1984), 167.

28. Quinnell Henrietta, "A Sense of Identity: Distinctive Cornish Stone Artefacts in the Roman and Post-Roman Periods," in *In Search of Cult,* edited by Martin Carver (Woodbridge, UK: The Boydell Press, 1993), 74, 75.

7

KEEPING ORDER

BRITISH LEADERSHIP

The western and eastern halves of Britain responded very differently to the changes of the fifth century. In the east, many Britons emigrated. The remainder merged with the Saxons both culturally and in marriage. In the west, an independent movement of British power not only developed that drew on its recent Roman past but also reached back to its Celtic heritage. The largely disused hill-forts of the west became focal points of British society. Not only were they reoccupied but also rebuilt. Miles of new earthwork fortifications were constructed along boundaries and around towns. The new earthen walls erected around Verulamium and Chichester demonstrated not only their continuing urban importance but also the ability of British leaders to mobilize armies of large groups of laborers for long-term projects. An effective regional government was in place.

Britons were accustomed to looking out for their own interests and confronting imperial authority. Already several usurpers had arisen in Britain and challenged Rome.

Constantine

Several would-be usurpers were elected in Britain. Constantine ran a military campaign against Rome from AD 407 to 411. Orosius derisively claimed he was "elected from the lowest ranks of the military, solely on the basis of the hope engendered by his name"[1] because it had been the name also of the first Christian emperor, Constantine the Great. After crossing to Gaul, Constantine did not fare so well with his would-be allies.[2] In AD 409, Alaric was also advancing on Rome. Constantine apparently hoped that he could maneuver himself into the position of becoming Honorius's ally against the barbarians under Alaric, but Honorius did not agree. Constantine, his son Constans, and his primary followers were dead in AD 411.

Magnus Maximus

Imperial historians give the impression that Britons were the troublemakers of the empire. Orosius, author of *Historium Adversum Paganos* (or *History against the Pagans*), in AD 417 told in Book VII about the general Magnus Maximus (AD 335–388), who was created emperor by the army in Britain. In a bid to seize Rome, Maximus crossed with the army to Gaul, defeated, and killed the Emperor Gratian.[3]

Orosius did not explain Maximus's motives further, but more can be found in Zosimus. A Greek historian and high-ranking official in the east, Zosimus wrote a history of the Roman emperors from Augustus to the early fifth century. Zosimus was not popular with the medieval Christian historians because he was a pagan and not afraid to show an antagonism to the Church. In Book IV of the *Historia Nova*, written in the early sixth century, Zosimus explained that Gratian's own neglect of the armies made the soldiers rebellious, especially the Britons. Maximus, in turn, felt he likewise had been ignored and not given the honors due him.[4] For a while, Maximus succeeded. Gratian was killed, and Emperor Theodosius agreed to make the Briton a coruler while secretly plotting against him.

Sozomen, author of the *Historia Ecclesiastica* written in Constantinople ca. AD 439, observed that charges of usurpation were beginning to plague Maximus, making inroads on his support. His fatal error, however, was tactical. While Maximus prepared a naval expedition, he left the Alps unguarded. Theodosius crossed the Alps and brought final defeat to the Britons and their Celtic allies.[5]

Maximus was taken prisoner and put to death. He lived on, however, in the Welsh imagination. Many of his followers perhaps fled back to Wales bringing heroic tales of their adventures under Maximus's command. In the kingdom of Gwynedd, northern

Wales, there stood a Roman fort named Segontium. The ruins of the Roman auxiliary fort lay on the outskirts of Caernarfon and may be visited today. The fort was named after the River Seiont and is clearly identified in several ancient documents describing Roman military installations in Britain. Although there is no historical evidence that Magnus Maximus ever set foot inside Segontium, the Welsh epic cycle of stories, called the *Mabinogion*, placed him and his legendary wife, Elen, there. The Welsh name for Segontium was Caer aber Seint, the "many-towered fort at the mouth of the Seiont." Maximus, or Macsen Wledig to the Welsh, became famous among the Britons for his earlier battles against the Picts and Irish. When he claimed the imperial title, the Welsh already looked upon him as a heroic defender. Macsen Wledig and Elen, his British princess, were often adopted as the legendary progenitors of important Welsh lineages.[6] They became the founders of the Welsh kingdoms. Their authority to rule was mystically ordained. In one of the tales of the *Mabinogion*, "The Dream of Macsen Wledig," Macsen saw and fell in love with Elen in a dream. Upon awakening, he discovered the real Elen and married her. The island of Britain was given to her as a gift, and she caused great strongholds and many roads to be built. The many hosts of Britons followed her rather than Macsen. Together, they marched on Rome to claim the entire empire, and in the Welsh version, Macsen is successful: "the emperor sat on his throne, and all the Romans did him homage."[7] Macsen and Elen became the rulers of a mythical golden age of Wales much like Arthur and Guinevere ruled Camelot. If it was any consolation, no other usurper ever raised so great a threat against Rome.

Peasant Rebellion

In the fourth century, large areas of the Roman Empire fell into unrest and disorder. Zosimus declared that the Britons and other Celts were obliged to throw off Roman rule due to the force of barbarian attacks. When there was no protection forthcoming from Rome, Britons were forced to take to their own defense. Armorica (modern Brittany) and other Gallic provinces did likewise. With no other value remaining in Roman rule, the provincial Roman officials were expelled.[8] Other historians asserted that the loss of Britain by Rome was not Rome's choice. The year usually chosen by the ancient and medieval authors for this momentous event was AD 410. Within half a century, Roman material culture practically vanished from Britain. How did this happen?

One view focuses on dissent from the lower classes composed primarily of tenant farmers and slaves. The tenant farmers, or peasants, worked the land but did not own it. They supplied the landowner with both their labor and much of the harvest, being allowed to keep only a portion of their efforts. Some historians have argued that a peasant uprising occurred in Britain and quickly brought down the upper class.[9] However, this theory, though compelling, lacks evidence. No written evidence confirming such a peasant revolt has been discovered. However, some slight evidence points to a similar revolt sweeping through Armorica, a land with which the Britons had close ties.

The effects of rebellion could be felt without a full revolt taking place. In Britain, the removal of armies to conquer or defend the empire left the peasants unprotected from growing unrest while also removing much needed supplies. As historian Neil Faulkner has suggested, the rebellion could simply have been one of refusal: refusal to pay rents, perform labor service, or provide any other return to the landlord for the use of the land. With the peasants standing together in their refusal to cooperate, the landowning class, without the army present to back it up, would be helpless.[10]

Villa Decay

The peasant rebellion hypothesis sees the problem as originating at the bottom of society and moving upward. Other explanations focus on a top-down process. As seen in Chapter 3, the decay of the villa system left the upper class without the means to maintain the economy. The collapse of the economy made governing impossible. If the transportation and market economy faltered, then villa goods could not be sold. Villas were profit-making enterprises that supported urban artisans, construction, fortifications, road networks, and all the trappings of civilization. Some villas produced surpluses of crops; others made pottery or iron. Without a working market economy, there would be no means of distributing surpluses. With the collapse of markets, every community strove for self-sufficiency. Lands continued to be cultivated, and small farms were maintained independently. Only the elites could not continue as they were before.

Excavations of farms like Bradley Hill (see Chapter 5) demonstrate that farms likely shared resources and labor. It was logical for farms originally under the umbrella of a villa to continue to work as cooperatives. The landowning family might remain the leaders of the community, but now they would act so by communal consensus. Their home would become simpler. They would cease to appear like Roman elites in the archaeological record. British elites may have had bigger homes, finer textiles, and more food, but these nuances are not preserved in the ground. As for wealth in metal or mineral form, the British seem to have been very adept at saving such objects and passing them on to the next generation.

Not every villa transitioned from the fourth century to the fifth in the same way. There are cases of abandoned villas. Some villa families must have emigrated. Some could have been killed. Others moved to the west. Did some peasants rebel violently against landowners? This possibility cannot be excluded. Complex change was happening all around. The one thing that was lost was not necessarily the upper class but its Roman cultural identity.

British Tyrants

In the areas still dominated by Britons, Gildas declared in his Latin writings that the Britons were ruled by *tyranni*—that is, tyrants. Did *tyranni* in the Latin vocabulary of Gildas's day mean the same thing as "tyrants" in modern English? In Book 27 of *De Excidio Britanniae*, Gildas wrote that the British kings were *tyranni*. He added that kings were ungodly men frequently engaged in plunder of the innocent. They were adulterous, taking numerous wives and harlots. They broke oaths, imprisoned the innocent in chains, and fought wars among themselves. On the basis of this account, tyrant appears to be the correct word to describe them.

Digging deeper into linguistic comparisons, Christopher Snyder posits that for Britons, a *tyrannus* (singular) was not really different in behavior than a *tigernos* in their native language. The pronunciation of the two words was close despite the spelling. A *tigernos* in Welsh and Breton texts designates simply a "lord" with no negative implications of character. For Latin writers, who often played with the sounds and meanings of words, this coincidence of sound would allow for a convenient pun. The pun is so obvious to any literate person of the time that Gildas does not explain it and carries on with it as if *tyrannus* and *tigernos* were the same thing. Gildas appears to use his pun as "proof" that the *tigernos* were evil men. There is no real logic in the argument, no evidence, only rhetoric. That is why Gildas continued with a litany of different accusations that served to bolster his meaning.

What inspired Gildas's charges were the series of usurper generals in the fourth century. In the third and fourth years of the reign of Gratian (ca. AD 382–384), the first *Gallic Chronicle* holds two entries about Magnus Maximus, both labeling him a tyrant: "Maximus was made a tyrant by his troops in Britain" and "Maximus the tyrant overcame the Picts and Scots who were engaged in making attacks."[11] It remains unclear whether Maximus was a tyrant because he was a military leader or because he led a rebellion against Rome.

On the question of changing political leadership in Britain, there is little more than Gildas's testimony for what happened. He also told of disasters that ensued when the Romans left. Gildas is the source of the information that Scottish and Pictish tribes came as "dark swarms" and attacked the Britons. Scots, in this instance, refers primarily to certain tribes from Ireland. They were the Scotti who came out of Ireland and settled parts of the west coast of Britain including areas to the north that now bear their name as Scotland. The Picts originated out of what is called Scotland today. According to Gildas, Hadrian's Wall became the battle line between Britons and the northern Scots and Picts.[12]

Hadrian's Wall was built under Roman supervision beginning in AD 122 when Emperor Hadrian ordered the northern frontier to be marked by fortifications. The construction, including the series of forts and fortlets along the wall, took six years. (Corel)

Gildas did have some curious ideas about the wall's history, describing it as having been built much later than it was. He thought it had been built by the British on Roman advice only when the Romans had refused to stay and help the British fight. The foolish Britons first built a wall of earth that did nothing to keep out invaders. Upon appealing to the Romans for more advice, they then built a proper wall of stone. They also erected stone forts along the south coast—that is, the Saxon shore forts. Finally, the Romans gave the Britons a final round of advice, which included "manuals on weapon training."[13]

The factual errors about the wall in *De Excidio Britanniae* leave questions about what other mistakes or misconceptions might be advanced in the text. The eastern portion of Hadrian's Wall, for more than half its length, was built of stone in the original plan, never of earth. The western part was initially built of turf as native fortifications had always been made, but there were defended gateways or fortlets along the whole length occurring every Roman mile of distance. A ditch ran in front of the wall. Another ditch with embankments on either side ran just south of the wall. The wall was built under Roman supervision beginning after AD 122 when Hadrian visited Britain and ordered the northern frontier to be marked by fortifications. The construction, including the series of forts and fortlets, took six years. Emperor Antoninus Pius, successor to Hadrian, tried to extend the Roman frontier northward and built the Antonine Wall in AD 142. Likewise of stone, and also fronted by a ditch, defense of the Antonine Wall was abandoned by AD 196. After that, all Roman defenses were concentrated along Hadrian's Wall. Although some repairs and new construction were made along Hadrian's Wall in the late fourth and early fifth centuries, Gildas's story of Britons begging Romans to come and build it, at that time, scarcely makes sense. Britons of the fourth century desired to be *rid* of Roman rule. The empire was in too much chaos to be able or willing to help. Roman provincial military units were too unruly and possibly more inclined to threaten and harass civilians with demands than to protect them. Late fourth-century renovations of military instillations could not have come free of cost to citizens and peasants. Romano-British relations had been strained for some time.

From *De Excidio*, Books 19–26, come more lurid descriptions of unspecified attacks from the north. Citizens were put to flight, pursued by enemies. Massacres and plundering left them leading lives like "wild animals." The remnants sent a letter to Agitius, a high-ranking Roman, pleading for help in AD 446. Only when they placed their trust in God, not man, did they begin to prevail against their enemies.[14]

Despite tales of widespread famine and plundering, archaeology has shown evidence only of peasants pursuing their farming chores for generations. Although some formerly cultivated lands were wholly or partly abandoned, other regions continued to be worked with vigor. Villas and towns were not sacked and burned. However, they were carefully scoured of useful objects, systematically dismantled for stone, renovated for other uses, or left in ruins to decay. The alleged letter from the Britons to Agitius (or Aëtius in some versions) does not ring true and is not supported by other contemporary sources. Martin Henig declares it a probable fabrication.[15]

According to the pollen analysis and climatological research reviewed by Petra Dark (see Chapter 1), famine could have been a localized problem due to cooler and damper weather patterns. In preindustrial agricultural societies, occasional crop failure and subsequent famine is common enough, and when this occurs, weak individuals—the young, sick, and elderly—suffer the most mortality. Nevertheless, there are no signs in the archaeological record that famine was widespread or significantly worse in fifth-century Britain than elsewhere.

As for the allegations of widespread lawlessness and resistance fighting, increased lawlessness would not be a surprise given the absence of an organized military to enforce civil order. Lacking a central government, policing had to be organized on a local level. The remaining leaders in towns and on the former villa estates were the logical individuals to organize "citizen watches" to look out for the welfare of local people. They would have also selected armed posses to deal with the outlaws.

In the end, the British leaders never learned from their mistakes. Gildas declared that even the victories gained by trusting in God did not make things right. The Britons remained wicked and sinful, in spite of all their suffering and successes. For Gildas, faith in God's will was the deciding factor. The Britons' independent efforts to help themselves were of no use. This was when British leaders gathered in a council led by the "proud tyrant" Vortigern and voted to invite the Saxons to Britain as a mercenary army to help fight the northern tribes.[16] Since Anglo-Saxons clearly came to Britain and acted as mercenaries in the beginning, this part of Gildas's story is generally accepted although there is no other corroborating evidence for the council led by Vortigern. Gildas felt that Vortigern bore most of the blame for bringing the Saxons to Britain. In truth, there is no telling but that the Saxons largely invited themselves. They clearly sought lands for settlement and had harried the southeast British shore before. With the Romans and usurper armies gone, the Saxons, like the Scots and Picts, saw a power vacuum they could use to their advantage.

Ambrosius and Arthur

There were still Britons capable of escaping overseas. The foolish and perhaps wicked overlord Vortigern was forgotten. In his place, Ambrosius Aurelianus, a man of good breeding and standing according to Gildas, arose to rally the Britons. Ambrosius's family had come from proper Roman roots. Gildas believed that only Roman roots, not British roots, gave a man the moral authority to rule in Britain. Gildas was decidedly Romano-centric in his views. Ambrosius's leadership allowed the Britons to defeat the Saxons at last. Mount Badon is one of those victories, but Ambrosius is not quite given the credit for that one. Arthurian interpretations of these passages abound. Arthur is sometimes identified as Ambrosius, but because Ambrosius was too "Roman" to be a hero of the British people, the more Celtic personification of "Arthur" was invented. Other arguments have been made for Vortigern being the real Arthur. Curiously, Mount Badon was mentioned in such a way as to avoid naming the victor at that battle, leading many to suggest that Gildas disapproved of Arthur as well and to the extent that he would not even memorialize his name in writing. Gildas's chronological references to the battle of Mount Badon have usually been placed around AD 496. The traditional date of the authorship of *De Excidio* is AD 540 although there has been growing academic dissension over that chronology.[17] Although Gildas was fuzzy on events of the second century when Hadrian's Wall was built, he may have known more accurate details from half a century earlier.

The Llandaff charters reveal something of post-Roman concepts of kingship. The Latin manuscript book called the *Liber Landavensis* contains copies of 158 charters, or records of land grants, given to the bishopric of Llandaff in southern Wales. The earliest charters originated in the mid-fifth century. Such survivals of early charters are extremely rare. They show that southern Welsh kings of the post-Roman centuries were concerned with guaranteeing the transfer of large tracts of land between individuals and would occasionally themselves give land to the Church. The charters also reveal that most royal successions were from father to son or from uncle to nephew. It was also possible for brothers to rule as co-kings. The lands controlled by these kings were generally small by comparison to later kingdoms. It was not until the seventh century that one dynasty of southern Welsh kings, the Meurig, dominated others and ruled a larger territory, on account of Meurig victories over the Saxons.[18]

THE END OF THE ROMAN MILITARY ORGANIZATION

The written evidence for fifth-century changes in military order gives only limited information. More answers can be obtained through archaeology. In this case, it is also fruitful to look at the records of fourth-century Roman Britain in order to understand how the province operated during its final decades. One area where considerable work has been done is Roman military history. Both documentary evidence and excavation reports of military sites, especially forts, provide a good picture of circumstances.

The question of who were the soldiers on the frontiers of late Roman Britain has provoked considerable comment. Only a few usurpations and military uprisings have been mentioned, but numerous smaller ones occurred throughout the Roman period. There was frequent tension between the civilian administration of the province and the army. Misappropriations of finances and supplies by the governors and high bureaucrats were all too common. The emperor and his Roman advisors seemed more concerned with eliminating opportunities for the army to mobilize, and perhaps rebel, than to hear and address grievances.

Written records for Roman Britain are spotty after the second century. Despite Rome's reputation for organization, few records concerning the governors and other officials of Britain have survived. What fragments of information about personnel exist have mainly come out of letters preserved in Gaul or elsewhere outside of Britain.

Typically, one imagines that the civilians and soldiers in fourth-century Britain were two distinct groups of people, but archaeological research has shown that this is not actually the case. The fort of Caerleon in southeast Wales demonstrates this observation.

Caerleon

The legionary fort is situated in modern Gwent on the River Usk and was called *Isca Silurum* by the Romans, in recognition of the

British tribal kingdom of the Silures. It was large enough to house a fully manned legion of about 5,500 men. Designed like a town, Roman forts contained a grid of streets and neighborhoods for the different ranks and activities. Built in the decade of the 70s, most believe that Caerleon was garrisoned until the mid-fourth century by the Second Legion Augusta, although the legion was sometimes away up north for decades on other duties. When they were in residence, excavated trash heaps reveal that the soldiers ate meat from cattle, sheep, goat, and pig, and they or their suppliers hunted roe deer, red deer, wild boar, and hare. Shellfish from the sea were also utilized. The remains of limpet, mussel, oyster, and cockle shells are evident. Some wolf and fox bones were also discarded. Romans liked to hunt these animals for sport, but such hunting was also useful because the carnivores did damage to the domestic herds and flocks. The pelts were also desirable possessions or valuable trade items.

The fortress at Caerleon had its own amphitheater, built during the first construction period. It was large enough to accommodate the entire legion. The amphitheater may have been used for entertainments such as gladiatorial bouts, but its purpose was to provide a suitable ground for parades, displays, and exercises. Rebuilt twice, it was last renovated in the third century.

Remains of the amphitheater at the Roman fort of Caerleon in southeast Wales. The fort, known as Isca Silurum, was likely garrisoned until the mid-fourth century and at one time held as many as 5,500 men. (Tyler Bell)

Caerleon was one of three legionary fortresses that stayed more or less in use throughout the Roman period. The others were Chester and York. Although occupied in the fourth century, the style and character of the habitation changed. The changes are so unexpected that some people argue that the fort was no longer used by the Second Legion. Instead, civilian "squatters" had come inside and were using the buildings.[19]

In one respect, it is difficult to determine what a normal pattern of use might include. The fort was rarely fully occupied. Sections of it fell into disuse at different times. However, at the beginning of the fourth century, major changes occurred. A number of essential structures—the principia or headquarters building, the amphitheater, the hospital, and the baths—all fell into disuse. Most of the active living area relocated to certain barrack groups. On the other hand, fourth-century pottery and coins were scattered throughout the fort area. Roman soldiers were usually paid their wages with coins although they may also have been paid "in kind" with food and other necessities in later years.

From experience with numerous fort excavations in Britain and elsewhere, archaeologists have learned that Roman soldiers tend to drop and lose their coins fairly frequently. Often they were paid with freshly minted coins, so the age of the coins indicates more or less when they were lost. If the number of coins from a particular time is greater, then the number of legionnaires in the fort is higher, and similarly, if there are few or no coins lost for a time, then few or no soldiers were present. At Caerleon, lost coins become far fewer after ca. AD 348.[20] The automatic conclusion is that the soldiers had left. But had they?

The Caerleon investigation looked closely at trash disposal and street renovations in the fort. During the first several centuries, trash was dumped outside the fort. By the fourth century, the occupants were merely disposing their trash into disused buildings, such as the baths. Probably, the baths had fallen into disrepair, and the occupants did not have the means and inclination to fix them. Even if repaired, the baths would require a constant supply of wood fuel and a number of servants or slaves to heat the water hypocaust system. Perhaps, the occupants of Caerleon were no longer so Roman in their ways to enjoy the ritual of the baths.

Some of the streets were resurfaced, so the occupants were not unwilling to make any repairs. The main road (*via principalis*) and the eastern rampart road were improved. Some areas in the barracks in the eastern quadrant and just outside the walls of the fort, in the civilian settlement called the *vicus,* were also repaired. Andrew Gardner, who evaluated the evidence from Carleon, concluded that it is impossible on the basis of the remains to determine whether soldiers or civilians are using the fort in the fourth century. The internal dumping of trash does not argue against soldiers because soldiers in second-century Caerleon also dumped trash into fort alleys.[21]

The pottery scattered at Caerleon resembles pottery found in civilian settlements. In many ways, the occupants of Caerleon were behaving as if they were civilians, but it is still possible that they were also soldiers—or local people who look upon themselves to defend the local fort for the benefit of the neighborhood. By the late fourth century, it may no longer be possible to divide people living around Caerleon and other forts into separate civilian and military categories.[22]

Traditionally, soldiers were gathered from all over the empire as small units. These units were then mixed together into larger units and legions. Like the Second Legion in its first three centuries in Britain, they did not stay stationed in one place. Having no particular attachments to a location, the soldiers identified mostly with the army as their home and with the military as their identity. On the other hand, if a unit of legionnaires is left to defend one fort for decades, then it starts to become accustomed to that place and to associate with the local people. Personal relationships, even families, flourish, and the identities of the soldiers become directly associated with that place. There is no way of estimating the number of soldiers at Caerleon at any one time. There could have been as few as one "century" of men.[23]

This change is the impression given by Caerleon. The soldiers living inside the fort became more intimately connected with the population of the countryside and especially to the people living in the *vicus* just outside the fort walls. These men were not high-status individuals and probably interacted with the natives on an equal basis. The vicus residents supplied the soldiers with necessities. It is unclear what might have been exchanged for these items. Since there was no longer as strict a barrier as once existed between the soldiers and the local people, civilians may have moved within the fort. For example, at the fort on Hadrian's Wall at Housesteads, archaeologists have found that the barracks were converted into somewhat roomier "chalets" for soldiers and their families—an eight-man room being utilized instead by one soldier and his family.[24] The soldiers did occasionally lose their small coins, but they were more careful not to drop other things of value, nor did they necessarily dress distinctively from the local people. In other words, we cannot expect to find many artifacts that can only be associated with soldiers—neither special buckles, armor, nor weapons—to prove that a military presence was still active at Carleon.

Birdoswald

The Roman fort known as Birdoswald is found on Hadrian's Wall just west of the point where the original stone portion of the wall ended. Birdoswald was originally built of stone, unlike the original turf wall extending from Birdoswald to Bowness on the west coast. The fort's actual Roman name may have been Camboglanna. It was occupied by Roman troops from about AD 122 when the wall was constructed until the end of the Roman period after which it continued to be used by Britons in the fifth century. The British residents may have been descendents of the last troop garrisons. To the north of the wall near Birdoswald were several outpost forts that were probably bases for troops watching for hostile activity. Birdoswald was connected by a northward road leading to an outpost fort called Bewcastle. Other wall forts had similar connections to outposts. Roman settlement was not confined to the lands south of the wall. Villas and farms operated north of the wall and played an important role in the production of food and supplies for the northern troops.

Three legions did the basic work of building the wall: the Second Augusta based at Caerleon, the Sixth Victrix based at York, and the Twentieth Valeria Victrix based at Chester. The three legionary fortresses in Caerleon, York, and Chester saw the longest and most consistent operation during the Roman period. The legionaries were not simply trained soldiers. Many of them were professionally skilled in engineering and construction. Otherwise, such monumental building tasks would never have been so well accomplished. With all the necessary road, wall, and fort construction, all legionaries spent quite a bit more time digging earth and fitting stones than fighting battles.

Forts on the wall like Birdoswald were not garrisoned by legionaries but by auxiliary troops. Legionaries were citizens of Rome, and due to their elite status, their numbers in the military were limited. In order to have more troops available for duty, the army recruited natives from all over the empire for both infantry and cavalry service, but these native soldiers were given lesser, auxiliary rank. The auxiliary's contract required him to serve in the army for 25 years. After his discharge, he and his descendents would be given Roman citizenship, and he would then also have the right to enter into legal marriage (no other marriages were recognized by Rome). The auxiliary was often moved far from his birthplace when assigned a post in the army. One inscription at Birdoswald (*RIB* 1909) refers to a cohort of auxiliaries from Thrace, far to the east of the empire.[25]

Birdoswald was an active community busy with everyday routines. Excavations have revealed workshops for blacksmithing, granaries, a bake-house with large bread ovens, and gardens for vegetables and herbs. The granaries had special, ventilated floors that were meant to keep the large and essentials stores of grain dry and free from mold if not mice. In the late third century, the fort seems to have been abandoned by the military for a time, and evidence for this is taken from the condition of the drainage ditches. Birdoswald was built on low-lying, boggy land. Ditches and drains were constructed to keep the building foundations dry. Run-off from the drains went into the big ditch that surrounded the fort. The drains and ditch had to be kept clear of vegetation and silt so that the drains would not back up. Apparently, at the end of the third century, the drains became clogged, and waterlogging damaged some of the fort buildings, including the commander's residence.[26] Such damage would not have been allowed to happen if any garrisons had been stationed there.

The late fourth century brought renewed invasions by northern tribes. In AD 360, 364, and 367, attacks by the Picts and the Scots troubled the northern regions. Finally, Theodosius was sent by Rome to manage the northern defenses. The forts were regarrisoned and renovated to improve defenses. The area remained a problem. Although usurpers such as Magnus Maximus were drawing off large numbers of troops from Britain for their continental campaigns, and though the emperor was also taking troops from Britain to defend Rome, the garrisons defending Hadrian's Wall did not seem to be significantly reduced in number.[27]

During most of the fourth century, the problematic drainage ditches were kept repaired and cleared of debris. The ventilated floor of the south granary was taken out and filled in. Apparently, the building had been given another use, but what that was cannot be determined. The roof of the north granary collapsed after mid-century. The building was neither repaired nor reused, but the stones were occasionally taken for reuse elsewhere while rubbish collected inside. The Birdoswald garrison no longer had need of the huge Roman granary buildings, but sufficient grain storage was probably accomplished elsewhere using sheds built in the native British style. The much smaller garrison of the fourth century had plenty of room to construct new storage facilities. The fort was redesigned for the contemporary needs of the soldiers and, of course, their families who now lived with them.[28]

At Birdoswald, there is clear evidence that occupation did not cease in the fifth century. The departure of Roman authority and even Roman wage payments—whatever those had amounted to in recent years—did not change the job description or the day-to-day routine of this garrison. Imagine the employees of a business continuing to run its shop after the disappearance of its owner and financial department. Yet, this was what happened, and it reveals that the Birdoswald garrison had already divorced itself from Rome. The empire was no longer needed. The fort belonged to its inhabitants, and they worked to protect themselves. This same feeling must have pervaded many of the other forts and towns of Britain where people still found a reason to stay and maintain services.

The foreign character of the auxiliary recruits had changed over the fourth century. The primary pool for recruits became northern native Britons. Familiar law required that a soldier's son must also become a soldier, creating in effect a hereditary military class of families. The sons of commanders may often have inherited their fathers' posts and the social status that came with such positions.[29] Higher status was motive enough to maintain the military garrisons with local men. The necessity to protect their families provided the rest of the motive.

Birdoswald and the other wall forts no longer had large garrisons. In fact, their strength after Roman rule was just a fraction of the garrisons that had been barracked in the second century. They could not have repelled a major attack, but it does not appear that the Picts and Scots were causing significant trouble inland. Most of the attacks, however many there were, appear to have occurred further south with the attackers arriving by sea.

The picture from Birdoswald tells the story that garrisons of native northern British men, descendents of career soldiers, chose to remain in fortified places and carry on with the business of defending Hadrian's Wall. The farmers of the surrounding countryside were glad to have the garrison stay to defend the land. Most of the garrison's "pay," for at least a generation already, had probably been food and other goods required from these same farmers as payments in kind. Such payments continued without the benefit of Roman rule. Very little in fact needed to change. Out of such a situation, the commander's family could develop into the local hereditary-ruling family, the soldier families into his band of trained warriors, and the people into his supportive subjects.[30] The situation could scarcely have been better tailored by the Romans beforehand for the reconstruction of native British society.

Archaeologists have been unable precisely to date the end of the post-Roman population within Birdoswald. It may have departed finally, for unclear reasons, in the early sixth century or not until sometime in the seventh century.[31]

LATE- AND POST-ROMAN ADMINISTRATION

Roman Policy

The policy of keeping the local leadership in its social and political place helped stabilize newly absorbed provinces. The Romans preferred to delegate basic governmental tasks, especially tax collecting, to local leaders. The higher officials, removed from contact with the people, were Roman.

Latin was used as the language of government and administration. All documentation was recorded in Latin. Learning and cultural matters were conducted in Latin. The British language was continued to be spoken, but it was not written. A large portion of the British upper class was probably bilingual. Having high status and being considered educated depended on the ability to speak, read, and write Latin.

A man could make a place for himself in Roman society by being a civil administrator, but real advancement in the provinces usually required a military career. Leading officers in the army were ambitious and sought opportunities to assert power. Britons were unhappy with the inept and unethical government handed down by the last Roman administrators. More disturbing than invading tribes and barbarians, the troubles inflicted on Britons by their own imperial leaders contributed to the popular support received by usurpers.

Increasing corruption was characteristic of late Roman Britain. The Roman political system had always operated in part through patronage that allowed ambitious men outside of Rome to link up with patrons closer to the government's core. Their patrons would assist them in getting noticed and advancing in their careers.

Although not foolproof, the system could work well if favoritism did not get out of hand and behavior remained somewhat ethical. In the later empire, however, many political relationships focused on economic gain, using public resources and alliances to make private profits. Patronage was not doled out fairly. The government became increasingly less efficient and unable to respond to emergencies.[32] The anonymous author of a tract titled *De Rebus Bellicis* proposed tax relief and reforms of the coinage system for greater fiscal regularity, availability, and accountability. He decried the excessive greed of the provincial governors and accused officials of juggling pay books, allowances, and muster lists of the military recruits: "To these men the enlistment of recruits, the purchase of horses and corn [grain]...are time-honored sources of profit and the eagerly awaited opportunity for robbery."[33] Returning to a reliable monetary standard and making payments in coin would help. Amounts paid in coin, whether by the people for taxes or by officials for supplies, were easier to track and monitor. In the later empire, when the supply of coinage was deteriorating and increasing numbers of payments were allowed to be made in kind—by transfer of the supplies themselves rather than with their worth in coin—there was far more opportunity for unethical officials to put aside a little for themselves and inaccurately report what and how much was received.

Corruption and Rebellion

Technically, Britain was not one single province in its original organization, but two. In the early fourth century, the Emperor Diocletian reorganized Britain into *four* provinces. The divisions were likely made so that one provincial governor could not control too many garrisons. Rome was always fearful of rebellion, particularly given the number of times it had been attempted in Britain. A fifth province was also created after the widespread barbarian and internal unrest of AD 367–370. All five provinces taken together were a *diocese* that was ruled by a *vicarius*, or vicar.

One aspect of the reorganization that frustrated Britain's leaders was their inability to appeal directly to the emperor. Although the vicar ruled all of Britain, under the reorganization even he did not have direct access to the emperor. Instead, the vicar answered to the praetorian prefect of Gaul. The endless levels of bureaucracy were a great hindrance to real efforts to achieve good government. Furthermore, the larger bureaucracy cost money, making taxes higher.

Much of the tax revenue was earmarked for the military, and the military had considerable control of who was governor, thus aggravating the taxation problem.[34] After retiring from a professional military career, Ammianus returned to Rome and wrote, in or around AD 393, a history, *Res Gestae Divi Augustae,* based in part on personal experience. Concerning yet another usurpation attempt in Britain led by Magnentius in the AD 350s, Ammianus wrote that Emperor Constantius sent a certain Secretary Paul to instill loyalty back into Britons. The outcome could not have been what Constantius had in mind. Paul exceeded his instructions, fabricating charges and unjustly imprisoning men of freeborn status. It was a public relations scandal. Provincial Vicar Martinus threatened to resign in protest. Paul responded with more intimidation, claiming he would put the vicar, the tribunes, and other leaders in chains. This led to a physical confrontation between the two men. Ammianus claimed that Martinus tried to kill Paul, but failing that, Martinus took his own life.[35] Having failed to resist Paul and left in a position where he would be thoroughly humiliated and executed as a criminal, Martinus took the only remedy he had left: suicide. In the Roman world, suicide was still an honorable recourse to irremediable adversity.

Paul was notorious, but he epitomized the disdain with which Roman emperors often treated the Britons. If some Britons were rebellious, then it did not matter who or how many were punished, just so long as no one would want to rebel again.

These were not Britain's only troubles with Rome. Britain was one of the places where political exiles were sent to be kept out of the way. In one known case, the exiled individual, Valentinus, gathered together other exiles in Britain along with disgruntled troops, and led yet another rebellion, ca. AD 370.[36] He succeeded in taking over a large territory before he was defeated. Valentinus's success in banding together the exiles in Britain along with ordinary Britons for such an enterprise demonstrates that the Britons were not happy with their place in the empire. The lands that Valentinus controlled for a short while were the lands collected into the fifth and last province of Britain, presumably separated out at that time so that those within who had sided with the rebels could be treated more harshly and with greater watchfulness.

In the empire as a whole, the numbers in the military increased during the fourth century as needs for security and defense increased nearly everywhere. However, the military was not treated equally in all parts of the empire. The outer provincial troops lost status, while a new type of mobile army, the field army, led by aristocratic counts appointed by Rome, held the higher regard and received greater benefits. Britain was not allowed a field army of its own. Meanwhile, British troops and even British commanders were increasingly of native origin and fulfilling hereditary duties in the military. They naturally resented the privileges of the foreign field armies. The British commanders had no hope of real advancement in the Roman military structure because they no longer had any opportunity to connect with Roman officials and gain their patronage. All these factors caused a shift in British military loyalties away from Rome as an authority and toward a British ideal of self-determination under British rulers. For a long time, there was no conscious goal of independence, but the continual appearance of military usurpers in Britain demonstrates a standing British urge to take what Rome would not permit: an opportunity for career advancement within imperial ranks. Rome would not allow Britain equality within the empire, so Britain reacted by threatening to dominate it.

Although the imperial military increased in size overall, the British garrisons decreased in the fourth century. Part of the problem was the result of the several campaigns led abroad by British usurpers. But additionally, troops were removed from Britain by Rome in order to defend other parts of the empire. In the second century, Britain claimed between 45,000 and 53,000 troops in residence. Troop estimates for the late fourth century range from 12,000 to 33,500 men. Security in Britain was at risk, even disregarding the effects of corruption and endemic rebellion.

The increase in size of the imperial military highlights another of Rome's problem. There was a shortage of citizens willing and able to take on military careers. Conscription, or the drafting of soldiers, became a widespread practice. The Roman landholders did not want to lose their laborers to the army, so the provinces were conscripted more heavily. Many of the conscripts from the outer provinces, still suffering from the effects of conquest, had little love for Rome. Some of the recruits were more inclined to assist the enemy rather than fight them on behalf of Rome. In Britain, some of the spies used by the garrisons to gather intelligence on native movements were found to be passing information to the enemy.[37] This is hardly surprising, under the circumstances.

SUCCESSOR NATIVE KINGDOMS

The power vacuum left by the Romans was in many places filled by reconstituted native kingdoms. These were not the same kingdoms that had existed before the Romans came. Too much had changed for those kingdoms to be recreated in their original form. Rather, these were similar political entities incorporating what could be salvaged, and what was worth salvaging, from the Roman organization. These kingdoms gained legitimacy and held the allegiance of the people because they promised protection from external attacks. The British rulers also needed to collect taxes both in kind and in labor in order to pay for defenses, but the success that they had for two centuries and that they maintained longer in Cornwall, Wales, and Scotland testifies to their ability to govern effectively.

Most discussion of the post-Roman kingdoms starts in the seventh century when contemporary written sources start to offer some useful details. This book is about the preceding centuries, so we will attempt to piece together what happened before the written sources appeared. Scholars can deduce from Roman records that most of the pre–Roman British tribal territories were maintained as entities in the Roman period. Tribal centers were replaced by administrative towns of the type called *civitas capitals*. The only tribe not to have had an associated *civitas* by the fourth century, so far as can be determined, were the Ordovicians in northern Wales. Why they would be different is not known, and perhaps they did have an administrative center somewhere. The complete list of tribal entities and towns (the modern name is given here) from the Roman period, from roughly north to south, is as follows:[38]

Tribe	Town
Carvetii	Carlisle
Brigantes	Aldborough
Parisi	Brough-on-Humber
Ordovices	?
Cornovii	Wroxeter
Corieltauvi	Leicester
Iceni	Caistor-by-Norwich
Demetae	Carmarthen
Silures	Caerwent
Dobunni	Cirencester
Catuvellauni	St. Albans
Trinovantes	Colchester
Atrebates	Silchester
Cantiaci	Canterbury
Belgae	Winchester
Regni	Chichester
Durotriges	Dorchester
Dumnonii	Exeter

Using a variety of textual sources and inscriptions on stones, it is possible to piece together the identities of the major kingdoms that formed in Britain after the fourth century. Ken Dark identifies six definite kingdoms (Gwynedd, Powys, Ceredigion, Brycheiniog, Dyfed, and Dumnonia) and three more for which there is less evidence (Dobunni, Gwent, and Glywysing). Most of these are in or along the eastern boundary of modern Wales. Ceredigion may not have appeared until the seventh century.[39] Archaeological methods comparing the geographic distribution of sites and artifact types have helped to clarify the extent of each of these territories.

An examination of the post-Roman kingdoms shows further continuity. The pre-Roman tribal polities reemerged after the Roman administration is discontinued. Clearly, they existed as a political undercurrent throughout the period of Roman rule. Some cases are obvious: the Dumnonii become the kingdom of Dumnonia. The Dobunni also appear to survive with their name intact. The Silures become Glywysing; the Demetae become Dyfed; Cornovii become Powys (others place the Cornovii in Cornwall, however); and the Ordovices become Gwynedd. In the east, the *civitates* become the basis for the early subdivisions of the Anglo-Saxon kingdoms. The Cantiaci become Kent; the Iceni become East Anglia; the Belgae become Wessex, among others. It seems as if, despite the loss of local populations, the Anglo-Saxons did not build their political units on a clean slate but followed a pattern of land divisions and boundaries that had existed since before the Romans.

Not all these British kingdoms, mentioned here, came into existence all at once. In the fifth century, Gwent may have been a part of Glywysing, not to be separated until the sixth century. The same is true for Brycheiniog. Later in the sixth century, the Anglo-Saxons began to make inroads and conquered by this date the Catuvellauni, Trinovantes, and Dobunni. The last kingdom to hold out and remain independent, at least in its western part, was Dumnonia.[40] Sadly, there is a long history of events here that is mostly lost to us.

As difficult as it is to map the major political units—the kingdoms of the British—it is far more problematic to discern the smaller political units existing within these kingdoms. Traces of these early subdivisions can be seen in the oldest surviving property divisions and related place-names. In Wales, the West Midlands, and Cornwall, there are shadows of these ancient units. The divisions were all similar to the early medieval "hundred" or a land area responsible for providing 100 fighting men in times of trouble.

Hundreds were grouped together into subkingdoms supervised by high-ranking landowners loyal to the king. Since the king could not conceivably organize and administer to such a large area by himself, he needed to be able to rely on subordinates who could collect his revenues (in kind) and deliver fighting men whenever necessary.[41] In some areas, the hundreds appear to coincide with older Roman estates. Most boundaries were drawn along stable features such as rivers, lines between hills, other major landscape features, and Roman roads.

The administrative, productive, and market functions of urban centers in the west were in many cases moved to hillforts. The elites, along with their entourage and servants, lived on the hillforts, and at sites like South Cadbury, archaeologists have discovered the typical aisled, rectangular, timber-built hall seen now repeatedly in post-Roman contexts. This style of living and public structure for holding large feasts and entertaining guests became characteristic of the British kings and subkings. There was room for both kings and his warriors at public occasions celebrated in the halls. Feasting while negotiating agreements, alliances, marriages, and other matters of state was an ancient tradition that had also been important to the Romans. Certainly, the Britons would not have done otherwise.[42]

Small towns and villages may have continued to function, although archaeological evidence is slim. Large towns and urban centers no longer functioned as such because urban services could not be maintained. Other primary concerns were an inability to garrison extensive walls or to provide food and other necessities of life to a large population. *Civitas* populations became small and may have been transitory rather than permanent.

HILLFORTS

Hillforts were constructed as places of fortification, power, authority, public gathering, marketplaces, refuge, and in later centuries for spiritual retreat. There were many hillforts in Britain before the Romans came. Because they were seats of British power, the Romans systematically destroyed most of their defenses and forbade their occupation. Alternatively, some of the largest pre-Roman centers were turned into *civitas* capitals. In the fifth century, Britons returned to their old hillforts, renovated them, and built new ones in strategic locations. Some hillforts were built as nearby successors to the largely abandoned Roman *civitas* towns.

The *civitas* capital of Exeter in Dumnonia had access to a port at Topsham in Roman times. This port was frequented by Mediterranean traders rounding the Iberian Peninsula. It was an important trading point for picking up Cornish tin, essential for the manufacture of bronze implements and ornaments. After the Roman departure, Exeter and its port no longer saw activity. However, trade did not cease. The hillfort at Castle Dore appears to have been one of many places along the southwest coast where continental traders continued to call.

The structure of post-Roman hillforts included earthen defenses of ditches and ramparts. The elevation of the ramparts could be reinforced with stones to prevent erosion. Larger hillforts had multiple ditches and ramparts. Today visitors only see the undulating earth, but when in use, these ramparts were often topped with palisades of logs or stone walls. The logs have decayed to nothing aboveground, but the stone walls were taken down to provide building stone for use elsewhere.

Hillforts were situated at locations suitable for their purpose. Defensive forts were built on coastal promontories, high elevations, important crossroads including waterways, and on territorial boundaries. Promontories and high elevations enabled the defenders to see approaching enemies long before they arrived. Advanced warning gave local residents the opportunity to bring their families, domestic animals, and other valuables within the fort. Forts guarding harbors kept the peace and gave security to valuable cargos so that markets and special deliveries for the local elites would not be interrupted. Forts set on inland boundaries protected territorial claims and were the first line of defense against invasion.

Hillforts varied in size as well as purpose. The largest ones were usually meant for the protection of large settlements. Medium-sized ones could accommodate a royal household and its servants, retainers, and specialized craftsmen producing and repairing all manner of materials. Blacksmiths, leather tanners, leather and bone workers, potters, carpenters, millers, and bakers were all necessary to keep the household well provided. Special markets and public assemblies might also be accommodated in these medium-sized forts. Monastic communities occupied somewhat smaller sites, and some hillforts were large enough only for a small family and a few cattle. The smallest forts were not likely to be defensive at all but meant as animal enclosures. A single ditch and rampart topped by a fence kept a small number of animals from straying.

The Southwest

The fifth- and sixth-century British kingdom of the southwest was called Dumnonia. The present-day county of Cornwall in the extreme southwest of England and parts of Devon just to its east were closely linked at the end of the Roman period to the part of France known as Brittany and formerly as Armorica. There are numerous settlements along the opposing coast of France showing strong cultural resemblances to the Britons and in essence occupied by relations of the Britons. Both of these regions continued to be ruled by their British kings in the early Middle Ages, and their language dialects were once hardly distinguishable.[43] The Britons of Cornwall had lost most if not all of their neighbors to the Saxons by the end of the eight century, but they kept their independence until the 10th century. That is why they retain a strong cultural identity separate from the rest of England today. The story of the Bretons in France is similar.

We have already seen that the fifth-century Britons in the southwest knew about luxury goods from the Mediterranean and had contacts with faraway places. Not all this awareness of the wider world had been learned only from the Romans. Before the Romans conquered Britain, some British tribes had already made changes in their culture through the influences of culture contact. Like other tribes on the continent that had made early contacts with Roman merchants and other travelers, the Durotriges of Somerset copied social patterns that they had seen, including the construction of towns, the minting of their own coins for use in international trade, and the consumption of Mediterranean goods such as wine and olive oil.[44] All this had happened before the Romans had arrived. Not every British tribe took these steps, but they learned quickly of these other ways of living and trading and could follow suit if they wished. Having had that ability prior to Roman rule, they certainly were able to adjust on their own after Roman rule. After the Romans came, town life was further encouraged, but hillfort construction and occupation was never fully abandoned in the southwest. Many hillfort sites show some signs of Roman period occupation, probably intermittent or limited, and occasionally Romano-Celtic temples or dedicated altar stones have been found, indicating that pre-Christian people under Roman religious influence had worshiped there.

Signs of Christianity appear in all things with the coming of the fifth century. Cemeteries display Christian burial without grave goods. Romano-Celtic temples are replaced by small wooden Christian churches. There are no certain archaeological signs of monastic communities yet, not even at Glastonbury where it has been long thought that one of the earliest communities began.

Hillforts such as Cadbury-Congresbury and South Cadbury are significantly refortified at this time. Trading sites such as Tintagel and harbors for the reception of cargoes by sea have been located along the south coast at places like Bantham Sands and Mothecombe (see Chapter 6). In the fifth century, the southwest was watchful but thriving. The troubles increased in the sixth century. The ancestors of the West Saxons, called the Gewisse, began pushing back the Britons in Dorset and Somerset. The *Anglo-Saxon Chronicle* lists a number of battles or raids aimed at the southwestern Britons beginning in AD 501. The Anglo-Saxon names of Port, Bieda, Maegla, Wihtgar, Cerdic, Cynric, Ceawlin, Cutha, Cuthwulf, and Cuthwine are given in connection with battles fought and villages taken although certainly not all was victory for the Saxons. The *Anglo-Saxon Chronicle* prefers to report success, but three of these names are reported to have died without explanation ca. AD 593. We should not take the claims of the *Anglo-Saxon Chronicle* literally, especially since the events of these early centuries were compiled much later and then reworked with information taken from other unknown sources. What we can surmise is that Anglo-Saxon warbands were harrying the Britons and snatching bits of territory here and there.

One Saxon incursion, listed under AD 577, appears to have had much greater consequences:

> 577. In this year Cuthwine and Ceawlin fought against the Britons and slew three kings, Coinmail, Condidan, and Farinmail, at the place which is called Dyrham, and they captured three cities, Gloucester, Cirencester, and Bath.

Compared to the previous entry, dated AD 571, that describes the Battle of Biedcanford, which ended with the taking of four "villages" called Limbury, Aylesbury, Bensington, and Eynsham, the symmetry of these two entries is suspicious—as is the chronicle's claim that this is the beginning of the West Saxon nation, or "Wessex." From four villages, the Saxons move on, six years later, to three towns. Again, we should be suspicious of the details. Battles at those places may have occurred. All the captured villages and towns may have been taken at one time or another in the sixth century, but the blitz campaigns were not necessarily so efficient. Smaller skirmishes at more frequent intervals would be more likely.

Nevertheless, historians have pointed to the Dyrham battle as one that probably allowed the Saxons to reach the western coast by the Bristol Channel.[45] This would have been a strategic connection for water transport and also effectively cut off (by land but not by water) the southwestern Britons from the Welsh Britons.

There are a number of long earthworks, called dykes, crisscrossing the landscape of southern and western Britain, and given the protracted struggle over these lands for a period of about 200 years, we can guess that these dykes represent a series of renegotiated boundaries and defended lines between the Britons and Saxons. More will be said below about some of these dykes. British settlements in the disputed territories could have survived for some time. Saxon (or British) victories did not mean that large chunks of territory exchanged hands or that boundaries were redrawn. The battles on the ground were far more immediate experiences for the people involved than the peasants trying to pursue their farming and herding tasks nearby. These ordinary people were only concerned with escaping danger to themselves and protecting their possessions as well they could. Crops in the field would have to be abandoned to chance, but harvested supplies might be hidden or taken in wagons and flocks and herds could be driven into the forests or to nearby hillforts, if available, for more protection. A victory or defeat in one location did not necessarily change the reality for people living 50 miles away. Victorious warbands did not effectively win territory. The only way that the Saxons could fully wrest land from the Britons and claim it as their own was gradually to settle their own people in the territory and eventually outnumber the Britons so that Saxon ways and Saxon culture would dominate the daily lives of everyone living there.

In Cornwall itself were found the descendents of the pre-Roman Dumnonii. Unlike the Durotriges, the Dumnonii never made their own coinage and did not create any large town-like settlements. Most of their hillforts were the size of defended farmsteads, and there were over 1,500 of these small forts scattered about, but mostly in western Cornwall. They were also known for their promontory forts: fortified points extending over the sea with earth ditch-and-rampart defenses protecting the approaches from behind. Compared to the Romanized parts of Britain, Cornwall was decidedly rural.

What gave the Dumnonii a foothold in the wider world were its sources of raw tin and lead. Cornwall was particularly famous as a source for tin, an essential ingredient for making bronze. Tin was also combined with lead to make pewter, often used for plates and utensils. Dumnonians, even before the arrival of the Romans, collected tin ore from streambeds and smelted it into ingots that were then used in trade as a form of money. The exploitation of tin for the making of bronze in Cornwall actually dates back to about 2000 BCE, for Cornwall also has its own sources of copper.[46] The Romans did not get involved in Cornwall's mineral resources until the late third century. Formerly, the Spanish tin mines were large suppliers of the western empire, but civil disturbances in Spain disrupted the mining industry and tin trade. When the Romans finally realized that Cornwall could be an effective supplier of tin and also of lead for water pipes and pewter, they were quick to build up the industry. Nevertheless, Roman villas, towns, temples, and the Roman way of life did not appear west of the town at Exeter in Devon.[47] That *civitas* was the administrative capital of the Dumnonii and called *Isca Dumnoniorum*. The relatively small number of stones with Irish ogham inscriptions point to a limited immigration of Irish settlers, either directly from Ireland or else by way of southern Wales. Not all Irish contacts were for the purpose of settlement; undoubtedly, there was much trade over the Irish Sea too.

Inscriptions, later Welsh poetry, later Welsh genealogies, and the story of the "Dream of Macsen Wledig" in the *Mabinogion* drop occasional names of Dumnonian kings in the fourth and later centuries. One of them is named Cynan, or sometimes Conan Meriadoc. Cynan accompanied Macsen (known to the Romans as Magnus Maximus) in his bid to usurp the imperial throne and title. Cynan is given the credit for founding the kingdom of Brittany in northern Gaul. The Breton kings counted the kings of Dumnonia as their ancestors. Another Dumnonian king whom Gildas named Constantine, but whose name could also be given as Custennin, was linked to Arthur in legend as his cousin.[48] An inscription stone found near the hillfort at Castle Dore gives a memorial to Drustanus, son of Cynfawr (Latin "Cunomorus"). "Drustan" is considered to be the Cornish, or possibly Pictish, form of "Tristan."

A poem that comes down to us from the sixth century, written allegedly by a poet, Taliesin, in the court of Cynan, conjures up images and riches with which archaeology cannot compete.[49] Cynan is depicted as a great warrior and leader who was generous with gifts to his followers in the way that leaders should be. He was the master of lands, possessor of horses and richly made objects. As the poem instructs, Cynan was successful both in battle and in protecting his own dominions. Judging from the names of his enemies, Cynan did battle with other Britons. These are not Saxons who threatened his lands.

South Cadbury Castle

South Cadbury Castle is a hillfort that has long had Arthurian associations. Antiquarians of the sixteenth century thought that it might even be "Camelot." The primary excavations were conducted by Leslie Alcock who also excavated Dinas Powys. Like Dinas Powys, South Cadbury was heavily fortified with substantial sixth-century habitation and activity. The major difference, however, was in size. South Cadbury is much taller and bigger and has more extensive fortifications than any other fort in Britain, with rings of ditches and embankment surrounding 18 acres—equivalent to nearly 14 football fields. Hundreds of men, 870 by one estimate, would be needed to defend all those ramparts.[50] The fort was not

South Cadbury Castle is a major hillfort in Somerset that has long held Arthurian associations. Antiquarians of the 16th century thought that it might be "Camelot," and this reputation has survived to the present day. Excavated in the 1960s, it was found that South Cadbury had been heavily fortified in the post-Roman period with substantial sixth-century habitation and activity. (Nick Sarebi)

much needed in Roman times, but visitors came in the third century when a Romano-Celtic temple was built atop it. In the latter part of the fifth century, a sudden outburst of activity brought new and better defenses along with many timber buildings inside the walls. By this time, the Mediterranean imports are numerous. This occupation pattern continued until the hillfort was abandoned at around AD 600. South Cadbury is one of three hillforts in Britain during the fifth and sixth centuries—the other two are Cadbury-Congresbury and Tintagel—where there is an exceptionally large amount of imported pottery.

At a high point on the hilltop, Alcock found a rectangular wooden hall measuring 52 feet long and probably the high court feasting hall. There were also smaller rectangular buildings and round buildings that would have been put to a variety of uses. Later, the walls and what Alcock called a "fighting platform" were reinforced with stone-robbed Roman buildings presumably nearby. The timber gate and other features demonstrate that the South Cadbury carpenters had sophisticated skills with wood. So far only 6 percent of the hilltop has been excavated. Parts of South Cadbury that Alcock expected to show craftworking and other intensive activity were not found or were "under some eight feet of hill-wash."[51] Alcock left such deep deposits for a later investigation, which has not yet occurred.

South Cadbury's location positions it to serve as a guardian hillfort for Dumnonia against the growing Saxon presence in Wessex. Along with Dinas Powys and Cadbury-Congresbury, the major hillfort defenses mark a line protecting all the southwestern lands. Cadbury-Congresbury is the only other site that is of a size approaching South Cadbury, although it is only a quarter as big. There is also some question about the nature of its defensive earthworks, but full consideration shows the fort to have been built with suitable rampants and even with watchtowers.[52] How these forts were meant to function together or if they did function cooperatively is impossible to know. How the population was distributed over the landscape and how many men could be mustered for emergencies is likewise unknown. We do not have enough information about fifth- and sixth-century events and demographic conditions to understand what tactics the Britons might choose or what necessities they would need to accommodate.

Wales

Several kingdoms organized in post-Roman Wales at a very early date. Gildas, writing perhaps ca. AD 540, named a certain king

Vortipor who was "tyrant of the Demetae" and Maglocunus called the "dragon of the island." Vortipor probably held the region of southwest Wales where the Demetae were found in pre-Roman times. "Maglocunus" appears to be Maelgwn of Gwynedd who died ca. AD 547, and his island may be Angelsey off northwest Wales. The origin of the Welsh kingdom of Gwynedd has been debated, but most likely it developed out of the pre-Roman Ordovicians. Other kings of Angelsey and Gwynedd also asserted their dominance and claimed or were given superlative titles such as "great king," "wisest and most renown," and, from Bede describing Cadwallon (an early seventh-century king), "king of the Britons."[53]

Gwynedd and Powys, associated with the *civitas* capital of Wroxeter, were rival kingdoms. Post-Roman Wroxeter saw considerable new building and continued use (see Chapter 3). If the Cornovii lands were here, then the Cornovii ruler built an urban court at Wroxeter in the fifth century. Christopher Snyder suggests that in the sixth century, the court was relocated to a safer site on a nearby hillfort called The Wrekin.[54] Another hillfort, named Bryn Euryn and found by modern Colwyn Bay, might be the "stronghold of the bear" and was associated with the subkingdom of Rhos, located between Powys and Gwynedd.[55] Bryn Euryn occupies a strategic position of coastal defense to the east of and a short distance from the Degannwy and Conwy Mountain hillforts, which could have been part of Gwynedd. The northern and western coasts of Wales needed to remain watchful against Irish and other raids, thus the large and closely related hillforts.

The kingdoms and subkingdoms of Wales took shape in close connection with the landscape of Wales. The coastal areas and river valleys were more densely populated, but huge areas of the interior lie at high elevations, were not suitable for agriculture, and were difficult to traverse. These areas today are preserved as Snowdonia National Park. The kingdoms held mainly to the lowlands and the promontories and hills overlooking them.

The kingdom of Dyfed in southwest Wales may have had Irish forebears, and ogham memorial stones in Dyfed reveal Irish names. An Irish tradition tells of a tribe named the Déisi who left Ireland and settled there. In Roman times, the region of Dyfed was quite rural and covered by a number of Roman villa estates, and after the Roman departure, various subkingdoms seem to have formed there, judging from the ogham inscriptions. The old villas themselves seem to have provided a basis for later land divisions, more than is usual. Continuity of settlement of occupation here is strong.

Somewhere into this picture fits the fortification and seat of power located at Dinas Powys. This hillfort is the area that fell under the domain of Gwent. Less is known of Gwent's early history, but the Roman town of Caerwent (see Chapter 3) and the Silurians were part of it.

Welsh rulers, like those in Cornwall, were leaders of warbands. Later rulers kept poets, or bards, with them. The bards made poetry that praised the ruler and his deeds, but incidentally also recorded a kind of history for people to remember. The structure of the poetry enabled the memory to recollect the exact words more readily. For this reason, the oldest poetry may be more trustworthy as a source of history than other later texts.

The North

One of the early northern kingdoms was Deira in the vicinity of York. The Britons may have ruled this kingdom for a brief period, but the Saxons soon were in control. York was one of the cities that appears to have had camps of German mercenaries around it, and this situation surely contributed to early Saxon takeover. North of Deira was kingdom of Bernicia, and to the west by Carlisle was the kingdom of Rheged. Somewhere within this region may have occurred the battle of Catraeth, linked by the poetry of Aneirin to the Roman fort of Catterick (Latin *Cataractonium*). York, Catterick, Aldborough, and a number of other town and fortress sites in this area have shown signs of post-Roman timber building and use. Some historians surmise that the battle of Catraeth may actually have been fought when a British warband came to challenge a Saxon occupation of Catterick or another nearby site.

Aneirin, like Taliesin, was a sixth-century British bard. The epic poem *Gododdin* is attributed to him. The *Gododdin* is a long series of elegies memorializing fallen British heroes, the warriors of Mynyddawg Mwynfawr the Wealthy from Din Eidyn (i.e., Edinburgh in Scotland). The poem tells that they fell in battle against the men of Deira and Bernicia, who might have been Saxons. Historians date the battle at Catraeth approximately to AD 600. The problem with using the poem for historical information is that many of the verses could have been later additions by other authors, making it is impossible to know which parts of the poem were original. Unfortunately, no other documentation for the Battle of Catraeth survives.

The poem emphasizes great slaughter. Warriors from as far as Gwynedd came to the northeast of Britain. Names of unknown leaders and their warbands are mentioned, and "death confronted them." One aspect of the poem is confusing, for elegies appear to be given for the fallen on both sides of the battle. Alliances and kin relationships were complex. The meters of the poem are not consistent and argue for various authorships. It is the atmosphere of dread in the *Gododdin* that makes it interesting as a literary work:

> A war-band steadfast in battle, shields shattered.
> And though they were being slain, they slew.
> Not one to his own region returned.[56]

The British settlements along Hadrian's Wall were discussed previously in this chapter, particular with regard to the fort at Birdoswald. Despite legends of battle and roving warbands, archaeology can only give us a picture of watchfulness and the construction of defensive settlements.

There are also post-Roman British kingdoms forming north of the wall. Some of the tribes who had been the enemy are now also British and face many of the same dangers as their counterparts to the south. From the sources and at some point from the fifth through the eighth centuries, we see the formation of Gododdin, Strathclyde, and Dalriada, in addition to separate populations of Picts. Gododdin itself, the Battle of Catraeth notwithstanding, may be the land centered on present-day Edinburgh. The *Annals of Ulster* indicate that in AD 638, the fortress at Din Eidyn fell to Northumbria. This could have been the end of Gododdin.

The kingdom of Elmet, centered on Leeds, is not well understood, but tradition contends that it held out against the Saxons of Deira under Edwin to defeat the Elmet king Ceredig ap Gwallog in AD 616. Whatever happened, the lands of "Elmedsætna" are listed in the seventh-century Mercian *Tribal Hidage* (see below). Beyond Elmet to the north and west lay the land of Cumbria where the kingdom of Rheged was founded. Supposed to have been overrun by Edwin in the same campaign that took Elmet, the conquest was rather less than complete in this rugged northwestern corner of England marked by extremely difficult terrain and isolated valleys. Cumbria, the land of the Cymry, centered on Carlisle, was claimed but not so fully controlled by Romans. The Anglo-Saxons had some settlements in the lowlands but did not reach into the mountainous fell-lands, nor did they develop any political dominance throughout the area. The Scandinavian Vikings occupied many of the valleys and established farms and had a stronger effect on Cumbrian culture. The area was not really incorporated into the English nation until the Normans extended their influence there around the 12th century (despite their earlier ineffectual claims). Parts of Cumbria remained contested between England and Scotland for several more centuries. The people of Cumbria today, like those of Cornwall, speak a different dialect and maintain a pervasive sense of "non-English" identity.

Strathclyde and Dalriada lasted as kingdoms until the coming of the Scandinavians in the ninth century, after which their separate identities remained in spite of political suppression. Both were in the west with Dalriada further to the north. Dumbarton ("Fortress of the Britons" near modern Glasgow) was the capital of Strathclyde. In the sixth century, the Strathclydians adopted Christianity in noticeable numbers and, in an effort to combat the Saxons who now held Bernicia to the east, they made an alliance with the Cumbrians on their southern border to create a common defense. There are some signs of a back-and-forth struggle for power between the British and the Northumbria, and the Irish may have had a hand in the power struggles as well. The ruling family of Dalriada was largely Irish in origin. The British Scots maintained their hold on these two kingdoms for several more centuries.

The Picts, a separate people in other parts of Scotland, were not yet organized into larger political territories. There were no hillforts and no archaeological evidence of kingship among the Picts until the eighth or ninth century. However, inscriptions and medieval chronicles from Scotland and also Ireland establish royal reigns dating back to the mid-fifth century. Either way, the Picts remained peripheral to British history in the fifth and sixth centuries.

BRITONS AMONG ANGLO-SAXONS

As has already been made clear, our knowledge of the political history of fifth- and sixth-century Britain is sketchy, and our ability to describe daily life in detail is limited. In the eastern, southern, and midland regions of Britain, where Saxon dominance came early, our efforts are complicated by a confusing picture of who was who. One advantage that we have when we encounter Saxons—however when they are still pagans—is that pagan burials contain artifacts included as grave goods, items to accompany the dead on their journey in the afterlife. Christian British burials are virtual empty of all objects because early Christianity forbade giving any material things to the dead. The practice was considered thoroughly pagan, and therefore even a functional pin and or small sentimental gift was unacceptable for Christians.

Cemeteries, however, whether pagan or Christian, can tell us a lot about the community of living who had left their dead behind. Depending on the state of preservation caused by the specific chemistry of the local soil, whether the bones are hard and intact or decayed into fragments, archaeologists might be able to recognize hereditary traits that mark family groups (rarely possible), or signs of disease, malnutrition, or injury that can tell us about living conditions in the community.

Archaeologists in the past have been attracted to pagan graves because of the informative value of the grave goods that they expect to find. Early Christian graves have been frustrating to interpret or even date within a time frame of five or more centuries. For this reason, there has been much less excavation of Christian graves. In recent years, however, more sophisticated scientific tests have become available to archaeologists, and in the not so distant future—with more affordable DNA tests, other chemical tests for human disturbances in the soil, and more precise dating techniques—the focus of burial archaeology will change from the things intentionally included in the grave to the human remains themselves. Already in recent decades, archaeologists have studied the transition from Romano-British (non-Christian, usually third century) burial to earliest British Christian burial within the same community. Cemeteries that were then in use for pagan burial often continued in use and received Christian burials. The Britons felt that ground sacred for burial was suitable for either pagan or Christian rites. It was very important to follow the correct ritual with an individual burial, but it was not important to choose a location dependent on the ritual. Only quite a bit later, in the seventh century at the earliest in eastern Britain and somewhat later elsewhere, is there any movement toward creating churchyard cemeteries where nothing but Christian burial would be permitted.

One such transitional rite cemetery, Queenford Farm in Oxfordshire, was discussed in Chapter 4. Here we found a hard-working community of farmers who showed the stresses of their labors in their bones. We also noted that infant mortality (and sometimes maternal mortality) was high. In Chapter 5, a close look was taken at Bradley Hill in Somerset. A small farmstead operated by several generations of a farming family worked hard and revealed the same stresses of heavy labor that were seen at Queenford. Because of the high levels of mortality, such small family farms could easily die out in any generation where conditions were harsher or luck was poorer than usual. This reminds us that we should not be surprised to see small settlements abandoned. If there were no or too few adults left to operate the farm, then the survivors must leave and move in with relatives or take servant positions elsewhere.

EARLY ANGLO-SAXON KINGDOMS

Most of what we think we know about the coming of the Anglo-Saxons to Britain was written by Bede around AD 731 in his *Ecclesiastical History of the English People (Historia Ecclesiastica Gentis Anglorum)* and in the *Anglo-Saxon Chronicle*. Bede is the more careful historian and will sometimes alert his reader to the qualifications of his information. For instance, when Bede began a statement with the Latin word *perhibentur* ("they are said"), it means that he is relating an oral tradition or some other source of which he is not confident. Although we might not choose the same standards for judging information as Bede, we generally have more confidence in what he wrote.

The *Anglo-Saxon Chronicle,* on the other hand, adopts traditional explanations for events, some of which are not likely to have been based on fact at all. Take, for example, the founders of Anglo-Saxon kingdoms as related in the chronicle: Cerdic and Cynric of the West Saxons, Stuf and Wihtgar of the Isle of Wight on the south coast, and Ælle and his sons of the South Saxons. Each founding group appears as a pair of heroes (or a pair of generations). Each arrives fully intent to conquer, fights some battles, and succeeds. Each kingdom is quickly and firmly established.[57] This pattern is a model for origin stories than any kind of factual account. The reality was a much more gradual process that did not immediately involve any intent of conquest. In the fifth centuries, small groups of Germanic immigrants were arriving for various reasons: to fight as mercenaries, to trade, and to find some land to settle on in a country where there was less shortage and crowding than back in their own homeland. If Britain had climatic problems and bad growing seasons leading to food shortages, then so did northern Europe. In the sixth century, population pressure and political competition led to more confrontations between Briton and Anglo-Saxon. New, incoming Germans might be more like the warriors prepared to fight and take land, as described in the chronicle, than their predecessors, but we should not imagine armies arriving in numerous ships, leaping on land, and preparing for battle until very late in the sixth century and also in the seventh. It is important to remember that the chronicle was rewritten and compiled in the late 9th and early 10th centuries under the direction of King Alfred of Wessex. The Anglo-Saxons of Alfred's day were much more familiar with the ways of the contemporary Scandinavian Vikings than they were with the ways of their own ancestors. In many ways, the chronicle reenvisions the founding Anglo-Saxons very much like the methods of conquest used against the Anglo-Saxons by the later Vikings.

As a result of trying to stick to the tradition that "Anglo-Saxons came and conquered," the chronicle tries to date the founding of the various kingdoms much too early. Historians have studied the names and relationships and determined that the earliest dates for known kings of any sort among the Anglo-Saxons would have to lay in the mid-part of the sixth century. Since even Bede placed the first coming of German warriors to the mid-fifth century, and archaeologists have shown that, in fact, the mercenaries arrived much earlier while other Germans were arriving even before the Romans left, the gap in time between the initial arrival of the Germanic people and the first formations of kingdoms is well over a century. Furthermore, the sixth-century beginnings of the Anglo-Saxon kingdoms still depict a society that is fragmented and trying to organize itself. It may well be true that Anglo-Saxon political organization did not manage to compete with the British kingdoms until the seventh century. Furthermore, if the British kingdoms had managed to be better consolidated and unified, the outcome might have been far different. In short, the Anglo-Saxons were better at unification than the British, and that was the key to their success.

The first Anglo-Saxon political units to form in England were smaller than the kingdoms that are known in the seventh and eighth centuries. There is one historical document in particular that demonstrates this fact. The *Tribal Hidage* gives a list of the different population groups mainly in the kingdom of Mercia and indicates the size of their lands. It may have been first compiled and written down during the reign of Wulfhere (AD 658–675), and its purpose would be to indicate how much tax in kind was owed by each of these lands to the king. The list begins with a number of small groups not all of which can be identified (e.g., Sweordora, Hicca, Wihtgara, etc.) and ends with other major parts of England: East Angles, East Saxons, Kent, South Saxons, and West Saxons. These last names were most likely added much later. There is no way of knowing because the oldest copy that still exists dates from

400 years after the *Tribal Hidage* was originally drawn up. What the beginning of the list tells us is that even in the second half of the seventh century, the owners of land the size of a Roman estate, or several estates combined, were still the dominant authorities in their area. By the late seventh century, these local authorities did owe revenue to an overlord, or king, but at an earlier date, in the sixth century, we can surmise that the smaller unit still operated much more independently.

How this transition of power was made is conjecture, but the change does not become significant until the seventh century. We can, however, safely conclude that Anglo-Saxon power, like British power, was built on the development of a professional warrior elite and the provision of local defense and security in exchange for food and other supplies from the simple farmers. As with the British, it is also likely that initial conflicts were among Anglo-Saxon warbands striving for supremacy. Only once leaders emerged to whom other Anglo-Saxons acknowledged dominance were these leaders able to turn their forces on the British in an effort to increase their lands—and their revenues. The nature of the warrior elite class is preserved for us in the genealogies of the Anglo-Saxon kings. These king lists, preserved later, often claim that the progenitor of the line was Woden, who is the god of war and of warriors.[58] In *Historia Brittonum* attributed to "Nennius" (but "Nennius" was a fictional identity of the anonymous author), the royal lines of Bernicia, East Anglia, Mercia, and Deira are all descended from Woden. This same kind of claim was made by the royal line of the Ynglings in eighth-century eastern Scandinavia. Part of the creation of the concept of hereditary royalty involves a belief that kings are born to be kings because their bloodlines are related to the gods and therefore superior. There is no better god for proving the worth of kings than the god of war, for it was in war that the unity of purpose created by kingship gave advantage to a people. In war, they could get more land and more riches.

Barbara Yorke has recently evaluated the documentary evidence on the early Anglo-Saxon kings. For the separate lines of East and West Kent, the East Saxons, the East Angles, and Mercia, no dates prior to the seventh century can be attached to any of the known or perhaps fictitious early kings. Northumbria in the sixth century was two kingdoms: Deira and Bernicia. Æthelfrith of Bernicia is said to have reigned over both kingdoms from AD 592 to 616. He was preceded by Ælle of Deira who was also an historical figure, although the dates of his reign are uncertain.[59] Among the West

Saxons, Yorke believes there has been considerable chronological distortion concerning the dates of the first two kings: the dates are too early and the reigns are suspiciously long. Cerdic (AD 538–554) and Cynric (AD 554–581) may have been kings in that order, but perhaps their power was exerted later in the sixth century. The third king, Ceawlin (AD 581–588) is more realistically recorded in the annals.[60]

DEFENDED BOUNDARIES

Hillforts were a primary way for the Britons to defend their territories. There were no comparable types of elevated defended sites held by the Germanic immigrants. Important Anglo-Saxon sites would eventually be surrounded by ditches and timber walls. Many other smaller sites, such as villages and farmsteads, seem to have had no walls. This does not necessarily mean that the Germanic people were less concerned about the need for defense. It may mean that British hillforts were not entirely about creating a defensible structure. The small farmstead forts may have taken their form in part because the earthen ring was a preferred style of building. The larger hillforts may have in part been designed to have an imposing appearance that would impress the local population with the status of the people who dwelled within. Both style and function were a part of British hillfort design.

Another form of defense only briefly mentioned so far was the building of earthwork dykes along boundaries. In the past, historians and archaeologists assumed that all dykes were the work of later Anglo-Saxons. Recently, this view has been challenged with better excavation and dating of the dyke sites. Sometimes, interior timbers can be dated by the use of radiocarbon or dendrochronological techniques. Usually, however, archaeologists must rely on artifacts found buried under the bank within the earthwork structure. The dates of pottery and the rare coin tell us the earliest possible date for the construction of the embankment.

Wansdyke and Wat's Dyke are two stretches of earthwork that many now believe date to the fifth or sixth century. Wansdyke exists as at least 2 stretches, about 12 miles each, running in an east–west direction in Somerset by Bath and in Wiltshire. Archaeologically, Wansdyke lies directly over layers that are Romano-British in date. It also has, according to Ken Dark, a pagan name attached to it by early Anglo-Saxons, so therefore it would be unlikely to date to a later (seventh) Christian century. The Anglo-Saxons did not build

Although bearing an Anglo-Saxon name from the pagan period ("Wans" is linked to the god Woden), Wansdyke connected a series of British hillforts and marked British boundaries in Somerset and Wiltshire. (Last Refuge/Robert Harding World Imagery/Corbis)

it, however. The dyke connects British hillforts and is aligned in such a way as to make sense only in British contexts. The sites to the south of Wansdyke have much more Mediterranean pottery than the British sites to the north. Dark suggests that the dyke, which faces north (its ditch is on the north side), was a boundary erected in the fifth century by the post-Roman Durotriges tribe to the south.[61] The hillforts connected to Wansdyke are just south of the line.

Wat's Dyke, also dated to the fifth century, faces west and at least 30 miles of it can be seen on the eastern border of Wales. Wat's Dyke runs parallel to the more recent Offa's Dyke, built by the Saxon king Offa in the eighth century, but Wat's Dyke was not built by Anglo-Saxons. The Saxons in the midlands and elsewhere on the frontier did not build dykes in the fifth century. It is a tactic they seem to have learned from the Britons but were only able to adopt in Middle Saxon times. The most likely explanation is that Wat's Dyke was originally built by the kingdom of Powys as a boundary against Gwynedd.

Other dykes exist as well, but many of them and large stretches of existing dykes have certainly been destroyed by farming practices throughout the centuries. Another southwestern earthwork is the Bokerley Dyke also dated to the fifth century. In East Anglia, a handful of short dyke remains are found scattered about. Two of these, near Cambridge, face southwest (Fleam Dyke and Devil's Dyke). Further to the north are Fossditch and Bichamditch, both facing east. These may have been built by the Britons in the early fifth century, or some stretches could also be Saxon imitations of a British type of defense structure. There is no way of knowing without excavation.

WEAPONS

The British warriors certainly had an array of weapons, but we are singularly ignorant of the details of these objects. Since most British graves were empty of grave goods as in accordance with the Christian rite and we have not identified any representative group of warrior burials (those containing weapons of war) as British rather than Saxon, we have no weapons to study. Weapons were too valuable to lose, and the scrap metal from broken weapons could be reused. However, the wider world of northwestern Europe shared basic similarities of technology, and there is no reason to expect that British weapons were much different from Germanic weapons. It is this group of objects, found in graves, that we can discuss.

The types of weapons normally encountered are swords, shields, spears, short swords or long knives, and battle axes. Helmets might be worn, but most of these were probably made of thick leather rather than metal. Full helmets of metal would be very valuable items but probably considered cumbersome in combat, and their finds are extremely rare. The four earliest Anglo-Saxon helmets found in Britain up until now all seem to date to the seventh century (this includes the famous helmet found in the Sutton Hoo burial). Some agricultural implements—woodcutting axes, scythes and sickles, pitchforks, and others—could and did double as weapons when need demanded. Some weapons—such as wooden bows and iron-tipped wood arrow shafts—would rarely survive from complete decay in burial contexts. Hunting weapons—spears, bows and arrows, and knives—could have been just as easily taken to battle as to the forest to hunt deer. Archaeologists and historians often forget about the lowly slingshot, a weapon used by the Romans, among others. Slingshots were also used in hunting and could have been a common and ordinary possession. The slingshot itself would hardly survive in burials, but the stones or metal balls that it shot just might be there, if only these ambiguous small round objects could be recognized for what they were. Finally, most people, men and women, carried personal knives with them for a myriad of simple routine tasks, including cutting meat at meals.

Swords were the hardest weapon to make well, and warriors would naturally distinguish between a sword made of iron with some impurities and one that had been worked much harder by the blacksmith to remove the weaknesses in the metal. A poor sword was unbalanced, prone to breakage or bending, and unable to hold a sharp edge. A well-made and valuable sword was balanced and swung easily, did not break under stress, and could be keenly sharpened. Swords might vary according to their length, weight, and whether they were double- or single-edged. Most swords of the period were double-edged, pointed, and of considerable weight so that a well-aimed blow would do immense damage. All these specifications have to do mainly with the blade itself that ended at the handle with a single tang or prong. Around this tang would be constructed a handle or "grip." Most grips were made of tightly wound leather strips or other fibers. The grip material would wear out comparatively quickly and would have to be replaced, while a good blade could last for decades or generations. Above the grip was the "guard," a protective crosswise piece that stopped an opponent's blade from cutting the swordsman's hand. Guards could have distinctive designs and styles that would identify their place and time of origin. Since guards could also be replaced from time to time, the origin of the guard was not necessarily the same as the origin of the blade. The final important piece of a sword is the "pommel." Pommels were placed on the other side of the grip from the guard and acted both as a counterweight and as a brace for the hand to counteract the centrifugal force of a swing that might pull the sword out of the hand. The decorations on the pommel could also be distinctive.[62]

Spears and axes both had wooden handles, so the archaeologist is able to find only the spear or axe head. Shields also were mostly of wood. Only the centerpiece that held the wooden slats tight and perhaps some other riveted iron plates would survive. The centerpiece is called the shield boss and is usually bowl-shaped. Inside the shield boss would be an iron handle where the bearer would hold on to the shield.

Swords were always a sign of high status and probably were limited to the professional warriors of a king and regional leader. Many men who might have to fight in battles as needed did not own their own swords. These men would depend on long knives, spears, axes, and any other hunting or household tool that was accessible to them. Battles were generally conducted on foot. Although horses were ridden, perhaps more by the Britons in the early centuries than by the Anglo-Saxons, the animals were for transport to the battle site, not for direct combat. Once battle commenced, the warrior dismounted and fought on foot. The stirrup was unknown in post-Roman Britain. Knowledge of stirrups came from China and did not reach Europe until the eighth century. Without proper stirrup technology, the rider could not stay securely seated on his horse. If he attempted to fight from horseback, he would have too much difficulty trying to stay balanced or prevent himself from falling off should the horse rear up.

ANGLO-SAXON DEVELOPMENTS

Laws and Governance

Many Anglo-Saxon regions of the fifth and sixth centuries were not yet organized into kingdoms. Communities or regional settlement groupings, guided by local leaders who were heads of extended families, dotted the landscape. By the end of the sixth century, the kingdom of Kent in the southeast had taken shape in time to receive the visit of St. Augustine of Canterbury. Bernicia, Elmet, Deira, Lindsey, and other kingdoms have more shadowy origins. Some may have begun as British polities that were later dominated by Anglo-Saxon warlords. Archaeologists look at the density of settlements over the landscape and the select number of exceeding rich or "princely" burials to determine that greater power is now being concentrated in the hands of the few and populations are gathering around central geographic focal points. Some place names ending in -*wic* may already signify greater organized trading, which generally requires a measure of social control and crime regulation so that foreign traders and their goods can be assured safety.

Only in the seventh century did the Anglo-Saxons develop the trappings of kingdoms seen in palace-based (Yeavering) and monastic (Jarrow) communities. The trading *emporia*, such as Hamwic and Lundenwic, grew in size. These kinds of settlements housed organized governing, spiritual and economic leadership that had not existed before.

Among the early Anglo-Saxons, law was based on customary practice and oral tradition. The only surviving written law of the sixth century of immediately thereafter came from the reign of Æthelberht of Kent, AD 560–616. The text begins with the statement, "These are the dooms which King Æthelberht established in the days of Augustine." When Pope Gregory the Great decided that the Anglo-Saxons were ready for conversion to Roman Christianity, he sent the mature and respected prior whose monastic rule Gregory himself had lived under. Part of the impetus for sending a mission to Britain was political. The Britons were already firmly Christian, but their religion was founded in a third-century set of beliefs and ritual. The independent-minded Britons were not always willing to follow the theological decisions of Rome. Gregory wanted to bring the Anglo-Saxons directly under Rome's wing before they fell under the influence of the Celtic Church. Therefore, St. Augustine arrived in Canterbury in AD 596. He had considerable success, achieving the conversion and baptism of Æthelberht in the following year. Yet again, there is a political angle to this conversion. Æthelberht, like other European kings struggling to establish their royal power in a society that knew little of kingship, undoubtedly saw his baptism as a certificate of membership in the elite circles of world leadership. With the Pope's backing and the conversion of Æthelberht's own people, kingship in Kent would stand on a solid and recognized footing.

The transition from a large and complex Germanic chiefdom to a full-fledged kingdom brought the need for more organization. Anglo-Saxons had been accustomed to laws held in memory and legal decisions made by a meeting of the most powerful men. The facts of the case were taken from testimonies and judgments reflected the value of the reputations of the plaintiff and defendant. The Anglo-Saxon idea of punishment was much like the system used in Viking Scandinavia for several more centuries. Lesser crimes such as theft, damage to property, or the harming or killing of a servant could be exonerated quickly by paying a suitable price in compensation to the victim, that is, the owner of the stolen goods or master of the servant.

Murder of someone of higher status, however, was sometimes too serious to be given a price tag. In such instances, when the crime caused too much community upset, the perpetrator was banished. One form of banishment was the most severe—outlawry. Although Germanic society before kings did not practice direct capital punishment, it had a means of causing the death of a man who had gone too far to be tolerated. If a man were outlawed, that decision put him "outside the law" and the protection the law offered. An outlaw lost all his property and could be pursued and killed by his enemies. No one was allowed to help or hide the outlaw, or they too could suffer. It was an effective solution when a community was disrupted by violence or if allowing the parties and their families to fight might lead to a large blood feud. In the case of a blood feud, the communal decision to take one side of the argument in its early stage would save lives and property in the long run.

Outlawry is only mentioned in preserved written sources as a punishment of free males. There is no evidence, but informal capital punishment may have been applied to servants and females as deemed necessary. In these cases, masters and male family members would have the authority to judge and act. Early justice was not so much about making the right decision as finding a way to reduce conflict and stabilize social relationships. Even in the 9th and 10th centuries, in the event there were no credible witnesses of freeman status, the innocence or guilt of the defendant was typically decided by the testimony of oath-helpers who declared the honesty of their friend in public assembly. In essence, whoever gathered the most influential supporters to the court hearing won his case. In this way, it was publicly demonstrated how the community at large wanted the case decided.

Public execution by order of the king's law and the existence of execution cemeteries on the desolate rural boundaries of political units is not attested by documents or archaeology until the later Anglo-Saxon period with some suggestion of late seventh-century executions at the Sutton Hoo royal site on the east coast. Royal power was slow to develop the authority to perform capital punishment.

Æthelberht's Laws

The written laws of Æthelberht begin with the statement that they were made in the days of Augustine, and their very existence is a sign of his influence. Given the papal desire to bring the Anglo-Saxons into the continental European-fold and Æthelberht's natural wish to consolidate and increase his power, taking the

Kentish laws to the level written law code was a logical step. Christian influence is seen immediately in the new first law describing compensation for theft of church *frith* or property. The fines are serious indeed. The property of God or the church is compensated at 12-fold the value, a bishop's property at 11-fold, a priest's at 9-fold, a deacon's at 6-fold, a clerk's at 3-fold, and so on.

Normally, fines or *bots* designated in the law are of a fixed amount, but these fines pertaining to the Church were much higher multiples of value. The end result was to grant high legal status to the Church, its agents, and its property—higher status than held by most members of the society.

The remaining laws are traditional in nature, although it may be true that offenses to the king and those who serve him have risen in value. The third law, for example, states that if the king is receiving hospitality at anyone's house and someone commits an evil deed while the king is present, the evildoer automatically is charged twice the penalty.

The paying of compensation immediately leads to questions of personal value. Since all persons are clearly not equal, offenses must be valued according to the social status of each person involved. There were, for example, graduated fines for raping female servants or slaves. Violating one of the king's female servants cost 50 shillings, taking his grinding slave brought a fine of 25 shillings, and the third-class (unspecified occupation) servant in the employ of the king required only 12 shillings of compensation.

Differences among owners were also essential conditions for deciding the fine. Although, as mentioned above, a king's female servant was worth a compensation of 50 shillings (paid of course to the king, not to the servant who received no compensation), an earl's female cupbearer brought only 12 shillings for the same infraction. Compared to the 50 shillings awarded for the comparable king's servant, this rule clearly defines the new relative worth of an earl (*eorl*) compared to a king even though an earl is the highest-ranking nobleman after the king.

Separate and distinct fines were delineated for different forms of bodily harm inflicted on a freeman. Rules 33 through 72 describe numerous forms of injury in graphic detail. Women's rights have interested Germanic studies scholars for generations. It has often been asserted that women in Germanic society had more rights than their Romanized counterparts. This appears true from a perusal of Æthelberht's laws using the assumption that the traditional laws have not changed much beyond accentuating the status of the king. Rule 78 states that a wife who bore a live child is entitled to half her husband's property should he die first. Otherwise (rule 81), the property goes to her father's relations. Naturally, in return, they must look after her and find her a new husband. Rules 79 and 80 make provision for divorce. If the wife goes away with the children, she is given half the property. Should the husband decide to keep the children, he must give her the inheritance of one child in exchange. Such a generous attitude toward divorce impressed Europeans for centuries and has been surpassed in modern society only in the past two generations.

Wealth and Money

Unlike the Britons, Anglo-Saxons had never been accustomed to using coins or any form of money at face value. They collected foreign coins only for the value of their metal. For daily mundane exchanges, they bartered with whatever they had. For exchanges of greater value or with foreigners, they might use a metal standard measured by weight of silver, bronze, or iron in any form to match the agreed value of the goods they desired. Gold was too rare among Anglo-Saxons to be a means of payment in trade. Other metals might be valued by their weight, but silver was most typically used. Silver and bronze were metals that a person could carry by wearing them. Prosperous men and women both wore numerous pins and ornaments of all kinds: necklaces with pendants, neck rings, arm rings, and rings on their fingers. Garments were secured with large decorated pins or brooches. Ornamental chains were attached to brooches or used as belts. For making a high-value payment, any of these items could be removed and used according to its metallic worth. If the item were too big for the value of the payment, an appropriately sized piece was broken or cut off to match the price to be paid.

Anglo-Saxons also gave gifts for favors or services rendered. This action may appear to be a wage paid for work performed, but since the gift was neither contracted nor promised ahead of time, its giving was optional and therefore considered a gift. The value of the gift was at the giver's discretion, but Anglo-Saxon society valued generosity. A reputation for stinginess did nothing to improve a man's social status.

Symbols of Power

The Anglo-Saxons shared numerous cultural ideas and beliefs with the Scandinavians. The Anglo-Saxon god Woden was in many ways the same deity as the Norse god Odin. In the seventh century, there were strong cultural connections between the kingdom of East Anglia and Sweden. Objects found at the royal burial of Sutton Hoo in eastern England closely resemble contemporary objects found in eastern Sweden. It has also been argued that the Wulfingas Dynasty of Sweden was linked in personal ways to the Wuffing royal house of East Anglia.

Although Britain has not produced many gold artifacts during the post-Roman period, contemporary Swedish elites prized gold objects including a type of medallion called bracteates. Bracteates were used in ritual deposits and had clear spiritual associations. The growth of early kingship in Sweden was connected to the establishment of new rituals and cult places that were now controlled by the first royalty. The gold objects bear a complex style of animal and abstract art that is connected to the religious beliefs legitimizing the centralization of authority. Unlike the Anglo-Saxons, it would be five centuries before the Swedes became Christian, so these changes reflect a purely pagan development of kingship. Yet, as shown above, the East Anglian Anglo-Saxons, at least, had a close connection to the eastern Swedes where many of the bracteates and similar ritual objects are found.

The C-type bracteates bear a runic inscription translated as "High One." This refers to Odin, and the symbolism of these bracteates relate to Odin, the chief god of Norse mythology and the god most worshiped by rulers and warriors. He is also characterized by powerful magical and healing powers.

The D-type bracteates depict snake-like animals alongside isolated human motifs such as a foot or a hand. These images have been interpreted as Odin fighting monsters although this idea is not fully accepted. What is important is that these bracteates represent important mythological religious themes, and the themes support Odin's kingship of the gods. By extension, the earthly king also has greater powers and rules his human subjects by right of godly example.

Some bracteates types are found on the east coast of England, principally in Kent. Over time, the designs become exceedingly abstract and difficult to recognize, but if the bracteates are lined up in sequence to their Swedish origins, the connection to Woden/Odin symbolism is tempting. The origins of Anglo-Saxon kingship in Kent and southeast England generally are connected first to developments in pagan Sweden and additionally to Roman Church and continental connections.

NOTES

1. Stanley Ireland, *Roman Britain: A Sourcebook* (New York: St. Martin's Press, 1986), 166.

2. Ireland, *Roman Britain*, 166.

3. Ireland, *Roman Britain*, 158, 159.

4. Ireland, *Roman Britain*, 158, 159.

5. Ireland, *Roman Britain*, 160, 161.

6. Frances Lynch, *A Guide to Ancient and Historic Wales: Gwynedd*, revised ed. (Cardiff, UK: Cadw: Welsh Historic Monuments, 2001), 103, 111.

7. Gwyn Jones and Thomas Jones, trans., *Mabinogion* (London: J. M. Dent & Sons, Ltd., 1970), 87.

8. Ireland, *Roman Britain*, 168, 169.

9. Neil Faulkner, *The Decline & Fall of Roman Britain* (Stroud, UK: Tempus Publishing, Ltd., 1986), 256, 257.

10. Faulkner, *The Decline & Fall of Roman Britain*, 256.

11. Robert Vermaat, "The Gallic Chroniclers of 452 and 511," *Vortigern Studies: British History 400–600*, http://www.vortigernstudies.org.uk/artsou/chron452.htm.

12. Ireland, *Roman Britain*, 169.

13. Edward James, *Britain in the First Millennium* (New York: Oxford University Press, Inc., 2000), 96 and Robert Vermaat, "Text of Gildas: de Excidio et Conquestu Britanniae (Parts 1 and 2, chapters 1-37)," *Vortigern Studies: British History 400–600*, http://www.vortigernstudies.org.uk/arthist/vortigernquotesgil.htm, a reprint of a part of Hugh Williams, ed. and trans, *Gildas, The Ruin of Britain &c.*, Cymmrodorion Record Series No. 3 (London: Nutt, 1899), http://www.ccel.org/ccel/pearse/morefathers/files/gildas_02_ruin_of_britain.htm.

14. Ireland, *Roman Britain*, 170.

15. Martin Henig, *The Heirs of King Verica, Culture and Politics in Roman Britain* (Stroud, UK: Tempus Publishing, Ltd., 2002), 127.

16. Ireland, *Roman Britain*, 171.

17. N. J. Higham, *King Arthur: Myth-Making and History* (New York: Routledge, 2002), 29.

18. Christopher Snyder, *An Age of Tyrants, Britain and the Britons, A.D. 400–600* (University Park: Pennsylvania State University Press, 1998), 87.

19. Andrew Gardner, "Military Identities in Late Roman Britain," *Oxford Journal of Archaeology* 18, no. 4 (1999): 405.

20. Gardner, "Military Identities in Late Roman Britain," 407.

21. Gardner, "Military Identities in Late Roman Britain," 408.

22. Gardner, "Military Identities in Late Roman Britain," 408.

23. By this time, the military century consisted of 80 men, not 100, and 6 centuries made a "cohort," while 10 cohorts made a legion.

24. Tony Wilmott, *Birdoswald Roman Fort: A History* (Carlisle, UK: Cumbria County Council, 1995), 36.

25. Description and translation provided by "Togodumnus," *Banna, Hadrian's Wall Fort and Settlement, Birdoswald, Cumbria,* http://www. roman-britain.org/places/banna.htm#rib1909.

26. Wilmott, *Birdoswald Roman Fort,* 35.

27. Wilmott, *Birdoswald Roman Fort,* 37.

28. Wilmott, *Birdoswald Roman Fort,* 40.

29. Wilmott, *Birdoswald Roman Fort,* 43.

30. Wilmott, *Birdoswald Roman Fort,* 44.

31. Wilmott, *Birdoswald Roman Fort,* 44.

32. Martin Jones, *England before Domesday* (Totowa, NJ: Barnes & Noble Books, 1986), 144.

33. Jones, *England before Domesday,* 158.

34. Jones, *England before Domesday,* 146–148.

35. Ammianus Marcellinus, Book XIV, 5, 6–8, see Ireland, *Roman Britain,* 147.

36. Jones, *England before Domesday,* 162.

37. Jones, *England before Domesday,* 168.

38. Ken R. Dark, *Civitas to Kingdom, British Political Continuity 300–800* (London: Leicester University Press, 1994), 100, 101.

39. Dark, *Civitas to Kingdom,* 110, 111, 119.

40. Dark, *Civitas to Kingdom,* 133–136.

41. Dark, *Civitas to Kingdom,* 157.

42. Dark, *Civitas to Kingdom,* 180.

43. Christopher Snyder, *The Britons* (Malden, MA: Blackwell Publishing, 2003), 157.

44. Snyder, *The Britons,* 157.

45. Snyder, *The Britons,* 159.

46. Malcolm Todd, *The South West to AD 1000* (New York: Longman, Inc., 1987), 109.

47. Snyder, *The Britons,* 162.

48. Snyder, *The Britons,* 166.

49. Joseph P. Clancy, *The Earliest Welsh Poetry* (London: Macmillan and Co., Ltd., 1970), 23, 24.

50. Snyder, *Age of Tyrants,* 179.

51. Leslie Alcock, *Was This Camelot? Excavations at Cadbury Castle 1966–1970* (New York: Stein and Day Publishers, 1972), 180–182.

52. Snyder, *Age of Tyrants,* 182.

53. Snyder, *The Britons,* 185.

54. Snyder, *The Britons,* 188.

55. Snyder, *The Britons,* 188.

56. Clancy, *The Earliest Welsh Poetry,* 43.

57. Barbara Yorke, *Kings and Kingdoms of Early Anglo-Saxon England* (New York: Routledge, 1997), 3.

58. Yorke, *Kings and Kingdoms,* 16, 17.

59. Yorke, *Kings and Kingdoms,* 76, 77.

60. Yorke, *Kings and Kingdoms*, 132, 133.

61. Dark, *Civitas to Kingdom*, 117, 125.

62. A detailed drawing of an Anglo-Saxon sword hilt and pommel can be found on pages 14–15 of the article, Hilda R. Ellis Davidson and Leslie Webster, "The Anglo-Saxon Burial (Woodnesborough), at Coombe Kent," *Medieval Archaeology* 11 (1967): 1–41, republished by the Archaeology Data Service, http://archaeologydataservice.ac.uk/catalogue/adsdata/arch-769-1/dissemination/pdf/vol11/11_001_041.pdf

8

MATTERS OF LIFE
AND DEATH

Britons and Anglo-Saxons suffered from diseases and injuries typical of their work, daily experience, and environmental hazards. A survey of these conditions observed in burial remains reveals the demographic makeup of the population: the age and sex ratios of the living and the growth of communities. The study of cemeteries also reveals family groupings, occasional catastrophic events leading to many deaths, and, under certain conditions, the arrangement of social statuses among the people using the cemetery. Burial evidence can also give clues regarding beliefs about the afterlife and the spiritual world.

MORTALITY AND POPULATIONS

Archaeologists are interested in the patterns of death within a society. They want to know about people's chances for survival, how many children were born into families, and how long everyone was likely to live—that is, their life expectancy. Estimates can be calculated from burial remains. If bone preservation in the ground is adequate, the approximate age and sex of the bodies can be determined. Some definitions are necessary. Mortality is the proportion of deaths to population size over a given period of time. Birthrate or natality is the proportion of births to population size over a given period of time. It is often expressed as the number of live births per 100 or 1,000 persons in the population per year. With good cemetery evidence, it is not hard to discuss the mortality, natality, and life expectancies of a single community, but there is always some room for error in the estimates due to missing burial evidence or false assumptions about the extent of the area occupied by the community.

If population estimates are made for a number of neighboring communities, the data can then be combined to create a regional estimate. However, the potential for inaccuracy multiplies dramatically as more estimates are combined. Although some experts will attempt to make regional estimates or give some idea of the population of Britain as a whole at a given time, these numbers need to be taken with caution. The problem encountered when analyzing larger groups, such as all the Anglo-Saxons in England or the Britons in Wales, is that many of the relevant cemeteries and settlements are not yet known, excavated, or have been damaged with their remains forever lost. The effort to put a close and accurate date on sites depends on how closely archaeologists are able to date the remains. Although large-scale population estimates would be useful, there is no way to make them reliable. The earliest historic benchmark for population estimates in England dates to AD 1086 when the Normans attempted a survey of the people and resources of their new land. This work was put together into *The Domesday Book*. The survey contains many gaps, but taking those into account, estimates of 2.5 million and up for the English population in AD 1086 have been proposed.[1]

Comparative studies of different populations in Europe from the late Roman period and subsequent centuries shows that there is no significant change in the mortality rates of the various populations.[2] At no time, compared to other times, did significantly more people throughout Europe die due to plague, starvation, or other disaster. In cases when infant burials are recovered, which is not often since infants and very young children were frequently disposed of by different means than accorded to adults, then about 40 percent of the dead were age 5 or under. Older children had a mortality rate ranging from about 6 to 19 percent within the population, depending on local conditions of disease and nutrition. Females of childbearing age (from about age 17 to 35) were more likely to die than males. Childbirth was always a risky undertaking. After age 35, male and female life expectancies gradually equaled out, with the majority of the oldest surviving persons often being female. The important observation is that there was little sign of death occurring at comparatively younger ages after the fourth century. Nothing in the cemetery evidence shows that the demise of the Roman Empire made life more precarious throughout Europe.

In Britain, there is no archaeological evidence from burials that either children or adults were dying at measurably greater rates from any cause, be it famine, disease, or violence. Nevertheless, landscape surveys of remains have indicated that the population might have decreased. A possible explanation may be a reduced birthrate or natality. Post-Roman families may simply have chosen to bear fewer children. With the same percentages of infants, children, and adults dying from the usual causes, a reduction in birthrate lowers population size in a matter of several generations.

DISEASES AND INJURY

Paleopathology

The study of ancient disease is called paleopathology. The work of Charlotte Roberts and Keith Manchester on the archaeology of disease is recommended.[3] Paleopathologists analyze human remains, microbe evidence in soil samples, written texts, and any other available pieces of evidence for clues about what made people sick in the past. Some noteworthy physical conditions found by archaeologists to have been present in post-Roman Britain include the following:

- *Tuberculosis.* Tuberculosis affects the lungs and respiratory system and is usually a problem in crowded and urban environments. Its incidence in the fifth and sixth centuries was rare since most of the population was dispersed in rural areas.

- *Hydrocephaly.* Hydrocephaly (i.e., any brain condition causing a oversized skull) is rare in human populations, but one Romano-British adult and a Saxon teenager have been documented with the condition. Their intelligence may have been normal, but the hydrocephaly could have caused physical problems handicapping these persons and limiting their ability to contribute necessary labor.

- *Leprosy and other deterioration diseases.* Different forms of leprosy have existed throughout history. In Britain, it was a rare disease in the early Middle Ages and disappeared by the 16th century. Medieval writers were not consistent and might refer to any degenerative disease as "leprosy." True leprosy had devastating effects. The degeneration of the skin and other soft tissues visible from the outside would be accompanied by less visible but traumatic bone loss on the inside. The details of degeneration caused by leprosy, particularly on skulls, are sometimes visible on well-preserved remains, but a diagnosis is not so simple. Advanced syphilis caused similar bone damage.

- *Anemia and poor diet.* Anemia may have been a common health hazard in fifth- and sixth-century populations. Without sufficient sources of iron in the diet—usually obtained from meat products but also from oat and wheat bran, wheat germ, lentils, and other beans—anemia can appear. Depending on the crops utilized and the quantity of food available, preindustrial rural populations can be at risk. Common symptoms are fatigue, pallor, shortness of breath, and irregular heartbeat. Certain bone changes occur in severe or prolonged cases, and these can be identified by paleopathologists. At Poundbury, a well-known Romano-British cemetery in Dorset, 230 out of 752 individuals, or over 30 percent of the burials, were found to show signs of anemia.

- *Arthritis.* Osteoarthritis caused by wear and tear on joints exposed to daily, hard manual labor was a common condition in adult members of the population. Even teenagers were not immune to joint damage. People were accustomed to carrying, pulling, and pushing heavy loads. Arthritic damage can occur anywhere on the skeleton and generally indicates the joints of the body that were most heavily stressed during life. For this reason, the study of joints in skeletons informs researchers about the work performed by historic and prehistoric populations.

- *Dental decay.* Before the availability of beet or cane sugar as a sweetener in the diet, the primary source of any sweetening was honey, and the main source of carbohydrates in the diet among Europeans was bread made from wheat, rye, oats, or barley. Potatoes and corn are foods originating from the Americas and therefore not known in Europe until the Elizabethan Age. Interestingly, Europeans accustomed to a wheat-based diet and who immigrated to America suffered from noticeable increases in dental decay after switching from predominantly wheat to corn consumption. Increased use of sweetened and corn-based foods correlates with an increased incidence of dental decay in Europeans. Sugar did not appear in Britain until the 12th century, so it is not responsible for post-Roman dental caries. However, a comparative study of teeth from Romano-British, Anglo-Saxon, and medieval cemeteries revealed that the Anglo-Saxons, on average, had far fewer cavities than the other two groups. This difference could have been due to diet or cultural behaviors.

- *Dental wear.* Another source of damage to teeth was wear and tear. Fragments of rock were incorporated into food by the normal methods of preparation. Grains were ground into flour with stone querns. In the process, stony grit broke off the quern stones, mixed with the flour, and became part of the food that people ate on a daily basis. The grit gradually chipped and ground down tooth enamel so that damaged teeth were more likely to suffer breakage and dental decay.

- *Dental abscesses, periodontal disease, and tooth loss.* A tooth becomes abscessed when its nerve tissue becomes infected. Today, patients with an abscess must go to the dentist for a root canal, a procedure that removes and replaces the infected tissue, essentially leaving the tooth dead. This procedure is necessary because if left unattended, the tooth infection can spread into the body and lead to death. Before root canals were possible, the only recourse was to pull the bad tooth out. Occasionally, an abscessed tooth heals itself, but if there is a great deal of pain, then removal is the best option. Extraction would also become important if a tooth were badly broken, or if gum disease caused an infection. In one study of dental problems in an Anglo-Saxon cemetery, it was found that from 4 to 11 percent of teeth were deliberately extracted during life. Tooth loss among the Romano-British (during all Roman centuries) was higher than among the Anglo-Saxons. The mean tooth loss in life for the Romano-British is almost 14 percent, while it stands at just 7 percent for Anglo-Saxons. Unfortunately, there is no available a study of British teeth from the post-Roman period, and many of the data on Saxon teeth come from monastic cemeteries where the monks were interred and date to the seventh century or later. The quality of food and overall health in monastic communities was better than for the population as a whole.

- *Enamel hypoplasia.* This term describes the horizontal rings surrounding teeth after growth has been seriously disrupted during childhood and adolescence. Either malnutrition or severe illness might be the cause. Enamel hypoplasia was not a serious problem among the Britons and Anglo-Saxons on the whole, but it marked the appearance of local or short-term fluctuations of nutrition and health in populations. Under such circumstances, hypoplasia affected the children of high-ranking families, marked by burial with valuable grave goods, as much as others whose burials were poorer or of lower status. Whatever traumas of famine or illness that children and adults both faced, the advantages of high social status seem not to have made much difference.

- *Effects of violence.* Beginning in the sixth century, some Saxon burials show obvious indications of battle injuries. At Fishergate cemetery in the city of York, 16 males, mostly young adults, exhibited traumatic cut damage to the bones of their limbs and spine. Furthermore, the majority of injuries were on the left side of the body, implying that both attackers and victims were predominantly right-handed, as would be expected. In close-range combat with knives, swords, axes, and clubs, most injuries occur on the arms and head. When longer-range weapons were used, injuries were more varied. One battle victim from Eccles, Kent, died of an arrow lodged in his spine. Not all victims of violence were male. Another of the Eccles skeletons bearing weapon injuries was identified as a woman. Was she a bystander, attempting to protect her home and children, or fighting alongside the men?

- *Injuries.* Broken bones were a serious problem because most efforts to set bones were unsuccessful. Simple fractures without any dislocation of bone could heal if the patient were allowed ample time to rest. Dislocated breaks and shattered bones were much more troublesome, often resulting in permanent disability or even death or amputation from infection. Did every village have someone with the knowledge and skill to set such breaks back in place and to splint the bones securely until they grew back together? Apparently, this was not the case. To accomplish the accurate set of broken bones without the advantage of modern X-rays and surgical repairs was often difficult. Many long bone breaks, especially in the legs, healed incorrectly when the broken ends overlapped and couldn't be pulled apart to be correctly positioned. The affected leg was permanently shortened by as much as several inches.

  Bones were not broken just in battle. There were many opportunities to break bones while performing the routine tasks of daily life. Stress injuries and fractures to the bones of the spine (affecting the vertebrae) were caused by heavy lifting or pulling. Such injuries, along with accidental skull injuries, falling injuries, and all kinds of battle wounds, were frequent in males, although women also sustained their share of accidental or violently inflicted injury.

- *Cultural practices.* A custom that has sparked much discussion is the occasional decapitation (beheading) of both Romano-British and Anglo-Saxon individuals found in cemeteries. It is not likely that the individuals were executed in this manner. More likely, the beheading occurred after death and was part of the burial ritual. Beheading of the dead may represent fear that the ghost of the person would come back to haunt the living. Persons suspected of witchcraft or feared for some other reason may have been treated this way as a part of a pagan ritual designed to prevent the dead from disturbing the living.

The Question of Fifth-Century Plague

Throughout the millennia of human history, conditions of health, good or poor, has often played a decisive role. Starvation due to climate change, war, or conquest was common. Epidemics changed populations and their leadership. However, diseases strike not only humans but also the plants and animals on which they depend. Some diseases are efficiently lethal, while others just weaken the body, making it incapable of thriving as it might. Some are chronic and stay with the body for a lifetime. Some are highly contagious, while others strike rarely but never quite go away once contracted. Now and then, a deadly disease becomes epidemic and sweeps over a broad geographic area killing thousands of people in just a few seasons. These occurrences are a fearsome event even today as we monitor the mutation of new flu strains each year.

Plague used to be counted as a major factor in the "downfall" of Roman Britain and the rest of the empire. Plague was blamed for the loss of many British lives and the presumed disappearance of British culture after the Romans left. People envisioned only a weakened remnant of Britons remaining. These were quickly overrun by the opportunistic Saxons. Near the beginning of his famous work, *De excidio Brittonum,* or *The Ruin of Britain* as it is translated, Gildas mentioned a "famous pestilence." He was quite clear on the subject. Since the pestilence was "famous," everyone must have known about it. Many historians have taken Gildas for his word on the deadly plague at face value, but when they look for other evidence of mass death, little is to be found.

Plagues were significant divine events in the Old Testament, and they were rarely mentioned by any Christian writer during the early centuries without some pointed reference to God's wrath and judgment of the stricken people as the root cause of the devastation. In fact, plagues often seemed to symbolize the wrath of God expressed in response to wrongful deeds and behavior. The plague is not only a story of the past, but also becomes a warning from the writer on behalf of God against future transgressions. Gildas was strongly motivated to "strike the fear of God" into the hearts of his fellow Britons. He used the story of plague for this purpose, but despite all the vivid imagery of his text, he rarely gave useful details, such as who, where, and when. Who died? Where did people die? When did they die? As for "when," Gildas did address the timing of the "famous" British pestilence. He implied that it occurred before Vortigern's ill-fated invitation to the Saxons; this would date the pestilence to sometime before AD 445 according to Gildas's chronology. So far, so good, but no other author writing close to this era ever mentioned the presence of plague in or near Britain. There was a later plague during Emperor Justinian's reign in the second half of the sixth century, well-documented by other writers, but this occurred after Gildas had written *De Excidio*. Gildas's story of plague stands alone.

Other fifth-century chroniclers from Europe mention various tales of local plagues, but none can be followed beyond a small region or anywhere near Britain. For example, a plague struck briefly in Spain in AD 443. Another in Constantinople in AD 445–446. A third in Italy in AD 452–453. Could a similar localized plague have struck in Britain? Possibly, but Gildas did not give as many details as the other writers. His plague description was entirely vague. In fact, he might have been speaking in religious metaphors and not talking about a real plague, after all.

Another reason to question Gildas's testimony about pestilence comes from his choice of words. He was writing in Latin and at times used the word *lues* to describe the plague. Words such as *plaga* or *pestis* would have been more common choices. *Lues* in Gildas's time was used to imply not only plague but a moral sickness.[4] Was Gildas speaking literally or metaphorically when he declared that a pestilence had passed through Britain? An argument can be made that Gildas's *lues* is a figure of speech and that he did not intend to deceive readers with a story of real plague. The double meaning, to him, would have been obvious. Britain suffered from moral plague.

Archaeologists have not found convincing evidence that plague struck Britain at its most vulnerable moment. Improper and possibly hurried burial of bodies at Wroxeter, Caerwent, and Cirencester has been suggested as a sign that rampant disease was causing public disorder but do not necessarily demonstrate plague. Both of the best cases are based on remains excavated over a century ago. The accuracy of both the excavation method and analysis of the finds is questionable. Archaeology is a much more exact process today than it once was. The Wroxeter bodies were said to have been left in the hypocaust system of the Roman public baths. Hypocausts are the underground channels constructed for spreading heat throughout floors and walls. Is it fair to call this action irregular and improper burial? If that area of the city had already been abandoned, then reusing the area as cemetery would have been convenient and reasonable. The reuse of old ruins, even those from another culture, as a "house" for the dead is an occasional practice across human societies. The early Anglo-Saxons sometimes buried their dead in the ancient burial mounds of millennia earlier. In this case, the last urban dwellers used Roman ruins for city cemeteries. Although the early Caerwent archaeologists thought that perhaps the bodies they found were simply abandoned among building ruins, more careful examination of the evidence decades later revealed that the dead had all been deliberately buried. In Cirencester, bodies were claimed to have been found buried haphazardly in a post-Roman ditch. Reexamination revealed that the potsherds found in the ditch with the bodies dated to the late Middle Ages, so the burials likely were of the same date and the ditch was not as old as once thought.[5]

The Justinian plague of mid-sixth century left a footnote on British history. King Maelgwn of Gwynedd was said to have died of it, but there is no other evidence that it had a noticeable long-term impact on Britain's population.[6]

The preceding discussion of evidence shows what archaeologists look for when seeking signs of epidemic. When a great many people die in a short span of time, the survivors have difficulty giving proper burial to all of the dead. Religious rules might require inhumation and forbid the more efficient method of burning. Survivors might fear having contact with the dead. Depositing bodies in existing pits and ditches or digging mass graves were common solutions. Customary funerary ritual was often minimized or abandoned. Such events are taken as signs of public emergency. However, mass burials are not always the sign of devastating plague. A long, cold winter with months of food shortages would strike down many people, especially the young and the old.

Battles can also be the cause of mass burials although the dead left behind on the battlefield sometimes did not receive burial at all unless their relatives came to find them. Many dead on battlefields were left to the elements, animals, and insects to remove their traces. If the dead were placed in a mass grave, there are telltale signs. The bodies in the graves would be mostly young males. Analysis of the bones would show severe injuries from sharp and blunt weapons. The bodies may also have been buried at a much later date after obvious exposure to weathering and animal scavenging. Bones would appear dried out, cracked, and fragmented. There were tooth marks from gnawing. Bones would become separated leaving no sign of intact bodies.

Some historians point to a different plague that occurred in the sixth century around AD 544 or 545. The Irish annals mention such an occurrence.[7] If the Irish plague were as destructive in Britain, it might have given the Anglo-Saxons an advantage, and the resulting British deaths might have cleared enough territory of resistance so that the new Anglo-Saxon kingdoms could get a foothold. Yet, as

Malcolm Todd has pointed out, if the plague wiped out Britons, then it surely affected Anglo-Saxons as well. There is no apparent reason why plague should be an advantage for one group and not another. The only argument that might be offered is that if a plague were devastating in Ireland but had not reached England from the east via the North Sea, then the Britons, who had more interaction with the Irish, would likely suffer more exposure to the contagion than the Saxons. On the other hand, since Britons and Saxons made constant contact for trade and personal relations, then the Irish plague theory falls apart again.

Plague and other epidemic diseases such as small pox may not have had significant impact on fifth- and sixth-century events, but disease and infection factors accounted for many of the health concerns of ordinary people. Other infectious diseases could be lethal or cause permanent impairment to health in the absence of modern antibiotics or treatments to alleviate dangerous symptoms. Modern immunization programs have changed the impact of disease on society. Polio, leprosy, tuberculosis, measles, and rubella are now rare diseases where vaccinations are used. Appendicitis, meningitis, bronchitis, influenza, and pneumonia were once deadly but now can be treated with confidence. Any minor infection or injury could once become critical and progress into a lethal case of blood poisoning (septicaemia) or gangrene before antiseptics and antibiotics were used. Early medieval people in Europe did have a store of herbal healing knowledge and remedies of some effectiveness, but these did not have widespread availability and use. Mostly, people relied on their bodies' natural immune defenses.

THE ARCHAEOLOGY OF CEMETERIES

Human societies throughout history and prehistory have disposed of their dead in a wide variety of ways. Many bury bodies in the ground. Others burn the dead and scatter or bury the ashes. Some place their dead on elevated platforms or in trees and leave them to decay and disintegrate in time. Where burial in the ground was difficult, perhaps because bedrock lay too close to the surface or because the ground was frozen, a body could instead be covered over with a mound of earth and stone. The ancient Egyptians built entire mountains—the pyramids and tombs—to cover their royal dead. In the ancient Mediterranean, underground stone chambers called catacombs, often running through miles of galleries, were constructed to store the bodies of the dead. Oftentimes, in underground chambers, the dead are not left alone once deposited. Once the soft tissues of the body decayed and the dry bones were remained, they were then collected and sorted by type into common collection areas of skulls, long bones, and so on, in order to make more room for future generations.

In the old city of New Orleans where the water table is near the ground surface, burial in aboveground crypts has been the traditional practice. Bodies were placed in aboveground family- or community-owned crypts where by tradition they were left in peace for "a year and a day." By then, in the intense Louisiana heat, the remains were mostly dust that was swept to the back, and the crypt was made available for another lodger. The names of all those interred are carved in stone on the outside.

Since the late 19th century, it has been understood that burial in urban areas can contaminate the groundwater. During medieval and early modern times, people in Europe and America were often buried in dense cemeteries surrounding urban churches. This practice was discouraged when it was realized that decaying bodies buried in wooded boxes contaminated local wells and water sources. New "garden cemeteries" like the famous Mount Auburn Cemetery near Boston were created on the outskirts of cities, and only rural churches, for the most part, maintained the practice of burial in the churchyard.

Literally, hundreds of thousands of Britons and Saxons—perhaps millions would be a better word to use—lived and died in Britain during the fifth and sixth centuries. There should be many burials to find, but only the burials of the smallest fraction of these have been excavated by archaeologists in recent decades. Many more single burials and cemeteries were found and casually destroyed by construction work, field plowing, or were randomly dug up in the past by amateur antiquarians or treasure hunters looking for bits of jewelry, swords, and other treasures.

The dead in Britain during the fifth and sixth centuries were both cremated and inhumed. Christian rules dictated against cremation because the clergy considered it a pagan practice. Cremation had also become unpopular among pagans and converted provincial populations in the late Roman period who wished to copy the Roman elite. In fifth-century Britain, the common assumption has been that only the Anglo-Saxons were likely to cremate their dead. The contemporary Britons would inhume their dead according to Christian practice.

Because of these religious differences, British and Saxon cemeteries would always be separate and distinct since the two groups did not tolerate each other well, or so many have assumed.

Lankhills Cemetery

Recent archaeological discoveries carried out alongside reevaluations of the documentary sources have shown otherwise. Not only did Saxons and Britons mix together in life, but they also were buried in the same cemeteries in death. This fact was recognized already in the 1970s at the Lankhills Cemetery excavation at Winchester, Hampshire. At Lankhills, approximately 450 late Roman burials were excavated ranging in date from ca. AD 310 to 410. Use of the cemetery ended with the Roman departure. The cemetery, like many Roman cemeteries, was situated off a Roman road, in this instance covering the distance from Winchester to Cirencester. As the fourth century wore to an end, fewer of the dead were being buried with grave goods. The Lankhills people were converting to the new religion of Christianity and gradually giving up the idea of burying important possessions with the dead.[8] Such a change in custom and fundamental belief does not come easily. People showed reluctance to abandon the old practices completely at first, in case by doing so their loved ones would be deprived of afterlife necessities. Worse, failing to give the deceased what was rightfully theirs could make their ghosts angry or vengeful. Trusting the teachings of new religion was a slow process that took several generations to complete the abandonment of the old rituals.

Out of the hundreds of burials at Lankhills, one group of six graves stands out. All six dated very closely to the decades from AD 390 to 410, but at first glance, they are not at all alike. Their grave goods or furnishings are much more variable and numerous than typical of late Romano-British burial. Some of the unusual objects in these six burials include weapons and pierced animal teeth used as pendants or other decoration. The meaning of the animal teeth pendants can only be guessed. The range and number of objects and the sudden appearance of this type of burial at Lankhills without any derivation from previous burials suggests that these six persons were early Anglo-Saxon arrivals who might have come to Winchester prior to the Roman departure. Six burials make for a noticeable group of immigrants during the last two decades of the cemetery's use. Furthermore, the local population included them in their own cemetery. The newcomers were not excluded because they were foreigners, pagans, feared, or hated.

Early Christian cemeteries throughout the vast rural areas of this period were not yet placed in parish churchyards. That practice was a later medieval development. Like their pagan counterparts, these Christian cemeteries were situated apart from settlements. Rural people followed Romano-British tradition, placing burials next to and even under house floors and other buildings. The excavation of the late fourth-century Romano-British Christian farmstead, Bradley Hill in Somerset (see Chapter 5), shows how this was done.

Unlike Lankhills, a number of urban cemeteries in use during the late fourth century remained in use in the fifth century. If British people left the towns, they did not go far, and they returned to the same urban sacred ground to bury their dead for several more generations. By the mid-fifth century, most of these cemeteries were finally abandoned. What had happened? As the Anglo-Saxons spread throughout eastern and southern England, the mixed populations of Saxon and British took on a much more Germanic cultural character. The Britons eventually mixed their dead with Anglo-Saxon burial practices, having found themselves in some localities now members of a society dominated by Anglo-Saxons. The Germanic settlers were not attracted to the old urban cemeteries.

Elsewhere in Cornwall, Wales, and Scotland, where Britons were dominant, native patterns of funeral ritual prevailed. A large number of memorial stones dot the landscape. These may or may not have stood as tombstones placed over the burial of the person memorialized in the inscription, but the stones have been found throughout the west of Britain. The monuments would not necessarily be tombstones marking a burial location but rather memorials placed where passersby could easily view the inscription. Such stones are also typically moved with the passage of centuries. They might be reused as new boundary markers or as building or paving stone for other construction. The absence of a burial accompanying the stone is to be expected.

Londinium

One example of an urban cemetery that continued in use after the Romans left is the eastern cemetery in Londinium. From the first century into the fifth, many generations were buried. Excavated burials include 104 cremations and 575 inhumations. The graves were placed into a natural gravel bed. Gravel has long been a valuable raw material for paving and building, and the quarrying of this gravel bed started in medieval times. Many burials were uncaringly destroyed or damaged in the process.

During the first two centuries of the cemetery's use, cremations had been more popular than inhumations. Gradually, in accordance with Christian belief, inhumation supplanted the use of cremation until the practice of cremation finally disappeared in the fourth century. Most of the inhumations were buried in wooden coffins made of boards and iron nails, but two bodies were inside molded coffins made from lead, a sign of wealth and high status. About one-quarter of the dead had grave goods with the body including a variety of food and drink vessels, jewelry, hobnail boots (typical footwear in Roman times), coins, buckles, combs, mirrors, and a gaming set. None contained weapons, and no one was arrayed like a warrior.

Stone foundations and postholes in the soil amid the graves revealed that miniature timber or stone houses had been built over some of the graves. Although graves containing personal objects for the dead have been presumed to be pagan or recently Christian convert burials, those lacking grave goods cannot assume definitively to be Christian. Lack of grave goods may indicate poverty, slave status, or Christian relatives taking charge of the funeral arrangements. It may also indicate that the gifts given were organic in materials and had completely decomposed over the centuries. None of the objects in the graves showed any kind of Christian symbolism. Datable fifth-century associations come from just three inhumations. Two had specific pins and brooches that come from the continent and are sometimes associated with people of rank in the government or the military. One other burial contained a pair of valuable German brooches. Signs of professional status or occupation, if they appear without other objects in the burials, might in this early century have been buried with either Christians or pagans.

It is unfortunate that so much of the cemetery is missing due to damage. There should be more fifth-century burials. Even though post-Roman London had many abandoned buildings, and the extensive "dark earth" area indicated that wattle-and-daub settlements of native British type had been constructed, the town continued to attract foreigner merchants and visitors of note and personal wealth, some of whom died away from home and were buried at the eastern cemetery.

RITUALS, BELIEFS, AND ANCESTORS

Rituals are an important means by which human communities remind all their members what behaviors are expected of them. Wedding ceremonies include vows and representations explaining the meaning of marriage and how the new couple should act, not only to each other but toward the community as well.[9] Modern graduation ceremonies emphasize the meaning of past achievements and the need for future goals. Some rituals reenact an event from the historical or mythological past. Taking communion in a Christian church is an example of a reenactment ritual.

All rituals, in one way or another, are intended to teach people what to think and how to act according to the rules accepted by the whole society. Subportions of society have their own special rules and rituals as well. People who work together in an office or department will plan after-work gatherings for themselves or weekend picnics including their families. The function of these activities is to help the group members to feel more emotionally connected. For groups whose regular activities include danger or violence, be they early medieval warrior bands, firemen, or urban gangs, their rituals may require behaviors and the making of bonds that fall outside what is expected for the rest of society.

Another universal aspect of ritual, if it is religious ritual, is the ability of ritual to put the ordinary individual in direct contact with the spiritual realm. Religious rituals inform people what the gods, nature spirits, or ancestors want of them. Ritual may also provide a way for the supplicant to make requests to spiritual powers. Ancestor spirits, deities, and Christian saints could all give assistance in times of need when contacted through offerings and prayers.

Another way of looking at rituals is to observe them as repetitive behaviors that mark eternal, unchanging, and timeless realities. The ritual expresses the belief that something is occurring exactly the way it has occurred many times before. Many rituals mark the event of some life passage such as marriage, birth, or death. Today, people circumvent this purpose of ritual by personalizing ceremonies, but that idea is atypical of most human societies. In fact, this is the common reality about rituals, even when people believed they must not be changed. A quick study of American social history will tell us that funeral ceremonies and periods of observed mourning in America have changed in many ways and have incorporated many foreign traditions over the past two centuries. Nevertheless, the perceived sameness of ritual can make the experience appear timeless and spiritual.

Ritual also reassures people that the powers of the spiritual world will be satisfied with human behavior. Satisfied spirits are more likely to treat humans benevolently. Germanic tribes in their homelands commonly gave offerings of sacrificed humans, animals, and valuable objects to their gods by depositing these into a lake or bog.

According to the classical writers who described this practice, the sacrificed objects and people were usually the weapons and prisoners taken in battle. The Germans gave a portion of these spoils of war to their gods in order to thank them for the victory. Not all were sacrificed, of course. The remaining weapons would have made valuable prizes for the victors to keep while the surviving prisoners were used for labor or sold as slaves for a profit.

Anglo-Saxons in England apparently did not continue the practice of making offerings in sacred lakes and bogs, but their provision of many valuable grave goods in burials may have been a new kind of ritual intended to substitute for the old way.[10] It has been a puzzle to some archaeologists why the Anglo-Saxons provided so many grave goods for their dead relatives when their distant relations in the German homelands did not deposit quite so many objects in burials. Were the Anglo-Saxons unable to leave votive deposits because there were no sacred waters in Britain? Did sacred waters exist only in the homeland? Perhaps, they decided that their dead must take offerings with them to give to the gods. Later, in the eighth and ninth centuries when Christianity had taken a firm hold of England, the Anglo-Saxons shifted once more to leaving special gifts in deposits underwater, this time in the English rivers. Many valuable items have been discovered in the beds of streams, lakes, and rivers. Perhaps because Christianity effectively forbade putting gifts inside burials, Anglo-Saxons compensated by finding another way to appease the ancestral and other spirits. These changing rituals for depositing offerings did not represent new and different religious beliefs, but rather, they were adjustments of the same beliefs and rituals made to changing circumstances.

We have seen how the process of Christian conversion in a population was gradual. Roman missionaries first made successful contact with the Anglo-Saxons in AD 597 when St. Augustine of Canterbury arrived in Kent and converted King Æthelberht. Throughout the seventh century, wealthy Anglo-Saxon elites who claimed to be Christian continued to leave jewelry and other objects in the graves of their dead relations. Oftentimes, the pieces bore the symbolism of the Christian cross, which was ironic because early Christian practice frowned on burying any object whatsoever with the dead. Old habits die hard.

Grave goods deserve a closer look. There are several reasons why people put gifts in burials. First, the gifts might have been meant for gods, spirits, or other ancestors and would travel to the otherworld with the recently deceased. On the other hand, the gifts might have been intended for the personal use of the deceased.

A modern statue of Queen Bertha dedicated in 2006 at Canterbury alongside a statue of her husband, King Æthelberht of Kent. The statues were erected near the medieval gate of St. Augustine's Abbey. Augustine converted Æthelberht and was made the first archbishop of Canterbury. Bertha may well have been instrumental in her husband's conversion because she had been raised a Christian in France. (Sharon Leelaratne/123RF Stock Photo)

Since the dead lived on in the otherworld, they naturally wanted to have their prized possessions with them so that they could fully enjoy their new existence. From a functional point of view, however, the funeral ceremony was also an opportunity for the family of the deceased to remind everyone of the departed's former status in life. In the case of the wealthy and powerful, the funeral was a critical time to express what an important person she or he had been. A successful funeral might play a part in the inheritance or wealth or power. Burying grave goods served to impress upon all the witnesses how much prestige the whole family held. Such symbolism was especially important if the deceased were a powerful and charismatic leader who left behind a widow and young son. The family would not want to lose any of its social standing with the death of its patriarch, so the funeral became a public recognition of the son who would someday reach manhood and step into his material and social inheritance.

All three of these interpretations of Anglo-Saxon burial ritual may have elements of truth. One of the fascinating things about ritual is that it never seems to have only one explanation, and it often means different things to different people. The Old English poem *Beowulf*, which originated as an oral tradition in the North Sea area during the early post-Roman centuries, reveals the ambiguity of the meaning of funerary ritual. The king of the Scylding tribe has died. His body was laid to rest at the foot of a mast on a magnificent ship. Great treasure, weapons, and foreign gems were deposited around it. In the poet's imagination, the ship sails out upon unknown seas to a mysterious destination.[11]

The funeral described in the poem *Beowulf* has similarities to the famous Sutton Hoo burial site where the East Anglian King Rædwald was buried along with his treasure inside a ship. This time, however, the ship did not sail away but was buried under an earthen mound. Other rich and not so rich burials have also been found in the vicinity. The dead king of the poem has all the proper kingly qualities of being loved, wealthy, and generous with gifts. He is placed in a ship with a spectacular treasure, but instead of being buried in the earth, his ship is set adrift across the water to the otherworld, by a path that the living cannot follow. Was the treasure a gift meant only for the king, or were the king and treasure together a gift for an otherworldly power? Did the early Anglo-Saxons believe that the dead rejoined their ancestors? That may well have been the case, but the poem ends by asking its own question, where do the dead go?

The Anglo-Saxon preference for making rich burials in England, compared with elite graves in their homeland, is one noteworthy change. Another noticeable behavioral change by the Anglo-Saxons was their reuse of prehistoric monuments belonging to earlier cultures. Although these sites had no personal connection to the Anglo-Saxons, the latter often adopted such places as sacred ground.[12] One example out of many is found at Bowcombe Down on the Isle of Wight. Here, Anglo-Saxon burials are inserted into a much older pair of Bronze Age barrows, and additional smaller Anglo-Saxon mounds surround the group. The Bronze Age barrows are several thousand years older than the Anglo-Saxon graves. Perhaps, the Anglo-Saxons believed that by appropriating a site that was sacred to very ancient Britons, the Anglo-Saxons would gain a kind of ownership over Britain.

The Anglo-Saxons who came to Britain were an unorganized collection of small groups who shared basic cultural characteristics but who were not of the same "people." They came from different tribes and differed in many details, nor did they recognize themselves as one people once they were living in England. Although there is no written history to confirm it, there is reasonable certainty that the Germanic immigrants at first fought with each other about as often as they fought the British. They were, after all, rivals for the same prize—possession of the land. Ultimately, the Anglo-Saxon domination of the Britons depended on the former's ability to find unity. They adapted to British conditions by adopting new kinds of ritual and legends that became shared and unifying experiences for all of them. The different groups sought symbolic and ritual ways through offering deposits and burials to link themselves and their ancestry to the new land rather than to their different places of origin in the homelands across the water. They insinuated themselves into the sacred spaces of the ancient Britons. They kept genealogies glorifying their forebears at the time of their arrival, but these lineages did not extend back before their arrival in Britain. They kept no remembered history before the migration. There was no going back.

COMMUNITIES AND KIN GROUPS

People are social beings and naturally form themselves into groups and communities. At the core of all relationships lies the family, and other patterns of relationship are based upon it. In the fifth and sixth centuries, no one had a sense of belonging to one large country encompassing the British Isles. Political units were much smaller. As already noted, after the departure of the Romans, the Britons abandoned the Roman form of administration and reformed approximately into their former tribal groups. As each group jockeyed for power and territory among themselves and a warrior elite eventually took over political leadership, small British kingdoms formed. Some of these were swallowed up by larger and more powerful British neighbors as the sixth century approached, but there was never adequate unification of the British people before the kingdoms succumbed, one by one, to Anglo-Saxon dominance in the seventh and eighth centuries. Then the tables turned again. The Anglo-Saxon kingdoms themselves had not yet fully unified when they were faced by powerful Viking raiders also seeking new lands beginning in the late eighth century.

For the ordinary Briton and Anglo-Saxon, the battles for conquest were something best avoided altogether. Life was mostly a matter of planting crops for food and providing for the family. The kingdoms and their warrior leaders were, more often than not, necessary annoyances that intruded only when revenues in crops and animals were being collected or when danger approached from outside. At such times, warriors were called upon to protect the people. Farmers also had no choice but to pick up their weapons and axes to defend their homes and villages. In all other respects, daily living involved a much smaller and more temperate circle of associations, obligations, and responsibilities. The average Briton and Anglo-Saxon depended on a broad network of family relatives—the kin group—to help her or him out when an extra hand in the field was needed or the family food supply ran dangerously short. What the family did not produce for itself had to be obtained through barter with neighbors or trade the occasional local market. For the average person, whatever goods or services could not be obtained in the immediate neighborhood had to be done without.

When the Saxons asserted themselves in eastern Britain, the displacement of eastern Britons to the western and southwestern parts of the country separated those fleeing danger from their personal networks of neighbors and kin. This separation must have been a hardship and could have made life more precarious for a while. As family members lost contact with each other, family identity naturally lost importance in the wider society. The identity of your father was no longer useful information since no one in your new location had known your father. Whereas men had formerly identified themselves as sons of their fathers, on fifth- and sixth-century memorial stones, texts began to emphasize places of origin, not patrilineages, as had been the tradition.

One man of Gwynedd was described on his memorial stone in Latin: "he was a citizen of Venedotia," the Latin name for Gwynedd. The intent of the text was to declare that this man moved to Gwynedd from far away and claimed his right to be counted among the people of Gwynedd. If he had been born in Gwynedd, the man would more likely be identified as a member of an established Gwynedd family. Also found in Gwynedd was the stone of a man who very likely fled Anglo-Saxon Northumbrian conquest of his former home in what had for a short while been the British kingdom of Elmet in the northeast. His stone states that he was "elmetiaco": he was an Elmetian still proud of his place of origin.[13] These memorial messages are indications of the breakdown of former British chiefdoms that had been based on well-known kinship and marriage relations. Movements of individuals away from their home territory made distant family relationships lose meaning and become altogether forgotten within a generation or two.

In a time of broken kinship networks, some people may have found a comforting substitute in Christian communities. Where could one turn as a lone rural farmer responsible for his wife and children and adrift in a strange landscape without reliable help from nearby brothers, uncles, and cousins in times of need? Christians had a tendency from the very beginning to treat the worship group as a surrogate family, and dislocated Britons appeared to have found the support they needed in the fellowship of Christian groups. From this perspective, the rapid late fourth- and fifth-century growth of Christianity in Britain is not at all surprising.

The Welsh saw an influx of Irish settlers from across the Irish Sea in the sixth century. The local population became substantially bilingual and ethnically diverse. They could even be described as trilingual, for some still remembered Latin. The people of Cornwall to the south received new Irish neighbors as well. Cornish archaeology shows that, in this part of Britain, new farmland was being taken from the forests and opened up for mixed farming—that is, for both the growing of crops and keeping of animals. The extra settlers required more land. The Welsh memorial stones show change as well. Some have inscriptions written in the older, traditional language of Latin with well-known memorial phrases such as *hic iacet* ("here lies…"), while the new, Irish-style stones bear vertical inscriptions and mimic the native ogham style of phrasing (see Chapter 7 for more on ogham script).[14] It appears that the Britons were accepting Irish immigrants into their lands without too much fuss.

Anglo-Saxon cemeteries in the early period exhibit a wide variety of burial customs. Some burials were marked with miniature houses built over them as if these were the homes in which the dead would live. Others were individually surrounded by ditches, while a small number of graves might be placed under earthen mounds. The mound seems to be the most prestigious of the burial customs, and it frequently signifies the presence of a rich burial. The central burial of the mound may also be directly surrounded by a group of burials that are possibly members of the same extended family. Archaeologists sometimes can determine kin-based groupings of graves in cemeteries.[15] These groups might take the form of tight, well-aligned rows of burials or other patterns that join the graves together. They may indicate family relationships among the dead or merely that a number of people had to be buried in quick succession due to a virulent and contagious illness in the region.

There are signs that Anglo-Saxon communities planned ahead for winter burial. It was difficult to dig a deep grave during the coldest part of winter when the ground was normally frozen. Ordinarily, the Anglo-Saxons had a habit of placing graves at a special orientation—that is, placing the head and the direction of the body in the grave according to a predetermined pattern. This practice was common throughout Europe. At Finglesham Cemetery in Kent, the excavators argued that all the graves are oriented toward the rising sun. Depending on the season of the year, the length-wise orientation of the new grave would vary according to the exact point on the horizon where the sun rose. A chart of the hundreds of grave orientations from Finglesham shows from the layout of the graves that this is a plausible explanation. There seems to be peaks in the number of graves dug in the early autumn and in the early spring. The excavators argued that the community, or each family as it chose, dug extra graves in the fall in anticipation of needing them during the winter. Other families or communities might have found themselves holding bodies aside until the ground softened and they could dig the necessary number of graves in the spring to catch up with their needs.[16]Thus, both times became busy seasons for grave diggers.

Studies of Anglo-Saxon family structure in the earliest centuries show that kinship relations were the strongest bonds in the whole society. Information from the laws and other written sources cannot properly explain early Anglo-Saxon society because the sources are much later than the post-Roman period and describe a much more complex society with many layers of personal statuses, from the king downward. The newer laws also contained many status-based obligations binding people who were not related as family. Anglo-Saxon mythology, including the legendary beginnings of the royal genealogies, suggests that important kin groups often believed themselves descended from a deity. All kin groups identified a common ancestor of special worth.[17] People, who did not otherwise know of a specific relationship between themselves but who shared the same common ancestor, would consider themselves related. Likewise, the living family male leader, or patriarch, held the highest status in the kin group. In recognition of their importance, the family patriarch and his wife were given considerably more wealth in their graves than other members of the same nuclear family.[18] It was a natural pattern in Anglo-Saxon society to grant greater status to the head of the group and also to his spouse. Similarly, children of important parents might be granted some status although they were too young to have any influence or to be known for any personal achievements. If a female child has been buried with valuable jewelry or a male child with weapons, then it must be concluded that these children were born into families of higher social rank, and the jewelry and weapons are there to demonstrate their inherited status.

Objects in the graves may also symbolize certain life transitions such as passage into adulthood or marriage. Females who were married would likely be treated differently in death than those who died maidens of marriageable age. Children and infants usually received less attention in death and might not even be given a proper burial at all. At some cemeteries, a particular style of brooch, called the saucer brooch, seemed to be associated only with mature, perhaps married, women. Girls were not given knives at death until they reached a certain age. Young boys very rarely had any sort of weapon unless their fathers held high status. Usually, only males approaching full adult stature were given weapons in burial. Some people were slaves or too impoverished and low status to be allowed any durable object of value in their grave. If they were given food offerings or objects made of organic materials such as cloth, leather, or wood, nothing would remain of these gifts after centuries of decomposition.

When inherited physical traits visible in skeletons have been studied, a correlation of physical traits with social status has sometimes been found. Those sharing the hereditary trait and judged to be related family members tended also to share the same inherited social status. At an Oxfordshire cemetery, individual males with one kind of skeletal trait, inherited within one elite family, were all buried with a set of weapons, while all the males with a different trait lacked weapons in their grave.[19]

The style of women's dress and the different kinds of dress fasteners, pins, and brooches, as well as other jewelry, were an important way to show membership in particular social or tribal groups. Men had identifiable traits of dress and ornament, too, but these were less obvious. Maintaining a specific style of dress would help social or occupational groups to identify themselves to one another. Family and tribal membership was an important part of one's identity and needed to be communicated, especially when traveling away from home—or to the otherworld. The larger society of all Anglo-Saxons depended on people being able to place themselves in relation to one another even if they were strangers. Regional comparisons of female graves have shown that the types of brooches and other dress fasteners mark not only the wearer's status but also her home area.[20] In this way, women who married far from their place of origin might stand out. Just as people today usually prefer to retain the style of dress and personal identity native to their place of origin, culture, or religion, Anglo-Saxons retained and broadcast identities through their regional styles.

PAGAN AND FOLK RELIGION

Druids

The members of the old Celtic priesthood were known to the Romans as the druids. As religious specialists, these men were local operators, not hierarchical as was the Catholic Church, but they probably had widespread links among themselves. Druids conducted rituals that were of great importance to the functioning of Celtic society. The British were one part of this Celtic society. The pre-Roman Celts depended on their religious leaders to keep the balance between the living world and the world of spirits. The druids were not so much like priests as they were like shamans: religious specialists found in many cultures who are able to communicate with the spirit world and do so on behalf of ordinary people. Such persons would know which sacrifices to perform to ensure that the crops, animals, and humans were all healthy and reproducing at a good rate. Sacrifices were made to keep the gods and spirits satisfied and benevolent. Requests given with offerings for good weather were made on schedule at the proper times, for no one could expect benevolence if people were inattentive to the gods. If something were wrong, if there were drought, or the cattle fell ill, the druids asked for advice and aid in putting matters right.

The Celtic druids were successors of earlier religious leaders who had constructed the stone megalithic monuments of northern and western Europe. Stonehenge in southern England is one of the best known of these monuments. We have long understood that some of these large megaliths dotting the landscape had both a calendrical and a ritual function. Each mid-summer, crowds still gather in awe and interest at Stonehenge in southern England to watch the sun rise over the heel stone. In fact, the stones of Stonehenge mark a number of calendric events throughout the year enabling the druids to know when to tell the farmers to sow seeds safely and when bringing in the harvest could no longer be delayed. These were life and death tasks that had to be done at the right time. However, the megaliths were not merely calendars. They were nothing less than the conduit for a divine message that the next phase in the cycle of life should begin.

What is to us the ordinary linear passage of time was to prehistoric people the miraculous annual rebirth of life on earth. They did not have our scientific certainty that this rebirth would naturally occur on schedule. For people who lived in the temperate parts of the globe that experienced the cycle of winter followed by summer, the rebirth of the landscape each year was a spiritually ordained event. Only those specialists who were trained to watch the changing stars and interpret the megalithic calendars could say when it was the right time to plant. Although any ordinary person might also watch for constellations in the sky and see all the myriad signs of spring, true knowledge came from the realm of deities and spiritual powers, and those who received it were the priests.

Spirits and Sacred Places

Celts observed their religious ritual out in nature—often at sacred springs, river banks, lake shores, and in wooded groves—anywhere far from the activity of ordinary daily life. For the Celts, sacred acts needed both distance and a natural environment. The spirits that belonged to these secluded, natural places were the opposite of humans in every way. They did not live in the temporal, waking world. They did not have recognizable forms or life histories. Sometimes, they did not even have gender, being neither male nor female, and their names might vary or be interchangeable with epithets or other descriptive phrases. Above all, they did not behave like humans or have any of the emotional motivations of humans.

Much information has been recovered from surviving stories of the beliefs of different groups of Celts, but there is room for argument about the exact meaning of their stories and symbols. While early Celts waited perhaps with just a little anxiety for the coming of spring, a luxuriant summer, and the hoped-for bountiful harvest, they also took steps to ensure that the spirits of nature remained supportive. Religious leaders would take a special seasonal consort, in a kind of ritual marriage. This act represented a union between the male power of virility and the female power of fertility and procreation. Such rituals based on sexuality and procreation would encourage the earth, and all that grew from it and lived upon it, to do likewise and be fertile.

Animal spirits played an important part in the Celtic universe. As in other cultures, some of the Celtic tribes had important animal spirit protectors. Such protectors are called totems by anthropologists. Tribal names recorded by the Romans reveal connections with animals that may have been the spiritual and protective totems relied upon by the members of the tribe: the Epidii were identified by name with the horse, the Bibroci with the beaver, and the Orci with the boar.[21] The people of these tribes would feel a special kinship with the horse, beaver, or boar spirit that represented not a single animal but all creatures of its kind. Furthermore, there might even have been an ancient belief that the people of the tribe descended from that same animal spirit.

In the spirit realm, humans found not only protection and their origin story but also reassurance of health and fecundity. The mother goddess was a most important figure standing not only for the fertility and well-being of humans, animals, and crops, but also often figuring as the ancestress of entire peoples. Other lesser spirits with similar, if less, encompassing responsibilities were oriented to specific places. There were deities for special types of landscape features: clearings or cultivated fields, exposed bedrock, river confluences, river fords, and fortified places. One name for the deity of fortified places was Dunatis. The Celtic names of rivers, lakes, and springs were names that identified the female spirits of each of these waters.

The Anglo-Saxon immigrants adopted many of these names and spirits. It may have been that the Germanic belief in similar spirits of nature led them to accept and respect these native spirits as real. The Anglo-Saxons changed the Celtic names of a number of places and locales to Germanic names, but the Celtic water names were frequently left untouched and have lasted to the present. In Christian times, the Welsh still had numerous holy "wells" that were natural springs of water—about 1,200 of these have been recorded. Many holy wells stood next to a sacred tree, an idea that was connected to the ancient and widespread cult of sacred trees. Special trees marked many of the sacred places of the Celtic world. The holy wells were transferred to associations with local saints and survived intact as Christian sacred places.

Hilltops and mountain summits were deemed sacred places because the land reached upward to the heavens. Such places were often dedicated to particular deities or spirits. These notions should cause us to rethink our entirely practical interpretation of hillforts and even the small fortlets that were constructed for single farm-steads. Did they serve another purpose besides being protective enclosures? The hill itself might have had a spiritual identity, and the warrior clan that held the place secure would have been in part dedicated to that same power. The otherworldly aura of hillforts gave the local leadership stronger authority to command the peas-ant folk around them, especially in times of danger when people were anxious for leadership and security. Even for post-Roman Christians, the old ideas would provide a comforting undercurrent to their religious beliefs. Christian doctrine was probably not well established or equally well understood everywhere, and Christian belief even among the most faithful harbored many so-called her-esies, as will be discussed below.

When the Romans brought their own gods to Britain, these gradually merged with the Celtic gods and spirits, but there were important differences in sacred spaces. Unlike the natural Celtic sanctuary placed distant from human activity, the Roman tem-ple was commonly built in an urban space. Temples defined and enclosed a sacred space within an urban area where a variety of people might attend. The temple used structural architecture to put boundaries on the sacred space—a far cry from the unbounded open-air space of Celtic sacred groves and clearings. Along with the temple architecture came statuary of anthropomorphic deities. Stone monuments, altars, and inscriptions completed the inorganic solidity of Roman sacred spaces. Roman religion had a much more solid and worldly aspect to it than did its Celtic counterpart. To the Romans, deities had distinct identities and appearances that were well known. They could be represented in stone in consis-tent ways, giving them a place in this world and a permanence among men. Roman deities had biographies and typical behav-iors that could be understood in human terms. By treating super-natural beings in this fashion, the Romans gained a measure of equality with them and some control over them, as well. To the un-Romanized Celt, this kind of solidity and control over the supernatural made no sense. The later Christians saw both Roman and Celtic religions as "pagan," but from the pagan perspective, not all pagans were alike.

The Romans knew better than to forbid the worship of native deities, for that kind of action would surely produce rebellion. Their primary goal was to make their conquered provincials as "Roman" as possible so that they would be more dependent upon and cooperative with the empire. Fortunately, Roman culture tolerated a diversity of religions. One ingenious means that the Romans used to tie a conquered people more closely to the Roman worldview was to equate Roman deities whenever possible with the native gods. As has been noted, the Celtic peoples of Britain and elsewhere did not originally endow their supernatural beings with strong personalities and vivid likenesses. These Celtic powers were spirits, disembodied for the most part, although they might occasionally be seen as male or female. They were the powers that inhabited rivers, hills, dense forests, the sun and moon, the storm clouds, and other aspects of the natural environment. Each of these aspects seemed to have a life force of its own. Yet, the Romans did have some success in drawing correlations.

Although it was no easy matter to make meaningful connections between Roman deities and Celtic spirits, a few combinations did work. Camulos, for example, was a kind of Celtic warrior god. His name was borrowed for Camulodunum, the Roman *civitas* that became modern Colchester. Some people today link this name to Camelot, the mythical seat of King Arthur's kingdom. Because of his warrior nature, he was linked to Mars (the Roman god of war). A sacrificial altar was found in Scotland with an inscription that reads "dedicated to the god Mars-Camulos." Worshipers of both Mars and Camulos could make use of this altar and its sacred environment.

Another connection is found in Maponus, a Celtic "divine youth" known for his beauty and probably representing some aspects of male virility. The "divine youth" figure was common in the classical and Celtic world. Maponus was connected by the Romans to their god Apollo, a similar sort of deity who probably once had more sexual overtones to his nature than is remembered in the popular, modern versions of his story. A current dictionary definition of Apollo declares that he was the god of healing, music, prophecy, and manly beauty—quite a mixed bag of attributes, but it is the last one that may be the original essence of the deity.

Sacred to both pre-Roman Celts and the Romans, the natural hot springs at Bath were frequented for healthful bathing and prayer. The Celtic goddess Sulis protected waters and offered health. The Roman goddess Minerva also possessed healing powers as well as governing wisdom and the arts. The Roman temple over the springs was built in the first century. (John Wallace/Dreamstime.com)

The female Celtic spirit named Sulis presided over the especially sacred, natural hot springs at Bath.[22] Many people wrote messages, prayers, and other supplications to her and then threw these words into her waters. Monuments to her from the Roman period link her name to the Roman Minerva, the goddess of wisdom and the arts but also, like Sulis and her waters, possessing healing powers.

The point of these three examples is that Romans devised the psychologically clever ruse of creating connections between the Roman culture and the native religious life of their new provincial citizens. This encouraged the Britons to feel themselves as part of the society that now dominated their lives. Within a few generations, it would leave an undeniably Roman imprint on the British self-image, particularly in the south and east of England where Roman control was greatest. Even if the leading British families remained the same, their continuing authority was now due to their Roman associations. Although most Britons still retained their gods into the third century, they started to think of them in a somewhat more Romanized way, carving stone monuments to them, making altars and inscriptions dedicated to them, separating them from the natural surroundings where they had originated by building temples of wood, if not of stone, and perhaps, in some quarters, taking them just a little bit for granted.

The general picture of religious change is peaceful, but some clues of turbulent religious change show up in the burials. Interpreting the finds is complicated. The religion of the late pagan Romano-British in the third and fourth centuries is a mixture of Celtic tradition and imported Roman cults, among which Christianity came late. The operative official policies of the time were recognition and tolerance of diversity. In this milieu, it is difficult to separate archaeologically the late pagans from the early Christians. In late Roman cemeteries, the common burial pattern consists of rows of plain burials without grave goods. Pagan cemeteries or burials did not have to be oriented east to west, like Christian graves, but they often were positioned this way for other reasons, so grave orientation is not a reliable clue to religious affiliation. The absence of grave goods might reflect that these people were early Christians, or it may simply mean that they and their surviving relatives were poor and could not afford to part with gifts of heirlooms for the dead. Food offerings, unless left in a pottery container, would not leave visible traces. Leaving gifts in Roman pagan graves may have been a practice that simply went out of fashion in the fourth century. For a long time, many archaeologists assumed that all row cemeteries without grave gifts must be late Roman and Christian. Research from the past several decades has opened up other possibilities. Such cemeteries may also be *late Roman and pagan* or *post-Roman and Christian*.

Lamyatt Beacon Romano-Celtic Temple

One burial site that shows a clear transition spanning the Romano-Celtic pagan period to the post-Roman Christian phase is Lamyatt Beacon, a hill in southeast Somerset in western Britain. Here, a Romano-Celtic temple, a number of votive deposits, and 13 out of 16 burials were excavated in 1973 after treasure hunters had done considerable damage to the site.

The construction of the temple is dated to the late third century on the basis of coin and pottery finds. Objects of later date show that it was used until the early fifth century. The central temple was skillfully built of cut stone and mortar, while other buildings at the site were constructed much more cheaply of timber. The temple had a roof made out of hexagonal slate tiles. In all, no expense was spared in either materials or workmanship in constructing the temple. Small niches were placed in the temple walls to hold statuettes or sculpted panels of gods. There was also one large freestanding stone statue of a god, probably Mars, the central deity of the temple. He is identifiable as Mars because of the tall shield at his left side.[23] Other gods depicted in stone or bronze at the temple were Apollo playing his lyre, bearded Jupiter, Mercury with his winged hat and shoes, Minerva holding a spear, and Hercules wearing a lion skin and holding a club.[24] The Roman god Mars was originally a god of war, but he became very popular with Celtic natives throughout the Roman world. Among the Celts, his character changed dramatically. Mars became a peaceful protector and even a healer.[25] At Lamyatt Beacon, however, Mars was still a Roman war god.

Mars and his Roman companions were not the only gods at Lamyatt Beacon. Among the votive deposits were discovered at least nine buried deposits of stag antlers. One pit containing antlers could be dated to the third century because it was underneath a building from that time. The meaning of the antlers is unclear, but they must be important because they occur at other sites as well. The excavator suggests that the antlers are connected in a roundabout way to the god Mars who was sometimes connected with the Celtic god Cernunnos. This god is believed to be the "the horned god" seen in numerous images, so-called because he was depicted with antlers coming out of his head. These images are as old as the fourth century BCE on the continent. The horned god had many animal and fertility connections and sometimes was depicted as triple-headed or three-faced. Sometimes, he is seen without his antlers, and some researchers believe that the antlers were part of a ritual that belonged to a particular part of the year. Sometimes, Cernunnos was shown with the ears or hooves of the stag as well. At other times, a snake was wrapped around his body. The snake is a common symbol of renewal, rebirth, and regeneration. Because the snake appears as a living thing crawling straight from the mud as if it was made out of the earth and because it can regrow damaged parts of its body, many cultures have used the snake as a symbol for the creation of life. Cernunnos, in his snake persona, is a fertility god protecting reproduction and abundance. Sometimes, Cernunnos is depicted with so many different kinds of animals that he is interpreted as a lord of animals.[26] Putting all this together, the antler deposits at Lamyatt Beacon suggest that a Celtic cult of Cernunnos was practiced there in connection with the Roman cult of Mars.

The temple of Mars and Cernunnos was situated to receive many visitors. Traces of a Roman road led straight to the temple site on Lamyatt Beacon. This road in turn connected to the major British thoroughfare called the Fosse Way. There is no clear evidence of the access road continuing beyond the temple, so it is possible that the road's only purpose was to enable visitors to reach the temple.[27] With such good public access provided to the site, religious activity at the temple must have been exceptionally high, at least during certain ritual events or festivals. Other similar temples exist in Somerset and nearby counties but never very near each other. Given the road access, the size of the site and its expensive construction, the statuary, and the mix of Roman and Celtic cults, the temple at Lamyatt Beacon must have served a large and diverse population from around the countryside during the third and fourth centuries.

The 13 burials tell us something of the people who lived at or near Lamyatt Beacon in later centuries. Only 12 of the burials excavated were identified by sex, and the results are lopsided: 11 females and 1 male. Two of the burials were radiocarbon dated to the sixth century and the eighth century, respectively. Radiocarbon test results can be corrupted by contaminated samples, so without further tests made, there is no knowing if the later date (or even the earlier date) is accurate. The placement of post-Roman burials at Romano-British temple sites is customary. Other examples of this behavior are seen in Wiltshire and at Maiden Castle in Dorset. The Christians of the fifth and sixth centuries behaved as if they wished to claim the sacred sites of previous pagan generations as their own.[28] This behavior mirrors the Anglo-Saxon burials on ancient barrows in the east and southeast. What is more curious is the excessive number of females. Even if the remaining four unexcavated burials were also male, this is a most unnatural sex ratio for an ordinary community. There are not enough burials here, nor comparable arrangements known from similar sites, so we really should not draw a firm conclusion. However, perhaps this small community represented an early monastic group that allowed both women and men, as the earlier communities sometimes did, but was mainly focused on female monastics.

PRE-AUGUSTINIAN (CELTIC) CHRISTIANITY IN BRITAIN

During the Roman period, Celts everywhere learned about Roman religious beliefs. They also were exposed to many other imported religions, particularly those from the East. Aside from the old Roman gods and the cult of worshiping the emperor as a god himself, Roman legionaries and auxiliaries in the British outposts, many of whom were foreigners from other far provinces, brought their own religions, including Christianity.

Christianity

At first, Christianity spread, if it can be said to have spread at all in any organized fashion, in a secretive and clandestine manner. The Romans tolerated any religion with only one proviso: the adherents must also acknowledge the emperor as a god. Only the Christians, of all followers of the diverse religions in the empire, were vocal in their refusal to do this one thing, and so they were the ones persecuted by the Romans. There were two reasons for this. The authorities at times charged the Christians as subversives trying to undermine the government with their refusal to worship the emperor. The general population, however, being mostly of the mind that worshiping many gods was the best insurance against calamity, was afraid of the Christians. These strange people insisted that there was only one true God, and they refused to acknowledge the others, even going out of their way to snub the other gods. Clearly, these insults offended all the other gods whose natural response would be to bring famine, disease, and manner of natural disaster to all people. This fear was pervasive throughout the empire by the third century, so when anything bad happened, the Christians were blamed.

Nevertheless, Christian ideas entered Britain in Roman times, even during the early centuries when it was not safe to be a Christian. Finds of pendants and other trinkets displaying Christian crosses, *chi-rho* designs representing Christ, and similar symbolism have been found. Yet, until the lifting of the imperial ban on Christianity in the early fourth century under Constantine, few professed his or her Christianity too publicly. And there were certainly no Christian churches for public gatherings. Gatherings of the faithful were held as quietly as possible in private places.

Eastern Mystery Religions

Another group of religions entering Britain were the so-called "mystery religions" from the east, characterized by elaborate symbolism and secret rituals or liturgies kept hidden from all but the select membership. These mystery religions were brought into Britain by mercenaries and other visitors from Middle Eastern and east

Mediterranean lands. The cults of Isis (from Egypt) and Mithras (from Persia) are two of the better known examples.

Many scholars will point out that early Christianity, in the form with which it came to Britain, also fits the definition of a mystery religion. Christianity had already developed a body of symbols associated with its beliefs, and services were conducted privately. Monastic communities of Christians did exist in the east, but these were not yet a part of western culture. Most Christians, especially in the west, were ordinary folk from the common lower classes. They had teachers who were versed in the scriptures and perhaps had possession of written texts from which they could read to the group. The initial organization of Christian clerical hierarchy was quite simple. "Bishops" followed in the footsteps of the apostles. The bishops taught and ordained priests, also called presbyters, who went about teaching and starting local groups of Christians, and the deacons were persons well versed in Christian beliefs who assisted the priests in various ways.

The Christian Church

The history of Christian persecution in the Roman Empire did not allow British Christians to feel safe in their own country until the latter half of the fourth century. During the reign of Emperor Flavius Valerius Constantinus, later called "Constantine the Great," lasting AD 306 until his death in AD 337, the tide turned dramatically in favor of Christians. Constantine's father was Constantius Chlorus who ruled as western Caesar under the preceding emperor Diocletian. In those days, the empire was ruled by separate eastern and western Caesars under the authority of the main emperor. As the Caesar of the Western Empire, Constantius resided in Eboracum, the Roman *civitas* in Britain that eventually became the city of York, and he was married to a British woman who was a Christian. Under his son, Constantine, the empire was once again united into one entity.

As emperor, Constantine changed many official policies including those on the management of religion. By the Edict of Milan, Constantine proclaimed general religious toleration and thereby freed the Christians from the former policy of official persecution. Constantine's efforts may have been less humanitarian and more oriented toward political stability for the empire at whatever the price. The Christians were a relatively small minority, but they were gathering increasing numbers of adherents. Constantine saw the state-sanctioned persecutions as divisive and destabilizing, and he himself publicly converted to Christianity, thus completing the reversal of Christianity's status within the empire. Once Christians were allowed freedom to worship, churches rapidly multiplied in the Roman towns and on villa estates.

As already observed, in late Roman times, at the temple of Sulis Minerva in Bath, visitors customarily wrote various requests, like prayers, on small rolls of lead and addressed these to the goddess. The rolls were then thrown into the waters of the hot spring. Fourth-century texts from these rolls reveal the coexistence of pagan and Christian belief without either dominating the other. One request, or curse, depending on your perspective, found in Sulis's waters came from a certain Annianus. He asked Sulis-Minerva, " 'Whether pagan or Christian whosoever...has stolen from me...six silver coins from my purse, you, lady goddess are to extract...the blood of him who has invoked this upon me' Annianus, son of Matutina wrote this curse."[29] Since Annianus used the word "pagan," scholars suspect that he was implying himself to be a Christian, for the word is only known to have been used by Christians in describing non-Christians.

The Celtic Church

By the post-Roman period in Britain, the Roman Catholic Church and its administrative organization was already beginning to take shape throughout the Mediterranean world, but the spiritual lives of Christians in the remote land of Britain, although free from persecution if not the occasional prejudice, remained community-centered and relatively unhampered by any larger, centralized earthly authority. It was not until the mission of St. Augustine of Canterbury sent by Pope Gregory I arrived in Kent in AD 597 that the authority of Rome established a first firm foothold in Britain. By that time, the homegrown ways of the Celtic Church were comfortably established in Cornwall, Wales, Ireland, and the Celtic north.

Signs of early Christian communities appear in Britain although the character of the communities is impossible to describe with clarity. Although most archaeologists today believe the site of Tintagel to have been mainly devoted to trade, excavations in the yard at Tintagel of a parish church have revealed some very early communal activity. Fifth-century burials—two in slate-lined graves and two under stone-and-earth burial mounds—along with a stone memorial pillar of unknown purpose and imported Mediterranean pottery show that fifth- and sixth-century Christians might have worshiped and buried their dead here. An enclosure around the cemetery may have been added in the late sixth century, giving it a resemblance to a number of known seventh- and eighth-century Christian community enclosures.[30] Since the site of this activity was later occupied by a parish church, it is reasonable to assume that the church location was chosen following a continuous tradition of worship on this spot. The early medieval British Christians who worshiped here may have lived here or come from nearby.

By the latter part of the sixth century, the kingdoms of the Britons are reputedly all Christian to some degree, or at least in name. Rheged, including Cumbria in the northwest corner of modern England, was Christian and alleged to have a monastic community at Whithorn founded by St. Ninian (a claim neither proven nor disproven by modern excavation). The people of Gododdin near Edinburgh were Christian. The Strathclydians had their founder saint, Kentigern, and a possible Christian community near the site of Glasgow's current cathedral.[31] The fifth and sixth centuries were a time of small-scale local organization for both Christianity and the Britons.

The most convincing signs of Christian belief are found on the memorial stones commemorating the important dead. The sixth-century memorial stone to Voteporix, king of Demetia (i.e., Dyfed), gives his name along with the archaic Roman title of "protectoris" and the symbol of the Celtic Christian cross in a circle. The message is written in both Latin and ogham.[32] Crosses or *chi-rho* symbols are obvious indicators of Christian affiliation, and the oldest memorial stones displaying these signs can be dated no earlier than AD 500. Prior to that time, overt signs of Christianity are not found on memorial stones although other clues suggest that Christianity was already spreading. References to Christians and Christian behavior, such as in the curse at Bath and the possible worship site at Tintagel, make this clear. The older memorial stones, from the fifth century and earlier, continued to be made following Roman custom with only Latin words and traditional phrases explaining the purpose of the stone. It cannot be said with certainty, but the effect of Irish immigration resulting in the meeting of the Irish Christian tradition with the British could have stimulated the innovation of including Christian symbols on memorial stones.

Not only death was marked by Christian symbolism and ritual. Written sources indicate that infant baptism for Christian families was becoming a common sacrament even in the fifth century.[33] Little else can be said about the practice. No surviving baptismal font in Britain is older than the seventh century.

Wherever there are remains of a church today that may have existed in an earlier form as far back as the seventh century, archaeologists often detect fifth- and sixth-century burials near or under the later structure. Religious sites did not often move from sites held sacred in earlier centuries. As at Tintagel, these same churches were likely to be rebuilt and made the parish churches of medieval times.

On the other hand, lesser sacred sites were abandoned. In Kirkcudbrightshire, southwestern Scotland, an enclosed cemetery, dated ca. AD 700, produced four graves oriented east to west in a row, a small rectangular stone oratory for religious devotions, and a round cell, or living hut. The arrangement reveals a snapshot of a local Christian community. Perhaps, only one person lived in this cell and performed regular religious observances in the oratory, but people would come for guidance and prayers and to participate in special services. A small number of dead were buried here. The number is so small that perhaps these were only the people who participated in the regular religious activities of the oratory: when one died, another stepped forward to replace him. The local population might have visited for guidance or blessing but seemed to have been buried elsewhere.[34]

A number of these small stone churches with a small group of graves nearby and perhaps a little round cell for a living inhabitant have been found, but none can be securely dated before the eighth century. There are several likely possibilities for Christian gathering places prior to the stone churches that are a century later than the time we are attempting to capture in this book. Christian gatherings likely had no permanent location but occurred in homes or some other building generally intended for another purpose. People could even gather in a convenient open outdoor location. Some itinerant Christian teachers, the forerunners of official priests but without any assigned church of their own, may have adopted the lifestyle of wandering from settlement to settlement to preach while receiving food and shelter in return. In that regard, if nothing else, they functioned as itinerant storytellers and entertainers. On the other hand, the earliest churches might have been built no differently than the ordinary homes of people—huts made out of wattle and daub on a timber frame. Such buildings would be round or rectangular just like all other structures, and their remains would be impossible to distinguish as religious meeting places.

EARLIEST MONASTIC COMMUNITIES

There are more hints of Celtic monasteries or religious communities in existence in the sixth century. One surviving record suggests that someone named "Constantine" went to live in a monastery in AD 589. Knowledge of Latin survives among some people, and logic tells us that Latin learning could only be maintained by the presence of Christian communities promoting theological study. Scraps of historical references suggest that there were urban bishops (*episcopus de civitate*) in York, Cirencester, London, and Lincoln already in the fourth century. These bishops must have at least led congregations within their cities, but they might also have headed up a network of rural connections in the surrounding countryside. In the fifth century, British bishops argued at councils in favor of the Pelagian doctrine (discussed below), and they had theological allies in Gaul. In the mid-fifth century, Patrick, who was made a bishop not by Rome but by the British Church, was sent to Ireland to convert all the peoples of that island. He later was made their patron saint. These simple facts taken from records of the period give a much more solid picture of early British Christianity than the archaeology alone can present.

Gildas had a reputation among his contemporaries as an expert on monasticism. One seventh-century writer told how Gildas was consulted "on the subject of monks who leave their monastery to seek a stricter discipline." Gildas stated a preference for moderate rather than extreme asceticism. It is believed that his reply is preserved in part in some of the *Fragmenta* of his writings.[35] In the second of the collected fragments, Gildas observed that those who practiced severe abstinence and deny themselves either meat or conveniences put themselves in danger of feeling superior to their brethren: "To these men death enters by the windows of pride."[36] Gildas might be responding to a sixth-century British monastic movement emphasizing an extreme restriction of food, shelter, and behavior in response to a prevailing belief that the clergy of earlier decades had been too corrupt and given to excess.

The archaeological signs of early monasticism are limited. In Caerwent (Venta Silurum), there are four stone buildings that archaeologists believe might be the reputed sixth-century monastery founded by the Irish saint Tathan.[37] Excavations at Glastonbury Abbey near the Tor in Somerset revealed a wattle-and-daub church and other similar buildings interpreted as oratories. The entire arrangement resembled early Irish monastic sites and has been dated to the late sixth or early seventh century. One associated find was identified as a copper censer, a container for burning incense, of eastern Mediterranean origin. The Christians at Glastonbury had trade connections with the Mediterranean and had the opportunity to obtain not only objects but also religious ideas from the eastern Byzantine Church.[38] Other sites in the British southwest, including Tintagel and Gateholm, were thought in the past to be early monastic sites, but current opinion is less certain.

Hagiographies, or saints' lives, called *vitae* in Latin, often tell stories of saints who came to live at or found monasteries in the early centuries. According to his *vita*, St. Petroc (or Pedrog) was born the son of a Welsh prince near the end of the fifth century. Educated in Ireland, he served as a missionary, spreading the faith. Around AD 518, he returned to Britain and settled in Cornwall, possibly bringing with him a group of Irish Christians. First, he settled at a monastery at Padstow, and then he built his own religious community at Bodmin, a place where a holy hermit named Guron already lived.

In Wales, other saints moved about the countryside as missionaries. The patron saint of Wales was David. St. David's *vita* gives the impression that large areas of Wales were determinedly pagan, especially where the tribe of the Deisi had settled. Some scholars believe that the *vita* of St. Bridget demonstrates that druids were still at work and influential in parts of Wales at the end of the fifth century when she was young. The tyrant Maelgwn of Gwynedd was said by Gildas to have had a great teacher (in spite of Maelgwn's corrupt behavior). The teacher is widely believed to have been Illtud. Saint Illtud's *vita* declares that "he was the most learned of all the Britons," and in the course of his life, he founded a monastery and became its abbot. Illtud's story provides an example of the common practice of married men taking on a monastic career. Before embarking on his monastic career, Illtud obtained his wife's permission to become celibate, and she in turn adopted a woman's ascetic life by moving to a cell in the mountains and devoting her life to assisting widows and the poor. The saints' lives suggest that a number of women became anchoresses in this fashion.[39]

In Scotland, much the same process took place. In Galloway, southwestern Scotland, a religious community appears to have been founded in the fifth century near Whithorn (only this later Saxon name for the place is documented). Here, St. Ninian is claimed to have established the first Celtic monastic community. Traces of buildings that could have been Ninian's monastery were uncovered in a 1990s excavation. Bede wrote that Ninian had studied in

Rome and was a "most holy man," probably also implying with this phrase that he was untainted by heresy since he had studied proper Christianity in Rome. Bede explained that Ninian built a stone monastery at Whithorn, and scholars today suspect that Bede got his information from his friend Bishop Pechthelm of Whithorn where the story of St. Ninian was already a strong tradition.

One of the best-known early saints was St. Columba of Iona. His origin was Irish. He was born in County Donegal in AD 521 as a prince of the royal Ui Neill family. He might have become high king of Ireland had he taken a different path in life. Columba studied

Appearing on a standing stone and accompanied by an encircled Chi-Rho cross, this early memorial text dated ca. AD 500 was found at the ancient Christian site of Whithorn in Galloway, Scotland. Known as the Kirkmadrine Stone, its inscription refers to two "holy and distinguished priests" (*sancti et praecipui sacerdotes*) who were named Viventius and Mavorius. The stone has been offered as proof that officiating Christian priests were practicing in a religious community at Whithorn in the sixth century. (G. Baldwin Brown. *The Arts in Early England*. London: John Murray, 1921)

under several scholars and was ordained priest in Dublin. At the age of 41, he left Ireland for Iona, an island off the west coast of Scotland. It is said that he forced the women living on Iona to leave the island so that he could found an all-male monastery there in AD 563. Eventually, other monastic foundations in mainland Scotland copied the rule of the Iona house.

There are other signs of early Christian communities throughout Scotland. A memorial stone at Kirkmadrine, erected ca. AD 500, tells of Viventius and Mavorius, *sancti et praecipui sacerdote*, a phrase that can be translated as "the holy and outstandingly excellent bishops." Two such bishops would surely have a community surrounding them. Some believe the collective evidence of the memorial stones demonstrates that Christianity spread, if it did not dominate, throughout the northern British kingdoms from about AD 450 to 550. The more southerly of the Pictish population had contact with the Christian Gododdin of Scotland. Christians among the southern Picts claimed that Ninian was responsible for their conversion.[40]

Hermits

Hermits, or anchorites (female anchorites were called anchoresses), were another group who sought greater spirituality through isolation. In parts of the Mediterranean world, particularly Egypt, people who sought to live a holy Christian life thought that the best means to reaching a pure state would be to depart from society and live in a desolate landscape, such as the desert, where there would be no distractions from contemplation. Anchorites rarely lived in complete isolation, for they might receive visitors, especially those who were in need of spiritual help or healing. Anchorites differed from true monks in two ways. One, they sought to be solitary, while monks lived in communities and pursued many tasks as a group. Two, the lives of anchorites had no prescribed activities; they could do as and when they wished, whereas monks lived according to a rule and had to follow strict daily routines of work, learning, and religious observances. Eremitism (living as a hermit) spread in the West beginning in the fourth century as various writings of famous churchmen and certain hagiographies highlighted its goals and values.

In the West and in northern Europe, the isolated life of the desert was replaced by isolation in the forest, in fens and marshlands, and on uninhabited islands. There are legends of Irish monks sailing way beyond the known world in search of an isolated place to contemplate God, and some were evicted from Iceland when the first Vikings arrived there in the late ninth century. St. Benedict of the monastery at Monte Cassino in Italy wrote in his famous Rule, which has governed all Benedictine monastic houses down to the present day, that only monks who had first learned in the monastic community how to fight against the devil and resist temptation would be ready to go out alone and be anchorites. Benedict wisely saw the solitary life of the anchorite as more demanding than the communal existence of the monk or nun.

There is no way of knowing how many early Britons chose to live the life of anchorite or anchoress, but the written sources suggest that there were many. These were people who chose to embrace poverty and devote themselves to prayer and setting an example for other people. They received visitors who wished to be taught, healed, or receive advice. Those visitors with some means would leave gifts of food and other necessities. The nearby presence of a holy person was highly valued by the common people of the countryside who might believe that the holy person's prayers would bring special favor to all who lived near and looked after him or her.

HERESIES

Heresies are any set of religious beliefs that the church leadership or faithful majority deems to be wrong. In the first few centuries of Christianity, there was considerable confusion about what was and was not correct. Even the acceptable books of scripture, and their exact texts, were disputed. Councils of bishops were called at various times and places to discuss and decide the details of certain doctrines. This process continues today, but in the early centuries AD, there were many big questions to debate and decide, including the true nature of Jesus himself and what was required to obtain salvation. Occasionally, a set of doctrines was widely promoted and followed by many adherents before a church council decided to strike it down as heresy. To be a heretic (i.e., one who believes in a heresy), you would have to have once been an "insider"—a proper Christian who was then charged with having left the fold due to willful, improper belief. It was worse to be a heretic than a pagan.

The Church knew that disagreements about the core beliefs of Christianity could not be allowed. If differing points of view were permitted, the Church would quickly splinter into fragments as small groups decided on their own interpretations of scripture. The Church could not have power without being united under one set of doctrines and one hierarchy of authority. Only its leadership, following correct bureaucratic procedures, could decide doctrinal questions and organize the faithful so that they may follow the true path. If a heresy was found, defined, and judged false, then it had to be stamped out quickly and with force so that people would understand and accept its wrongness. There was no room for compromise. The crime of committing heresy—merely believing in heretical teachings—became punishable by death, according to a decision handed down in AD 380.

While the Church in Rome was initially tightening its hold on doctrine, the Christians of Britain were still too geographically remote to feel the effect. For a time, they enjoyed the dangerous freedom to develop their church and doctrine according to their own preferences and with little effective oversight from Rome. This freedom ended with the advent of St. Augustine's mission sent by Pope Gregory. From a modern perspective, it is surprising that Celtic and Roman Christianity remained so much alike. The British bishops, in fact, were never unaware of broader developments on the continent, and they did participate in a number of episcopal councils held on the continent. Nevertheless, the British clergy did not feel pressured to conform to the ideas and ways of the Roman Church until the sixth century.

Pelagianism

The principle heresy found in Britain during the post-Roman Arthurian decades is Pelagianism. Pelagius, who died in AD 418, was a British-born monk who taught a rigorous morality and a strong regard for law. It is an irony that his teachings became heresy. He allegedly believed that humans could discipline themselves, and by their own force of will, achieve their salvation. Since none of his own writings have been preserved—and none of his students' writings, if any existed, have been preserved—scholars have pieced together the content of Pelagianism from hints in various sources.

Pelagius thought that all Christians needed to take the dictates of scripture more seriously. Baptism was supposed to be a kind of rebirth. All Christians should seek perfection; perfection was not just the monks. Pelagius disagreed with Augustine of Hippo who wrote in his *Confessions* that humans must necessarily and inevitably sin even after baptism.[41] For Pelagius, this attitude was a kind of pagan fatalism. Instead, humans should be held individually responsible for their own morality.

Pelagius had numerous supporters, but too many Christians were not prepared to make the level of commitment in their lives that he demanded. Church leaders likewise had low expectations of ordinary Christians. Pelagius's opponents preached that humans were controlled by the divine will. It is difficult to say exactly what Pelagius believed because most of his ideas were recorded by his enemies, particularly Augustine. Because his ideas quickly fell out of favor, no one wrote a proper biography of Pelagius.

Pelagius has often been accused of denying that grace or divine will had any importance, but this is not true. God gave humans a sense of right and wrong and the will to choose. Grace and divine will existed beyond those capacities. Grace was the revelation of God's purpose, which humans must seek. This was not the same as Pelagius's demand that humans seek perfection. Pelagius's opponents accused him of overestimating the human ability to distinguish good and evil and make correct choices. In AD 412, that opposition gained force when one of Pelagius's followers was accused of promoting false teachings, including that Adam was created mortal and would have died whether or not he had sinned and that infants at birth are in the same state that Adam was in before he committed his sin. These teachings and others conflicted with the accepted doctrine of original sin. After this event, Pelagius had to defend himself against increasingly vocal critics.[42] He died or was excommunicated (there is disagreement over what became of Pelagius) ca. AD 418, but other prominent members of the Church tried still to defend his teachings. They lost the struggle after the condemnations against Pelagius made by the Council of Orange in AD 429, the same year that Germanus of Auxerre visited Britain.

In AD 429 and 431, Bishop Germanus of Auxerre and Palladius were both sent separately to Britain to seek out and pursue heretics. Some argue that Palladius was sent to convert the Irish, but there was a large element of combating heresy in the instructions given to both missionaries. Heresy was a more dangerous problem than paganism, for all the reasons cited above. And if Germanus had meant to preach to the common people like a missionary, he would have communicated in the British language. As it was, he did not know or bother to learn British and only spoke Latin. Germanus's search for heresy required only that he speak with the elites of British society where his Latin would be understood.

A monk by the name of Agricola was spreading Pelagianism throughout Britain at the time. Pelagius himself spent these years in Rome and in the Holy Land. Bishop Germanus approached the leading Pelagians of British society intending to make them see the error of their ways and to instruct them in the need to submit to the doctrines of Rome. The bishop's biographer, Constantius, described these meetings with the British Pelagians and could not resist observing that the Pelagians were wealthy and well dressed. Apparently, this showed that they were not sufficiently devout. In fact, Constantius's description of their dress, houses, and towns is often used as primary evidence for the vigorous survival of the Romano-British lifestyle, even two decades after the disappearance of Roman authority. Germanus's visit seems to have centered on the *civitas* of Verulamium (later the city of St. Albans) in Hertford-shire, East Anglia. If accurate, the recorded history of Bishop Germ-anus in Britain presents a picture of a still-thriving fifth-century Romano-British society undeterred by the German mercenaries in their midst. British Christians were still confident in their way of life and their religious choices.

There are hints in the sources that Britons resisted Roman author-ity over what was judged to be correct Christian doctrine. First seen historically in the confrontation with Germanus, leading Britons were concerned about maintaining a unified and organized British countryside capable of defending itself against barbarian invaders. British Christianity helped to unify the former province made up of many political rivals. When Bishop Augustine came to Canterbury in AD 597, as a representative of Pope Gregory, he experienced a similar resistance from Britons still holding to the vision of a uni-fied and independent British Christian land.

ANGLO-SAXON CHRISTIANITY

For the duration of the post-Roman period, the Anglo-Saxons felt very little attraction to Christianity and its beliefs. In religious and all other ways, they demonstrated a desire to be different and to avoid adopting British language, manner of government, and any other aspect of culture, nor did the Celtic Church attempt to con-vert them.

Anglo-Saxons in Winchester

For the most part, the early Anglo-Saxons stayed in the rural areas, but gradually they took over some of the less-occupied or aban-doned urban areas. One of the Roman towns that experienced a more severe fifth-century collapse than most is Venta Belgarum (modern Winchester). Venta Belgarum later became the capitol of Anglo-Saxon Wessex and arguably the first capitol of England, but in the fifth century, it had fallen into rapid decay. Only a small group of people remained living there. Archaeologists have found former streets blocked by new houses and other domestic buildings, while old Roman structures were unoccupied and in ruins. Such odd behavior may have been due to wet weather conditions making drainage a problem: the street surfaces were the driest available. Or perhaps, the people just preferred their traditional style of architecture. Later in the fifth century, the large south gate built of stone collapsed into the street, but the continuing traffic simply went over the rubble rather than clearing it away or attempting to repair it. No one was in charge of maintaining the town's facilities—there was no effective town government; it was just a place occupied by residents and those who passed through.

Winchester continued to be occupied in this fashion. By the end of the sixth century, all but two of the city gates allowing access through the still-standing Roman walls were deliberately blocked. The residents were creating a defensive fort out of a Roman town. Judging from the distribution of Anglo-Saxon pottery, most of the occupants during the post-Roman centuries were Anglo-Saxon, and if anything, their numbers increased over time.[43] Anglo-Saxons were not at all accustomed to maintaining public buildings or managing larger populations in towns. Towns required public maintenance and administration. The Roman way of gaining popular support by providing good streets, drainage and sanitation, market spaces, governmental institutions, temples, and recreational areas was foreign to the Anglo-Saxons. Their haphazard use of urban space was not so much a sign of general disorder as merely an indication of the more individualistic way that the Anglo-Saxons preferred to occupy spaces. They carved up Winchester into individual lots with complete disregard for the existing structure and organization, but it suited them.

There is no sign of Christianity in Winchester's urban space or in the surrounding cemeteries. The Anglo-Saxons remained clearly pagan in their beliefs. Christianity came to them in the seventh century by decree from the ruling families of the newly forming Anglo-Saxon kingdoms. After Augustine brought the idea of an English Church whose hierarchy and theology would reinforce the authority of the infant Anglo-Saxon kingdoms, Christianity spread rapidly through the upper class of Anglo-Saxon society. The process began in the southeast in Kent but moved quickly to the West Saxons in their kingdom, which was known as Wessex. Winchester lay at the heart of Wessex, and the first minster church of Winchester was founded by the mid-seventh century.

Alliance of Rome and England

What brought Christianity to the Anglo-Saxons, in part, was the prior foundation of Christianity among the Britons that enabled the conversion of their enemies in the seventh century. As already seen, the British Church was well enough evolved and organized to clash forcefully with the Roman Church when Augustine brought his demands to Britain just before the seventh century. From Bede, we read how the missionary Augustine, after meeting with the Anglo-Saxon king in Kent, went west to meet with the British bishops. Here he wanted to persuade them to abandon the errant ways of the Celtic Church that no longer matched Rome's rules. There were a number of doctrinal differences, but one large source of conflict was the calculation of the date of Easter.[44] Having failed to convince the British bishops by argument, Augustine proposed a kind of spiritual power challenge: both sides would try to heal a blind man through prayer. First, the British bishops failed; then Augustine succeeded, according to Bede who is telling the story from the side of the alleged winners. Still, the Britons insisted on consulting first with their own people, and Augustine prophesied their defeat.

Whether or not this story is pure legend, Bede has told us that the bishops of Britain had a well-established church and their own way of observing the Christian liturgical calendar. That this memory is linked clearly to Augustine's arrival means that it is well dated and more likely to be an accurate account in general terms, if not in the specifics. In other words, Augustine tried to order the British bishops to submit to the rule of Rome, but they refused. The British Church was used to its independence. Despite the vagueness of archaeological information concerning the early church in Britain, we can be confident from Bede's words that a fully organized church had developed in Britain by the end of the sixth century. Since the fourth century, the British Christians had been able to go their own way, and they resented being told after so many generations that they were, in essence, doing it wrong and would have to take orders from Rome.

British defiance of the Roman Church led to Augustine's (and Rome's) alliance with the willing Anglo-Saxons who undoubtedly recognized a power alliance opportunity when they saw one. Augustine could more easily exert his missionary effort over these Germanic people who were not yet converted. The Anglo-Saxon kingdom of Kent was taking form and provided an ideal political and economic framework for the Roman Church to enhance in order to gain a foothold in Britain. Since the Anglo-Saxons felt a long-standing antagonism to British ways and ideas, they would also be attracted to an opposing form of Christianity. This road took the Anglo-Saxon kings far along their way to becoming kings recognized in the company of the rulers of continental Europe. An alliance with Rome put the Anglo-Saxons on the global political stage, while the Britons became history and legend.

NOTES

1. Heinrich Härke, "Kings and Warriors: Population and Landscape from Post-Roman to Norman Britain," in *The Peopling of Britain: The Shaping of a Human Landscape,* edited by Paul Slack and Ryk Ward (Oxford: Oxford University Press, 2002), 145–175.

2. György Acsádi and János Nemeskéri, *History of Human Life Span and Mortality* (Budapest, Hungary: Akadémiai Kiadó, 1970), 227–231.

3. Charlotte A. Roberts and Keith Manchester, *The Archaeology of Disease,* 3rd ed. (Ithaca, NY: Cornell University Press, 2005).

4. Malcolm Todd, " 'Famosa Pestis' and Britain in the Fifth Century," *Britannia* 8 (1977): 321.

5. Malcolm, "Famosa Pestis," 323.

6. Härke, "Kings and Warriors," 148.

7. J. R. Maddicott, "Plague in Seventh-Century England," *Past and Present* 156, no. 1 (August 1997): 7–54.

8. Martin Biddle, "Winchester," in *Ancient Europe 8000 B.C.–A.D. 1000, Encyclopedia of the Barbarian World,* edited by Peter Bogucki and Pam J. Crabtree, Vol. 2 (New York: Charles Scribner's Sons, The Gale Group, 2004), 501–507.

9. Deborah J. Shepherd, *Funerary Ritual and Symbolism: An Interdisciplinary Interpretation of Burial Practices in Late Iron Age Finland,* BAR International Series No. 808 (Oxford: British Archaeological Reports, 1999), 33, 34.

10. Sally Crawford, "Votive Deposition, Religion and the Anglo-Saxon Furnished Burial Ritual," *World Archaeology* 36, no. 1 (2004): 88.

11. Charles W. Kennedy, trans., *Beowulf, the Oldest English Epic,* Vol. 2 (Oxford: Oxford University Press, 1968), 30–53.

12. Howard Williams, "Monuments and the Past in Early Anglo-Saxon England," *World Archaeology* 30, no. 1 (1998): 104.

13. Charles Thomas, *Celtic Britain; Ancient Peoples and Places Series* (London: Thames and Hudson, 1986), 51.

14. Thomas, *Celtic Britain,* 115.

15. Shepherd, *Funerary Ritual and Symbolism,* 18, 19.

16. Martin Welch, *Discovering Anglo-Saxon England* (University Park: Pennsylvania State University Press, 1992), 74, 75.

17. C. J. Arnold, *An Archaeology of the Early Anglo-Saxon Kingdoms,* 2nd ed. (New York: Routledge, 1997), 177.

18. Welch, *Discovering Anglo-Saxon England*, 82.

19. Arnold, *An Archaeology of the Early Anglo-Saxon Kingdoms*, 189.

20. Arnold, *An Archaeology of the Early Anglo-Saxon Kingdoms*, 190.

21. Thomas, *Celtic Britain*, 28.

22. Thomas, *Celtic Britain*, 26.

23. Roger Leech, Martin Henig, Frank Jenkins, et al., "The Excavation of a Romano-Celtic Temple and a Later Cemetery on Lamyatt Beacon, Somerset," *Britannia* 17 (1986): 270–272, 274.

24. Leech et al., "The Excavation of a Romano-Celtic Temple," 276, 277.

25. Miranda J. Green, *Dictionary of Celtic Myth and Legend* (London: Thames and Hudson, Ltd., 1992), 140.

26. Green, *Dictionary of Celtic Myth and Legend*, 60, 61.

27. Leech et al., "The Excavation of a Romano-Celtic Temple," 272.

28. Leech et al., "The Excavation of a Romano-Celtic Temple," 274.

29. "Roman Baths Museum," *Museums Libraries Archives: Discovering UK Collections*, http://www.cornucopia.org.uk/html/search/verb/GetRecord/2963. Compare Jean Manco, "*Aquæ Sulis* to *Aquæmann*," *Bath Past: Saxon, December 5, 2004*, http://www.buildinghistory.org/bath/saxon/aquaemann.shtml.

30. Christopher Snyder, *An Age of Tyrants, Britain and the Britons, A.D. 400–600* (University Park: Pennsylvania State University Press, 1998), 187.

31. Thomas, *Celtic Britain*, 99.

32. Thomas, *Celtic Britain*, 51.

33. E. A. Thompson, *Saint Germanus of Auxerre and the End of Roman Britain* (Woodbridge, UK: The Boydell Press, 1984), 18.

34. Thomas, *Celtic Britain*, 137.

35. Snyder, *Age of Tyrants*, 126.

36. Text transcribed by Roger Pearse, Ipswich, UK, 2003 from Hugh Williams, *Gildas*, Part I, Cymmrodorion Record Series No. 3 (London: Published for the Honourable Society of Cymmrodorion by David Nutt, 1899), http://www.tertullian.org/fathers/gildas_04_letters.htm

37. Snyder, *Age of Tyrants*, 153.

38. Snyder, *Age of Tyrants*, 178.

39. Daniel J. Mullins, *Early Welsh Saints*, trans. from Welsh by Harri Pritchard Jones (Llanrwst, UK: Gwasg Carreg Gwalch, 2003), 13–19.

40. Thomas, *Celtic Britain*, 99, 100.

41. Robert L. Wilken, "Pelagius," in *Encyclopedia of Religion*, 2nd ed., editor-in-chief Lindsay Jones (Detroit, MI: Macmillan Reference USA, 2005), 7025, 7026.

42. Wilken, "Pelagius," 7025, 7026.

43. Biddle, "Winchester," 504, 505.

44. The story of the Easter controversy is best known from Bede's *Historia Ecclesiastica Gentis Anglorum*, Book 3, Chapter 25. http://classiclit.about.com/library/bl-etexts/bede/bl-bede-3-25.htm

GLOSSARY

Abbeys—According to many sources, any community, where monks or nuns live together under a communal rule governing duties, behaviors, and worship, may be called a monastery. If any difference between a monastery and an abbey is recognized, it is usually one of degree. An abbey is a larger, more influential monastery controlling lands and properties. The term "abbey" is most commonly used within the Benedictine Order.

Alloys—Alloys are formed by mixing together two or more metals. The first metal used in antiquity for making things was copper. This metal was soft enough to be pounded and shaped cold. When melted and mixed with a small amount of tin, a technique first developed in the third millennium BCE, copper became bronze, a considerably harder metal capable of being turned into a usable knife or weapon. Bronze could also be molded into intricate ornaments and became the basis for many pieces of jewelry. Special accessories were covered in silver or gold gilt. Although bronze oxidized in time and developed a green patina, it did not rust like iron. On the other hand, when iron technology was mastered and iron became available, around the 7th century BCE in northern Europe but as early as the 13th century BCE in Asia Minor, its far greater strength made it the preferred metal for tools and weapons. Other alloys exist including a combination of silver and gold used in early coinage and called *electrum*.

Anglo-Saxon, Saxon, German, and Germanic—To avoid confusion, this book uses the term "Anglo-Saxon" for all persons and cultural materials of German origin found in Britain after the mid-fifth century AD. The term "Anglo-Saxon" is used in this book in preference over "Saxon" because it is conceptually more inclusive. The first Germans came from different German territories and are best not described by the name of one particular group even though that name is shorter and more convenient. Other books sometimes use simply "Saxon" as a synonym of Anglo-Saxon. The term *"Germanic"* is a linguistic term and refers to the language of the Germans rather than to the people or their culture.

Archaeology (sometimes spelled, Archeology)—Archaeology as an academic discipline comprises the method and theory behind the excavation out of the ground and analysis of past material culture. Today, excavation does not take place until a clear research design has been developed. Archaeologists are trained to utilize the field methods best applicable to different landscapes and research questions. Modern archaeology enlists many kinds of laboratory techniques to help glean additional information from objects and structural features in the landscape.

Artifacts (sometimes spelled, Artefacts)—For archaeologists, an artifact is any object that has been made, modified, or used by humans. Generally, the word is used in reference only to portable objects, that is, an object that can be picked up and moved. A hearth set in the ground or building foundations, which are not portable, are called *features*.

Barbarians—Once a term that was considered improper, vague, and even derogatory, historians and archaeologists have embraced the word to describe the European tribes who opposed the overlordship of the Roman Empire particularly during its late phase.

Brythonic Languages—Also called Brittonic, this is one of two branches of Celtic languages documented in the British Isles. Brythonic consists today of the Welsh, Cornish, and Breton languages, but it is also the usual general term used to describe the language spoken by Britons before, during, and after the Roman period. The other Celtic language branch is the Goidelic, also known as Gaelic. This branch includes the Scottish, Irish, and Manx (from the Isle of Man) languages.

Burial Rite: Cremation and Inhumation—Burial rites encompass the different means by which people choose to dispose of their dead. In post-Roman Britain, the acceptable choices were cremation and inhumation. Cremation consists of the burning of the body on a funeral pyre after which its ashes are generally buried. The Germans and early Anglo-Saxons usually preferred this rite and buried the ashes in specially made pottery urns. The Britons and later Anglo-Saxons used the inhumation rite, or burial of the intact body in the earth. Wooden coffins were often used. Occasionally, for wealthy persons, coffins were made of other more valuable materials such as lead. The poor might not have any coffin at all but were wrapped in a simple cloth shroud.

Carbon-14 Dating—See **Radiocarbon Dating.**

Clerics—A cleric in the early Roman Catholic Church might be a deacon, priest, or bishop. He was well educated and often scholarly, could write in Latin, and perform bookkeeping tasks. A cleric might also be a monk, but not necessarily.

Cremation—See **Burial Rite.**

Dendrochronology—Colloquially known as tree-ring dating, dendro-chronology is an archaeological dating method applied to preserved pieces of wood found in excavated site layers. Since annual tree growth produces rings that vary in form with respect to local weather conditions, it is possible to match up pieces of wood (from the same species of tree and locality) with overlapping ring patterns to create a timeline of tree rings leading all the way up to the present. Newly found pieces of wood can then be dated by matching them to the timeline of rings. In northern Europe, some areas have a dendrochronological record going back more than two millennia. Dendrochronology is the only archaeological dating method that can give an exact date.

DNA (Deoxyribonucleic Acid)—The molecules carrying the genetic instructions for the formation of all living organisms are analyzed by archaeological labs in order to make species identifications from visually indeterminate remains or to ascertain the genetic health of human populations. As DNA testing becomes simpler and less expensive, analysis of skeletal and dental DNA from human graves will assist in identifying family groups and the biological sex of individuals, even of children prior to puberty whose sex is otherwise not skeletally distinguishable.

Domestication—The act of controlling and modifying the characteristics of populations of wild animals (fauna) and plants (flora) by selecting individuals with desirable traits and causing them to breed. This process has created numerous new species of useful farm animals and crops over the past 10 millennia and more. Cattle were bred to produce more milk, sheep more wool, and swine more meat. Large animals were selected for docile behavior. Wolf domestication produced the working and protective breeds of dogs. In the fields, different grains were made more productive and easier to process. Nearly, all crops and animals raised by farmers undergo a selection process.

Elites—Anthropologists use the term "elite" to refer to anyone in any society who is a leader, has wealth, or otherwise is attributed high status within the society.

Excavation—The best-known field method used by archaeologists to investigate a site. Excavation is a planned digging program designed to locate underground artifacts and features and is preceded by a surface survey of the area. Surveys look for stray finds on the surface or the remnants of ruins still exposed. Sometimes, oddities of the landscape or vegetation reveal that foundations exist below ground level. Once a site is located, it rarely is excavated entirely. A more ethical practice is to sample areas of the site and leave other areas untouched so that future archaeologists armed with different research plans and improved excavation methods can investigate and offer additional opinions.

Fauna—See **Domestication.**

Features—See **Artifacts.**

Flora—See **Domestication.**

Heresy—Christian heresies were beliefs that challenged dominant or official belief. By the fourth century, councils of bishops were increasingly called to decide on issues being debated among the different Christian communities. Once a decision on a particular matter was made, continuing belief in the heretical views drew punishment, excommunication, and even a death sentence. Many heretical ideas concerned the nature of the trinity or of Jesus Christ, but the chief heresy discussed in this book, Pelagianism, dealt with the degree to which humans practiced free will.

Hillforts—Sites that appear defensive but may also have been elite seats of power, or simple residential properties, animal corrals, and all forms of occupation in between. The symbolic meaning of a hill in Celtic mythology lends support to the idea that not all hillforts were defensive in nature. The surrounding ditches and ramparts were boundaries as well as defenses. The hill itself is likely to have held meanings of sacred space and close connections with the spirit world. The boundary ditch marked the hill space as separate from the outside secular world. Some hillforts were clearly lived in, others not necessarily so.

Hoards—Whenever the social or natural order became weak, people have sought to preserve their valuables from theft by burying them in the ground. Most hoards were undoubtedly recovered when times improved or need arose, but occasionally, neither the owners nor their heirs came back. Hoards, having been buried in secret locations away from settlements, are usually discovered by accident during plowing or construction work. In Britain, the contents are mainly coins and other objects made of precious metals.

Inhumation—See **Burial Rite.**

Kingdoms—Political units ruled by kings. In general, it was the king's responsibility to maintain an armed force capable of protecting the people and property within the kingdom's territory. It was the people's responsibility to support the king, his entire household, and retinue with mandatory donations of labor, food, and other products. In the post-Roman centuries, kingdoms began as small units and gradually through conquest, marriage alliance, and the resulting consolidation of territories, the dimensions of surviving kingdoms grew. At first, there was no firm rule for the inheritance of royal power from father to son although both

Singular Noun Ending	Example	Plural Noun Ending	Example
-us	tyrannus	-i	tyranni
-a	colonia	-ae	coloniae
-um	municipium	-a	municipia
-as	civitas	-ates	civitates

Britons and Anglo-Saxons appeared quickly to emulate this continental pattern.

Latin Singulars and Plurals—In this book, Latin names usually have been adapted with modern English plurals in order to avoid confusion. However, this practice has not always been appropriate. The table below shows the plural forms of the most common categories of Latin nouns. Only the nominative (subject) case is provided:

Monasteries—See **Abbeys.**

Monks—See **Clerics.**

Ogham Script—Ogham is an ancient script or alphabet used for inscriptions since before AD 500 primarily in Ireland but also in Scotland, Wales, England, and the Isle of Man. The letters were formed by linear strokes carved into stone or wood. Existing examples are mainly visible on gravestones, memorial stones, and boundary markers.

Pagans—Like *barbarians,* this was once a term that was considered improper, vague, and even derogatory. Historians and archaeologists have embraced *pagan* to describe any native European who had not yet been converted to Christianity.

Palynology—Palynology is the study of pollen. Plants contain pollen particles that although microscopic survive buried in soil for millennia. Archaeologists frequently collect soil samples from excavated sites and extract the ancient pollens in different layers and features for study. Determining which plants were present at the site or in the feature reveals what plants people may have been eating or using for the production of textiles. Wild plants can be differentiated from domesticated species. Plant species present at a particular locale can also reveal the presence and degree of agricultural or forest clearing activities. Pollens are always in the air, depending on the season, and fall at an expected rate onto the ground surface. Those that fall onto the surface of still bodies of water, such as lakes, settle down in the sediments of the lake bed. Palynologists drill and remove cores of soil from suitable lake beds to study the changes in pollen deposition over the centuries. Depending on the identification of the species present, conclusions can be drawn about overall changes in climate, such as whether the years became wetter, drier, warmer, or colder.

Parchment—Neither Romans nor medieval clerics had paper for writing. Romans chose to use either papyrus, made from the native reeds of the

Nile River, or parchment, made from animal skins. Sheep skins were the most desired. When cleaned, processed, and stretched thin, the skins were dried and cut into sheets for binding into books. (Romans often preferred to connect and wind long pieces of parchment onto scrolls.) Particularly, fine quality parchment was called vellum. In an age when books were handwritten and made to last, parchment was the ideal material in the variable seasons of medieval climate. Although they could be destroyed by waterlogging, mold, fire, vermin, and certain insects (bookworms!), parchment books stored in clean, dry conditions might survive many centuries even if regularly handled and read.

Post-Roman versus Sub-Roman—In the context of Britain, some authors use the terms "post-Roman" and "sub-Roman" interchangeably or assign a special meaning to sub-Roman. The term "sub-Roman" may be taken to indicate the latest decades of the fourth century and the earliest decades of the fifth century when the official Roman presence was in the process of departing from Britain. Sometimes, the use of sub-Roman implies a rapid deterioration of culture in general and may suggest a Roman bias in the source. This author feels it is more objective to use only the term "post-Roman" and to apply it to the entire period from the end of direct Roman administration to the ascendancy of the seventh-century Anglo-Saxon kingdoms.

Radiocarbon Dating—The technique of radiocarbon dating, also called carbon-14 dating, enables archaeologists to obtain an approximate age of certain kinds of artifacts if they are somewhere between 50,000 and 500 years old. The process works on organic materials, principally bone, wood, and plant fibers, especially if these materials have been exposed to fire and became charred during the period of their use. Radiocarbon dating depends on the radioactive isotope carbon-14 and its particular rate of decay. Unstable carbon-14 has a half-life of about 5,700 years, and the isotope is ubiquitous throughout the atmosphere and in all living organisms, including humans. Everything that is living, according to its size, carries a similar proportion of the isotope within its body. Once the organism dies, no new isotopes enter the body, but those inside it continue to breakdown into the stable isotope nitrogen-14, as the isotopes normally decay, according to the 5,700-year half-life rate. When an artifact is tested for dating purposes, the ratio of carbon-14 relative to nitrogen-14 is measured to determine approximately how many years it has been since the plant, animal, or person died and new carbon-14 ceased to be ingested.

Sherds—Any broken pieces of pottery found in an archaeological context may be referred to as sherds. Although sometimes still popularly called shards, archaeologists use the term "sherd."

Tree-Ring Dating—See **Dendrochronology.**

Tribes—In anthropological terms, tribes are a smaller social group, rarely more than a few thousand people, who select a headman to organize their activities. The headman does not normally receive wealth for performing this role, nor do his sons automatically inherit their father's status. Tribal organization is common among simple farmers and pastoralists (animal herders). However, in northwestern Europe from Roman times through the early Middle Ages, the larger and more complex social groups, such as found among the Britons and Anglo-Saxons, were more appropriately called chiefdoms. Chiefs rule larger populations, up to tens of thousands of people, as well as obtain much more tangible status and wealth from their position of leadership, both for themselves and for their heirs. Some of the smaller post-Roman kingdoms might have been more appropriately called chiefdoms. This book has used the designation of "tribe" with reference to Britons and Anglo-Saxons because that is the term typically used by other authors.

Typology—The systematic arrangement of artifacts into types on the basis of shared characteristics is called typology. Shared characteristics may include shape, design, size, method of manufacture, and materials used. When archaeologists lack information about the way objects were used by their owners, arranging related objects into types can reveal chronological information through the discovery of an orderly progression of forms. Typological studies are often complex and may also reveal relationships based on culture, kinship, gender, and status.

Tyrants—A derogatory term used mainly by Gildas and derived from the Latin *tyrannus* to mean "usurper." British leaders who seized power in the fifth century were said by Gildas to have no proper authority to rule since their power had not been made legitimate by Rome. Similarly, the leaders of the fourth-century rebellions were also usurpers and therefore tyrants.

Villas—The villas were large rural Roman estates employing many laborers and slaves for farming and manufacturing activities. Depending on local resources and the business interests of the villa owners, villas could engage in craft work as well as food production, but they were not self-sufficient. The villa economy was dependent on a thriving market economy for the sale of excess villa wares and the purchase of items not produced by the villa. Villas sometimes generated a great deal of wealth as can be seen in the remains of mosaic floors, hypocaust heating systems, frescoed walls, and elaborate architectural work.

Vita—As early as the third century, Christians began writing specialized biographies of the venerated Christian saints and martyrs. In later centuries, esteemed kings like the ninth-century Alfred of Wessex also merited being memorialized in a *vita*. Unlike the modern biography, these works focused on describing the mystical, spiritual, miraculous, or proselyting behavior of a great Christian. Another term sometimes used for *vita* is "hagiography."

Wattle-and-Daub—A Celtic method of wall construction in which pliable branches were woven into panels that were lashed together. The wall was then covered in plaster to make it solid and windproof. See also **Woodland Management.**

Woodland Management—Living in a small and densely occupied land compared to the later frontier nations of the western hemisphere and elsewhere, the Britons early understood the necessity of conserving timber resources, both for building and for fuel. Not only crops were sown, but woodland tracts were set aside for encouraging the growth of particular tree species. Several techniques were developed to increase wood growth. A tree with multiple trunks may be cut down during the dormant winter period. If enough of the base is left behind, the stump will produce new shoots in the spring that will in turn be cut down when they reach maturity in a pattern called coppicing. A variant of this practice involved cutting the initial trunk at a height of about six feet. From this trunk, lateral and upward branches grew. Called pollarding, this method was useful on lands that were also pastures for browsing animals. Raising the growth portion of the tree above the ground prevented excessing animal damage to the new shoots. It is important to remember that Britons did not usually need thick tree trunks or wide planks of lumber. Their wood needs, except for a small number of main structural support posts, mainly required the production of branches between one-half to two inches in diameter for use in creating wattled (woven) panels for walls, to be daubed with mud, and for reinforcing muddy tracks in wetlands.

BIBLIOGRAPHY

Acsádi, Gy., and J. Nemeskéri. *History of Human Life Span and Mortality.* Budapest, Hungary: Akadémiai Kiadó, 1970.

Alcock, Leslie. *Was This Camelot? Excavations at Cadbury Castle 1966–1970.* New York: Stein and Day Publishers, 1972.

Alcock, Leslie. *Economy, Society and Warfare among the Britons and Saxons.* Cardiff, UK: University of Wales Press, 1987.

Arkenberg, Jerome S. "The Laws of Æthelberht, King of Kent, 560–616 A.D." In *Medieval Sourcebook: The Anglo-Saxon Dooms, 560–975,* edited by Paul Halsall, transcribed and modernized from Oliver J. Thatcher, ed., *The Library of Original Sources,* Vol. IV: *The Early Medieval World,* 211–239. Milwaukee, WI: University Research Extension Co., 1901, http://www.fordham.edu/halsall/source/560–975dooms.asp.

Arnold, C. J. *An Archaeology of the Early Anglo-Saxon Kingdoms,* 2nd ed. New York: Routledge, 1997.

Aston, Mick, Bruce Eagles, David Evans, et al. "Early Medieval." In *The Archaeology of South West England, South West Archaeological Research Framework, Resource Assessment and Research Agenda,* edited by Chris Webster, 169–188. Taunton, UK: Somerset Heritage Service, Somerset County Council, 2007, http://www1.somerset.gov.uk/archives/hes/downloads/swarfweb.pdf.

Aylett, John. "Roman Britain: The Villas." *British Heritage* (September 2003): 44–51.

Barber, Bruno, David Bowsher, and Ken Whittaker. "Recent Excavations of a Cemetery of 'Londinium.'" *Britannia* 21 (1990): 1–12.

Biddle, Martin. "Winchester." In *Ancient Europe 8000 B.C.–A.D. 1000, Encyclopedia of the Barbarian World,* Vol. 2, edited by Peter Bogucki and Pam J. Crabtree, 501–505. New York: Charles Scribner's Sons, The Gale Group, 2004.

Bidwell, Paul. "Mediterranean Pottery from Bantham Sands, South Devon." *Study Group for Roman Pottery Newsletter* 35 (November 2003).

Blackmore, Lyn, and Alan Vince. "The Origins of Lundenwic? Excavations at 8–9 Long Acre." *London Archaeologist* 10 (2004): 301–305.

Blair, Ian. "The Anglo-Saxon Prince." *Archaeology Magazine* (September– October 2005): 25–28.

Bonifay, Michel. "Post-Roman Imports in the British Isles: Material and Place." *Antiquity* 82 (2008): 1122–1124.

Brigham, T. "A Reassessment of the Second Basilica in London, A.D. 100–400: Excavations at Leadenhall Court, 1984–1986." *Britannia* 21 (1990): 36–40.

Burnett, Andrew. "Clipped Siliquae and the End of Roman Britain." *Britannia* 15 (1984): 163–168.

Campbell, Ewan. "The Archaeological Evidence for External Contacts: Imports, Trade and Economy in Celtic Britain AD 400–800." In *External Contacts and the Economy of Late Roman and Post-Roman Britain,* edited by K. R. Dark, *Studies in Celtic History,* Vol. 16, 83–96. Woodbridge, UK: The Boydell Press, 1996.

Carver, Martin. "Lost, Found, Repossessed or Argued Away—The Case of the Picts." *Antiquity* 85, no. 330 (2011): 1479–1483.

Cave, Roy C., and Herbert H. Coulson, eds. *A Source Book for Medieval Economic History.* New York: Biblo & Tannen, 1965.

Chamber, R. A. "The Late- and Sub-Roman Cemetery at Queenford Farm, Dorchester-on-Thames, Oxon." *Oxoniensia* 52 (1987): 35–69.

Chew, Sing C. "Globalisation, Ecological Crisis, and Dark Ages." *Global Society* 16 (2002): 333–356.

Clancy, Joseph P. *The Earliest Welsh Poetry.* New York: Macmillan, 1970.

Clutton-Brock, Juliet, "The Animal Resources." In *The Archaeology of Anglo-Saxon England,* edited by David M. Wilson, 373–392. London: Methuen and Co., Ltd., 1976.

Cooper, Nicholas J. "Searching for the Blank Generation: Consumer Choice in Roman and Post-Roman Britain." In *Roman Imperialism: Post-Colonial Perspectives,* edited by Jane Webster and Nick Cooper, 85–98. Leicester, UK: University of Leicester, 1996.

Cotterill, John. "Saxon Raiding and the Role of the Late Roman Coastal Forts of Britain." *Britannia* 24 (1993): 227–239.

Crabtree, Pam. "Sheep, Horses, Swine, and Kine: A Zooarchaeological Perspective on the Anglo-Saxon Settlement of England." *Journal of Field Archaeology* 16, no. 2 (1989): 205–213.

Crabtree, Pam. "West Stow." In *Ancient Europe, 8000 B.C.–A.D. 1000, Encyclopedia of the Barbarian World,* edited by Peter Bogucki and

Pam J. Crabtree, Vol. 2, 500, 501. New York: Charles Scribner's Sons, 2004.

Cramp, Rosemary. *Whithorn and the Northumbrian Expansion Westwards: Third Whithorn Lecture, 17th September 1994.* Whithorn, Scotland: Friends of the Whithorn Trust, 1995.

Crawford, Sally. "Research Issues in the Post-Roman to Conquest Period in Warwickshire." *Seminar 4—West Midlands Regional Research Framework for Archaeology.* Birmingham, UK: University of Birmingham, 2002, http://www.birmingham.ac.uk/schools/iaa/departments/archaeology/research/wmrrfa/seminar4.aspx.

Crawford, Sally. "Votive Deposition, Religion and the Anglo-Saxon Furnished Burial Ritual." *World Archaeology* 36, no. 1 (2004): 87–102.

Crummy, Philip. "Colchester between the Roman and the Norman Conquests." In *Archaeology in Essex to AD 1500,* edited by D. G. Buckley, CBA Research Report No. 34, 76–81. London: Council for British Archaeology, 1980.

Cummins, W. A. *The Age of the Picts.* Stroud, UK: Sutton Publishing Ltd., 1999.

Cunliffe, Barry. *Iron Age Communities in Britain, an Account of England, Scotland and Wales from the Seventh Century BC until the Roman Conquest,* 2nd ed. London: Routledge & Kegan Paul, 1978.

Dark, Ken R. *Civitas to Kingdom, British Political Continuity 300–800.* London: Leicester University Press, 1994.

Dark, Ken. *Britain and the End of the Roman Empire.* Charleston, SC: Tempus Publishing, Inc., 2002.

Dark, Ken, and Petra Dark. *The Landscape of Roman Britain.* Stroud, UK: Sutton Publishing, Ltd., 1997.

Dark, Petra. *The Environment of Britain in the First Millennium A.D.* London: Gerald Duckworth and Co., Ltd, 2000.

Davies, Sean. "The Battle of Chester and Warfare in Post-Roman Britain." *History* 95, no. 318 (April 2010): 143–158.

Denison, Simon, ed. "Gemstone Evidence for Late Roman Survival," *British Archaeology: News* 52 (April 2000), http://www.britarch.ac.uk/ba/ba52/ba52news.html.

Dickinson, Tania M. "An Anglo-Saxon 'Cunning Woman' from Bidford-on-Avon." In *In Search of Cult,* edited by Martin Carver, 45–54. Woodbridge, UK: The Boydell Press, 1993.

Dickinson, Tania M. "Review Article: What's New in Early Medieval Burial Archaeology?" *Early Medieval Europe* 11, no. 1 (2002): 71–87.

Dodgshon, R. A., and R. A. Butlin, eds., *An Historical Geography of England and Wales,* 2nd ed. San Diego, CA: Academic Press, 1990.

Drewett, Peter, David Rudling, and Mark Gardiner. *The South East to AD 1000, a Regional History of England.* London: Longman Group UK, Ltd., 1988.

Drinkwater, J. F. "The Usurpers Constantine III (407–411) and Jovinus (411–413)." *Britannia* 29 (1998): 269–298.

Driver, Jonathan C. "Zooarchaeological Analysis of Raw-Material Selection by a Saxon Artisan." *Journal of Field Archaeology* 11, no. 4 (1984): 397–403.

Edens, W. Julian. "Saint Gildas and the Pestilent Dragon: A Meander through the Sixth-Century Landscape with a Most Notable Guru." *The Heroic Age* 6 (Spring 2003), http://www.heroicage.org/issues/6/gildas.html.

Ellis, Peter, et al. "North Leigh Roman Villa, Oxfordshire: A Report on Excavation and Recording in the 1970s." *Britannia* 30 (1999), 199–246.

English Heritage. *Research on Tintagel Castle*, http://www.english-heritage.org.uk/daysout/properties/tintagel-castle/history-and-research/research/.

English Heritage. *Significance of Wroxeter Roman City*, http://www.english-heritage.org.uk/daysout/properties/wroxeter-roman-city/history-and-research/significance/.

Faulkner, Neil. *The Decline and Fall of Roman Britain*. Charleston, SC: Arcadia, 2001.

Fischer, Svante, and Jean Soulat. "The Typochronology of Sword Pommels from the Staffordshire Hoard." *Portable Antiquities Scheme*, http://finds.org.uk/staffshoardsymposium/papers/svantefischerandjeansoulat. Paper given at the Staffordshire Hoard Symposium held at the British Museum, London, March 2010.

Fitzwilliam Museum, *Checklist of Coin Hoards from the British Isles, c.450–1180*, http://www.fitzmuseum.cam.ac.uk/dept/coins/projects/hoards/index.list.html.

Fowler, P. J. "Agriculture and Rural Settlement." In *The Archaeology of Anglo-Saxon England*, edited by David M. Wilson, 23–48. London: Methuen and Co., Ltd., 1976.

Fulford, Michael G. "The Interpretation of Britain's Late Roman Trade: The Scope of Medieval Historical and Archaeological Analogy." In *Roman Shipping and Trade: Britain and the Rhine Provinces*, edited by Joan du Plat Taylor and Henry Cleere, CBA Research Report No. 24, 59–69. London: Council for British Archaeology, 1978.

Fulford, Michael G. "Byzantium and Britain: A Mediterranean Perspective on Post-Roman Mediterranean Imports in Western Britain and Ireland." *Medieval Archaeology* 33 (1989): 1–6.

Fulford, Michael G., J.R.L. Allen, C. Gaffney, J. Gater, George C. Boon, and Isabel Figueiral. "Iron-Making at the Chesters Villa, Woolaston, Gloucestershire: Survey and Excavation 1987–1991." *Britannia* 23 (1992): 159–215.

Fuller, B. T., T. I. Molleson, D. A. Harris, L. T. Gilmour, and R.E.M. Hedges. "Isotopic Evidence for Breastfeeding and Possible Adult Dietary Differences from Late/Sub-Roman Britain." *American Journal of Physical Anthropology* 129, no. 1 (2006): 45–54.

Gaffney, Vincent L., Roger H. White, H. Goodchild, et al. *Wroxeter, The Cornovii, and the Urban Process: Final Report on the Wroxeter Hinterland Project, 1994–1997*, Volume 1: *Researching the Hinterland*. In *Journal of Roman Archaeology*, Supplementary Series No. 68 (Portsmouth, RI: Journal of Roman Archaeology, 2007), http://www.journalofromanarch.com/supplements/S68.pdf.

Gambash, Gil. "To Rule a Ferocious Province: Roman Policy and the Aftermath of the Boudican Revolt." *Britannia* 43 (2012): 1–15.

Gardner, Andrew. "Military Identities in Late Roman Britain," *Oxford Journal of Archaeology* 18, no. 4 (1999): 403–415.

Gerrard, James. "Recent Work on the Dark Age Site of Mothecombe." *Study Group for Roman Pottery Newsletter* 35 (November 2003), http://www.romanpotterystudy.org/newsletter/SGRPnewsletter35.pdf.

Gerrard, James. "Rethinking the Small Pig Horizon at York Minster." *Oxford Journal of Archaeology* 26 (2007): 303–307.

Gildas. *De Excidio Britanniae, Six Old English Chronicles, of which Two Are Now First Translated from the Monkish Latin Originals*, edited by John Allen Giles. London: G. Bell & Sons, 1891. Published online by Paul Halsall, ed., *The Internet Medieval Source Book*, http://www.fordham.edu/halsall/basis/gildas-full.asp.

Green, Miranda J. *Dictionary of Celtic Myth and Legend*. London: Thames and Hudson, Ltd., 1992.

Green, Miranda J. *Celtic Myths*, 2nd ed. Austin: University of Texas Press, 1995.

Grimmer, Martin. "British Christian Continuity in Anglo-Saxon England: The Case of Sherborne/Lanprobi." *Journal of the Australian Early Medieval Association* 1 (2005): 51–64.

Halsall, Paul, ed. *Medieval Sourcebook: Notitia Dignitatum (Register of Dignitaries), c. 400*. New York: Fordham University, November 1998, http://www.fordham.edu/halsall/source/notitiadignitatum.html.

Halsall, Paul. "St. Vincent de Lerins: The 'Vincentian Canon', AD 434—From Chapter 4 of the Commonitorium A.D. 434." Originally published in T. A. Moxon, ed., *Cambridge Patristic Texts*, 1908. *Ancient History Sourcebook*, January 1999, http://www.fordham.edu/Halsall/ancient/434lerins-canon.asp.

Handley, Mark A. "The Origins of Christian Commemoration in Late Antique Britain." *Early Medieval Europe* 10, no. 2 (2001): 177–199.

Härke, Heinrich. "Early Anglo-Saxon Military Organisation: An Archaeological Perspective." In Military *Aspects of Scandinavian Society in a European perspective, AD 1–1300*, edited by Anne Nørgård Jorgensen and Birthe L. Clausen, 93–101. Copenhagen, Denmark: Danish National Museum, 1997. Paper from an international research seminar held at the Danish National Museum, Copenhagen, Denmark, May 2–4, 1996.

Härke, Heinrich. "Early Anglo-Saxon Social Structure." In *The Anglo-Saxons from the Migration Period to the Eighth Century: an Ethnographic Perspective,* edited by J. Hines, 125–170. Woodbridge, UK: The Boydell Press, 1997.

Härke, Heinrich. "Kings and Warriors: Population and Landscape from Post-Roman to Norman Britain." In *The Peopling of Britain: The Shaping of a Human Landscape,* edited by Paul Slack and Ryk Ward, 145–175. Oxford: Oxford University Press, 2002.

Härke, Heinrich. "Population Replacement or Acculturation? An Archaeological Perspective on Population and Migration in Post-Roman Britain." In *Celtic Englishes III,* edited by H. L. C. Tristram, 13–28. Heidelberg, Germany: Anglistische Forschungen, no. 324, 2003.

Härke, Heinrich. "The Anglo-Saxon Weapon Burial Rite: An Interdisciplinary Analysis." *Opus (Moscow)* 3 (2004): 197–207.

Härke, Heinrich. "Gender Representation in Early Medieval Burials: Ritual Re-affirmation of a Blurred Boundary?" In *Studies in Early Anglo-Saxon Art and Archaeology: Papers in Honour of Martin G. Welch,* edited by S. Brookes, S. Harrington, and A. Reynolds, British Archaeological Report No. 527, 98–105. Oxford: Archaeopress, 2011.

Hart-Davis, Duff. *Fauna Britannica.* London: Weidenfeld & Nicolson, 2002.

Harvey, David C., and Rhys Jones. "Custom and Habit(us): The Meaning of Traditions and Legends in Early Medieval Western Britain," *Geografiska Annaler. Series B. Human Geography* 81 (1999): 223–233.

Henig, Martin. "Roman Britons after 410," *British Archaeology* 68 (December 2002).

Henig, Martin. *The Heirs of King Verica.* Charleston, SC: Tempus Publishing, Inc., 2002.

Henig, Martin. "British Bretons. Review: The British Settlement of Brittany," *British Archaeology* 72 (September 2003).

Heroic Age Staff. "Early Medieval Tintagel: An Interview with Archaeologists Rachel Harry and Kevin Brady." *The Heroic Age* 1 (1999), http://www.mun.ca/mst/heroicage/issues/1/hati.htm.

Higham, N. J. *The English Conquest: Gildas and Britain in the Fifth Century.* Manchester, UK: University of Manchester Press, 1994.

Higham, N. J. *King Arthur: Myth-Making and History.* New York: Routledge, 2002.

Higham, Nick. "Literary Evidence for Villas, Towns and Hillforts in Fifth-Century Britain." *Britannia* 25 (1994): 229–232.

Hill, John M. *The Cultural World of Beowulf.* Toronto, ON: University of Toronto Press, 1995.

Hillgarth, J. N. *Christianity and Paganism, 350–750, the Conversion of Western Europe,* revised ed. Philadelphia: University of Pennsylvania Press, 1986.

Hills, Catherine. "Roman Britain to Anglo-Saxon England." *History Today* 40 (1990): 46–53.

Hills, Catherine. "Spong Hill." In *Ancient Europe, 8000 B.C.–A.D. 1000, Encyclopedia of the Barbarian World,* edited by Peter Bogucki and Pam J. Crabtree, Vol. 2, 496–497. New York: Charles Scribner's Sons, 2004.

Hudson, Benjamin. "Time Is Short: The Eschatology of the Early Gaelic Church." In *Last Things, Death, & the Apocalypse in the Middle Ages,* edited by Caroline Walker Bynum and Paul Freedman. Philadelphia: University of Pennsylvania Press, 2000, 101–123.

Hugh, William, ed. and trans. "Fragments from Lost Letters of Gildas." In *Gildas, The Ruin of Britain &c.,* transcribed by Roger Pearse, Cymmrodorion Record Series No. 3, 257–271. London: Nutt, 1899, http://www.tertullian.org/fathers/gildas_04_letters.htm.

Hurst, J. G. "The Pottery." In *The Archaeology of Anglo-Saxon England,* edited by David M. Wilson, 283–348. London: Methuen and Co., Ltd., 1976.

Ireland, Stanley. *Roman Britain: A Sourcebook.* New York: St. Martin's Press, 1986.

James, Edward. *Britain in the First Millennium.* New York: Oxford University Press, Inc., 2000.

Jarus, Owen. "Did the Scots Visit Iceland? New Research Reveals Island Inhabited 70 Years before Vikings Thought to Have Arrived," *Unreported Heritage News,* http://www.unreportedheritagenews.com/2010/12/did-scots-visit-iceland-new-research.html.

Johns, Catherine, and Roger Bland. "The Hoxne Late Roman Treasure." *Britannia* 25 (1994): 165–173.

Johnson, Mark. "The Saxon Monastery at Whitby: Past, Present, Future." In *In Search of Cult,* edited by Martin Carver, 85–89. Woodbridge, UK: The Boydell Press, 1993.

Johnson, Stephen. *Later Roman Britain.* New York: Charles Scribner's Sons, 1980.

Jones, Gwyn, and Thomas Jones, trans. *Mabinogion.* London: J. M. Dent & Sons, Ltd., 1970.

Jones, M. U. "Mucking and the Early Saxon Rural Settlement in Essex." In *Archaeology in Essex to AD 1500,* edited by D. G. Buckley, CBA Research Report No. 34, 82–86. London: Council for British Archaeology, 1980.

Jones, Martin. *England before Domesday.* Totowa, NJ: Barnes & Noble Books, 1986.

Jones, Michael E. *The End of Roman Britain.* Ithaca, NY: Cornell University Press, 1996.

Jones, W. T. "Early Saxon Cemeteries in Essex." In *Archaeology in Essex to AD 1500,* edited by D. G. Buckley, CBA Research Report No. 34, 87–95. London: Council for British Archaeology, 1980.

Justinian. "*Codex Justinianus:* Return of Fugitive Slaves & Coloni, c. 530 [XI.48.xii.]." In *A Source Book for Medieval Economic History,* edited by Roy C. Cave and Herbert H. Coulson. Milwaukee, WI: The Bruce Publishing Co., 1936. Reprinted in Paul Halsall, ed., *Medieval*

Sourcebook, http://www.fordham.edu/halsall/source/codexXl-48-xii.html.

Kelley, D. W. *Charcoal and Charcoal Burning.* Princes Risborough, UK: Shire Publications, Ltd., 1996.

Kennedy, Charles W., trans. *Beowulf, the Oldest English Epic.* London: Oxford University Press, 1968.

Kennedy, Maev. "Discovery of Ancient Tunny Fish Paste Gives Inkling of Roman Taste." *The Guardian,* July 9, 2002, http://www.guardian.co.uk/uk/2002/jul/09/arts.humanities.

Knight, Jeremy K. "From Villa to Monastery: Llandough in Context," *Medieval Archaeology* 49, no. 1 (2005): 93–107.

Konstam, Angus. *The Forts of Celtic Britain.* Oxford: Osprey Publishing, Ltd., 2006.

Kulikowski, Michael. "Barbarians in Gaul, Usurpers in Britain." *Britannia* 31 (2000): 325–345.

Laing, Lloyd. *The Archaeology of Late Celtic Britain and Ireland, c. 400–1200 AD.* London: Methuen and Co., Ltd., 1975.

Leech, Roger, E. M. Besly, R. F. Everton, and Elizabeth Fowler. "The Excavation of a Romano-British Farmstead and Cemetery on Bradley Hill, Somerton, Somerset." *Britannia* 12 (1981): 177–252.

Leech, Roger, Martin Henig, Frank Jenkins, et al. "The Excavation of a Romano-Celtic Temple and a Later Cemetery on Lamyatt Beacon, Somerset." *Britannia* 17 (1986): 259–328.

Lloyd, Bronwynn M. "Roman Britain to Germanic England: A Settlement Study of Military Sites in Northern England from AD 300–600." *Culture, Society and Praxis* 7, no. 1 (2008): 23–42.

Lo, Lawrence K. "Ogham." *AncientScripts.com,* 1996, http://www.ancientscripts.com/ogham.html.

Lynch, Frances. *A Guide to Ancient and Historic Wales: Gwynedd,* revised ed. Cardiff, UK: Cadw Welsh Historic Monuments, 2001.

Maddicott, J. R. "Plague in Seventh-Century England," *Past and Present* 156 (August 1997), 7–54.

Manco, Jean. "*Aquæ Sulis* to *Aquæmann.*" *Bath Past, Saxon,* December 5, 2004, http://www.buildinghistory.org/bath/saxon/aquaemann.shtml.

Mason, Austin. "Buried Buckets: Rethinking Ritual Behavior before England's Conversion." *Haskins Society Journal* 20 (2008): 1–36.

Matthews, Keith J. "What's in a Name? Britons, Angles, Ethnicity and Material Culture in the Fourth to Seventh Centuries." *The Heroic Age* 4 (Winter 2001), http://www.heroicage.org/issues/4/Matthews.html.

Mattingly, David. *An Imperial Possession, Britain in the Roman Empire.* New York: Penguin Books, 2007.

May, Jeffrey, and Peter Weddell. "Bantham: A Dark Age Puzzle." *Current Archaeology* 178 (2002): 420–422.

Miles, David, ed. *Archaeology at Barton Court Farm, Abingdon, Oxon: An Investigation of late Neolithic, Iron Age, Romano-British and Saxon Settlements,* CBA Research Report No. 50. Oxford: Oxford Archaeological Unit Report 3, 1986.

Mommsen, Theodor, et al. *Monumenta Germaniae Historica, Chronica Minora,* Vol. 9, bk. 1. Berlin, Germany: Weidmann, 1826–, 617–666.

Moran, P. F. "St. Patrick." In *The Catholic Encyclopedia.* New York: Robert Appleton Company, 1911, http://www.newadvent.org/cathen/11554a.htm.

Morris, Chris. "Not King Arthur, But King Someone." *British Archaeology* 4 (May 1995), http://www.britarch.ac.uk/ba/ba4/ba4feat.html.

Mullins, Daniel J. *Early Welsh Saints,* translated from Welsh by Harri Pritchard Jones. Llanrwst, UK: Gwasg Carreg Gwalch, 2003.

News Editor. "Rare Early Saxon Village in Midlands." *British Archaeology: News* 26 (1997), http://www.archaeologyuk.org/ba/ba26/BA26NEWS.HTML#village.

News Editor. "In Brief: Dyke Redated." *British Archaeology: News* 49 (November 1999), http://www.britarch.ac.uk/ba/ba49/ba49toc.html.

Nuttall, Nick. "New Light Cast on Dark Ages." *The Times* (London), August 22, 2000: 11.

Owen-Crocker, Gale R. *Dress in Anglo-Saxon England,* revised ed. Woodbridge, UK: The Boydell Press, 2004.

Pattison, John E. "Integration versus Apartheid in Post-Roman Britain: A Response to Thomas et al. (2008)." *Human Biology* 83, no. 6 (December 2011), http://digitalcommons.wayne.edu/humbiol/vol83/iss6/.

Pearson, Kathy L. "Nutrition and the Early-Medieval Diet." *Speculum* 72 (1997): 1–32.

Powlesland, D. "Early Anglo-Saxon Settlements, Structures, Form and Layout." In *The Anglo-Saxons from the Migration Period to the Eighth Century: An Ethnographic Perspective,* edited by John Hines, 101–124. Woodbridge, UK: The Boydell Press, 1997.

Project Gutenberg. *The Anglo-Saxon Chronicle,* translated by the Rev. James Ingram. London: 1823, with additional readings from the translation by Dr. J. A. Giles. London: 1847, http://ebooks.gutenberg.us/WorldeBookLibrary.com/aschron.htm.

Quinnell, Henrietta. "A Sense of Identity: Distinctive Cornish Stone Artefacts in the Roman and Post-Roman Periods." *Cornish Archaeology* 32 (1993): 29–46.

Rackham, Oliver. *Trees & Woodland in the British Landscape, the Complete History of Britain's Trees, Woods & Hedgerows,* revised ed. London: Phoenix Press, 1990.

Rahtz, Philip. "How Likely Is Likely?" *Antiquity* 49 (1975): 59–61.

Roberts, Charlotte, and Keith Manchester. *The Archaeology of Disease,* 3rd ed. Ithaca, NY: Cornell University Press, 2005.

Rogers, Penelope Walton. *Cloth and Clothing in Early Anglo-Saxon England, AD 450–700*, CBA Research Report No. 145. York, UK: Council for British Archaeology, 2007.

"Roman Baths Museum." *Museums Libraries Archives: Discovering UK Collections*, http://www.cornucopia.org.uk/html/search/verb/GetRecord/2963.

Roman Britain Organisation. *"Cohors Primae Thracum*—The First Cohort of Thracians," RIB 1909. *Banna, Hadrian's Wall Fort and Settlement, Birdoswald, Cumbria*, http://www.roman-britain.org/places/banna.htm#rib1909. Based on R. G. Collingwood and R. P. Wright, *The Roman Inscriptions of Britain*, Vol. 1. Oxford: Clarendon Press, 1965.

Ross, Anne. *Pagan Celtic Britain, Studies in Iconography and Tradition*. New York: Columbia University Press, 1967.

Schofield, John. "Saxon London in a Tale of Two Cities." *British Archaeology* 44 (1999), http://www.britarch.ac.uk/ba/ba44/ba44regs.html.

Shepherd, Deborah J. "Evidence of Violence from Anglo-Saxon Cemeteries." Paper presented at the annual meeting of the International Medieval Congress, Western Michigan University, Kalamazoo, Michigan, May 1997.

Shepherd, Deborah J. *Funerary Ritual and Symbolism: An Interdisciplinary Interpretation of Burial Practices in Late Iron Age Finland*. Oxford: British Archaeological Reports 808, 1999.

Shepherd, Deborah J. "The Elusive Warrior Maiden Tradition—Bearing Weapons in Anglo-Saxon Society." In *Ancient Warfare*, edited by Anthony Harding and R. John Carman, 219–248. Stroud, UK: Sutton Publishing, Ltd., 1999.

Sherlock, Stephen J., and Martin G. Welch. *An Anglo-Saxon Cemetery at Norton, Cleveland*, CBA Report No. 82. London: Council for British Archaeology, 1992.

Smithsonian National Museum of Natural History. "Difficult Lives." Exhibition on *Written in Bone: Forensic Files of the 17th-Century Chesapeake*, Washington, DC, February 7, 2009–January 6, 2014, http://anthropology.si.edu/writteninbone/difficult_lives.html.

Snyder, Christopher A. *An Age of Tyrants, Britain and the Britons, A.D. 400–600*. University Park: Pennsylvania State University Press, 1998.

Snyder, Christopher A. *The Britons*. Malden, MA: Blackwell Publishing, 2003.

St. Patrick. *The 'Confessio' of Saint Patrick*. Grand Rapids, MI: Christian Classics Ethereal Library, http://www.ccel.org/ccel/patrick/confession.pdf.

Stewart, Bob. *The Waters of the Gap: The Mythology of Aquae Sulis*. Bath, UK: Bath City Council, 1981.

Straker, Vanessa. "Early Medieval Environmental Background." In *The Archaeology of South West England—South West Archaeological Research Framework: Resource Assessment and Research Agenda*, edited by C. J. Webster, 163–168. Taunton, UK: Somerset County Council, 2008, http://www1.somerset.gov.uk/archives/hes/swarf/publications.htm.

Swift, Ellen. "Object Biography, Reuse and Recycling in the Late to Post-Roman Transition Period and Beyond: Rings Made from Romano-British Bracelets." *Britannia* 43 (2012): 167–215.

Sykes, Bryan. *Saxons, Vikings, and Celts.* New York: W. W. Norton, 2006.

"The Treasure Act." *Portable Antiquities Scheme,* http://finds.org.uk/treasure/.

Thomas, Charles. *Celtic Britain: Ancient Peoples and Places Series.* London: Thames and Hudson, 1986.

Thomas, Mark G., Michael P. H. Stumpf, and Heinrich Härke. "Evidence for an Apartheid-like Social Structure in Early Anglo-Saxon England," *Proceeding of the Royal Society, B: Biological Sciences* 273, no. 1601 (October 2006): 2651–2657.

Thomas, Mark G., Heinrich Härke, Gary German, and Michael P. H. Stumpf. "Limited Interethnic Marriage, Differential Reproductive Success and the Spread of 'Continental' Y Chromosomes in Early Anglo-Saxon England." In *Simulations, Genetics and Human Prehistory (McDonald Institute Monographs),* edited by S. Matsumura, P. Forster, and C. Renfrew, 61–70. Cambridge: McDonald Institute for Archaeological Research, 2008.

Thompson, E. A. *Saint Germanus of Auxerre and the End of Roman Britain.* Woodbridge, UK: The Boydell Press, 1984.

Thornhill, Philip. "St. Alban and the End of Roman Britain." *The Mankind Quarterly* 41, no. 1 (2000): 3–41.

Todd, Malcolm. " 'Famosa Pestis' and Britain in the Fifth Century." *Britannia* 8 (1977): 321.

Todd, Malcolm. *The South West to AD 1000.* New York: Longman, Inc., 1987.

Todd, Malcolm. *A Companion to Roman Britain.* Hoboken, NJ: John Wiley & Sons, 2008.

Trustees of the British Museum. "Silver-gilt Sword Pommel." *British Museum Explore/Highlights,* http://www.britishmuseum.org/explore/highlights/highlight_objects/pe_mla/s/silver-gilt_sword_pommel.aspx.

van Leusen, Martijn. "The Wroxeter Hinterland Project." In *Pattern to Process: Methodological Investigations into the Formation and Interpretation of Spatial Patterns in Archaeological Landscapes.* PhD diss., Rijksuniversiteit Groningen, Groningen, Netherlands, May 30, 2002, http://www.scribd.com/doc/36539145/Pattern-to-Process-Methodological-Investigations-Into-the-Formation-and-Interpretation-of-Spatial-Patterns-in-Archaeological-Landscapes.

Vermaat, Robert. "The Gallic Chroniclers of 452 and 511." *Vortigern Studies: British History 400–600,* http://www.vortigernstudies.org.uk/artsou/chron452.htm.

Vermaat, Robert, ed. "The Sources on Vortigern—The Text of Gildas: *De Excidio et Conquestu Britanniae.* (Parts 1 and 2, chapters 1–37)." *Vortigern Studies: British History 400–600,* http://www.vortigernstudies.org.uk/arthist/vortigernquotesgil.htm.

Vermaat, Robert. "The *Vergilius Romanus:* The First British Book? Vergil MS Vat. lat. 3867 = *Romanus.*" *Vortigern Studies: British History 400–600,* http://www.vortigernstudies.org.uk/artlit/vergilius.htm.

Vince, Alan. "West Midlands Post-Roman Research Agenda; Ceramics." *Seminar 4—West Midlands Regional Research Framework for Archaeology.* Birmingham, UK: University of Birmingham, 2002, http://www.birmingham.ac.uk/schools/iaa/departments/archaeology/research/wmrrfa/seminar4.aspx.

Wacher, John. *Roman Britain.* London: J. M. Dent & Sons, Ltd., 1978.

Walters, Bryn. "Exotic Structures in 4th-Century Britain." In *Architecture in Roman Britain,* CBA Research Report No. 94, edited by Peter Johnson with Ian Haynes, 152–162. Walmgate, UK: Council for British Archaeology, 1996.

Ward-Perkins, Bryan. "Why Did the Anglo-Saxons Not Become More British?" *English Historical Review* 115, no. 462 (June 2000): 513–533.

Welch, Martin. *Discovering Anglo-Saxon England.* University Park: Pennsylvania State University Press, 1992.

Wenham, S. J. "Anatomical Interpretations of Anglo-Saxon Weapon Injuries." In *Weapons and Warfare in Anglo-Saxon England,* edited by Sonia Chadwick Hawkes, 123–139. Oxford: Oxbow Books, 1989.

White, Roger. "Wroxeter, Rich in a Wealthy Land." *British Archaeology,* 17 (September 1996), http://www.britarch.ac.uk/ba/ba17/ba17feat.html.

Whitehall Farm Roman Villa and Landscape Project. "A Practical Experiment in the Use of Local Materials in the Iron Smelting Process, Whitehall Farm, Nether Heyford 2001." http://www.whitehallvilla.co.uk/htmlfiles/smelt2001.html.

Whyman, Mark. "Invisible People? Material Culture in 'Dark Age' Yorkshire." In *In Search of Cult,* edited by Martin Carver, 61–68. Woodbridge, UK: The Boydell Press, 1993.

Wilken, Robert L. "Pelagius." In *Encyclopedia of Religion,* editor-in-chief Lindsay Jones, 2nd ed., 7025, 7026. Detroit, MI: Macmillan Reference USA, 2005.

Williams, Ann, Alfred P. Smyth, and D. P. Kirby. *A Biographical Dictionary of Dark Age Britain, England, Scotland and Wales, c. 500–c.1050.* London: B. A. Seaby, Ltd., 1991.

Williams, David, and Cesar Carreras. "North African Amphorae in Roman Britain: A Re-Appraisal." *Britannia* 26 (1995): 231–252.

Williams, Howard. "Monuments and the Past in Early Anglo-Saxon England." *World Archaeology* 30 (1998): 104.

Wilmott, Tony. *Birdoswald Roman Fort: A History.* Carlisle, UK: Cumbria County Council, 1995.

Wilson, David M. "Craft and Industry." In *The Archaeology of Anglo-Saxon England,* edited by David M. Wilson, 253–282. London: Methuen and Co., Ltd., 1976.

Wood, Ian. "Before and After the Migration Period." In *The Anglo-Saxons from the Migration Period to the Eighth Century: An Ethnographic Perspective*, edited by John Hines, 41–64. Woodbridge, UK: The Boydell Press, 1997.

Woodfall, David, photographer, and Kenneth Taylor, text. *Natural Heartlands: The Landscape, People, and Wildlife of Britain and Ireland*. Ramsbury, UK: Airlife Publishing, Ltd., 1997.

Y Chromosome Consortium. "A Nomenclature System for the Tree of Human Y-Chromosomal Binary Haplogroups." *Genome Research* 12, no. 2 (February 2002): 339–348, http://genome.cshlp.org/content/12/2/339/F1.expansion.

Yorke, Barbara. *Kings and Kingdoms of Early Anglo-Saxon England*. New York: Routledge, 1997.

INDEX

Abandonment, 21, 37, 98, 119, 246.
    See also Deserted Villages
Acidic soils, 2–3, 28, 52, 94,
    125, 129
Alloys, 32, 152, 179
Alps, 7, 184
Altars, 207, 261–63. *See also*
    Shrines; Temples
Ambrosius Aurelianus, 191
Amphitheaters, 33, 60, 68, 102,
    193–94
Amphorae, 53, 157, 173
Ancestor beliefs, 46, 248–52, 257
Aneirin (poet), 214
Angelsey, 44, 175, 213
Anglo-Saxon Chronicle
    (manuscript), 72, 169, 208, 218
Anglo-Saxons, overview, 71–75,
    96–97, 100–102, 106–7
Animal sacrifice. *See* Ritual
Animals, domesticated, 14, 86,
    129; cats, 134; cattle, 130; dogs,
    133–34; donkeys, 133; draft ani-
    mals, 80, 127–28, 133; goats, 132;
    horses, 133; pigs, 130; poultry,
    132; sheep, 131
Antonine Wall, 13, 42, 189
Apartheid hypothesis, 112–13
Aqueducts, 59–60, 64, 68
Archaeology, excavation methods,
    28–29, 99, 132, 161, 217, 242;
    experimental archaeology, 151.
    See also Flotation
Architecture, 4, 31, 68–69, 79, 261,
    280
Armorica. *See* Brittany
Army, Roman, 32, 35, 37, 41, 47,
    66, 69, 184, 192–99, 202
Arthritis, 95–96, 238
Artisans. *See* Craftsmen
Augustine of Canterbury, Saint,
    35, 170, 225–27, 250, 269, 277–81
Authority, 26, 30, 33, 37, 43, 59,
    168, 183, 191

Bantham Sands, 172, 208
Barley. *See* Grains, cultivated
Barns and byres, 118, 141–42

Barter. *See* Trade

Barton Court Farm, 20–22, 84, 124

Basilicas, 66, 68, 73, 81, 102, 166

Baths (structures), 15, 33, 64, 67,
68, 78, 102, 118, 194, 242. *See also*
Hypocausts; Personal hygiene

Beans, 120, 123, 125–27, 137, 238

Bears. *See* Hunting

Bede, The Venerable (cleric), 15,
26, 45, 104, 169, 213, 218, 281

Beer, 123, 130, 138

Bees. *See* Honey

Beowulf (epic poem), 136, 252

Birdoswald, 196–99, 215

Birds: fowl, 3, 129, 132; hawks, 133

Birth. *See* Pregnancy

Blades: knives, 5, 15, 49, 54, 108–9,
134, 148; seaxes, 108; swords,
49, 54, 108, 149, 159, 162, 223–25,
240, 245

Boar. *See* Hunting

Boats, 3, 63, 149, 155, 172–73

Bone abnormalities. *See* Skeletal
analysis

Bradley Hill, 140–43, 186, 217, 247

Bread, 94, 122–25, 136, 154,
197, 238

Britons, overview, 25–55, 111–13,
212–18

Brittany, 38, 39, 42, 185, 207, 210

Bronze, 32, 43, 152–54, 164, 177,
180, 209, 229

Buckwheat. *See* Grains, cultivated

Buildings: cellular, 45, 173;
rectangular, 32, 97, 118,
141; round, 97, 118;
subterranean, 143

Burials, 216–18, 244–46; Christian,
91, 93–95, 207; cremation, 49,
54, 75; inhumation, 50, 54; mass,
241–43; pagan, 46, 49–50, 71,
108–11, 135, 160, 166, 223; sites
(cemeteries), 32, 53–55, 141–44,
229–30, 246–53

Byzantine culture, 32, 175, 273

Cadbury-Congresbury, 154,
208, 212

Caerleon, 195–96

Caerwent, 81–82, 93, 164, 203, 214,
242, 272

Cairns (stone), 46

Canterbury, 35, 170, 203, 225–26,
250, 269, 279

Carbohydrates. *See* Nutrition

Carlisle, 169, 203, 214–15

Catterick, 69, 214

Cemeteries. *See* Burials

Cereals. *See* Grains, cultivated

Chalk, 2, 16, 122

Charcoal, 4–5, 52, 80, 139–40,
150–51

Charters, 66, 119, 191

Chester, 68, 194, 196

Christianity. *See* Religion

Churches, structures, 76, 98, 155,
208, 245, 267, 269, 271

Cirencester, 68, 73, 203, 208,
242–43, 272

Civil war. *See* Power struggles

Civitas (plural, *civitates*), 31, 67–69,
81–82, 203, 205–6, 210

Climate change, 6–8, 13, 17–18,
85–86, 240

Clothing, 49, 93, 109–10, 129, 132,
136, 141, 161

Coins, 28, 39–40, 62, 99, 168–69,
176, 180–81, 194–95; and Anglo-
Saxons, 229; and British tribes,
207. *See also* Hoards

Colchester, 66, 165–67, 203, 262

Colonia (plural, *coloniae*), 65–66,
69, 166

Columba, Saint, 45, 274

Commerce. *See* Trade

Conquest of Britain, 29–30, 60, 67,
71–72, 202, 218, 254

Constantine I (emperor), 34, 98,
177, 267–68

Constantine III (usurper), 38, 178,
183–84

Conversion, religious, 36–37, 45–47, 98, 142, 226, 250, 272, 275, 281

Coppicing, 138–39

Corn drier, 127, 141

Cornovians, 78–81, 203, 204, 213

Cornwall, 31–32, 42–43, 48, 69

Coroticus, Letter to (Saint Patrick), 36–37

Craftsmen, 33, 147–48, 163–67; at market and royal sites, 75, 89, 98, 173, 206

Cremations. *See* Burials

Crop rotation. *See* Shifting agriculture

Crops, 9–12, 18, 21–22, 85–86, 120–27; villa production of, 186; at West Stow, 143. *See also* Grains, cultivated

Cultivation, 12, 17–19, 120–36

Cults. *See* Religion

Cumbria, 3, 43, 215–16, 270

Currency. *See* Coins

Dairy products, 10, 14, 120, 129, 131–32, 138. *See also* Protein

Dalriada, 44–45, 215–16

Dark earth, 75, 79, 248

De Excidio et Conquestu Britanniae (manuscript), 22–23, 44, 48, 187–91, 241–42

Deer. *See* Hunting

Defenses, 37, 65, 73, 82, 166, 189, 197, 206–9. *See also* Cadbury-Congresbury; Dinas Powys; Hillforts; South Cadbury Castle

Demography, 51–52, 107–8, 237

Dendrochronology, 52, 221

Dentition. *See* Teeth, human

Deserted settlements, 119–20, 164, 166, 205, 212, 218, 253, 279

Devonshire, 69, 152, 172, 207, 210

Diet. *See* Nutrition

Dinas Powys, 134–35, 153–55, 157, 164, 211–12, 214

Disease. *See* Illness

Ditches, 61, 68, 170, 197, 206, 211, 221, 243, 256

DNA, 97, 108–13, 217

Druids, 258–59

Dumnonians, 31–32, 69, 173–74, 181, 203–4, 207–11

Dux bellorum (military title), 26–27

Dykes, 80–81, 170, 209, 221–23

East Anglia, 10, 49, 54, 135, 136, 204, 220. *See also* Sutton Hoo

Easter controversy, 35, 281, 283n. 44

Edict of Milan, 34, 98, 268

Eels. *See* Fishing

Elites. *See* Status

Elmet, 215, 225, 255

Embankment. *See* Ditches

Emigration. *See* Migration

Empire, Roman: 87; and Christianity, 268–69; overview, 7, 32–35, 85–86, 168–69, 177; and provincial decline, 185–87

Environment, 1–23, 47, 94; in contagious disease, 237

Epidemics. *See* Illness

Erosion, 20, 64, 128, 206

Ethnic identity, 47, 52, 71, 74, 96; blurring of, 144; ethnic markers, 100–101; and political power, 104–7; in Wales, 255

Excavation. *See* Archaeology

Exeter, 32, 68, 203, 206, 210

Experimental archaeology. *See* Archaeology

Factories. *See* Manufacturing

Famine, 18, 20, 123, 190; in gildas, 23, 44; and health, 239

Farming. *See* Animals, domesticated; Cultivation

Fashions and styles, Roman, 32–33, 41–42, 68–69; adapted by Britons, 78–79, 101–3; burial practice, 264; styles and identity, 99–100; trained bears, 136

Fens. *See* Wetlands
Fibers: flax, 21, 120, 126; hemp, 9,
    11–12, 126; wool, 14, 17, 86, 129,
    131–32
Fields, 3–4, 9–13, 29; relocation of,
    8, 18, 20–22, 62, 82; rotation of,
    11, 84
Fishing, 2, 29, 120
Flotation, 124
Food preservation, 126–27,
    131, 138
Food production. *See* Animal
    husbandry; Cultivation
Footwear, 65, 94, 126, 142, 147, 168
Foreign imports, 39, 181; at
    southwestern hillforts, 153, 212
Forests. *See* Woodlands
Forts, overview: hillforts, 47, 65,
    73, 80, 152, 155, 261; Roman
    forts, 32–33, 72, 185, 193, 196–99,
    214; as seats of power, 205–16,
    221–23
Free people, 91
Frocester Court villa, 53, 55
Furnishings, 29, 41, 92, 98, 155;
    and the illusion of poverty,
    101–2

Gallic Chronicles (manuscript),
    48, 188
Germanus, Saint (Bishop of
    Auxerre), 35–36, 278–79
Gildas (cleric), 22–23, 26, 48,
    189; on tyrants, 43–44, 187–91;
    on pestilence, 241–42; on
    monasticism, 272–73
Glass, 33, 99, 130, 153–55, 158, 163;
    at Tintagel, 174
Glastonbury Tor, 53, 208, 272–73
Gloucester, 66, 208
Gododdin (epic poem). *See* Aneirin
Government: British government,
    38, 42, 169, 183, 190, 199–205;
    final breakdown, 280; Roman
    government, 13, 27, 30, 60, 64,
    159, 168, 180

Grain drier. *See* Corn drier
Grains, cultivated: barley,
    120, 123–25, 130; bran, 238;
    buckwheat, 9, 11; in diet, 238;
    grains at West Stow, 143; oats, 8,
    21, 123, 125; rye, 9, 12, 120, 123–
    25; wheat, 9, 21, 120, 123–25,
    127, 137
Granaries, 60, 118, 197–98
Grasses, 2, 10, 129–30, 132
Grave goods, 54–55, 93–94,
    109–10, 207, 216; in high status
    graves, 239, 252; problems
    with, 217, 223, 246, 248, 250, 264.
    See also Burials

Hadrian's Wall, 13, 36, 42, 76,
    188–89; the Wall forts, 195–99
Hagiography. *See* Saint's life
Helmets, 136, 149, 159, 223
Hemp. *See* Fibers
Hengist and Horsa, 71–72, 169
Herbs, 126, 136, 138, 197, 244
Heresy, 35–36, 274, 276–78
Hermits and anchorites, 53, 273,
    275–76
Hillforts. *See* Forts
Historia Brittonum (manuscript),
    26, 220
*Historia Ecclesiastica gentis
    Anglorum* (manuscript), 26, 218
Historia Nova (manuscript), 184
Hoards, 39, 43, 147, 169, 176–77;
    at Barton Court farm, 21–22; at
    Traprain Law, 47. *See also* Hoxne
    hoard; Patching hoard
Honey, 9, 134, 138, 238
Hospitality and generosity,
    228–29
Houses. *See* Buildings
Hoxne hoard, 177–80
Hunting, overview, 3, 14, 16, 120,
    134–36, 143; of bear, 16, 136, 213;
    of boar, 130, 136; of deer, 16, 135,
    143; pelts, 16, 135, 136, 143
Hypocausts, 194, 242

Illness: disease, 217, 235–38, 241, 244; epidemics, 240–41; mortality, 190, 217–18, 235–37; plagues, 240–44
Immigration. *See* Migration
Ine's Laws, 106
Infants, 95–96, 141–42, 217, 236–37, 257; baptism of, 270; and original sin, 278
Inhumations. *See* Burials
Injuries, 239–40, 243; at Queenford Farm, 96. *See also* Skeletal analysis
Insects, 14–15, 22, 161, 243. *See also* Vermin
Ireland, 33, 36, 42, 46, 69, 213, 273
Iron, 5, 148–52, 154
Isle of Man, 43

Jutes. *See* Anglo-Saxons

Kent, 71, 72, 91, 107, 169, 179, 225–30; Æthelberht (king), 250–51
Kentigern, Saint (Bishop of Strathclyde), 46, 270
Kilns, 4, 41, 99, 139–40, 156, 166
Kin groups, 253–58
King lists, 45, 220
Kingdoms, 26, 44, 48, 71, 76, 82, 109; in the west, 153, 173–74, 202–5; in Wales, 185
Knives. *See* Blades

Language: Brythonic, 30–31, 35; Latin, 30–31, 35
Laws, 106, 190, 225–29
Leather, 67, 155, 158–59
Liminality, of sacred places, 47
Lincoln, 51, 66, 71, 73, 272
Linen, 126, 161, 163. *See also* Textiles
London, 8, 50–51, 66, 71, 73–75, 169–71; Londinium, 170, 247–48
Looms, 109, 143, 156, 160–63, 166
Lullingstone villa, 91–92

Londinium. *See* London
Lynchet, 120–21

Magnus Maximus (Macsen Wledig), 184–85, 197, 210
Malt, 123
Manufacturing, 27, 30, 33, 38–39, 67, 72; at villas, 93, 98, 100; at home, 156–57
Manure, 10, 84, 131–32
Manuscripts, 22, 27, 158, 174–75
Marginal land, 17–20, 30, 120
Markets. *See* Trade
Marshes. *See* Wetlands
Mead, 134, 138
Mediterranean influences and culture, 153, 157, 172–74, 181; at Glastonbury, 273; and hermits, 275; and southwestern ports, 206, 212, 222, 269
Memorial stones, 175, 210, 213–14, 247, 254; with Christian influence, 270, 275
Mercenaries, 41, 44, 47–51, 69
Mercia, 80, 171, 215, 219, 220
Metal ores, 4–5, 33, 62, 148–54, 210
Mice. *See* Vermin
Midlands, 11, 122, 171, 204
Migration, 15, 49, 83, 110, 210, 253, 270
Milk. *See* Dairy products
Mines and mining, 7, 60, 150–52, 210
Missionaries, 37, 46, 107, 170, 273, 278; Saint Augustine, 250, 281
Mithras, 33, 268
Mitochondrial DNA, 108, 111–12
Monasteries, 53, 173, 206, 208, 226, 239, 266, 272–76
Mosaics, 41, 92, 98, 102
Mothecome, 172, 208
Mucking, 50, 71, 84
Municipium (plural, *municipia*), 66–67, 69

Nennius (pseudonym), 26–27, 220
Ninian, Saint, 46, 270, 273–75

Nutrition: carbohydrates, 9, 122, 124–25; general diet, 122–26, 136–38, 238; proteins, 124–26, 129–31

Oats. *See* Grains, cultivated
Offa's Dyke, 80, 222
Ogham script, 44, 210, 213, 255, 270
Ores. *See* Metal ores
Original sin, doctrine of, 36, 278
Orkney Islands, 3, 45
Orosius (historian), 183–84
Outlawry, 135, 190, 227
Ovens. *See* Kilns

Paganism. *See* Religion
Palynology (pollen studies), 8–13, 17, 126
Parchment, 22, 158, 174–75
Pastures, 3–4, 9–10, 13, 16, 138, 144; for army veterans, 66; later pasture management, 128, 130
Patching hoard, 39
Patrick, Saint, 36–37, 45, 90, 103–4, 272
Peasants. *See* Status
Peat, 2–3, 14, 138
Pelagius, 35–37, 277–78; and doctrine of free will, 36
Pelts. *See* Hunting
Personal hygiene, 152–53
Pewter, 32, 152, 210
Picts, 42–43, 155, 185, 188, 197–98, 216
Plague. *See* Illness
Plants, domesticated. *See* Crops
Plows, 9, 20, 29, 118–24, 127–29
Plumbing, 68. *See also* Aqueducts; Sewers
Poetry, 136, 210, 214–15, 252
Pollens. *See* Palynology
Potsherds. *See* Sherds
Pottery, 4, 32, 41, 49–52, 78, 94; Mediterranean, 222, 269; site finds, 54–55, 73–74, 79, 280; stylistic concerns, 99–100

Power struggles, 20, 29, 37, 43, 70; military rebellion, 200–2; the peasant rebellion, 185–86; among tyrants, 187–88, 216. *See also* Gildas, on tyrants
Pregnancy and birth, 95, 142, 235–38, 249; and rebirth, 259, 265; baptism, 277–78
Preservation of remains, 15, 28, 79, 124, 129, 217, 235
Protein. *See* Nutrition

Queenford Farm cemetery, 94–96, 217

Radiocarbon dating (Carbon-14), 52, 73, 80, 94
Raids on Britons, 27, 38, 43–44, 70, 72, 82; and role of hillforts, 93, 213
Rampart. *See* Ditch
Rats. *See* Vermin
Rebellion. *See* Power struggles
Refugees, 13, 40
Religion, overview: Christianity, 35–37, 266–82; paganism, 258–68; ritual and sacrifice, 16, 34–35, 47, 50, 128, 249–50, 258–59; spiritual places, 259–64, 270–71. *See also* Liminality
Rheged, 106, 214–15, 270
Rivers. *See* Waterways
Roads, 7, 27, 30, 50, 59–60; and native tracks, 3, 60, 64; Roman construction of, 60–62; after the Romans, 62–64
Rodents. *See* Vermin
Roman Empire. *See* Empire, Roman
Rural life, 71–72, 76, 78, 82–86, 118–44
Rye. *See* Grains, cultivated

Sacrifices. *See* Religion
Saint's life, 35, 46, 273
Salt, 3, 131, 136, 138

Saxon Shore forts, 189

Saxons. *See* Anglo-Saxons

Scots, 42–44, 188, 197–98, 216

Scribes, 22. *See also* Manuscripts

Scythe and sickle, 129

Sewers, 68. *See also* Aqueducts; Plumbing

Shellfish. *See* Fishing

Sherds, 99, 114n. 10, 157; on site, 50, 53, 55, 78, 80, 172–73, 243

Shifting agriculture, 11, 84–85

Ships. *See* Boats

Shoes. *See* Footwear

Shrines, 33, 65. *See also* Altars; Temples

Sickle. *See* Scythe

Skeletal analysis, 95–96, 108, 111, 237–40, 257. *See also* Injuries

Slaves. *See* Status

Social unrest, 27, 42, 84–85

Soils, 2–3, 8, 10–13, 18, 117, 122, 124–29; acidity of, 28, 52; and agriculture, 84, 85, 120; on archaeological sites, 75, 94, 139

Somerset, 8, 11, 20, 85, 139–40, 143, 264

South Cadbury Castle, 205, 208, 211–12

Spices, 136

Spirits, supernatural, 259–64. *See also* Religion

Spong Hill, 54–55

Statuary and carved monuments, 175, 213, 247, 254, 255, 263, 265, 270, 275

Status: elites, 35, 38, 78, 81, 89, 91–92, 109–10; peasants, 38, 39, 51, 90, 93, 96; slaves, 43, 45, 89–91, 93, 94, 106, 144

Stone, masonry or building, 68–70, 73, 81

Sunken-featured building (SFB). *See* Buildings, subterranean

Sutton Hoo, 135–36, 223, 227, 230, 252

Symbol stones (Pictish), 46–47

Taliesin (poet), 210, 214

Taxes, 27, 36, 38, 59, 68, 174, 200, 203

Teeth, human: decay, 238–39; damage, 124, 238–39

Temples, 264–67. *See also* Altars; Shrines

Textiles, 154–55, 161–63; tanning of, 159. *See also* Fibers

Thames, River, 50, 71, 74, 171

Thetford, 134–35

Threshing, 123–24

Tin, 32–33, 99, 152, 168–69, 173, 179, 181; and trade, 206, 209–10

Tintagel, 32, 154, 164, 172–74, 208, 269–71, 273

Tools, 5, 49, 54, 81, 108–10, 117, 127–29, 135

Towns, 37–39, 50–51, 64–82

Tracks. *See* Roads

Trade: barter, 147, 180–81, 254; local, 254; long distance, 157, 168–69, 175; markets, 167–68, 171–74, 186, 205

Traprain Law, 47

Travel, 7, 59, 62–63, 121, 139, 148, 164, 171, 258. *See also* Roads

Tree rings. *See* Dendrochronology

Tribal Hidage (manuscript), 215, 219–20

Tribes, concept of, 25

Urban life, 59–60, 64–65

Vale of Wrington, 119

Vellum. *See* Parchment

Venta Silurum. *See* Caerwent

Vergilius Romanus (manuscript), 175–76

Vermin, 14, 134

Verulamium, 66, 70, 183, 279

Vicus (plural, *vici*), 67–68, 195

Villages, 29, 71, 78, 119–20, 128, 171, 205, 221

Villas, 9, 13, 41, 55, 78–85, 90–93, 118

Viroconium. *See* Wroxeter

Vita (plural, *vitae*). *See* Saint's life
Vortigern, 48, 70, 190–91, 241.
   See also Gildas, on tyrants
Votadini, 47

Wages, 33, 62, 140, 147, 176, 194
Wales, 13, 40, 42, 44, 47, 191,
   212–14, 273. *See also* Anglesey;
   Caerleon; Caerwent; Dinas
   Powys; Magnus Maximus
Wall decoration: paintings, 41–42;
   textile coverings, 98
War. *See* Power struggles
Waterways, 8, 50, 74, 205, 206; as
   sacred places, 47, 250, 259–62
Wattle and daub, 73, 79, 84, 97,
   102, 118, 139
Weapons, 154–55, 189, 223–25, 246,
   250, 254, in burials, 50, 108–10,
   252, 257. *See also* Blades
Weather. *See* Climate
Weaving, 156, 162–63, 166
Wessex, 72, 106, 204, 208, 212, 219,
   279–80
West Stow, 15–17, 143–44
Wetlands, 7, 8, 10, 20, 85,
   121–22, 139
Wharves, 8

Wheat. *See* Grains, cultivated
Whitehall Roman villa, 151
Wild animals and plants, 3, 4–5,
   14, 16, 120, 130, 134–36, 138
Winchester, 72, 203, 246, 279–80
Wine, 157, 169, 173, 177, 207
Woad, 45
Wolves, 14, 16, 135. *See also*
   Hunting; Wild animal and
   plants
Women, role of, 35, 54, 95–96, 100,
   109–11, 154–55, 162, 228–29; in
   religious orders, 266, 273, 275
Woodlands, 10, 13, 118–19, 138–40;
   clearance of, 4, 12, 107. *See also*
   Coppicing
Wool. *See* Fibers; Textiles
Workshops. *See* Manufacturing
Written communication, 22–23,
   25–28, 44, 48, 106, 174–76, 192,
   226, 255; and Christianity, 268,
   270; and literacy, 31, 199
Wroxeter, 68, 76–81, 93, 203, 213,
   242

Y-chromosome, 111–13

Zosimus (historian), 38, 184–85

ABOUT THE AUTHOR

DEBORAH J. SHEPHERD holds a PhD in interdisciplinary archaeological studies and specializes in the early medieval archaeology
of Britain, Northern Europe, and Finland. She has been a Fulbright
scholar and taught at the University of Minnesota and elsewhere.